MŪLAMADHYAMAKAKĀRIKĀ
OF
NĀGĀRJUNA

Mūlamadhyamakakārikā of Nāgārjuna

THE PHILOSOPHY OF THE MIDDLE WAY

Introduction, Sanskrit Text, English Translation and Annotation

DAVID J. KALUPAHANA

MOTILAL BANARSIDASS PUBLISHERS
PRIVATE LIMITED • DELHI

6th Reprint: Delhi, 2015
First Indian Edition: Delhi, 1991

ISBN: 978-81-208-0774-7

MOTILAL BANARSIDASS
41 U.A. Bungalow Road, Jawahar Nagar, Delhi 110 007
8 Mahalaxmi Chamber, 22 Bhulabhai Desai Road, Mumbai 400 026
203 Royapettah High Road, Mylapore, Chennai 600 004
236, 9th Main III Block, Jayanagar, Bengaluru 560 011
Sanas Plaza, 1302 Baji Rao Road, Pune 411 002
8 Camac Street, Kolkata 700 017
Ashok Rajpath, Patna 800 004
Chowk, Varanasi 221 001

Printed in India
by RP Jain at NAB Printing Unit,
A-44, Naraina Industrial Area, Phase I, New Delhi–110028
and published by JP Jain for Motilal Banarsidass Publishers (P) Ltd,
41 U.A. Bungalow Road, Jawahar Nagar, Delhi-110007

To Professor N. A. Jayawickrema
(yo) ācariyo 'hosi mam' atthakāmo (*J* 5.20)

PREFACE

Almost ten years ago, I undertook a new translation of Candrakīrti's encyclopaedic work the *Prasannapadā*, a commentary on Nāgārjuna's primary philosophical treatise, the *Mūlamadhyamakakārikā*. After I had completed nearly ten chapters, I learned through one of my students about a similar attempt by Professor Marvin Sprung. I was about to give up my project, when my student, who had previously studied under Professor Sprung, shared with me a copy of Professor Sprung's translation of the first chapter. Comparing his and my translations, I discovered that Professor Sprung's translation was to some extent influenced by Stcherbatsky's work (*The Conception of Buddhist Nirvana*, 1927). I felt then that my effort would not be in vain, especially because I had expressed strong disagreement with Stcherbatsky's interpretation of the Buddhist philosophical tradition (see my *Causality, The Central Philosophy of Buddhism*, 1975).

To my surprise, Professor Sprung's translation, consiting of only seventeen chapters (including an incomplete rendering of Chapter I), appeared in 1979. As I plodded along through my own laborious work, I began to realize how Candrakīrti was gradually leading me away from Nagarjuna's philosophical standpoint. My suspicions were strengthened in 1981 when I visited India on a Smithsonian grant. Meeting with some scholars who were brought up in the Vedantic tradition, I found them to be extremely comfortable with Nāgārjuna as interpreted by Candrakīrti and less impressed by the teachings of early Buddhism as recorded in the Nikāyas and the Āgamas. My suspicion that Nāgārjuna and Candrakīrti were upholding two different philosophical standpoints compelled me to take a fresh look at Kumārajīva's *Chung-lun*, which is at least two centuries prior to Candrakīrti. Translating the entire *Chung-lun* into English and comparing it with Nāgārjuna's original Sanskrit text, I was pleasantly surprized by their similaries. I found no justification whatsoever in looking at Nāgārjuna through Candrakīrti's eyes when there was a more faithful and closer disciple of Nāgārjuna in Kumārajīva. This discovery diminished my enthusiasm for cleaning up my English rendering of the *Prasannapadā* for possible publication.

After translating both the Sanskrit and the Chinese versions of Nāgārjuna's treatise, I proceeded to annotate both according to my understanding of early Buddhism as well as later Buddhist traditions before Nāgārjuna. The annotation of the Sanskrit text alone turned out to be more extensive than anticipated. Furthermore, considering the difficulties that might arise in publishing this work with Sanskrit and Chinese texts side by side, and also with the Chinese characters in the body of the annotation, I decided once again to modify my project. The Sanskrit text is here presented with annotation and introduction. The Chinese text with commentary will appear subsequently as a companion volume.

I am not unaware of the controversy this work may engender. Hoping that it will be a healthy one, I intend to raise one major question regarding Nāgārjuna, especially in the light of the more recent research in the history of Buddhism. Professor Hajime Nakamura's monumental work, *Indian Buddhism* (1980), has provided more information regarding the history of Buddhist literature than any other work published so far. This carefully executed work not only deals with the contents and authorship as well as the chronology of most of the Buddhist texts, but also compares the different versions available in Sanskrit, Pali, Chinese, Tibetan, and Japanese. After a careful reading of this work, I cannot help recognizing an earlier stratum of literature that has so far been lumped together with all the literature that came to be called Mahāyānistic. This includes two famous pieces, the *Kāśyapaparivarta* and the *Vajracchedikā-prajñāpāramitā* (see Nakamura, p. 159). I wonder whether the original versions of these texts can be approriately called Mahāyānistic, even though they were preserved by the Mahāyāna schools. This objection, indeed, is not very difficult from that raised against considering the Nikāyas and Āgamas to be Hīnayānistic because they were preserved by the Theravādins, the Sarvāstivādins, or any other later tradition.

The major question that can be raised is: "Where would a philosopher like Nāgārjuna go in order to discover the Buddha's teachings?" This historical question has, to my knowledge, neither been raised nor answered. The *Saddharmapuṇḍarīka-sūtra* that highlights the Hīnayāna-Mahāyāna controversy was not yet written. That does not mean that the controversy was not known before Nāgārjuna. Even if the controversy had preceded Nāgārjuna, what were the canonical texts, embodying the pure Mahāyāna philosophical standpoint, that Nāgārjuna could have utilized in order to explain the Buddha's message?

A careful reading of Nakamura's work shows it to be futile to attempt to discover a pure Mahāyāna text that Nāgārjuna might have been able to depend upon. Before the compilation of the *Saddharmapuṇḍarīka*, one can hardly expect to find a carefully executed treatise that would explicate the Mahāyāna philosophy as it is presented by modern scholars. Since such sohisticated Mahāyāna sutras were not available to Nāgārjuna, he could not help moving on to the early discourses in the Nikāyas and the Āgamas in search of the Buddha's teachings, especially at a time when he realized that the problems were created not only by metaphysicians like the Sarvāstivādins and the Sautrāntikas, but also by more popular religious teachers like Aśvaghosa, who over-emphasised the function of "faith" in the emerging belief in a transcendent Buddha. A careful reading of Nāgārjuna's treatise will reveal that he was critical of both these trends. If Buddhaghosa were to be considered the model of a Theravādin and Candrakīrti or Sāntideva were to be looked upon as ideal Mahāyānists, neither the Buddha, nor Moggalīputta-tissa, nor Nāgārjuna would fit into their shoes.

The present work may come as a surprise to many who are familiar with my previous publications, especially because it repudiates many things that I have said about Nāgārjuna. In those earlier works, my major endeavor was to show how the Buddhism of the Buddha differed from both Sthaviravāda and Mahāyāna, and the latter included philosophers like Nāgārjuna. My main contention with scholars like Stcherbatsky and Murti has been in regard to the manner in which the former equated Sarvāstivāda with early Buddhism and the latter portrayed the Buddha as a half-hearted metaphysician introducing a theory of elements that came to be rejected by Nāgārjuna. I was prepared to accept Murti's interpretation of Nāgārjuna, while struggling to find ways in which that interpretation could be justified without sacrificing the empiricism of the Buddha. A more detailed study of both Māgārjuna and Candrakīrti has convinced me that the former still remains faithful to the Buddha, while the latter has moved more towards a Vedāntic interpretation, thereby initiating a process that culminated in the disappearance of Buddhism as a distinct ideology from the Indian scene a few centuries later.

ABBREVIATIONS

(Consult Kenneth Inada's *Nāgārjuna*, for a detailed bibliography on Nāgārjuna and the Mādhyamika school.)

A	*Aṅguttara-nikāya*, ed. R. Morris and E. Hardy, 5 volumes, London: PTS, 1885-1900.
AA	*Manorathapūraṇī*, [*Aṅguttara-aṭṭhakathā*], ed. M. Walleser, London: PTS, 1973.
Abhvt	*Abhidhammatthavibhavinī-ṭīka*, ed. D. Pannasara and P. Vimaladhamma, Columbo: Mahabodhi Press, 1933.
AD	*Abhidharmadīpa*, see *Adv*.
Adv	*Abhidharmadīpa with Vibhāṣāprabhāvṛtti*, ed. P. S. Jaini, Patna: K. P Jayaswal Research Institute, 1959.
AK	*Abhidharmakośa*, see *Akb*.
Akb	*Abhidharmakośa-bhāṣa*, ed. Pralhad Pradhan, Patna: K. P. Jayaswal Research Institute, 1967.
Ch'ang	*Ch'ang A-han Ching* (*Dīrghāgama*), tr. Buddhayaśas, *Taishō* No. 1.
Chung	*Chung A-han Ching* (*Madhyamāgama*), tr. Gautama Saṃghadeva and Saṃgharakṣa, *Taishō* No.26.
D	*Dīgha-nikāya*, ed. T. W. Rhys Davids and J. E. Carpenter, 3 volumes, London: PTS, 1890-1911.
Dh	*Dhammapada*, ed. V. Fausboll, London: Luzac, 1900.
DhsA	*Atthasālinī*, *Dhammasaṅganī-aṭṭhakathā*, ed. E. Muller, London: PTS, 1897.
DhsT	*Abhidhammamūlaṭīkā* [*Ṭīka* on *Dhammasaṅganī-aṭṭhakathā*], ed. D. Pannasara and P. Wimaladhamma, Colombo: Mahabodhi Press, 1938.
It	*Itivuttaka*, ed. E. Windish, London: PTS, 1889.
Karikā	See *MKV(P)*, *MKV(V)*.
Kp	*Kāśyapaparivarta of the Ratnakūṭa-sūtra*, ed. A. Stael-Holstein, Shanghai: Commercial Press, 1926.

Kvu	*Kathāvatthu*, ed. A. C. Taylor, 2 volumes, London: PTS, 1894-1897.
M	*Majjhima-nikāya*, ed. V. Trenckner and R. Chalmers, 3 volumes, London: PTS, 1887-1901.
Miln	*Milindapañho*, ed. V. Trenckner, London: PTS, 1962.
MKV(P)	*Mādhyamikavṛtti* (*Madhyamakakārikās*), ed. L. de la Vallée Poussin, *Bibliotheca Buddhica* 4, St. Petersburg: The Imperial Academy of Sciences, 1903-1913.
MKV(V)	*Madhyamakaśāstra of Nāgārjuna with the commentary; Prasannapadā by Candrakīrti*, ed. P. L. Vaidya, Darbhanga: The Mithila Institute, 1960.
PEW	*Philosophy East and West*, ed. Eliot Deutsch, Honolulu: The University Press of Hawaii.
PTS	The Pali Text Society, London
S	*Saṃutta-nikāya*, ed. L. Feer, 5 volumes, London: PTS, 1884-1904.
Sakv	*Sphuṭārthābhidharmakośa-vyākhyā*, ed. U. Wogihara, Tokyo: The Publication Association of Abhidharmakośavyākhyā, 1932-1936.
Sdmp	*Saddharmapuṇḍarīka-sūtra*, ed. H. Kern and B. Nanjio, St. Petersburg: The Imperial Academy of Sciences, 1912.
Sn	*Suttā-nipāta*, ed. D. Anderson and H. Smith, London: PTS, 1913.
Taishō	*Taishō Shinshū Daizōkyō*, ed. J. Takakusu and K. Watanabe, Tokyo: Daizo Shuppan Company, 1924-1934.
Thag	*Thera-therī-gāthā*, ed. H. Oldenberg and R. Pischel, London: PTS, 1883.
Thig	See *Thag*.
Tsa	*Tsa A-han Ching* (*Saṃyuktāgama*), tr. Guṇabhadra, *Taishō* No.99.
Tseng	*Tseng-i A-han Ching* (*Ekottarāgama*), tr. Gautama Saṃghadeva, *Taishō* No.125.
Ud	*Udāna*, ed. P. Steinthal, London: PTS, 1948.
VbhA	*Sammohavinodanī*, *Vibhaṅgaṭṭhakathā*, ed. A. P. Buddhadatta, London: PTS, 1923.

Vin *Vinaya Piṭaka*, ed. H. Oldenberg, 5 volumes, London: PTS, 1879-1883.

Vism *The Visuddhi-magga of Buddhaghosa*, ed. C. A. F. Rhys Davids, London: PTS, 1975.

CONTENTS

INTRODUCTION

THE MIDDLE PATH

Myths of huge proportions have developed around the spiritual and philosophical stature of various personalities in almost every school of Buddhism. Often these myths were inflated by sectarian rivalries that continued to plague the history of Buddhism, especially the rivalry between the two major schools, Theravāda and Mahāyāna. These prejudices tended to polarize the philosophical teachings of these two traditions though, in fact, they are similar if not identical. They are similar in being faithful to the basic teachings of the Buddha; they are also comparable in the way in which they rejected certain metaphysical ideas that continued to creep into the teachings.

The two aspects of the Buddha's teachings, the philosophical and the practical, which are mutually dependent, are clearly enunciated in two discourses, the *Kaccāyanagotta-sutta*[1] and the *Dhammacakkappavattana-sutta*,[2] both of which are held in high esteem by almost all the schools of Buddhism in spite of their sectarian rivalries. The *Kaccāyanagotta-sutta*, quoted by almost all the major schools of Buddhism, deals with the philosophical "middle path", placed against the backdrop of two absolutistic theories in Indian philosophy, namely, permanent existence (*atthitā*) propounded in the early *Upaniṣads* and nihilistic non-existence (*natthitā*) suggested by the Materialists. The middle position is explained as "dependent arising" (*paṭiccasamuppāda*) which, when utilized to explain the nature of the human personality and the world of experience, appears in a formula consisting of twelve factors (*dvādasāṅga*). The practical middle path is enunciated in the equally famous *Dhammacakkappavattana-sutta*, respected by most Buddhists as the first sermon delivered by the Buddha. Here the middle path is between the two extremes of self-indulgence (*kāmasukhallikānuyoga*) and self-mortification (*attakilamathānyoga*) and consists of the noble eightfold path (*ariyo aṭṭhaṅgiko maggo*) leading to freedom and happiness.

Throughout the history of Buddhism, Buddhists have endeavored to remain faithful to the doctrines enunciated in these two discourses, in spite of unfortunate divisions into Theravāda and Mahāyāna and in the face of enormous pressures, either from inside or from outside, either social or political, that forced them occasionally to deviated from the original message. For example, in the sphere of philosophical speculations, one of the sects belonging to the so-called Sthaviravāda, namely, Sarvāstivāda, presented a theory of "self-nature" or "substance" (*svabhāva*) and some of the Mahāyanists admitted a conception of "inherent thought of enlightenment" (*bodhi-citta*), both of which, as may be indicated in the following discussions, are theories contrary to the fundamental philosophical tenet of the Buddha, namely, "dependent arising" (*paṭicca-samuppāda*).

The practical middle path as enunciated in the famous *Dhamma-cakkappavattana-sutta*, which is complementary to or based upon the philosophical middle path referred to above, was more susceptible to variations. The analysis of the wide variety of religous practices that emerged in the two traditions, Theravāda and Mahāyāna, which appear to be contrary to the middle path enunciated in the above discourse may require a separate volume. The present treatment will therefore be confined to the philosophical middle path and its survival, in spite of the heretical interpretations that occasionally appeared in the Buddhist tradition. The survival of that middle position in philosophy can be attributed to reformers like Moggaliputta-tissa (little known among the Western scholars of Buddhism, in spite of the important role he played in the Buddhist council held during the reign of the Emperor Asoka of India) and Nāgārjuna. Such personalities have emerged from time to time and they have been responsible for the continuation of the Buddha's message. The activities of such reformers have either been ignored, as in the case of Moggaliputta-tissa, or exaggerated, as in the case of Nāgārjuna.

The present essay is not intended as an attempt to highlight the contributions of the less known figures—like Moggalīputta-tissa, whose famous treatise, "The Points of Controversy" (*Kathāvatthu*),[3] awaits a careful and sympathetic treatment by Buddhologists. On the contrary, this will be an attempt to put into perspective the philosophical and spiritual stature of Nāgārjuna, which has been exaggerated beyond limits, more by modern scholars than by the classical Buddhists.

NĀGĀRJUNA: THE MYTH

Nāgārguna has been considered the second Buddha and has occupied a second position in the line of patriarchs in almost all schools of Mahāyāna Buddhism, primarily because the adherents of these schools refused to recognize the spiritual status of thousands of Buddha's immediate disciples who, according to the Buddha's own recognition, had attained the same knowledge and understanding (*ñāṇa-dassana*) as well as the moral and spiritual perfection attained by the Buddha. While the intellectual and spiritual attainments of the immediate disciples are clearly portrayed in texts like the *Theragātha* and the *Therigātha*, no such information is available to us about Nāgārjuna's spiritual attainments except the account of his conversion to Buddhism and his scholastic activities referred to in a biographical account translated into Chinese by Kumārajīva.[4] Nāgārjuna's stature as the second Buddha derives, therefore, from his basic writings, which are generally looked upon as philosophical interpretations of the Mahāyāna sutras.

Kenneth Inada, who presented one of the most sympathetic analyses of Nāgārjuna's thought, has admitted that the veneration of Nāgārjuna "at times reached such ridiculous heights that his name was sanctified and stamped everywhere with reckless abandon even for purposes of frauding scriptural authority."[5] He was probably referring to the attempt on the part of some of the later Tantric writers to seek authority and sanctity for their ideas, which were undoubtedly influenced by some later Indian religious practices. Even if one were to ignore such excesses, it is possible to maintain that the exalted position accorded to Nāgārjuna yet reflects an uncritical and dogmatic attitude of some of the later Buddhists toward the spiritual ideal of early Buddhism. Such an attitude is reflected not only in some of the Mahāyāna texts but also in some of the Theravāda commentaries. For example, in the later Theravāda commentarial literature, an exalted status is accorded to the Abhidhamma in relation to the discourses, so much so that the Buddha had to ascend to the world of deities (*devaloka*) and preach the Abhidhamma to his "mother" who was residing there.[6] Such an admission, though intended to provide authority and sanctity to a body of literature that emerged long after the passing away of the Buddha, undoubtedly carried the implication that the Buddha's immediate disciples were not capable of understanding its contents. However, even though such an implication was there, the Theravādins did not elaborate this story in such a way that it would lead to the devaluation of the early ideal of an *arahant*. Yet, when a similar need was felt by the Mahāyānists to provide authority and sanctity to some of the later Mahāyāna texts such as the *Prajñāpāramitā sūtras*, which were obviously later than the Abhidharma treatises, they were not satisfied with merely saying that they were "great discourses" (*vaipulya-sūtra*), greater than those included in the Nikāyas and the Āgamas. They, in fact, proceeded to condemn the very ideal of an *arahant* embodied in those discourses and to criticize the spiritual attainments of the early disciples of the Buddha.

In this particular movement, the *Saddharmapuṇḍarīka-sūtra* leads the field.[7] The motivation or even the final goal of this movement may have been very noble. It was, in fact, one of the earliest attempts to unify all the conflicting ideas and ideals that were creating enormous rifts among the Buddhist community. Yet, the manner in which such unification was carried out led to increasing conflicts rather than to their reconciliation or appeasement.

Even a superficial glance at the history of Buddhism would reveal the existence of "monks" (*bhikṣu*) who deviated from the ideal and who falsely claimed spiritual attainments while leading a form of life inferior to that of ordinary lay people. Such monks were reported even from the time of the Buddha. The *Vinaya-piṭaka*[8] as well as the *Kāśyapaparivarta*[9] generate no sympathy for such miscreant monks, the latter branding them as a pack of dogs fighting each other for a morsel of food thrown at them.

Such selfish and dishonorable behavior on the part of certain monks may have been counter productive. Self-sacrifice and absolute altruism could emerge as noble ideals in such a context. However, such actions and reactions need not be a reason for condemning even the immediate disciples of the Buddha, *arahants* like Sāriputta, Moggallāna, and Kassapa, as people of "low aspirations" (*hīnābhiratā*),[10] and forcing them to disclaim their attainments in order to accept a new ideal, an ideal certainly contrary to the "middle path" enunciated by the Buddha in his very first discourse to the world. It is by following a "middle path" avoiding the two extremes of self-indulgence and self-destruction that the disciples of the Buddha attained the state of freedom called "the appeasement of dispositions" (*saṅkhāra-samatha*) and continued to work for the welfare and happiness of mankind. Very authentic records available in the *Thera-* and *Therī-gāthās* bear ample testimony to the ideal of the early disciples, and it is also an ideal recognized by Nāgārjuna, the champion of the "middle way" (XVII.1).

While the Theravādins elevated the Abhidhamma to an exalted position without devaluing the ideas embodied in the early discourses, the *Saddharmapuṇḍarīka* appears to have gone much further in dealing with this entire Buddhist philosophical and religious tradition beginning with the Buddha himself. It is responsible not only for condemning the early disciples, but also for down-playing the value of the early discourses. The discourses included in the Nikāyas and the Āgamas were considered to be inferior in content. The argument presented is that because the immediate disciples could not understand the deeper doctrine the Buddha had to preach an inferior and unsatisfactory doctrine to suit their intellectual capacity. Such a statement, however, has a hidden implication, namely, that the Buddha lacked the capacity to teach the deeper doctrines in a way that would be intelligible to the people who were in his presence. In the Mahāyāna tradition, the stage was thus made ready for a philosopher like Nāgārjuna, who is supposed to have best expounded the doctrine, to be elevated to the level of a second Buddha, nay, even to the status of a supreme Buddha more exalted than Sākyamuni. Thus, it is not surprizing to find some modern commentators proclaiming the view that the lotus bud that appeared in the world with the birth of the Buddha grew up and blossomed forth with the appearance of Nāgārjuna. In fact, a scholar like T. R. V. Murti has maintained that the Buddha even suggested a "theory of elements" (*dharma*), which came to be be rejected by Nāgārjuna when the latter presented his theory of "emptiness" (*śūnyatā*).[11] This undoubtedly places Nāgārjuna in a more exalted position than that occupied by the Buddha. Most classical and some modern scholars have thus created an atmosphere where the interpretation of Nāgārjuna's philosophy will have to assume a historical development and unfolding of doctrines that were merely suggested, not taught, by the historical Buddha. Some writers on Buddhism, intoxicated by this conception of the evolution of thought, have shown reluctance to recognize the sophistication with which philosophical ideas were presented by the Buddha 2500 years ago. Having miserably failed to perceive the philosophical ingenuity of the Buddha as reflected in the Nikāyas and the Āgamas, as well as the subsequent degeneration of that system in the later commentarial tradition, followed by a revival of the earlier system by philosophers like Moggaliputta-tissa and Nāgārjuna, these writers are insisting upon a gradual sophistication in Buddhist thought comparable to what one can find in the Western philosophical tradition.[12]

NĀGĀRJUNA: THE PHILOSOPHER AND GRAND COMMENTATOR

In the following pages, an attempt will be made to present Nāgārjuna merely as a grand commentator on the Buddha-word and to show that he did not try to improve upon the teachings of the Buddha. His work will be explained as an attempt to destroy the weeds that had grown around the Buddha's teachings as a result of some of the ideas expressed by philosophers of both the Sthaviravāda and the Mahāyāna traditions. It will be shown that the *Mūla-madhyamaka-kārikā* (hereafter abbreviated as *Kārika*) is a superb commentary on the Buddha's own *Kaccāyanagotta-sutta*, a commentary in which Nāgārjuna upholds every statement made by the Buddha in that discourse, bringing together more material from the other discourses as well, and then clearing the water muddied by the speculations of some of the metaphysicians of the later Buddhist tradition. The continuation of certain sectarian prejudices among the faithful adherents of Theravāda and Mahāyāna may be understandable. Critical scholarship, on the contrary, has a responsibility to remain unsmeared by such sectarian prejudices. Modern scholarship in Buddhism, which began with the recognition of this sectarian rivalry as representing a major split in Buddhist philosophical and religious ideology, has come a long way in asserting its untenability. However, scholars are now beginning to realize that the Theravāda/Mahāyāna distinction is an exaggeration and that the fundamental teaching of the Buddha has remained intact throughout the centuries. Now it is time to exorcize the terms Theravāda and Mahāyāna from our vocabulary. A major obstacle to the elimination of this distinction is the manner in which Nāgārjuna's philosophy has come to be expounded by a majority of modern scholars. The present translation of Nāgārjuna's *Kārika* and commentary upon each of the verses therein are intended as a corrective to this interpretation.

A careful study of the doctrines in the extensive corpus of Buddhist literature indicates very clearly how certain fundamental ideas have survived, in spite of the occasional appearance of concepts that conflict with the basic teachings of the Buddha and thus produce controversies among the Buddhist thinkers. Without undertaking a careful study of such instances, scholars have rather uncritically lumped together the early discourses of the Buddha and the summaries of their contents that came to be preserved in the so-called Abhidharma, together with all the interpretive texts compiled by some of the later commentators, either in the form of *vibhāṣā* or *aṭṭhakathā*, and criticized this whole corpus as being representative of Theravāda or Hīnayāna. The same is done with some of the Mahāyāna discourses (*sūtra*) and the treatises (*śāstra*). The contents of the discourses as well as of the Abhidharma literature are examined only in the light of such commentarial explanations and not independent of them. Modern scholarship has thus failed to extricate itself from commentarial traditions. There seems to be no justification for considering the discourses and even the early Abhidharma literature as sectarian works of the so-called Theravāda. Theravāda or Sthaviravāda in general, and Sarvāstivāda and Sautrāntika in particular, may be considered sectarian, but their sectarian views are found not in the discourses and the Abhidharma but in the commentaries that came to be compiled on these two bodies of literature. The elevation of the Abhidharma to the level of a supreme body of literature, more exalted than the discourses, is the work of these later commentators and not of the compilers of those Abhidharma texts. The Mahāyānists themselves, bothered by the substantialist thought of the Sarvāstivāda and Sautrāntika schools, endeavored to preserve the early teachings by emphasizing the negative aspect of the Buddha's doctrine, especially the doctrine of emptiness (*śūnyatā*). The *Kāśyapaparivarta* as well as the early Prajñāpāramitā literature represent this reaction to the substantialism of later Buddhism and this literature should be dissociated from the sectarianism that emerged as a result of the attempt at unification in treatises like the *Saddharmapuṇḍarīka*.

An attempt will be made in the following pages to show that even some of the more prominent philosophers of Mahāyāna were really trying to overcome such sectarian interpretations and go back to the non-sectarian form of Buddhism as embodied in the early discourses, without rejecting either the canonical Abhidharma texts that embody positive teachings or the early Mahāyāna sutras that emphasized the negative aspect of the Buddha's doctrine.

The present analysis will be confined to the work of Nāgārjuna in India. Once Nāgārjuna's philosophy is critically and objectively analysed, it will be possible to see whether there is any substance to the rivalry between the two major philosophical traditions, Mādhyamika and Yogācāra. That project has to be postponed to a later occasion.

A.K. Warder was one of the first to raise the question whether Nāgārjuna was a Mahāyānist.[13] His reason for raising that question was that in the *Kārikā*, which undoubtedly was Nāgārjuna's most significant work, no reference whatsoever is made to any one of the major discourses of the Mahāyāna tradition, not even to the famous *Prajñāpāramitā-sūtras*. Warder believed that the discourse in the Samyukta served as a source for Nāgārjuna's treatise, even though he did not specify them. The only discourse referred to by name is *Kātyāyanāvavāda*,[14] a discourse found both in the Pali Nikāyas[15] and the Chinese Āgamas.[16] This single most important fact has often been overlooked by most of the leading scholars who have written about Nāgārjuna.

Even where this fact has been noted, scholars have assumed that Nāgārjuna was merely referring to the Buddha's rejection of the two extremes of existence (*atthitā*) and non-existence (*natthitā*) in that discourse and that was all. So far, no published work on Buddhism (available to the present author) has treated the contents of the Buddha's discourse to Kaccāyana in detail before proceeding to analyse Nāgārjuna's thought. Assuming that Nāgārjuna was a Mahāyānist and, therefore, must have rejected any literature that came to be preserved by the Sthaviravādins, these scholars have proceeded to analyze the *Kārikā* in the light of their own prejudiced understanding of Mādhyamika philosophy. The ultimate result is bafflement and confusion. Not only are they reluctant to accept certain positive statements of Nāgārjuna in the *Kārikā*, they are also ready to abandon some of the most important chapters in that work either as later interpolations or as having no relevance to Nāgārjuna's thesis.

To assume that Nāgārjuna was a philosophyer who would merely pick out from the Buddha's statements only those that would support or fit in with his own preconceived notions is to do him great injustice. If he was rejecting a theory of elements suggested by the Buddha (as Murti seems to think), Nāgārjuan, who was one of the most fearless critics of metaphysical views, would have certainly said so. Nor is there any evidence to support the hypothesis that the "Admonition to Kātyāyana" (*Kātyāyanāvavāda*) that Nāgārjuna was referring to was a version different from the *Kaccāyanagotta-sutta* found in Pali and Chinese. The *Kāśyapaparivarta* of the *Ratnakūṭa* contains two discourses, both of which were addressed to Kāśyapa and which deal with the middle path. One of them refers to the middle path and explains it in terms of the twelve factors of the human personality (*dvādasāṅga*),[17] while the other explains the middle path in negative terms as "non-ceasing, non-arising, etc."[18] This latter version is not found in the Nikāyas and the Āgamas. Nāgārjuna was probably aware of the existence of both these versions and he understood their implications. His *Kārikā* was an attempt to explain the doctrine without rejecting the contents of any one of them. However, his reference to Kātyāyana, instead of Kāśyapa, is extremely significant, in that he was conversant with not only the contents of the *Ratnakūṭa* versions but also the version included in the Nikāyas and the Āgamas. For this reason the analysis of Nāgārjuna's philosophy as embodied in the *Kārikā* will be undertaken with a view to locating the sources of those ideas that are accepted by him and those that are criticized and rejected by him.

It is anticipated that an analysis of the *Kārikā* in relation to the "Discourse to Kātyāyana" as well as other discourses included in the Nikāyas and the Āgamas will lead to a better understanding of the Buddha's philosophy without exaggerating the so-called Hīnayāna-Mahāyāna distinction.

NĀGĀRJUNA AND KUMĀRAJĪVA

Recent scholarship in the history of Buddhist thought has emphasized a distinction between Indian and Chinese forms of Buddhism. Indian Buddhism is explained as an attempt to deal with causation through karma, while Sinitic Mahāyāna is seen as advocating causation through *dharma-dhātu*.[19] Early Buddhism, according to the proponents of this thesis, underwent a radical change when it was introduced into China. In order to deal with this question of transition, it would be necessary to provide a complete English translation of Kumārajīva's rendition of Nāgārjuna's *Kārikā* into Chinese. Richard Robinson made the first systematic attempt to deal with this problem of transition.[20] However, that was done on the basis of an inadequate examination of the first chapter of Nāgārjuna and Kumārajīva. A careful scrutiny of Kumārajīva's work has convinced me that the form of Buddhism introduced into China by him was not at all different from that of Nāgārjuna. Thus, if my contention that Nāgārjuna's philosophy is a mere restatement of the empiricist and pragmatic philosophy of the Buddha, the form of Buddhism introduced into China would also be the same as the original teachings of the Buddha with no paradigm changes. And this may account for the survival of Buddhism along side of the equally pragmatic philosophy of Confucianism, whereas it failed to survive in India in the face of a very strong idealistic tradition. The prevalent view—that Buddhism, because of its idealistic character, got absorbed into the idealistic tradition in India and failed to remain as a separate entity—needs careful scrutiny, especially when a leading philosopher like Nāgārjuna is not seen to advocate such an idealistic view. This calls for a detailed treatment of the Yogācāra tradition in Buddhism that has not yet been attempted.

NĀGĀRJUNA'S BUDDHA

Nāgārjuna's Buddha was no doubt Gautama (see *Kārikā* XXVII.30), the prince from the Sākyan country (presently part of Nepal) who attained enlightenment and turned out to be the most formidable opponent of almost every major philosophical idea that came to be presented by the Indians. In fact, as will be explained below, the philosophical atmosphere was so confused during the Buddha's day that sometimes he was forced to coin new terms to express his thoughts.

Two of the major philosophical theories that dominated the Indian scene during this time were (1) existence (*sat*, *astitva*), proposed and developed for centuries by Indian thinkers since the time of the early Vedas, and (2) nonexistence (*asat*, *nāstitva*), presented by the Materialists reacting against the traditional metaphysics. Existence or *astitva* was no ordinary empirical existence but the existence of a permanent and eternal substratum in man as well as in all aspects of nature. In man, it was the immutable self (*ātman*) that remained in bondage to the impermanent psychophysical personality and which returns to its ultimate abode, the universal self (*Ātman*), once it is freed from that bondage and reaches its ultimate moral status (*Brahman*). Attempting to explain the origin of this reality in man as well as in nature, some of the traditional philosophers settled for a conception of a creator god. As it is, this may not have generated much protest from the Buddha. However, the Indian philosophers were not satisfied with the simple notion of a creator god. At a very early stage, they asserted that this self (*ātman*) was created by a god or gods who determined that it belongs to one or the other of the four social classes: the priestly (*brāhmaṇa*), the warrior (*kṣatriya*), the merchant (*vaiśya*), and the servant (*śūdra*).[21] Thus, each individual's status was predetermined and unchangeable. It was this particular idea of creation that elicited the most vehement criticism both from the Materialists as well as from the Buddha.

Denying such a metaphysical self, the Materialists moved to the other extreme of advocating the annihilation of the human personaiity after death, and then also denied any moral responsiblity for human actions. Instead, they propounded a theory of the indestructibility of matter.[22]

Kaccāyanagotta-Sutta

The Buddha's discourse to Kaccāyana, a discourse whose authority was recognized by almost all the major philosophical schools of Buddhism, becomes meaningful only in the context of the philosophical views mentioned above. Following is the complete text of the discourse as reported by Ānanda:

Thus have I heard: The Blessed one was once living at Sāvatthi, in the monastery of Anāthapiṇḍika, in Jeta's Grove. At that time the venerable Kaccāyana of that clan came to visit him, and saluting him, sat down at one side. So seated, he questioned the Exalted one: "Sir [people] speak of 'right view, right view.' To what extent is there a right view?"

"This world, Kaccāyana, is generally inclined towards two [views]: existence and non-existence.

To him who perceives with right wisdom the uprising of the world as it has come to be, the notion of non-existence in the world does not occur. Kaccāyana, to him who perceives with right wisdom the ceasing of the world as it has come to be, the notion of existence in the world does not occur.

The world, for the most part, Kaccāyana, is bound by approach, grasping and inclination. And he who does not follow that approach and grasping, that determination of mind, that inclination and disposition, who does not cling to or adhere to a view: 'This is my self,' who thinks: 'suffering that is subject to arising arises; suffering that is subject to ceasing, ceases,' such a person does not doubt, is not perplexed. Herein, his knowledge is not other-dependent. Thus far, Kaccāyana, there is 'right view.'

'Everything exists,'—this, Kaccāyana, is one extreme.

'Everything does not exist,'—this, Kaccāyana, is the second extreme.

Kaccāyana, without approaching either extreme, the Tathāgata teaches you a doctrine by the middle.

Dependent upon ignorance arise dispositions; dependent upon dispositions arise consciousness; dependent upon consciousness arises the psychophysical personality; dependent upon the psychophysical personality arise the six senses; dependent upon the six senses arises contact; dependent upon contact arises feeling; dependent upon feeling arises craving; dependent upon craving arises grasping; dependent upon grasping arises becoming; dependent upon becoming arises birth; dependent upon birth arise old age and death, grief, lamentation, suffering, dejection and dispair. Thus arises this entire mass of suffering. However, from the utter fading away and ceasing of ignorance, there is ceasing of dispositions; from the ceasing of dispositions, there is ceasing of consciousness; from the ceasing of consciousness, there is ceasing of the psychophysical personality; from the ceasing of the psychophysical personality, there is ceasing of the six senses; from the ceasing of the six senses, there is ceasing of contact; from the ceasing of contact, there is ceasing of feeling; from the ceasing of feeling, there is ceasing of craving; from the ceasing of craving, there is ceasing of grasping; from the ceasing of grasping, there is ceasing of becoming; from the ceasing of becoming, there is ceasing of birth; from the ceasing of birth, there is ceasing of old age and death, grief. lamentation, suffering, dejection and dispair. And thus there is the ceasing of this entire mass of suffering."[23]

ANALYSIS OF THE KACCĀYANAGOTTA-SUTTA

The discourse is delivered in response to a fundamental question in epistemology: "What is a right view (*sammādiṭṭhi*)?" The *Brahmajāla-suttanta* refers to sixty-two varieties of views prevalent during the Buddha's day.[24] After his enlightenment, the Buddha realized that none of these were satisfactory. He was not willing to subscribe to any one of them. For this reason, many scholars of Buddhism have assumed that the Buddha did not have a view to present. For them, he had no sixty-third view to propound. If that was the case, the Buddha could have admonished Kaccāyana not to be bothered by any view, whether it was right or wrong, true or false. However, that was not the case.

The Buddha proceeds to enumerate two basic views that are prevalent in the world. The sixty-two views referred to in the *Brahmajāla-suttanta* represent, in one way or another, a proliferation of these two basic views of permanent existence (*atthitā*, Sk. *astitva*) and non-existence (*n'atthitā*, Sk *nāstitva*). He then provides reasons for rejecting both these views. The reasons are epistemological and therefore deserve detailed examination. "For him, who perceives with right knowledge, the uprising of the world as it has come to be, whatever view that is in the world about non-existence will not be acceptable."

The two terms of great epistemological significance that occur in the above statement are (1) "perceives" (*passati*) and (2) "right knowledge" (*sammappaññā*). There could be no mystery associated with the implications of the first of these two terms. *Passati* or "perceives" refers to simple, ordinary sense perception, *for* what is perceived is not something that is mysterious but simply the arising and ceasing of various phenomena in the world. It does not, at least in this instance, refer to a special or unique form of insight not shared by the ordinary people. What makes the difference is "right knowledge" (*sammap-paññā*, or simply *paññā*), and that difference is then explained in the next paragraph.

The perceptions or sense experience of the ordinary person in the world are generally "bound by approach, grasping and inclination" (*upāya-upādāna-abhinivesa-vinibandha*). They are colored by one's prejudices, by one's likes and dislikes. If a person is able to avoid such approach, grasping and inclination, if he does not follow his dispositions, then that person would not take a determined stand and say: "This is my [permanent] self." He would perceive phenomena in the world as arising and ceasing.

The perception of arising and ceasing of phenomena conditioned by various factors is available even to ordinary people who have not been able to completely free themselves from prejudices. Thus, there is a common denominator between the perceptions of an ordinary person and those of the enlightened one. However, the ordinary person continues to worry about a permanent and eternal substance behind phenomena or about a supreme being who is the author of all that happens in the world. He is assailed by doubts about what he perceives. One way of overcoming such doubts is to confine oneself to what is given, that is the causal dependence of phenomena, without trying to look for something mysterious. The Buddha realized that "When phenomena (*dhammā*) appear before the brahman who is ardent and contemplative, his doubts disappear, as he sees their causal nature."[25]

According to the *Kaccāyanagotta-sutta*, if a person does not make up his mind that there is a permanent and eternal self and continue to look for it, but, instead, merely understands things as they have come to be (*yathābhūtaṃ*), as for example, understands suffering (*dukkha*) as something that arises depending upon conditions, then he does not fall into doubt. In other words, instead of looking for mysterious causes one should start with whatever causes one can discover that are contributory to each situation. Of course, in most cases, past experiences are a good index. Thus, in order to attain such knowledge one does not have to go around looking for a teacher who would transmit that knowledge in a secret session or in some mysterious way. His knowledge would, in that case, not be other-dependent (*apara-paccayā ñāṇam ev 'assa ettha hoti*).

On the basis of such knowledge and experience, one is said to have "right view" (*sammā-diṭṭhi*). "Right view" in early Buddhism is contrasted with "wrong view" (*micchā-diṭṭhi*). These two are not contrasted in the way truth and falsehood are contrasted in the pre-Buddhist tradition. In the latter case, what is true is considered to be what exists (*sat*). Whatever exists, is real, and by definition whatever is real cannot be otherwise. According to this *a priori* definition, "truth" has to be something that exists *always*. Yet, what is given to the sense experiences is not available always. Hence it was assumed that what is true is something other than what is given to the sense experiences, and that remains always (*sassata*) and in everything. It is the ontological truth (*ātman*) as well as the moral truth (*brahman*) in everything.

As mentioned earlier, a theory of existence or a theory that says "everything exists' (*sabbaṃ atthi*) is wrong, not because it can be proved to be false, but only in the sense that it does not take into consideration the empirically given fact of cessation (*nirodha*). Hence, it is characterized as "confusion" (*musā*, Sk. *mṛṣā*), not as "non-existent" or "un-truth" or "falsehood" (*a-satya*).

Avoidance of the theory that "everything exists" does not, according to the Buddha, make the opposite view, namely "everything does not exist" (*sabbaṃ n 'atthi*), any more true. The reason for this is that this latter theory implies much more than a *simple denial* of a permanent and eternal substance in man (*ātman*) or in the universe (*brahman*). It implies complete discontinuity in phenomena or their annihilation (*uccheda*), and this too is a wrong view, not because, like the former, it can be proved to be false, but because it is partial in that some aspects of experience like arising (*samudaya*) cannot be accounted for by such a view.

The Buddha did not worry about discovering strictly logical arguments to reject any one of these views. He merely avoided these two theories in his explanation of existence. Hence his statement: "Without approaching either extreme, the Tathāgata teaches you the doctrine by the middle" (*ete te ubho ante anupagamma majjhena tathāgato dhammaṃ deseti*).

The Buddha clearly distinguished his philosophy from that of his contemporary, Sañjaya Bellaṭṭhiputta, who refused to make any pronouncements through fear that he would be found fault with.[26] It makes no sense to assume that the Buddha, after criticizing the two extreme views, avoided propounding any view or observed complete silence. Such an assumption would undermine the authenticity of almost all the doctrines attributed to the Buddha and would stand in the way of appreciating the greatness of this philosopher and spiritual leader whose message did not fade into oblivion, as in the case of the skeptic Sañjaya Bellaṭṭhiputta, but instead became a formidable world-view throughout the last twenty-five centuries. For this reason, the final conclusion of the *Kaccāyangotta-sutta* can in no way be ignored as a later interpolation by the so-called Theravadins.

In this final statement, the Buddha was attempting to explain the human personality as well as its experiences in the world in terms of the principle of dependence, without resorting to the two extreme views that he criticized earlier. In the first part of that explanation, he was describing the personality in bondage, as it evolves conditioned by "approach, grasping and inclination." This is the twelvefold formula (*dvādasaṅga*) presented in positive terms, describing the functions of ignorance, dispositions, and behavior prompted by such dispositions in the matter of propelling human beings into states of unhappiness and suffering as well as continued process of births and deaths. The negative statement explains how, as a result of the elimination of that ignorance and the development of insight, one comes to pacify one's dispositions and thereby eliminate suffering as well as the continued cycle of births and deaths. Such is the conclusion of the *Kaccāyanagotta-sutta*.

The *Kaccāyanagotta-sutta*, though brief, lays down in no unclear terms the basic teachings of the Buddha. Further elaboration of this philosophy is available in the huge collection of discourses of the Nikāyas and the Āgamas. Although denying existence and non-existence conceived of in such a metaphysical manner, the Buddha recognized existence and non-existence in a more empirical sense, such existence and non-existence being understood in terms of the experience of consequences or effects (*attha*, Sk. *artha*). Thus, while being aware of the metaphysical implications of the nominalized forms: "exist-ence" (*atthi-tā*) and "non-exist-ence" (*n' atthi-tā*), the Buddha continued to use the verbal forms "exists" (*atthi*) and "does not exist" (*n 'atthi*) to explain his view of existence.[27]

The existence of things as well as their arising and passing away are clearly expressed in the famous formula:

> When that exists, this comes to be; on the arising of that, this arises. When that does not exist, this does not come to be; on the cessation of that, this ceases (*Imasmiṃ sati idaṃ hoti, imassa uppādā idaṃ uppajjati. Imasmiṃ asati idaṃ na hoti, imassa nirodhā idaṃ nirujjhati*).[28]

Yet the linguistic conventions of his day did not provide the Buddha with technical terms to express this idea. The notion of self-causation (*sayaṃ katam*, Sk. *svayam kṛtam*) was prevalent in the tradition of his day, but unfortunately it carried with it the implication of a metaphysical self (*ātman*), permanent and eternal (*sassata*), which he wanted to avoid.[29] The idea of external causation (*paraṃ katam*, Sk. *para-kṛtam*) was not different from the Materialist view of annihilation, especially in its denial of moral responsibility.[30] A combination of these two views was also not satisfactory, for the Buddha was probably aware of the implications of the Jaina theory of causation that attempted to combine both.[31] Under such circumstances, it was almost impossible for him to express his understanding of existence. This may also have contributed to his initial reluctance to exlain his ideas after this enlightenment. However, he was equal to the task.

An attempt to explain the manner in which a phenomenon gives rise to or produces another phenomenon, how a cause gives rise to an effect, would have involved him not only in the task of unravelling the essence or substance in a cause that produces the effect but also in the job of predicting the effect arising from a cause with absolute certainty, a job for which he did not have the necessary empirical means. The Buddha decided to explain this process in terms of "dependence." He was thus led to speak of an event that has occurred (*samuppanna*) by tracing it back to a condition or set of conditions upon which it depended (*paṭicca*). Having analysed the process of becoming (*bhava*) in this manner, he laid down a principle that would explain future occurrences. Thus, from observing "dependently arisen" (*paṭicca-samuppanna*) phenomena, he asserted the principle of "dependent arising" (*paṭicca-samuppāda*). That terminology is indeed conspicuous by its absence in the pre-Buddhist Indian literature.

The old Indian term *dharma* was retained by the Buddha to refer to phenomena or things. However, he was always careful to define this *dharma* as "dependently arisen phenomena" (*paṭicca-samuppanna-dhamma*). Most of the controversies of the later Buddhists centered on this conception of *dharma*, and therefore the various uses of the term in the Buddha's discourses may be appropriately examined here.

The term *dhamma* (Sk. *dharma*) has four related uses in the early discourses.

(1) *Dhammā* (in the plural) meaning phenomena or things.[32] These are the dependently arisen phenomena referred to earlier. They may also be described as elements of experience.

(2) *Dhammo* (in the singular) meaning the uniformity of phenomena or things as represented by the principle of dependence (*paṭicca-samuppāda*).[33]

(3) *Dhammā* (in the plural) referring to things or phenomena evaluated as good or bad in an ethical sense.[34] While good is often designated *dhammā*, the notion of bad is expressed by its negation, *a-dhammā*.

(4) *Dhammo* (in the singular) expressing the uniformity of moral phenomena, which also represented the ideal or the standard of morality derived from the moral perfection attained by the saint. Hence, *nibbāna* or freedom is also called *dhammo*.[35]

In order to distinguish this notion of *dhamma* from the Indian conception where the term *dharma* meant reality (*ātman*), in an ontological sense, the Buddha utilized the conception of result or consequence or fruit (*attha*, Sk. *ar-*

tha) to bring out the pragmatic meaning of *dhamma*. For the Buddha, whatever is true or real (*bhūta*, *taccha*) is also what produces result (*attha-saṃhita*).[36] This pragmatic definition of truth or reality was more often used in explaining moral phenomena. Hence the reference to the three types of results or consequences or fruits:

1) bad, evil—*an-attha*, corresponding to *a-dhamma*.
2) good, beneficial—*attha*, corresponding to *dhamma*, and
3) ultimate good, ultimate fruit—*param' attha*, corresponding to *nibbāna*.[37]

BUDDHA'S CONCEPTION OF LANGUAGE AND TRUTH

While the term *dharma*, in the four contexts referred to above, may be taken as implying empirical truths, a more comprehensive use of the term is also available. In this case, the *dharma* (or *sad-dharma*) expresses the notion of "true doctrine," and without any hesitation this may be explained as a "true statement," a use that may be most appealing to the modern linguistic philosopher who is generally averse to metaphysics and insists that "truth" pertains to statements. The use of the term *dharma* in this sense at once renders futile any attempt to speak of a linguistically transcendent truth or reality in the Buddhist context.

Dependent arising is the middle path presented by the Buddha between the extremes of eternalism and annihilationism, of strict determinism and chaotic indeterminism, of absolute reality and nihilistic unreality, of permanent identity and absolute difference. Considering the manner in which he explained the middle position between these extremes, no one could maintain that this middle position is beyond linguistic description or transcends any form of verbal expression. In fact, the two terms that are generally utilized in the absolutistic systems of Indian thought to present such a standpoint, namely "indescribable" (*avācya*) and "indefinable" (*anirvacanīya*), do not occur in the early discourses of the Buddha. The term "undeclared" or "unexplained" (*avyākata*) occurs, but it is used to refer to problems such as the duration and extent of the universe, the identity of or the difference between the soul and the body, as well as the status of the *tathāgata after* death—these being problems that could not be explained on the basis of any empirical evidence.[38] For the Buddha, whatever is empirically given is also describable or definable without having to assume metaphysical standpoints.

Thus in the Buddha's view language is not, in itself, an inadequate means of expressing what is empirically given. Yet modern intepreters of Buddhism seem to assume that the Buddha considered language inadequate to express the truth about existence that he discovered. The evidence for such an interpretation is rather dubious. No attempt is made to examine the Buddha's own statements about his enlightenment, as recorded in such discourses as "The Noble Quest" (*Ariyapariyesana*).[38] Most books on Buddhism published in the modern world will attribute to the Buddha, as well as to his early disciples and even to the later ones like Nāgārjuna, a distinction between *sammuti* and *paramattha*. *Sammuti* (Sk. *saṃvṛti*) is explained by Candrakirti as language [40] and *paramattha* (Sk. *paramartha*) as ultimate reality or absolute truth.[41] The terms *sammuti* as well as *vohāra* occur in the early discourses.[42] *Sammuti*, (derived from *sam* + √ *man* "to think") literally means "agreement" and therefore, "convention". *Vohāra* (Sk. *vyavahāra*) means "usage." A rather lopsided interpretation of these two terms as implying "language" only has caused havoc in the explanation of the teachings of the Buddha as well as of Nāgārjuna. There seems to be no justification for confining the meanings of these two terms to language only.

Conventions (*sammuti*) are of various types—linguistic, social, political, moral or ethical, or even religious. Even a superficial glance at pre-Buddhist literary traditions would reveal the manner in which the Indians elevated linguistic, social, political, moral, and religious conventions to the level of absolute realities, permanent and eternal. The language of the Vedas became the absolute language, possessing miraculous powers. In spite of the existence of such languages as Dravidian and Chinese, which have nothing to do with the Vedic language, some educated Indian scholars still believe the Vedic is the mother of all languages. Therefore not a single syllable of it is to be tampered with. Another convention, the social order consisting of four castes, came to be considered absolute. Punishment awaited those who violated it or ignored it. Arjuna was to be rewarded for maintaining that social order. Political conventions derived their absoluteness from the absoluteness of the social order. A rules (*kṣatriya*) who ignores the advice of the spiritual leader and guide (*brāhmaṇa*) was doomed to failure, since he was thereby ignoring the law (*dharma*). The absoluteness of the moral and ethical conventions was equally recognized. No other form of morality except that which contributes to the preservation of the social system was permissible. Religious duties were specific and unalterable.

When, in the *Sutta-nipāta*, the Buddha spoke of *sammuti*, he was referring to all these different kinds of conventions.[43] According to him, these conventions have come to be depending upon specific conditions (*puthujjā*). They were not absolute and ultimate; they were not universally binding. The Buddha realized that when these conventions were considered to be absolute and ultimate (*paramaṃ*) they contributed to the worst form of dogmatism (*diṭṭhi*), which eventually led to all the conflicts (*kalaha*, *viggaha*) in the world.[44] These constituted the worst forms of obsession, obstruction, constraint, or bondage. Therefore, the Buddha claimed that a wise man (*vidvā*) does not approach (*na upeti*) such conventions.[45] This does not mean that he ignores all conventions. Instead, he understands their conditionality and as well as their fruitfulness without elevating them to the level of ultimate realities, thereby making them absolute, or simply ignoring them as absolutely unreal and therefore useless.

Freedom (*nibbāna*) could then be interpreted more appropriately as freedom from obsessions, obsessions *for* as well as *against* such conventions. The elimination of such obsessions or constraints (*papañca*) turned out to be more difficult than abandoning pleasures of sense, for if by freedom was meant only the latter, the Buddha could have attained enlightenment during the time he was practicing self-mortification.

Here again, the difficulty lies in adopting a middle path without accepting conventions as being ultimate or rejecting them as being useless. The uniqueness of the Buddha's philosophy lies in the manner in which a middle path can be adopted with regard to any convention, whether it be linguistic, social, political, moral, or religious. Since the present analysis of the Buddha's philosophy is undertaken only as a prelude to the examination of Nāgārjuna's thought, and since the latter was more concerned with the basic doctrines of the Buddha, our attention at this point will be focussed only on the way in which the Buddha adopted the middle path in dealing with linguistic conventions.

As pointed out above, the term *sammuti* was used in the early discourses to refer to all kinds of conventions. However, there were two terms that were very specifically employed to refer to linguistic conventions. They are *nirutti-patha* (the way of etymology) and *adhivacana-patha* (the way of definition). The *Saṃyutta-nikāya* contains an important discourse dealing with linguistic conventions, which are neither to be clung to as absolute truths, nor to be ignored as mere conventions. The discourse called *Nirutti-patha* runs thus:

> There are these three linguistic conventions or usages of words or terms, which are distinct, have been distinct in the past, are distinct in the present and will be distinct in the future and which are not ignored by the wise brahmans and recluses. Whatever material form (*rūpa*) that has been, which has ceased to be, which is past and has changed, is called, reckoned and termed 'has been' (*ahosi*) and it is not reckoned as 'it exists' (*atthi*) or as 'it will be' (*bhavissati*). . . . [This is repeated for the other four aggregates: feeling, perception, dispositions and consciousness.] Whatever material form has not arisen nor come to be, is called, reckoned or

> termed 'it will be' (*bhavissati*) and it is not reckoned as 'it exists (*atthi*) or as 'it has been' (*ahosi*). . . . Whatever material form has arisen, and has manifested itself, is called, reckoned, or termed 'it exists' (*atthi*), and it is not reckoned as 'it has been' (*ahosi*) nor as 'it will be' (*bhavissati*).[46]

The Buddha advised his disciples "not to cling to dialectical usage nor go beyond the limits of linguistic convention" (*janapada-niruttiṃ nābhiniveseyya sāmaññaṃ nātidhāveyya*).[47] Such being the middle position adopted by the Buddha regarding linguistic convention, it would be an extreme position to maintain that language is either ultimately real (as it was the case with the Indians who made *vac* a supreme god) or that it is useless when it comes to expressing ultimate reality.

For the Buddha, language derives its "meaning" (*attha*) when it is able to produce results (*attha*), and thus what is true (*bhūta*, *taccha*) is that which bears results (*attha-saṃhita*).[48] The Buddha did not recognize anything that is false to be productive of results. Truth in this sense can be equated with "meaningful" language. Thus, linguistic expressions that imply permanence and annihilation would be "meaningless" (*an-attha*) in that they do not communicate anything that is given in experience (*dhamma*), where experience is understood in terms of the felt results (*attha*) rather than in terms of an indefinable ultimate reality.

Having thus rejected the two views, namely, the traditional Indian view that the human personality consists of a permanent and eternal spiritual entity (*ātman*) and the Materialist view the denied such a spiritual entity and recognized matter (body) to be the only reality, the Buddha continued to speak of the psychophysical personality (*nāma-rūpa*), referring to it with such terms as "I" (*ahaṃ*) and "you" (*tvaṃ*) and even the term "self" (*atta*) when speaking of that personality.

With the emergence of Buddhism as a formidable philosophical and spiritual movement that undermined the very foundations of the traditional Indian philosophy and religion, Indian thinkers reformulated their substantialist world-view, presenting it in a more subtle and appealing form in the *Bhagavadgītā*. The notion of *dharma* embodied in this text may be analysed in terms of the three Buddhist categories presented above, namely, *an-artha, artha* and *paramārtha*. Instead of the pragmatic definitions of the Buddhists, the Indian thinkers were presenting a more substantialist interpretation where,

1) *an-artha* = the psychophysical personality (*nāma-rūpa*) which is unreal and which is contrasted with the real self (*ātman*).

2) *artha* = the permanent and eternal self (*ātman*) in man, the so-called *dehin* (the dweller in the body), which is in bondage because of attachment to the psychophysical personality, and
3) *paramārtha* = *paramātman*, which is the ultimate reality, the universal self identified with God.

Thus was inaugurated an enormous controversy between Buddhists and Indian philosophers that continued to rage for several centuries until Buddhism completely disappeared from the Indian soil as a philosophical and spiritual force around the seventh and eighty centuries, only to survive and flourish in the countries south and southeast of India as well as in the Far East.

THE PERIOD OF THE ŚRĀVAKAS

The survival of a pragmatic philosophy in the face of an extremely absolutistic tradition such as the one embodied in the *Bhagavadgītā* was not easy. One of the ways in which the Buddhists responded to that philosophy was by compiling the now famous Buddhist classic, the *Dhammapada*. As the title indicates, it was an attempt to counter the Indian absolutist and substantialist definition of *dhamma*. The Buddhist philosophers, confronted by the onslaught of Indian thinkers asserting the reality of the self (*ātman*), spent most of their time analysing what they called *dhamma* in order to show that there was no permanent and eternal self. As Kenneth Inada has rightly remarked, this represented "the most active, highly vibrant and competitive age in Buddhist history known as the Abhidharma period. . . . If there are high watermarks to be considered in Buddhist history, the Abhidharma period certainly rates a very high level, a level of great fermentation and flourishment of Buddhist thought. Ideologically speaking, no other period in Buddhist history, whether of the Theravada or Mahayana, or even national Buddhist developments such as in T'ang Dynasty China, could ever match, or come up to the level of activity as recorded during this period."[49]

Two complete sets of Abhidharma texts compiled during this period are available to us. One is preserved by the Theravādins consisting of the following texts:

1. – *Dhammasaṅgani*,
2. *Vighaṅga*,

3. *Dhātukathā*,
4. *Puggalapaññatti*,
5. *Kathāvatthu*,
6. *Yamaka*, and
7. *Paṭṭhāna*.

The other version was preserved by the Sarvāstivāda school and comprises one major work and six ancillary texts. They are as follows;

1. *Jñānaprasthāna* (attributed to Kātyāyanīputra),
2. *Saṅgītiparyāya* (attr. Mahā Kauṣṭhila/Śāriputra),
3. *Prakaraṇapāda* (attr. Vasumitra),
4. *Vijñānakāya* (attr. Devaśarman),
5. *Dhātukāya* (attr. Purṇa or Vaśumitra),
6. *Dharmaskandha* (attr. Śāriputra/Maudgalyāyana), and
7. *Prajñaptiśāstra* (attr. Maudgalyāyana).

That the Theravāda and Sarvastivāda schools preserved these two bodies of literature does not make them sectarian, any more than the discourses, preserved by any school, could be branded as such. Although the treatment of subject-matter in these two sets of works differs widely, the subject-matter is practically the same. Both deal with the categories into which the human personality as well as human experience came to be analysed in the early discourses where they receive a more discursive treatment. The analysis of human experience into aggregates, elements, and faculties, all of which were considered to be *dharmas* or elements of existence, seems to be the first and foremost concern of the Ābhidharmikas. Undoubtedly, the purpose of this analysis is to demonstrate the absence of a self or substance in these phenomena. Exhaustive analyses of the various types of relations that obtain among them were also undertaken, providing a sort of scholastic advancement in the study of such phenomena, but still not deviating from the fundamental teachings of early Buddhism. Examination reveals that these two processes in some way represent an attempt to deal with the same issues that the Buddha was concerned with, namely, "dependently arisen phenomena" (*paṭiccasamuppanna-dhamma*) and "dependent arising" (*paṭiccasamuppāda*). The knowledge of these two processes was looked upon as right understanding, which ultimately leads to the attainment of freedom (*nirvāṇa*).

Unfortunately, two of the schools that were involved in this Ābhidharmic enterprise were driven too far in their academic study of the *dharmas*, probably by the unrelenting criticisms levelled against Buddhism by the traditional schools of Indian philosophy. These schools came to be known as Sarvāstivāda and Sautrāntika.

The Sarvāstivāda concluded their analysis of *dharmas* with the recognition of ultimate discrete atomic elements which they were unable to put together even with a theory of four basic relations. The result was that they were compelled to admit a singularly metaphysical conception of "self-nature" (*svabhāva*) to account for the experienced continuity of such discrete phenomena.[50] This self-nature could not be looked upon as something impermanent and changing, for that would be to defeat the very purpose for which it was formulated in the first place. Therefore they insisted that this self-nature (*svabhāva*, *dravya*) of *dharmas* remain during all three periods of time, the past, the present and the future. No other conception could be more heretical in the eyes of the Buddhists who were avowed non-substantialists (*anātmavādī*).

The view that *dharmas* have self-nature had its impact on the conception of "dependent arising" (*pratīya-samutpāda*), the central conception in early Buddhism as well as in the early Abhidharma. Henceforward, "dependence" came to be explained on the basis of self-nature. It turned out to be no more different from the identity theory of causation (*satkārya-vāda*) formulated with such precision, using logical arguments, by the Sānkhya school of thought.[51] The relationship between these two schools of thought is so close that one can hardly discount mutual influences and borrowings.

One of the schools that reacted against this conception of "self-nature", other than the tradition represented by Moggalīputtatissa referred to earlier, was the Sautrāntaka school of Buddhism. As its name implies, this school was openly antagonistic to the "treatises" (*śāstra*) and insisted upon returning to the "discourses" (*sūtrānta*) as sources for the study of the Buddha-word.[52] It considered the notion of "self-nature" as a theory of "self" (*ātma-vāda*) in disguise. However, for some inexplicable reasons they failed to realize that neither a theory of atoms (*paramāṇu*) nor a conception of moments (*kṣaṇa*) was part of the early Buddhist teachings, either in the discourses or in the Abhidharma treatises. On the one hand, they probably assumed that these two conceptions were not the root cause of all the confusion among the Sarvāstivādins. On the other hand, they felt that these two conceptions were, after all, not incompatible with the doctrine of impermanence (*anicca*, Sk. *anitya*) in the early discourses. Without abandoning atomism and momentariness, the Sautrāntikas proceeded to explain "dependence" and ended up recognizing a sort of non-identity theory of causation (*asatkārya-vāda*) comparable to the one proposed by the Vaiśeṣika school of Indian philosophy.[53]

Even though the Sautrāntikas were openly critical of the substantialist conception of *dharma* advocated by the Sarvastivādins, their reluctance to abandon the theory of moments (*kṣaṇa*) left them with the difficult task of explaining the experienced continuity in the individual person. The emergence of schools like "personalists" (*pudgala-vāda*) and "transmigrationists" (*saṃkrānti-vāda*),[54] closely related to and sometimes identical with the Sautrāntikas, is indicative of the solutions that this school had to offer in order to overcome the difficulties arising from the acceptance of a theory of moments.

The Sarvāstivāda and Sautrāntika schools thus presented a rather complicated set of theories, all contributing to philosophical confusion. The former perceived a "self-nature" (*svabhāva*) in the cause and emphasized the identity (*ekatva*) of cause and effect, while the latter, seeing no such "self-nature" but merely perceiving "other-nature" (*para-bhāva*), insisted upon the difference (*nānatva*) between cause and effect. The Sarvāstivāda conception of self-nature (*svabhāva*) was extended to all phenomena, including the human personality, while the Sautrāntikas, denying self-nature in phenomena, surreptitiously introduced a conception of self or person (*ātman*, *pudgala*) in a human personality.

MOGGALĪPUTTATISSA: THE FIRST REFORMER

The Russian Buddhist scholar Th. Stcherbatsky was one of the first among Western scholars to ignore the very significant differences between early Buddhism and Abhidharma on the one hand, and Sarvāstivāda and Sautrāntika interpretations of the "discourses" and Abhidharma on the other. For him, Sarvāstivāda was not only an *interpretation* of Abhidharma but *was* Abhidhama, and the early Buddhism of the discourses as well.[55] However, there was at least one disciple of the Buddha who was not willing to accept either the Sarvāstivāda or the Sautrāntika as the correct interpretation of Buddhism. This was Moggalīputtatissa. Critical scholarship unfortunately has blindly dismissed his views without much serious consideration, even though they are presented with clarity and logical acumen.

Almost 250 years after the Buddha and 300 years before Nāgārjuna, Moggalīputtatissa was responsible for the "great purge" in the Buddhist tradition. The Indian emperor Asoka, as he declared in his Minor Rock Edicts, was actually instrumental in unifying the Buddhist Order (*saṃgha*) by expelling the miscreant and schismatist monks and getting them to don white (lay) garments. Yet, the background for this great purge was prepared by Moggalīputtatissa when in his famous "Points of Controversy" (*Kathāvatthu*) he refuted the ideas presented by almost seventeen heterodox schools of Buddhism. "Moggalīputtatissa is said to have followed the method of discourse adopted by the Buddha—*satthārā dinna-naya-vasena*—at the time he established the *mātikā*, 'topics' of the *K[athā]v[atthu]*."[56] This monumental work is an attempt to go back to the early teachings, and in doing so the author, for the first time in Buddhist history, utilizes even abstract logic. Whether the use of such abstract logic is appropriate is not a matter that concerns us here. What is important is that Moggalīputtatissa was critical of certain ideas which were incompatible with the Buddha's philosophy.

The metaphysical theory of a person (*pudgala*), propounded by the Sautrāntikas and their allies, was the first of the metaphysical views to be taken up for criticism in the *Kathāvatthu*.[57] With great ingenuity and logical precision, Moggalīputtatissa destroyed the concept of a person propounded by the Sautrāntikas and established what may be called the non-substantiality of the human personality (*pudgala-nairātmya*).

With equally cogent arguments, he annihilated the Sarvāstivāda doctrine of *dharma* that implied substantial and eternal existence (*sabbaṃ sabbadā atthi*)[58] and established the non-substantiality of all *dharmas* (*dharma-nairātmya*]. These two uncontroverted achievements, recorded in one of the most authentic texts, have been completely ignored by those who attributed a substantialist theory of elements to the early Buddhist tradition.

EARLY MAHĀYĀNA: THE SECOND REFORM MOVEMENT

The same text highlights another controversy that was beginning to ruffle the minds of Buddhist thinkers during the third century BC and which became the topic of a heated debate during the first and second centuries AD. This pertained to the question whether the Buddha is transcendent (*lokuttara*). Moggalīputtatissa rejected the view, gradually gaining ground in the Buddhist tradition, which favored transcendence.[59] The biographies of the Buddha, like the *Mahāvastu*, were probably not yet written. Mahāyāna, with its conception of a completely transcendent Buddha, had not come into existence by that time. The *Saddharmapuṇḍarīka*, which is responsible for condemning the miscreant monks (*bhikṣu*) as well as the ideal of a saint (*arhant*) in early Buddhism, indicates a gradual growth with the final version assigned to the third century AD. In the earliest versions of some of the early Mahāyāna *sūtras*, such as *Vajracchedikā-prajñāpāramitā* and the *Kāśyapa-parivarta*, there is no mention of a *bodhisattva*.[60]

What sort of Mahāyāna can there be without the conception of a transcendent Buddha and the notion of a *bodhisattva*? It certainly ought to be different from the kind of Mahāyāna that one comes across in the available versions of the *Saddharmapuṇḍarīka* and other texts that include a condemnation of the early *arhant*-ideal.

Indeed the *Kāśyapa-parivarta*, even in the Sanskrit version which is not the earliest, will enable us to understand what that original Mahāyāna was. It was not the Mahāyāna that came to be deeply prejudiced against early Buddhism as well as Theravāda, for, as pointed out earlier, even though we find a strong criticism of the monk (*bhikṣu*), a criticism that may be accepted even by the Buddha and his disciples like Moggalīputtatissa, this criticism is not extended to the early ideal of the "worthy one" (*arhant*).

One of the most important series of discourses or instruction (*dharma-paryaya*) referred to in the *Kāśyapa-parivarta* as "the great pinacle of gems" (*mahā-ratna-kūṭa*), pertains to the "middle path" (*madhyamā-pratipat*).[61] Here we find a long list of middle paths, most of which are described in negative terms. However, side by side with the negative descriptions, one also discovers a positive description of the middle path in terms of the twelve factors of the human personality (*dvādasāṅga*). It is indeed an abbreviation of the *Kaccāyanagotta-sutta*, with Kāśyapa as the interlocutor or the person to whom the discourse is addressed.

The need for negative descriptions, especially at a time when Buddhahood was not yet looked upon as a transcendent state or as an Absolute, calls for an explanation. Available historical records indicate that some of the canonical texts that emphasized the doctrine of non-substantiality (*nairātmya*), and which included the work of Moggalīputtatissa, found a haven in Sri Lanka and other South East Asian countries after the third century BC. However, some of the early discourses as well as some of the Abhidharma texts were still circulating in India and came to be preserved in a Prakrit, slightly different from Pali. Yet, what came to be popular after the third century were the interpretations of the Buddhist metaphysicians, like the Sarvāstivādins and the Sautrāntikas. The early Mahāyāna that did not include either the concept of "transcendence" as applied to the Buddha or a notion of *bodhisattva*, but which emphasized a negative doctrine while at the same time preserving the positive assertions of early Buddhism, was therefore a response to the Sarvastivāda and Sautrantika metaphysics, rather than a reaction to the early Buddhism of the "discourses" or the Abhidharma.

Nāgārjuna's Mission

Nāgārjuna, who lived at a time when the Theravāda-Mahāyāna conflict had not degenerated to the level that is presented in the *Saddharmapuṇḍarīka*, therefore had an already different mission. It was indeed not the least different from the mission that lay before Moggalīputtatissa, to expose the untenability of certain heretical views that were gradually becoming popular in the Buddhist tradition. A careful reading of the *Kārikā* will reveal the fact that Nāgārjuna had all the help he needed to achieve this task. As mentioned before, even after the transference of the Pali canon to Sri Lanka, the discourses and the Abhidharma texts survived in India. Thus the discourses of the Buddha as well as the tradition of the disciples (*śrāvaka*) were available to Nāgārjuna. The humility with which Nāgārjuna bows down to the Buddha and the respect with which he treats the Buddha's disciples (*śrāvaka*)[62] are in complete contrast to the unsympathetic attitude of the later Mahāyānists toward the earlier Buddhist tradition.

In the following analysis of the *Kārika*, it will be shown that Nāgārjuna attempted to discredit heterodox views, especially those of the Sarvāstivādins and the Sautrāntikas, and establish the non-substantiality of all *dharmas* (Chapters III - XV) as well as the non-substantiality of *pudgala* (Chapters XVI - XXI) and thereafter to explicate the positive doctrines of the Buddha as embodied in the early discourses like the *Kaccāyanagotta-sutta*.

The present analysis is, therefore, contrary to the more popular interpretation of Nāgārjuna espoused by commentators like Candrakirti who emphasized the *reductio ad absurdum* (*prāsaṅgika*) method. It will be more sympathetic to the interpretations offered by Nāgārjuna's disciples like Bhāvaviveka and the more positive thinkers of the Mādhyamika school. While highlighting the ingenuity and philosophical maturity of Nāgārjuna, the present analysis will at the same time be unsympathetic toward the myth that Nāgārjuna was a second Buddha.

STRUCTURE OF THE *KĀRIKĀ*

Selections from the works of a major philosopher belonging to a tradition may be helpful in introducing that tradition but not in providing a complete view of that philosopher's thought. The reason is that when a philosopher presents his ideas in some form, he feels that everything he has said in that work is relevant to his thought. If anything that he has said is irrelevant to what he proposes to convey to his readers, he would be not only wasting his time, but also the reader's.

Attempts have often been made by modern scholars to pick out selections or chapters from the works of eminent philosophers of the East, hoping thereby to provide a complete and accurate picture of their ideas. Sometimes they are considered to be *essential* secitons or chapters, the implication being that the rest is inessential.[63] This undoubtedly has contributed to a great deal of misunderstanding and sometimes deliberate distortion of the author's ideas. Considering the unsatisfactoriness of such a method, the present analysis of Nāgārjuna's thought will be presented on the basis of an examination of his *Kārikā* taken as a whole, with every word, every verse, and every chapter in it treated as in integral part of that work. This is done in the absence of any concrete evidence that some portions of this work are not by Nāgārjuna.

A superficial reading of this work, with 448 verses divided into 27 chapters, could leave the reader with the impression that the text is repetitious. This wrong impression will disappear like a mirage if one keeps in mind the circumstances that led to the complication of this work, the motivation for writing it, the background in which it was written, and the goal that was to be achieved. Such considerations will enable one to see a carefully executed plan or structure in the *Kārikā*. In order to highlight this structure, the *Kārikā* will be analysed here into four major sections, without changing the sequence either of the individual verses or of the chapters.

Section I

This first section includes Chapters I and II, which deal with the most fundamental doctrines of Buddhism, causation and change. The problem of causation or "dependent arising" is taken up in the first of these. If this were a text written during the Buddha's day, this chapter would undoubtedly have dealt with theories of existence presented by the traditional schools of Indian philosophy advocating the reality of a permanent self (*ātman*) and the Materialist school that denied such a self (*an-ātman*) thereby denying the continuity of the human person as well as his moral responsibility. However, Nāgārjuna was living in the second century AD and his problems, as mentioned earlier, were created more by the Sarvāstivādins and the Sautrāntikas than by the non-Buddhist schools. This is clearly evident from the way in which Nāgārjuna begins his first chapter.

The first verse in this chapter refers to four different theories of causation or arising: (i) self-causation, (ii) external causation, (iii) both self- and external causation, and (iv) arising out of a non-cause. After enumerating four such theories, any further explanation would naturally commence with an analysis of the first of these four theories, self-causation (*svata-utpatti*). Thus, the four types of relations (*pratyaya*) referred to in the next verse should be taken as examples of the theory of self-causation (*svata-utpatti*), even though the most respected modern interpreter of Nāgārjuna, namely T.R.V. Murti, following the footsteps of Candrakīrti, took these four types of causal relations to represent the theory of external causation, and not self-causation.[64] He assumed that self-causation was presented by the Hindu schools and external causation was a theory advocated by the early Buddhists only. As explained above, the early Buddhist theory of causation cannot be placed under the category of either self-causation or external causation. Nāgārjuna was clearly aware of this and therefore, even though in the first verse he denied the possibility of any one of the four causal theories, in the second verse he recognizes four conditions (*pratyaya*) without denying them—though to make his analysis more comprehensive he denies a fifth condition. The denial comes only in the third verse, but what is important to note is that it is not a denial of the four conditions (*pratyaya*) but of the manner in which the condition is considered to be related to the effect. When Nāgārjuna said, "The self nature of an existent is not evident in the causal condition, etc." (*Na hi svabhāvo bhāvānāṃ pratyayādiṣu vidyate*, I.3), he was not rejecting or denying conditions, but only self-nature (*svabhāva*) that some philosophers were positing in the condition (*pratyaya*) in order to account for the arising of the effect. This is a quite clear indication that Nāgārjuna was not rejecting the Adhidharma theory of conditions but only its interpretation by some of the metaphysicians, in this particular case that of the Sarvāstivādins. As pointed out above, there is every evidence that it was the Sarvāstivādins who interpreted the theory of conditions (*pratyaya*) on the basis of a conception of substance (*svabhāva*). In the same verse, Nāgārjuna proceeds to deny external causation (*parata-utpatti*) or, more specifically, the conception of "other nature" (*para-bhāva*) advocated by the Sautrāntikas. If this background is kept in mind, the understanding of Nāgārjuna's ideas in the *Kārikā* is not as formidable as has been assumed.

Chapter II deals with the problems created—not by an empirical theory of change and impermanence (*anityatā*), for that was a fundamental conception of early Buddhism—by a more metaphysical theory of change and impermanence based on a logical or even a psychological theory of moments (*kṣaṇa-vāda*).

Section II

The second section includes thirteen chapters, beginning with an examination of sense faculties (*indriya*, Chapter III) and ending with an examination of substance (*svabhāva*, Chapter XV). The entire section is an attempt to establish the doctrine of the non-substantiality of phenomena (*dharma-nairātmya*) without having to get rid of any one of the categories such as the aggregates (*skandha*), spheres of sense (*āyatana*), and elements (*dhātu*), all of which were part of the early Buddhist teachings embodied in the discourses as well as in the Abhidharma. Almost all the important subjects dealt with in early Buddhism are taken up, once again not with the intention of rejecting them, but with a determination to rid them of any metaphysical explanation, especially of existence (*astitva*) and of non-existence (*nāstitva*), implying permanence (*śāśvata*) and annihilation (*uccheda*) which the Buddha was openly rejecting in the *Kaccāyanagotta-sutta*.

Section III

The third section includes eleven chapters from XVI to XXVI. It is a section that has caused confusion in the minds of many who wrote on Nāgārjuna's thought. First, many of the topics dealt with in the previous section are again analysed here. This gave the impression that the text is repetitive and therefore it is possible to ignore some of its parts when presenting Nāgārjuna's philosophy. For example, the examination of action and agent (*karma-kāraka*) was attempted in Chapter VIII, and a longer chapter (XVII) on the examination of the fruit of action (*karma-phala*) is included in this section. Secondly, this particular chapter (XVII) deals with the doctrine of karma in a more positive way, asserting the existence of a more appropriate view than the one criticized at the beginning of the chapter. Such an assertion seems to go against not only the doctrine of emptiness (*śūyatā*), as it is generally understood by modern scholars, but also the view that neither the Buddha nor Nāgārjuna had a view to propound.

However, reading the eleven chapters one cannot help coming to the conclusion that they were intended to establish the non-substantiality of the individual (*pudgala-nairātmya*) but not to eliminate the conception of an individual or person altogether. The conception of the individual involves the problems of bondage and freedom (*bandhana-mokṣa*) and, after defining these, five chapters are devoted to the problem of bondage. These five chapters are undoubtedly commentary on a verse that seems to have been extremely popular among the Buddhists and which both Nāgārjuna and Vasubandhu were conversant with, for we find the latter composing a whole treatise called *Karmasiddhiprakaraṇa*.[65] This verse is quoted by Candrakirti in his commentary, and runs thus:

Actions are not destroyed even by [the passage of] hundred myriads of aeons. Having reached the harmony of conditions and the proper time, they bear fruits for the human beings.

Na praṇaśyanti karmāṇi kalpakoṭiśatair api,
sāmagrim prāpya kālaṃ ca phalanti khalu dehinām.[66]

The denial of a permanent self (*ātman*) by the Buddha prompted his critics to insist that the Buddha could not satisfactorily explain the problem of moral responsibility. The present verse is only a summary of the Buddha's causal explanation of the doctrine of moral responsibility, not an admission of a permanent and eternal *karma*. In fact, the determinism that may appear with the reading of the first line, is immediately corrected with the conditionality specified in the second line. Three main topics are dealt with here: the imperishability of karma (*avipraṇāśa*), the harmony of conditions (*sāmagrī*) and the appropriate time (*kāla*). It is therefore not surprising to see Nāgārjuna inserting two chapters on "harmony" (*sāmagrī*, XIX) and time (*kāla* XX), after stating the "imperishability" of karma (XVII) and denying the existence of a permanent and eternal "self" (*ātman*, XVIII). To eliminate any one of these chapters as inessential to the understanding of Nāgārjuna's thought is, therefore, highly unwarranted.

After a clarification of the meaning of bondage (*bandhana*) in the context of a human being who is without a permanent and eternal self and who still continues to wander along experiencing births and deaths, happiness and suffering, Chapter XXII takes up a person who has attained freedom (*mokṣa*), who has "thus gone" (*tathāgata*) without having to wander along as a person in bondage. No other issue in Buddhist thought has been as misunderstood and misinterpreted, not only by the non-Buddhists, but also by the Buddhists themselves, as the conception of *tathāgata*. Probably for this reason, Nāgārjuna felt the need to begin his discussion of freedom with an examination of the conception of *tathāgata*. It will be shown that Nāgārjuna's analysis follows exactly the method of analysis given by the Buddha. The chapter that follows explains the reasons for such misconceptions (*viparyāsa*, XXIII).

Modern scholarship on Nāgārjuna has empahsized the conception of two truths to the complete neglect of his explanation of the four truths as enunciated by the Buddha. It will be shown that the two truths in Nāgārjuna are not an improvement on the four noble truths, nor a special insight on the part of Nāgārjuna, but an understanding of a doctrine that is already clearly expressed in the early discourses. This lengthy chapter (XXIV) concludes with a recognition of the four noble truths and the doctrine of dependent arising that is the foundation of the four noble truths.

The chapter on *nirvāṇa* (XXV) is a refutation of the absolutist interpretation of the notion of freedom and a determined attempt to go back to the non-absolutist form of Buddhism enunciated in the early discourses.

Contrary to the view of most modern scholars of Nāgārjuna's thought, Chapter XXVI (*Dvādaśāṅgaparīkṣā*) is here presented as an elaboration of the Buddha's own conclusion in the *Kaccayānagotta-sutta*. It deals with the Buddha's positive explanation of how a human being in bondage cân free himself from the mass of suffering.

Section IV

Nāgārjuna could have concluded his treatise with the previous section. However, he was aware that his most favorite discourse—the *Kaccāyanagotta-sutta*—began with the queston regarding "right view (*sammādiṭṭhi*). Nāgārjuna has already explained almost every aspect of the Buddha's doctrine and shown what constitutes a "right view" as against the "wrong or confused views" (*micchādiṭṭhi*) that appeared in the Buddhist tradition. Yet there were some views that the Buddha left aside without either asserting or denying them. These pertained to the ten, and sometimes fourteen, unexplained or undeclared questions (*avyākata*, Sk. *avyākṛta*). A treatment of these questions was needed before Nāgārjuna could make a final comment about the attitude of the Buddha, the "freed one" (*nibbuta*), with regard to all varieties of views, whether they be right or wrong. One could hardly expect a better conclusion to a text intended to bring about freedom from all obsessions (*prapañcopaśama*) than this last chapter. It represents an explanation of the highest form of freedom, that is, freedom from ideological constraints, that the Buddha as well as his disciples (*śrāvaka*) had attained and which made Buddhism one of the most tolerant religions ever to appear on earth.

ANALYSIS OF THE KĀRIKĀ

Part-I (Causality and Change)

1. *Conditions* (*pratyaya*). The Buddha's main philosophical insight, as has been shown, was expressed by the term "dependent arising" (*paṭiccasamup-*

pāda). It was presented against the four theories of self-causation, external causation, both self- and external causation and non-causation. Nāgārjuna, being a true disciple of the Buddha, is therefore seen as initiating his primary philosophical treatise by categorically denying these four causal theories (1.1). According to the Buddha, the four theories imply the existence or non-existence or both or neither, of a permanent existence, an eternal and substantial self (*ātman*). That same implication is assumed by Nāgārjuna when he used the term *bhāva* (instead of *bhava*) to refer to the entities that are explained in these four ways. Thus, in the very first stanza Nāgārjuna's denial pertains to a metaphysical existence (*bhāva*) and not to the empirical notion of becoming (*bhava*) characterized by arising (*utpāda*) and ceasing (*vyaya*).

In verse 2, Nāgārjuna refers to four types of conditions (*pratyaya*), emphatically declaring that there is no fifth. However, there is no categorical denial of the four conditions, compared to the denial of the four causal theories in the previous verse. The reason for this is very evident. Nāgārjuna, a very sophisticated philosopher, realized that the Buddha rejected the four causal theories mentioned in verse 1. He also knew that the later Buddhist disciples (*śrāvaka*) attempted to elaborate upon the Buddha's conception of "dependent arising" (*pratītyasamutpāda*) by formulating a theory of four conditions (*pratyaya*); these were the early Ābhidharmikas. He saw no reason for an outright rejection of the theory of four conditions.

However, in verse 3, he immediately takes up a particular interpretation of a condition (*pratyaya*) and negates it: "The self-nature of existents is not found in the condition, etc." It is not difficult to see what is being denied here. To Nāgārjuna, it seems that some philosophers were interpreting the Buddhist (Ābhidharmika) theory of four conditions (*pratyaya*) in terms of one or the other of the theories mentioned in verse 1, which the Buddha himself had rejected. Nāgārjuna could not have been unaware of the fact that the philosophers who spoke of conditions (*pratyaya*) at this early period in Indian thought were the Buddhists and not the non-Buddhists. Therefore, his attention is now directed to these Buddhist interpreters and not to the non-Buddhists.

As mentioned earlier, among the Buddhists the only school that gave a susbstantialist interpretation of phenomena (*dharma*) during this early period was the Sarvāstivāda school. Their theory of self-nature (*svabhāva*) came dangerously close to the Indian conception of self (*atman*). Nāgārjuna was, therefore, merely criticizing the view of the Sarvāstivāda school of Buddhists, who were suggesting a substantialist interpretation of the four conditions. Thus, the categorical denial in stanze 3 pertains to the view of the Sarvāstivādins, who assumed a self-nature or substance (*svabhāva*) of the existent (*bhāva*) *in* the conditions (*pratyaya*).

What sort of argument does Nāgārjuna present in order to deny the existence of self-nature? Murti and others who saw in Nāgārjuna's method a dialectic comparable to that of Immanual Kant have considered self-nature (*svabhāva*) and other-nature (*parabhāva*) as antinomies. This may be true. However, such a dialectic is not used by Nāgārjuna in his first refutation of the notion of self-nature. Nāgārjuna rejects self-nature, not because it is relative to other-nature, but because it is not evident (*na vidyate*). The argument from relativity is utilized to reject other-nature only and not self-nature. ("In the absence of self-nature, other-nature is also not evident.") What is found here is a simple and straightforward denial of self-nature on epistemological grounds, even though he does not elaborate upon that epistemology at this point. Throughout the text, one finds Nāgārjuna using the negated verb, *na vidyata*, and sometimes the present participle, *avidyamāna*. The former is often rendered as "not found," and in our translation preference is given to the more epistemologically oriented rendering: "is not evident." This emphasis is clearly evident from the manner in which he rejects "self-nature," as explained above.

In other words, Nāgārjuna appears more as an empiricist than as a dialectician who merely utilizes reason. Thus, the text begins with a simple denial of self-nature as something that is *not evident*. What Nāgārjuna means by evidence will be explained later on in this essay. If this point is kept in mind, it becomes rather easy to understand the rest of Nāgārjuna's analysis of conditions.

Thus, in the verse that follows (1.4), Nāgārjuna speaks of action (*kriyā*) and condition (*pratyaya*). In this case, neither the action nor the condition is denied. What is denied is the sort of relationship that is assumed between them, that is, inherence which emphasizes identity. The denial of identity is prompted by the fact that it is equated with "self-nature" (*svabhāva*) which, in its turn, was looked upon as a permanent entity. Difference was likewise denied because it was perceived as other-nature, which implied annihilation or lack of any continuity.

Verse 5 takes up the definition of a condition. A condition is such because depending upon it others arise. However, the reason why Nāgārjuna rejects this definition is not that it is not empirically valid, but that there is a rider attached to the definition. That rider implies that this dependence is eternal and permanent. In other words, that which is dependent and that upon which it depends are substantially connected through a relation of inherence. Hence, Nāgārjuna's queston: "So long as it [the effect] does not arise, why is it [the cause] not considered to be a non-condition?"

Verse 6 completes Nāgārjuna's general criticism of conditions. Most modern translators have failed to bring out the significance of this verse, primarily because the term *artha* (= effect, fruit, result, rendered into Chinese as *kuo*) failed to attract their attention. What is denied is, therefore, not the arising of an effect as ordinarily understood, but the arising of an effect that is already existent (*sato arthasya*) or one that is non-existent (*asato arthasya*). These again represent the identity (*satkārya*) or the non-identity (*asatkārya*) theories of causation presented by the Sarvāstivādins and the Sautrāntikas.

Verses 7-10 represent the criticism of the four types of conditions referred to at I.2 as interpreted by the Sarvāstivādins and the Sautrāntikas. If the *sat* (existent) and *asat* (non-existent) qualifying *dharma* (phenomena) are understood as implying "the substantially (*svabhāvato*) existent and non-existent," a qualification that Nāgārjuna often makes, then it will be easy to understand the nature of Nāgārjuna's criticism. This is especially so in verse 10 where, on the surface, it appears that Nāgārjuna was criticizing the Buddha's own statement: "When that exists, this comes to be," (*asmiṃ satīdam bhavati*). However, Nāgārjuna was very careful in dealing with this statement, for in the first line he was explicit with regard to the sort of existence he was criticizing, that existence being none other that "substantial existence" (*sat-tā*).

Verses 11-14 deal with several other aspects of the theory of causation such as the arising of an effect from a combination of conditions. It is indeed the concluding line of the last verse (1.14) that possibly can give rise to all the misunderstanding regarding Nāgārjuna's analysis of causal conditions. "In the absence of the effect, whence can there be a condition or a non-condition." It is easy to interpret this statement to mean that Nāgārjuna did not accept either a cause or an effect that is dependent upon a cause. To take it as a simple denial of cause and effect would be to ignore everything that Nāgārjuna has been trying to say earlier in the chapter, regarding self-nature (*svabhāva*) or substantial or permanent existence (*sat*). There seems to be no rationale for interpreting this statement independent of the basic premises with which he set out on his examination of conditions. To conclude: What is denied here is not the simple effect that depends upon the condition or conditions for its arising, but an effect that is either pre-existent, and therefore permanent, or non-existent because it is not pre-existent. It is also reasonable to assume that a similar denial pertains not to a simple cause or condition but to a cause or condition that produces an already existent or non-existent effect.

"Dependent arising" or casuality (*pratītyasamutpāda*) was, to reiterate, the principle in terms of which the Buddha was able to explain the functioning of phenomena (*dharma*) without resorting to a conception of permanent and eternal entity (*nitya ātman*). In other words, dependent arising explains the impermanence (*anityatā*) of phenomena that are dependently arisen (*pratītyasamutpanna*) without which no identification of "dependent arising" is possible. Because such phenomena are dependently arise, they are impermanent (*anitya*). Impermanence involves change and movement.

2. *Change or movement* (*gatāgata*). Chapter II of the *Kārikās* is an attempt to reconsider this conception of impermanence, i.e., change or movement. Such a reconsideration, like the examination of causality, was necessitated *not* by a desire to transcend it but by a desire to return to the original teachings of the Buddha. Here too the waters were muddied by the speculations of the Sarvāstivādins and the Sautrāntikas. In the first instance, Nāgārjuna was compelled to re-examine the conception of causality because these two schools were confronting each other as a result of the former's recognition of a self-nature or substance (*svabhāva*). Why did the conception of self-nature emerge at all? As we have seen, the two schools had wrongly conceived of change and impermanence.

The Buddha described time and temporality in a more empirical way when he said that the arising of phenomena, the change of what has come to be and their cessation are evident.[67] The three temporal periods of past (*atīta*), present (*paccuppanna*), and future (*anāgata*) in relation to phenomena were thus recognized. To refer back to the discourse on "Linguistic Conventions" (*Niruttipatha*) mentioned earlier, the Buddha even examined the three linguistic conventions (*adhivacana*) such as "existed" (*ahosi*), "exists (*atthi*) and "will exist" (*bhavissati*), pointing out that these should not be ignored.

However, in their enthusiasm to demarcate the boundaries of the three periods of time, the Sarvāstivādins and the Sautrāntikas were led to an atomic notion of time and temporality,[68] unaware of the dangers that lay ahead of them. In order to overcome the difficulties they faced as a result of their acceptance of an atomic conception of time, the Sarvāstivādins were bold enough to admit an underlying substance that remains unchanged, even though they did not realize that such a doctrine was incompatible with the Buddha's notion of non-substantiality (*anātman*). The Sautrāntikas, on the contrary, denying such a substance and claiming themselves to be the faithful interpreters of the discourses, still maintained the momentary destruction (*kṣaṇabhaṅga*) of phenomena. They did not realize that their conception of the momentary destruction of phenomena was forcing them to recognize a subtle transmigrating entity. Hence, they came to be characterized by their opponents as "transmigrationists" (*saṃkrāntivādin*).

Nāgārjuna's attempt, therefore, was to show that a speculative notion of time and temporality such as the one emphasized by the Sautrāntikas was not an empirically justifiable one. A modern critic of a similar conception of time, William James, has provided the following analysis:

> In short, the practically cognized present is no knife-edge, but a saddle-back, with a certain breadth of its own on which we sit perched,

> and from which we look into two directions into time. The unit of composition of our perception of time is a *duration*, with a bow and a stern, as it were—a rearward- and a forward-looking end.[69]

The very first verse in Chapter II suggests the kind of movement or motion that is under criticism: "What has moved is not being moved."

For someone to claim that what has already moved (= present), the underlying assumption is that even though there is a distinction in terms of temporality, there is indeed the sense in which what is being moved in the present is not different from what, on an earlier occasion, was also in a state of moving. This can easily give rise to the view that phenomena are in a constant flux, a continuous uninterrupted flow (*santati*). While such an explanation may account for the continuity of phenomena that are analysed into discrete events, it also explains the identity of each individual stream (*santāna*). This latter idea, carried to its extremes, led to the metaphysical notion of a subtle but substantial personality (*pudgala*), neither idential nor different from the aggregates (*skandha*). This is the school of "personalists" (*pudgalavāda*).

Thus, following the same method that he adopted in criticizing the substantialist notion of causality, Nāgārjuna focuses his attention on the metaphysical interpretations of ideas of change and movement, without attempting to deny the concepts such as "the moved" (*gata*), "the not moved" (*agata*), or "the present moving" (*gamyamāna*) *per se*. After a detailed analysis of the unhealthy consequences of such metaphysical interpretations, Nāgārjuna, in the end, specifies the sort of view he is criticizing when he maintained:

> An existing mover does not carry out the movement in any of the three ways. Neither does a non-existing mover carry out the movement in any of the three ways. Nor does a person carry out a movement, both existing and non-existing, in any of the three ways. Therefore, neither the motion, nor the mover, nor the space moved is evident. (II.24-25.)

The 'existing mover' (*sadbhūto gantā*) is indeed similar to the 'exitent' (*bhāva*) possessing self-nature (*svabhāva*) which was criticized in the previous chaper. The denial of motion, the mover, and the space moved is thus not a categorical denial but the denial of a substantialist interpretation of these phenomena.

Even though the refutation of the substantialist view of existence (*bhāva*, *svabhāva*) remains the primary concern in Chapters I and II, the ideas examined in Chapter I seems to be predominantly those of the Sarvāstivāda school, while Chapter II seems to concentrate more on the tenets of the Sautrāntikas, who were more aligned with the "transmigrationists" (*saṃkrāntivādin*) and the "personalists" (*pudgalavādin*).

The method developed in these two chapters provides a large framework on the basis of which the innumerable concepts are analysed in the chapters that follow.

Part II (Dharma-nairātmya)

As mentioned earlier, Chapters III and XV deal with almost all the major Abhidharma categories that are treated under general rubric "*dharma*." Of these various categories, the most important are aggregates (*skandha*), faculties/spheres (*indriya/āyatana*), and elements (*dhātu*). This is the order in which these are normally enumerated. However, Nāgārjuna was interested in epistemology, and therefore it is natural for him to take up the faculties (*indriya*) for examination at the very outset.

3. *Faculties* (*indriya*). Chapter III, verse 1, refers to the six faculties and their spheres. Yet, there is no denial of any one of them. This may be compared with Nāgārjuna's statement in Chapter I, verse 1, that refers to the four causal theories, all of which were instantly denied. However, in verse 2, Nāgārjuna criticizes a particular definition of "seeing" (*darśana*) and that definition involves "the perception of itself" (*svātmānaṃ darśanaṃ*). This undoubtedly is the Indian version of the Cartesian "cogito" which led to the belief in a permanent and eternal self during the period of the *Upaniṣads*[70] and continued to flourish in the speculations of the later Indian philosophical schools.[71] It is the definition that produced the most metaphysical of ideas, such as the conception of the "inner controller" (*antaryāmin*) that turns out to be the permanent and eternal self or soul (*ātman*). Any form of perception, for them, involved self-awareness as a necessary pre-condition, after which every other form of activity follows. In fact, later on Nāgārjuna devotes an entire chapter (IX) to an examination of this notion of an antecedent self. Whether this view influenced the Yogācāra conception of "self-perceiving consciousness" (*svasaṃvedaka-vijñāna*) remains to be seen. For Nāgārjuna, however, such a definition was not satisfactory, since it implies the conception of a substantial entity.

Here again, after making a categorical denial of "seeing" as "seeing itself," Nāgārjuna proceeds to draw the implication, as he did in his criticism of other-nature (*para-bhāva*, I.3), that "if seeing cannot see itself, how can it see another?" Such a criticism on the part of Nāgārjuna would still leave intact the Buddha's own explanation of perceptual experience in terms of the principle of dependence (*pratītyasamutpāda*). In fact, it is for this reason that later on

Nāgārjuna was able to speak of visual perception (*cakṣur-vijñāna*) as a product of causal dependence (see XXVI.4).

The criticism of "seeing" (*darśana*) in III.4 is similar to the criticism of causal condition in I.5. Nāgarguna assumes that the implication of the substantialist notion of "seeing" is that "seeing must always see." Thus, if the Sarvāstivādins were to recognize a "self-nature" (*svabhāva*) in "seeing", then it could possibly not be "not seeing" even on some occasions, for the very nature of seeing is to see. Therefore, when Nāgārjuna asserts that "there cannot be a non-seeing seeing" (*na apaśyamānaṃ darśanaṃ*), he was merely stating the substantialist definition of the Sarvāstivādins. Hence the second statement "seeing sees' (*darśanaṃ paśyati*) becomes a mere tautology and, as such, is not appropriate. The rest of the chapter deals with a criticism of all forms of perception conceived in the above manner, indicating that "grasping" (*upādāna*), etc. will remain inexplicable in such a context.

4. *Aggregates* (*skandha*). Of the five aggregates into which the human personality came to be analysed in the Buddhist tradition, Nāgārjuna takes up only the first, namely, material form (*rūpa*). After explaining Nāgārjuna's treatment of material form, Inada rightly remarks: "But all this does not mean that neither *rūpa* nor the elements cease to exist."[72] This confirms what we have said about Nāgārjuna's treatment of other concepts such as cause, effect, motion, or seeing. However, Inada's explanation of the reason for this needs to be qualified. He maintains: "Nāgārjuna is only trying to exhibit the fact that any conception or thing cannot be described by reference to a simple cause-effect relationship in order to establish its existential status." On the contrary, it seems that Nāgārjuna may not have any difficulty in maintaining that there is a simple cause-effect relationship between the four primary elements (*manbhūta*) and material form (*rūpa*), so long as that cause-effect relationship is understood as one of dependence, which was the Buddha's own view.[73] Yet, what is being introduced here is not such a simple theory of dependence of the effect upon the cause.

The conception of *kāraṇa* that Nāgārjuna refers to here is one of the six causes (*hetu*) referred to in the Sanskrit Abhidharma texts and interpreted by the Sarvāstivādins as a "unique cause," that is, "anything other than itself" (*svato 'nye kāraṇahetuḥ*).[74] In other words, it is any cause whose self-nature is different from that of the effect. The four great elements (*mahābhūta*) depending upon which the material form (*rūpa*) comes to be would be the *kāraṇa* of material form. Yet as a *kāraṇa* of material form it would be distinct from material form. It is this particular definition of *kāraṇa* that is criticized by Nāgārjuna. His reason for denying it is stated in IV.2: "If material form is separated from the unique cause of material form [i.e. the four great elements], it would imply that material form is without a cause (*ahetuka*)." However, Nāgārjuna's empiricist and analytical approach does not allow him to recognize an effect (*artha*) which is without a cause (*ahetuka*).

Existence (*bhāva*), which Nāgārjuna was often criticizing implied self-existence (*svabhāva*). The fact that the Sarvāstivādins defined not only material form, but also the other four aggregates—feeling, perception, disposition, and consciousness—as self-existent entities (*bhāva*) is evident from Nāgārjuna's statement at IV.7. Thus, Nāgārjuna's basic criticism of the Sarvāstivādins in this chapter is that they could not consistently speak of a unique cause (*kāraṇa*), while at the same time recognizing a cause and an effect that are related by way of self-nature (*svabhāva*). In other words, the notion of self-causation (*svatotpatti*) contradicts a "unique cause" (*kāraṇa*), for it is anything other than itself.

5. *Elements* (*dhātu*). In the early Buddhist tradition, the psychophysical personality was analysed into five aggregates (*skandha*) in order to show that there was no permanent spiritual entity or self (*ātman*) as recognized by the traditional Indian philosophers. Therefore, the psychic part of the personality was analysed in detail. In order to refute the view of the Materialists that the eternal entity is matter, not a spiritual or psychic entity, the Buddha once again analysed the human personality into six elements (*dhātu*) with a detailed examination of the physical part of the personality. Thus we have the category of elements consisting of earth (*pṛthvi*), water (*āpas*), fire (*tejas*), air (*vāyu*), space (*ākāśa*) and consciousness (*vijñāna*).

While the conception of a "unique cause" (*kāraṇa*) was introduced in the examination of the aggregates (*skandha*), the notion of "characteristics" (*lakṣaṇa*) is brought into the analysis of elements (*dhātu*). Though the term "characteristic" (Pali *lakkhaṇa*) occurs in the early discourses, there it is not used in the metaphysical sense in which it came to be employed by the Sarvāstivāda school. For the Sarvāstivāda, a characteristic (*lakṣaṇa*) represented the changing aspect of an entity (*dharma*), while self-nature (*svabhāva*) stood for the unchanging and eternal aspect. This particular notion of "characteristic" needs to be kept in mind when analysing the contents of Chapter V.

A "characteristic" is evaluated here in relation to an existent (*bhāva*) which possesses self-nature (*svabhāva*). For the Sarvāstivādins, this existent was a *dharma*. Hence, very often we find Kumārajīva utilizing the term *fa* (= *dharma*), in its restricted sense, to render *bhāva* (*yu*), which is an indication that he too was aware of the nature of the concept analysed by Nāgārjuna. Nāgārjuna's major endeavor here is to demonstrate the difficulties that arise when speaking of characteristics (*lakṣaṇa*) in relation to eternal or absolute existence (*bhāva*) as well as nihilistic non-existence (*abhāva*).

This analysis becomes all the more important because of the way *bhāva* and *abhāva* are treated here. Nāgārjuna's conclusion is significant: "Those people of little intelligence who perceive the existence (*astitva*) as well as the non-existence (*nāstitva*) of existents (*bhāva*) do not perceive the peaceful appeasement of the object (*draṣṭavya*)"(V.8).

In the Buddhist texts, including the *Kārikā*, we read more often about the appeasement of obsession (*prapañcopaśama*). However, for the first time, Nāgārjuna introduces the notion of the appeasement of the "object" (*draṣṭavyopaśama*). Why?

It was mentioned earlier that the Buddha's discourse on the aggregates (*skandha*) was intended to refute the notion of a spiritual self (*ātman*) and the discourse on elements (*dhātu*) was meant to reject the notion of a material self or eternal matter. If this supposition is correct, we have no difficulty in understanding the reasons for Nāgārjuna's introduction of the idea of appeasing the object. The objects of perception associated with the first five sense faculties are material. If the Materialists were looking for a self (*ātman*) in matter and the Sarvāstivādins were looking for a self-nature (*svabhāva*) in the same, the best advice a non-substantialist like Nāgārjuna could give such people is to "vaporize or liquify" the object, and avoid grasping after it. For Nāgārjuna, there was no difference between self (*ātman*) and self-nature (*svabhāva*). While they carry the same philosophical implications, their practical consequences are also similar, in that both lead to grasping and, therefore, suffering. Abandoning grasping (*upādāna*) for the object, one eliminates the metaphysical beliefs pertaining to eternal existence (*astitva*) and nihilistic non-existence (*nāstatva*). Hence the emphasis on the appeasement of the object. Indeed, "the appeasement of the object" (*draṣṭavyopaśama*) is the means by which one can realize the "non-substantiality of phenomena" (*dharma-nairātmya*) and it does not mean the elimination of the object.

Unless one were to keep in mind this particular context in which Nāgārjuna was emphasizing the "appeasement of the object," it would be easy to assume that here Nāgārjuna was justifying idealism (*vijñānavāda*). Candrakīrti's comments, unfortunately, lead to such unwarranted conclusions.[75]

6. *Lust* (*rāga*). The Buddha considered lust (*rāga*) to be the cause of most of the ills of life, the worst of these being bondage. Freedom (*nirvāṇa*) was thus defined as absence of lust (*vairāgya*). Not only did he speak of lust and absence of lust, he also often spoke of people who are lustful (*rakta*) and free from lust (*virakta*). Yet, all such statements were made with no assumption of a concealed substance (*svabhāva*) or of a mysterious spiritual or material personality. The analyses of faculties (*indriya*), aggregates (*skandha*), and elements (*dhātu*) were intended to demonstrate the futility of such assumptions. However, the Sar-

vāstivādins conceived of a substance in every element, while the Sautrāntikas posited a mysterious personality. Therefore, it became necessary for Nāgārjuna to examine the concepts of lust (*rāga*) as well as the lustful (*rakta*). A variety of unsatisfactory implications that arise out of the Sarvāstivāda and Sautrāntika interpretations is clearly presented in Chapter VI, with the conclusion: "Thus, with or without the lustful, lust is not established. Like lust, all things, with or without [accompaniments], are not established."

Once again, we should not forget the fact that the *dharmas* referred to here are those that were recognized by the Buddhist metaphysicians, not the empirical phenomena as defined by the Buddha and the early Buddhists.

7. *Conditioned* (*saṃskṛta*). The early discourses referred to three characteristics of the conditioned (*saṃskṛta*).[76] These were arising (*utpāda*), change of what has come to endure (*sthitasya anyathātva*), and ceasing (*vyaya*). In a similiar discourse, a definition of the "unconditioned" (*asaṃskṛta*) is provided and, in this case, it is said that the three characteristics mentioned above are not evident. It was, therefore, easy for some of the later Buddhists to leap to the conclusion that the "unconditioned" is also uncaused or independent (*apratītyasamutpanna*). This, evidently, was the intention of the Sarvāstivāda commentator, Yaśomitra, when he stated that the terms "conditioned" (*saṃskṛta*) and "dependent" (*pratītyasamutpanna*) are synonyms.[77] Yet, from other statements in the discourses, it is clear that this was not the case. For example, while the three terms *anicca* (impermanent), *saṃskṛta* (conditioned), and *pratītyasamutpanna* (dependent) occur together (though not as synonyms), to explain the nature of the world,[78], of their negative forms only *abhūta* and *asaṃskṛta* (together with *ajāta*, and *akṛta*[79]) are used to characterize nirvana. The negative form of *pratītyasamutpanna* does not occur. For this reason, it can be maintained that the term *saṃskṛta* has the specific meaning of "dispositionally conditioned," and is not identical in meaning with the term *pratītyasamutpanna* ("dependent").

Not only did the Buddhist metaphysicians ignore this subtle distinction and considered the concepts of "conditioned" and "dependent" as being identical, they also explained the "conditioned" in terms of their metaphysical notions of substance and their speculative notion of temporality referred to earlier. Nāgārjuna's lengthy chapter on the subject of "The Conditioned" (*Saṃskṛta*, VII) draws out all the implications of such metaphysics.

After rejecting the metaphysically conceived notions of arising (*utpāda*) and along with it all other related concepts such as "the present arising" (*utpadyamāna*) and "non-arising" (*anutpāda*), comparing all of them to the notions of "the moved" (*gata*), "the not moved" (*agata*), and "the present moving" (*gamyamāna*)(VII.14) which he had previously criticized. Nāgārjuna makes a very significant statement at VII.16: "Whatever that comes to be dependently, that is inherently peaceful. Therefore, that which is presently arising as well as arising itself are peaceful."

In the first place, here there is no denial of arising (***utpāda***) or that which is presently arising (***utpadyamāna***). By implication, there is no denial of cessation (*vyaya*) either. Secondly, there is no denial of "dependent arising" (*pratītyasamutpāda*) or that which is dependently arisen (*pratītya yad yad bhavati*). On the contrary, there is a very significant assertion: "Whatever is dependently arisen is inherently peaceful." Explaining the "elements" (***dhātu***) in a previous chapter (V), Nāgārjuna has shown how the belief in eternal existence (*astitva*, *bhāva*) and nihilistic non-existence (*nāstitva*, *abhāva*) lead to the unfortunate consequences such as grasping (*upādāna*) and, therefore, suffering (*duḥkha*). The avoidance of such perspectives and the adoption of the view that things arise and pass away dependently (*pratītya*) were considered by the Buddha and the early Buddhists as well as Nāgārjuna as being "inherently peaceful" (*svabhāvataḥ śāntaṃ*).

The significance of the use of the term *svabhāva* in the above context should not go unnoticed. The term *svabhāva* as well as its adverbial use, *svabhāto asti*, especially when qualifying existence, was condemned by Nāgārjuna throughout the work. However, in the present verse he was willing to use this very same term in an adjectival sense, qualifying *śānta* (peaceful).

The concepts of "the conditioned" and "the unconditioned", perceived in terms of substantial existence, are rejected here, and the notions of arising, duration, and ceasing, similarly conceived, are also abandoned as being illusory.

8. *Action and agent* (*karma-kāraka*). While "dependently arisen (*pratītyasamutpanna*) phenomena imply a process of natural occurence "unconditioned by dispositional tendencies" (*asaṃskṛta*) on the part of human beings, "dispositionally conditioned" (*saṃskṛta*) phenomena are the results of human deliberations (*saṃskāra*) or actions (*karma*). For this reason, after clarifying the notions of the "conditioned" and the "unconditioned," it was natural for Nāgārjuna to take a look at the notions of action (*karma*) and agent (*kāraka*). If these two were found to be real in a substantialist sense, then the lengthy analysis of "conditioned" phenomena in the previous chapter would appear faulty.

Therefore, Nāgārjuna begins with a substantial agent (*sadbhūta kāraka*) who performs a substantially existing action (*sadbhūta karma*) and his analysis demonstrates that such an agent as well as such an action, in fact, logically lead to a denial of action (*kriyā*), agent (*kartṛ*) as well as a cause (*kāraṇa*).

Verse VIII.5 represents an unequivocal assertion on the part of Nāgārjuna that such a substantialist view not only leads to the denial of action, etc., but also to an abandoning of discriminations and distinctions such as good (*dharma*) and bad (*adharma*) that are so relevant to the Buddha's conception of fruits (*phala*) of life, both worldly (= heavenly, *svarga*) and ultimate (= freedom from suffering, *mokṣa*). Not only the goal or fruit of life, but also the path that leads thereto or all the actions that produce such fruits, would thereby be rendered useless or meaningless (*nairarthakyaṃ*).

The statement at VIII.12 that both action and agent are dependently (*pratītya*) arisen and that there is no other perceivable manner in which these could be established (*nānyat paśyāmaḥ siddhikāraṇaṃ*) stands as an eloquent testimony to Nāgārjuna's vindication of the empirical standpoint of the Buddha and of early Buddhism.

9. *Antecedent state* (of the self) (*pūrva*). If there were to be no substantial action and agent, except the empirically given action and agent which are the results of dependence, how is it that metaphysicians came to assume the existence of such an eternal self or personality?

In Chapter IX, Nāgārjuna undertakes to show how the belief in a permanent and eternal entity arises as a result of the recognition of the existence of a personality *prior* (*pūrva*) to his experiences such as seeing, hearing, and feelings (IX.1). In other words, the Buddhist metaphysicians, following a method similar to that adopted by Descartes in Western philosophy, were positing a substantial entity and then proceeding to attribute the functions of seeing and hearing to that entity. It is hard to believe that a philosopher like Nāgārjuna was unaware that the Buddha's notion of non-substantiality (*anātman*) was the direct result of his rejection of such a perspective, very clearly expressed by the Buddha in a passage in the *Sutta-nipāta*: "Let him destroy the entire root of obsession, [namely, the belief] 'I think, [therefore] I am," (*mantā asmīti*).[80]

This indeed is an unequivocal rejection of the "cogito ergo sum" (*mantā asmi*) which contributed to the substantialist thought of the *Upaniṣads* as well as later Indian thought. Nāgārjuna's arguments shows how self-destructive such an assertion is. The implication of this assertion, as Nāgārjuna perceives, is that such a personality has to be separated from the experiences that emerge subsequently. Nāgārjuna wants to know how such a personality could be made known (*parjñapyate*) independent of such experiences (IX.3) thus implying that the *sum* (*aham asmi*) is dependent. If these experiences can be separated from the personality, it follows that they could occur even without such a personality (IX.4).

Having explained certain other implications of this metaphysical position, all of which he considers to be unsatisfactory, Nāgārjuna maintains that with regard to such a personality the concepts of existence and non-existence are not validly applicable.

10. *Fire and fuel* (*agnīndhana*). The futility of employing the example of the fire (*agni*) and fuel (*indhana*) in order to illustrate the relationship between a substantial action and a substantial agent is shown in Chapter X. It is indeed the most important metaphor used by the substantialists to establish the conception of a metaphysical person. The manner in which the Pudgalavādins utilized this metaphor is explained in detail by Vasubandhu in the final chapter of his *Abhidharmakośa-bhāṣya* (see annotation on Chapter X). Finally he refuses to recognize those who admit the reality of a self (*ātman*, *pudgala*) as well as those who uphold discrete substantial entities (*bhāva*), as people who are conversant with the true meaning of the Buddha's teachings (X.16). It is clear that the reference here is not to the non-Buddhist metaphysicians, but rather to the Buddhist metaphysicians who claimed themselves to be the true interpreters of the Buddha-word, namely the Sautrāntikas (= *pudgalavādins*) and the Sarvāstivādins (= *svabhāvavādins*).

11. *Prior and posterior ends* (*pūrvāparakoṭi*). The refutation of the prior existence of a substantial being or entity would still leave open the question regarding the beginning and end of things. Speculations regarding the beginning (*pūrva-koṭi*) and the final end (*apara-koṭi*) have occupied the attention of philosophers from the dawn of history. These speculations have given rise to a wide variety of beliefs, one of which is the substantial existence of a being (such as God) or an ultimate entity (such as primordial matter, *prakṛti*, sometimes referred to as *svabhāva*).[81] Realizing the epistemological problems involved in these speculations, the Buddha refrained from making any statements regarding such issues.

Chapter XI is intended to explain the Buddha's attitude towards such questions. Nāgārjuna was aware that the Buddha refused to make any statements about the prior end of the life-process. Hence his statement: "The Great Sage has declared that the prior end of the life-process is not known" (XI.1). However, the Sanskritization of the Prakrit term *anamatagga* (= "inconceivable is the beginning") as *anavarāgra* (= "without beginning and end") had already appeared in the Buddhist texts that Nāgārjuna was familiar with.[82] Taking this latter version of the Buddha's statement, Nāgārjuna maintains that there is neither a beginning nor an end, whereas the Buddha's own statement pertained to the epistemological difficulties.

Yet, Nāgārjuna's ingenuity was such that he was able to indicate the logical difficulties involved in any denial of either the beginning or the end. For he finds that "no middle can be conceived of that which is without beginning or end" (XI.2). Because of such logical difficulties, he maintains that prior and posterior as well as simultaneous states (of *saṃsāra*) are not appropriate. These logical difficulties arise primarily becaue entities are conceived of in a rather substantialist way. Thus, if birth were to be considered as being prior to old age and death, and birth as well as old age and death are substantial, that is, existing in their own nature (*svabhāva*), then there will be birth without old age and death, which implies immortality (XI.3). Moreover, if they were to be self-existent, there would be no causal connection between them (XI.4). Similar logical difficulties arise if they were considered as being simultaneous.

While the Buddha was unwilling to discuss the absolute origin and end of the life-process (*saṃsāra*) and yet continued to speak of things arising and passing away on the basis of causal dependence, Nāgārjuna had to deal with the notion of the life-process interpreted in a more substantialist way by the Buddhist metaphysicians. Therefore, after making the remark that the prior end of *saṃsāra* is not evident, a position upheld by the Buddha himself, Nāgārjuna proceeds to maintain that "the prior end of all *existents* is also not evident" (*sarveṣām api bhāvānāṃ pūrvā koṭi na vidyate,* XI.8), thereby rejecting all the views of the substantialists.

12. *Suffering (duḥkha).* After analysing the nature of existence and adoping a middle position between the two extreme views presented by his fellow Buddhist philosophers, Nāgārjuna focussed his attention on the problem of human suffering (*duḥkha*). Here again, it is difficult to believe that Nāgārjuna was unaware of the statements of the Buddha as recorded in the Nikāyas and Āgamas. His analysis of suffering follows exactly the line that was followed by the Buddha in the *Acela-kassapa-sutta* of the *Samyutta-nikāya.*[83] Herein, when a disciple by name Kassapa questioned the Buddha as to whether suffering is self-caused (*sayaṃ kataṃ dukkhaṃ*), the Buddha, without saying: "It is not so" (*no h'etaṃ*), which is a formal negation, merely remarks that "he should not speak so," or "should not put it that way" (*ma h'evaṃ*). Kassapa elicits the same response from the Buddha when he questions him as to whether "suffering is caused by another" (*paraṃ kataṃ dukkhaṃ*) or whether it is "caused by both self and other" (*sayaṃ katañ ca paraṃ katañ ca*) or whether it is "caused neither by oneself nor by another" (*asayaṃkāraṃ aparaṃkāraṃ*) and, therefore, of "spontaneous origin" (*adhiccasamuppannaṃ*).

The reason why the Buddha discouraged Kassapa from reflecting on the cause of suffering in this manner was that he felt that the first two views led to beliefs in permanence (*sassata*) and annihilation (*uccheda*) respectively. In the background in which the Buddha preached, to say that "one acts and the same person experiences the consequences" (*so karoti so paṭisamvediyati*) implied the existence of an eternal soul or self, and to maintain that "one acts and another experiences the consequences" (*añño karoti añño paṭisaṃvediyati*) was taken to mean annihilation, that is, absence of any connection between act and consequence. This was tantamount to a denial of moral responsibility. Avoiding these two extremes, the Buddha explained the relation between action and consequences as one of dependence.

It would be necessary to keep in mind that in the above context the Buddha was not denying the four theories of the causation of suffering. He was merely stating that the theories as presented were not satisfactory, because of the implications drawn by the metaphysicians. However, after warning that one should avoid such implications and explaining the dependence of such phenomena, the Buddha used similar linguistic expressions in order to explain his view of the causation of suffering. Recognizing one's responsibility for one's own actions, he was even willing to say: "An action is performed by oneself" (*attanā va kataṃ kammaṃ*),[84] so long as one does not assume the existence of a metaphysical agent or ignore any other factor that contributes to the situation.

Following the same method, Nāgārjuna (XII.1), instead of denying these possibilities, merely says that they are not proper (*na yujyate*). The reason for this is that "if [suffering] were to be considered self-caused, then it will not be dependently arisen" (XII.2). Here then is a distinction between self-causation and dependence, a distinction based upon the assumption or the non-assumption of a metaphysical agent respectively. Therefore, Nāgārjuna maintains: "These aggregates appear dependent upon these other aggregates." However, this latter view should not be taken as meanihg "external causation" (*parakṛta*).

Subsequently Nāgārjuna proceeds to show the logical difficulties involved in accepting either self-causation or external causation. And this criticism is then applied to the self-causation or external causation of any other existent (*bhāva*).

13. *Dispositions* (*saṃskāra*). The Buddha never claimed that all phenomena (*dharmāḥ*) lead to suffering (*duḥkha*). For him, all dispositions (*saṃskārāḥ*) or everything conditioned by dispositions (*saṃskṛta*) are subject to suffering or are unsatisfactory.[85] Thus, after explaining the conception of suffering, Nāgārjuna deems it necessary to discuss the conception of dispositions (*saṃskāra*). Chapter XIII is devoted to this question.

The non-absolutist standpoint of early Buddhism is clearly manifest in the Buddha's rejection of the sharp dichotomy between truth (*satya*) and falsehood (*asatya*) recognized in the Indian philsophical tradition. Instead of the true/false dichotomy, the Buddha spoke of truth (*sacca* = *satya*) and confusion (*musā* = *mṛṣā*),[86] indicating thereby that he was not advocating a notion of absolute or ultimate truth, comparable to the Atman/Brahman of the pre-Buddhist traditions.

Nāgārjuna was faithfully following the Buddha and the early Buddhists when he began his analysis of "dispositions" (*saṃskāra*) with a reference to this idea of "confusion" (*mṛṣā*). The relationship between "dispositions" and "confusion" needs to be carefully examined before any attempt to understand the Buddha's as well as Nāgārjuna's disquisition on the nature of dispositions.

A careful reading of the early discourses will reveal that dispositions are an inalienable part of the human personality. In the case of an ordinary unenlightened person, they are not eliminated even at death. Hence the possibility of his being reborn. However, they are completely eliminated in the *tathāgata* when he attains *parinirvāṇa*, that is, when he dies. Yet, there is no mention of the dispositions being *completely* eliminated in the enlightened one (*buddha, tathagata*) while he is still alive. What is achieved with the attainment of freedom (*nirvaṇa*) is the "appeasement of dispositions" (*saṃskāropaśama*). This very subtle distinction will become extremely important when we try to understand Nāgārjuna's treatment of "dispositions" (*saṃskāra*) in the present chapter.

William James explains human knowledge and understanding in the following manner: "The intellectual life of man consists almost wholly in his substitution of a conceptual order for the perceptual order in which his experience originally comes."[87] Elaborating upon this statement he says:

> The substitution of concepts and their connections, of a whole conceptural order, in short, for the immediate perceptual flow, thus widens enormously our mental panorama. Had we no concepts we should live simply "getting" each successive moment of experience, as the sessile sea-anemone on its rock receives whatever nourishment the wash of the waves may bring. With concepts we go in quest of the absent, meet the remote, actively turn this way or that, bend our experience, and make it tell us wither it is bound. We change its order, run it backwards, bring far bits together and separate near bits, jump about over its surface instead of ploughing through its continuity, string its stems on as many diagrams as our mind can frame.

Unless we attribute "omniscience" (*sarvajñatā*) to the Buddha, and that is knowledge of everything that has occurred, is ocurring and will occur in this world, a knowledge he refused to claim for himself,[88] we may end up turning him into a "sessile sea-anemone," if we are to deny him the need to *conceptualize*. In this process of conceptualizing, in "putting things together" (which is the literal meaning of *saṃskāra*), our interests play a dominant role. Interests are easily converted to likes and dislikes, and these latter are causes of most human suffering. We are, therefore, in a double-bind. We need the *saṃskāras* in order to live. On the contrary, they can contribute to most of our suffering (*duḥkha*).

Realizing this fact, the Buddha emphasized the need to pacify our dispositions rather than eliminate them completely. Thus, on the basis of experience we come to know that things are "dependently arisen" (*pratītyasamutpanna*) and then adopt the view that in the dim past this may have been the case and that in the future it may be the case.

In the eyes of the Buddha this represents a more comprehensive and, therefore, a more appropriate view (*samyag-dṛṣṭi*) rather than the more limited views: (1) which says: "Suffering is self-caused" (*svayaṃkṛtaṃ*), which is the result of our believing in a self (*ātman*) to the exclusion of every other factor, and (2) which says: "Suffering is caused by another" (*duḥkhaṃ parakṛtaṃ*), which is, in some sense, the result of our reluctance to admit our own responsibility. In both cases, our likes and dislikes have dominated our dispositions, and hence our perspectives push us in two different directions. Such dispositions, dominated by our likes and dislikes, eventually mislead us regarding many of our experiences and thereby contribute to our suffering and frustrations. In the Buddha's view, therefore, the cessation of suffering is synonymous with "non-grasping" after views[89] which comes about as a result of the appeasement of dispositions.[90] Cessation of suffering is *not* synonymous with not having views or not having dispositions. Rather, it is synonymous with the appeasement of dispositions.

It is very appropriate, therefore, that Nāgārjuna decided to write a chapter on the dispositions (*saṃskāra*) after his analysis of suffering (*duḥkha*). However, what is more important is that this chapter is entirely devoted to an examination of "views" (*dṛṣṭi*) as well as of the condition that give rise to "wrong-" or "confused views" (*mithyā dṛṣṭi*), namely, confusion (*mṛṣā*). In fact, the term *saṃskāra* occurs in the first verse *only*.

The entire chapter is devoted to an examination of the notions of the "existent" (*bhāva*), the "non-existent" (*abhāva*), "self-nature" (*svabhāva*), etc. and the manner in which these could be avoided by adopting the conception of "emptiness" (*śūnyatā*), without allowing that notion of emptiness to be an obsession. Hence his conclusion: "The Victorious Ones have announced that emptiness is the relinquishing of all views. Those who are possessed of the view of emptiness are said to be incorrigible."

We have rendered the term *niḥsaraṇa* occurring in the above verse as "relinquishing" in order to bring out the specific meaning that Nāgārjuna probably had in mind. Many interpreters of Nāgārjuna have explained "emptiness" (*śūnyatā*) as a "provisional view," thereby implying that the ultimate truth is beyond conceptualization.[91] The foregoing analysis of the Buddha's as well as Nāgārjuna's thoughts would mean that they indeed did not recognize a "non-conceptual truth or reality." For them, there is no way in which a "truth" could be understood non-conceptually, because, as mentioned earlier, truth in its most comprehensieve sense pertains to statements and thus involves conceptualization. However, conceptualizations can be comprehensive and therefore right (*samyak*), or limited and confused and therefore wrong (*mithyā*), and these depend upon the amount of prejudice that has gone into the formulation of the concepts. Thus, "emptiness" is a "view," a view not without identification, but which is identified with "the empty" (*idaṃ śūnyaṃ*). It is a view that helps the individual to attain freedom from views and upholding it as the absolute or ultimate truth without any reference to "the empty" would be the last thing either the Buddha or Nāgārjuna would advocate.

14. *Association (saṃsarga)*. The dispositions are instrumental in our forming of views on the basis of experience. It was also pointed out that if we were not to formulate such views we would be no different from the sessile sea-anemone. Dependent arising (*pratītyasamutpāda*), impermanence (*anityatā*), non-substantiality (*anātmatā*), emptiness (*śūnyatā*), etc. are all concepts which would be rendered meaningless unless they were to be identified with the "dependently arisen," "the impermanent," "the non-substantial," and "the empty" given to us in experience. They are views or theories formulated by stretching out our experiences into the dim past as well as the future.

However, some of the Buddhist metaphysicians, as explained earlier, had complicated the situation for Nāgārjuna by their analysis of experience into discrete momentary events. Such as analysis, which led to the formulation of the metaphysical notion of self-nature (*svabhāva*), also created other problems that these metaphysicians were never able to solve satisfactorily. One of them is the distinction they made between mind (*citta*) and matter (*rūpa*). In their ultimate constitution, these were explained as having completely distinct natures (*svabhāva*). Mind was considered to be im-material (*a-rūpa*) and matter was looked upon as being non-mental (*a-citta*).

Avoiding such a reductive analysis, early Buddhism was able to maintain that depending upon the eye, the visible form, and consciousness perception (*saṃjñā*) arises.[92] However, following that reductive analysis, the Buddhist metaphysicians experienced difficulty in explaining not only perceptual experience, but also conceptual formulation of such perceptual experience.

This accounts for the need to have a chapter on "association" (*saṃsarga*) following the chapter on the "dispositions" (*saṃskāra*). How is it possible to bring together into association (*saṃsarga*) the object (*draṣṭavya*) and the subject (*draṣṭṛ*) in order to have a visual perception (*darśana*)? Nāgārjuna begins this chapter with a denial of such a possibility. In doing so he is specifically denying the possibility of an association of events that are considered to be ultimately distinct, and this idea is being emphasized in Kumārajīva's translation of XIV.1. The problems of identity and difference that arise as a result of such a reductive analysis are once again clearly brought out in this chapter.

15. *Self-nature (svābhāva)*. The problem of association (*saṃsarga*), discussed above in the specific context of seer, object of seeing, and seeing, arose as a result of admitting a self-nature (*svabhāva*) in each one of these phenomena. This provided Nāgārjuna with an opportunity to come into grips with the most difficult issue he had to deal with, self-nature or substance. In our earlier discussions we have shown how the Sarvāstivādins utilized this conception to explain the relationship between a cause and an effect, Nāgārjuna's basic argument against this notion of self-nature is that it contradicts the conception of the occurrence (*saṃbhava*) of an event depending upon causes and conditions (*hetu, pratyaya*). Nāgārjuna's understanding of self-nature is that it is not made (*akṛtaka*) by anything else. It is not dependent upon causes and conditions for its existence; hence independent. A "caused substance," according to him, is a contradiction in terms. This analysis should, therefore, be supplemented by his analysis in Chapter I. As we have pointed out there, Nāgārjuna was not denying either dependently arisen phenomena or dependent arising. He was merely showing the inconsistency in explaining causally conditioned phenomena in terms of self-nature. It is in the present chapter that he is giving a definition of self-nature that contradicts the notion of dependent arising or causation. He says: "Indeed, an unmade self-nature is also non-contingent upon another," (*akṛtrimaḥ svabhāvo hi nirapekṣaḥ paratra ca*) (XV.2). The argument in Chapter I is then repeated to show that in the absence of self-nature, there cannot be other-nature (*parabhāva*). Buddha's famous discourse to Kātyāyana, discussed at length at the beginning of this Introduction, is then quoted in order to reject the "existent" (*bhāva*) or "self-nature" (*svabhāva*) and the "non-existent" (*abhāva*) or "other-nature" (*parabhāva*). These then are aligned with views regarding existence (*astitva*) and non-existence (*nāstitva*).

Existence (*astitva*) is further defined as the original or primordial existence (*prakṛti*), a conception developed in the Sāṅkhya school of Indian philosophy which had close affinity, if not identity, with the Sarvāstivāda conception of existence. The empirical and logical difficulties involved in this conception are then laid bare. Reiteration of the fact that the beliefs in self-nature and other-nature, in the existent and the non-existent, in existence and non-existence, lead to beliefs in permanence and annihilation respectively provides a conclusion to this rather significant chapter.

The topics taken up for discussion in this section (Chapters III-XV), as pointed out above, deal with elements of experience (*dharma*) which were originally explained in terms of dependence, but which were complicated by the introduction of the notions of self-nature (*svabhāva*) and other-nature (*parabhāva*), of metaphysical identity and absolute difference, by some of the later Buddhists. Nāgārjuna's attempt in this section was mainly directed at getting rid of the conception of self-nature or identity (the notions of other-nature or difference falling apart as a result). This is the way in which he attempted to establish the non-substantiality of elements (*dharma-nairātmya*). The non-substantiality of the human personality (*pudgala-nairātmya*) turns out to be his next concern.

PART III (Pudgala-nairātmya)

16. *Bondage and release (Bandhana-mokṣa)*. The recognition of a permanent and eternal self (*ātman*), even though it raised epistemological difficulties, enabled the early Indian thinkers to explain many ideas like karma and survival, bondage and release, in a more comfortable way. The Buddha's denial of such a metaphysical entity gave rise to enormous philosophical problems. The question was often raised: "Which self will be touched (or affected) by actions performed by a non-self."[93] So long as the doctrine of dependent arising was understood properly, the Buddhists could consistently descirbe the manner in which a person may be said to perform an action and reap its consequences. However, as emphasized earlier, the Buddhist metaphysicians created more problems with their interpretations of dependence than they solved. These metaphysical views were foremost in Nāgārjuna's mind when, after examining the problems relating to suffering, etc., he proceeded to analyse the problems of bondage and release (*bandhana-mokṣa*), action and consequence (*karma-phala*), and so on.

Bondage (*bandhana*) can be of several sorts. Human beings are fettered by the pleasant objects they perceive, the ideas they form, and finally the process of becoming (*bhava*) itself. Craving for becoming (*bhava-tṛṣṇā*) is looked upon in Buddhism as one of the most troublesome bonds. This craving for becoming, while leading to suffering in the present life, keeps the individual wandering in samsaric existence, subjecting him to repeated births and deaths. Death, personified as Māra, carries with it a snare (*pāsa*) which very few humans can escape. The present chapter, therefore, focusses its attention on this bondage to the life-process.

While the discussion of the Sarvāstivāda conception of self-nature (*svabhāva*) lingers along in the next few chapters, the Sautrāntika theory of a transmigrating personality (*pudgala*) emerges into prominence in the present section. When it is said that "dispositions transmigrate" (*saṃskārāḥ saṃsaranti*), what is assumed is that there is a subtle essence in the dispositions that enable them to be perpetuated. Nāgārjuna's argument here is more dialectical. If dispositions are permanent, then there is no point in speaking of their transmigration. For, transmigration implies moving from one position to another, disappearing in one place and appearing in another. If something is permanent, it is always present and there is no question of its ceasing and arising. On the contrary, if things are impermanent, in the sense of being completely destroyed (*uccheda*), they will never transmigrate. Nāgārjuna, therefore, maintains that if a human being is looked upon in the above manner, it is not possible to speak of his transmigration (XVI.1).

The impression one gets from the available translations of XVI.2 is that Nāgārjuna rejects the theories of aggregates (*skandha*), faculties (*āyatana*), and elements (*dhātu*).[94] Yet, what is clearly stated here is the early Buddhist position: "It may be assumed that a person transmigrates. Yet such a person, sought for in the fivefold way, in the aggregates, spheres and elements, does not exist. Who then will transmigrate?"

Thus, the transmigration that is denied is that of a subtle personality. However, if transmigration is understood as the continuation of the factors of the human personality on the basis of causal dependence, Nāgārjuna may not have any objection against it.

The notion of bondage that is criticized turns out to be the bondage of a substantial entity to such things as dispositions. It is similar to the notion one finds in the Indian tradition where the permanent "self" (*ātman*) is said to be in bondage to the psychophysical personality which is impermanent. Hence Nāgārjuna's argument that anything that is of the nature of arising and passing away (*utpāda-vyaya-dharmin*) is neither bound nor released. What is being criticized here is not the simple notions of bondage and release but those that take into consideration a substantial subject and its attributes.

The concluding verse could easily lead to much misunderstanding if the significance of the relative terms "where/there" (*yatra/tatra*) are ignored. The context specified here with these relative terms is what came to be discussed before, namely, the assumption of a substantial subject and the attribution of various attributes to it. Thus, in a context *where* some substantial subject is attributed with something called freedom (*nirvāṇa samāropa*) or is stripped of the life-process (*saṃsārāpakarṣaṇa*), *therein* there is no sense in making a discrimination (*vikalpa*) between freedom and bondage, for what is real, namely, the substantial subject, will remain the same. Or else, *where* nirvana is "reified" (*samāropa*) and the life-process is eliminated (*apakarṣaṇa*), *therein* too there is no sense in making such discriminations. These being totally different from one another, the knowledge of one would have no relevance to the understanding of the other.

17. *Action and consequence (karma-phala)*. Buddhism, in contrast to the theistic religions of India, advocated human responsibility in the case of bondage as well as release. Chapter XVII that follows therefore deals with the notions of human action (*karma*) and its consequences or fruits (*phala*).

Inada's analysis of this very lengthy chapter is very confusing. He assumes that verses 1–19 contain the popular views on karma, while in verse 20 Nāgārjuna finally explains the true position of the Buddha who spoke of "emptiness" (*śūnyatā*).[95] Yet, verses 2 and 13 unequivocally attribute certain views to the Buddha, as well as the Pratyeka-buddhas and the Śrāvakas. The contents of this chapter therefore deserve careful scrutiny.

The doctrine of karma is clearly stated in XVII.1: "Self-restraint as well as benefitting others—this is the friendly way and it constitutes the seed that bears fruit, here as well as in the next life."

If Nāgārjuna was a Mahāyānist, as many have portrayed him to be, then he certainly could not deny this "friendly way" (*maitraṃ dharmaṃ*), for otherwise he could not qualify as a *bodhisattva*. Restraining oneself and benefitting others are actions that need to be recognized by a *bodhisattva*. These are here described as bearing fruit (*phala*) in this world as well as in the next. Nāgārjuna was not unaware of the fact that according to the Buddha, actions are to be defined in terms of volition (*cetanā*). While volition itself could be considered an action, anything that is volitional also falls under the category of action. This is the implication of the Buddha's statement in *Aṅguttara-nikāya*[96] and Nāgārjuna is seen to elaborate on this statement at XVII.2.

Nāgārjuna asserts that according to the Buddha there are two main types of karma: volition and volitional. These are further analysed into a variety of karmas that were also recognized in the early Buddhist tradition. He gives no indication that all these karmas are not real in the sense that they do not produce fruits or consequences. However, in XVII.6 he raises a question which clearly embodies the particular form of inquiry carried out by the Buddhist metaphysicians with which he disagrees. The inquiry is as follows: "Does karma remain even at the time it has not attained maturity? (*Tiṣṭhati apākakālāt?*).

There can be little doubt as to who would raise such a question. While a pragmatic Buddhist may say that karma is what it is because it produces consequences or fruits (*phala*), a substantialist could not resist asking the question: "Yet, does not the effect (*phala*) pre-exist, before karma reaches its maturity?"

Such metaphysical inquiries, as pointed out earlier, led to the belief in an underlying substance (*svabhāva*), which was criticized and rejected by Nāgārjuna in Chapter I. And here Nāgārjuna is once again asserting the view that such inquiries lead to the belief in permanence (*nityatā*). If one were to reject such a notion of permanence, then karma and effect are separated in such a way that once the karma ceases, it will not produce any consequences (*niruddhaṃ sat kiṃ phalaṃ janayiṣyati*). Thus we are back again in the permanence-annihilation (*śāśvata-uccheda*) syndrome.

Verse 7 introduces the notion of a series (*saṃtāna*) upheld by the atomistic Sautrāntikas, and the difficulties this generates are then examined in the few verses that follow.

It is rather unfortunate that this new situation arising from the metaphysically oriented question raised in verse 6 came to be ignored by those who dealt with verse 12. The term *eṣā* (this, such) in XVII.12 refers specifically to the sort of thinking (*kalpanā*) involved in XVII.6 and Nāgārjuna maintains that such thoughts engender a multitude of insuperable difficulties (*bahavaś ca mahataś ca doṣāḥ*). It is this particular way of thinking that is considered to be inappropriate (*nopapadyate*).

Indeed, at XVII.13, Nāgārjuna suggests another way of thinking (*kalpanā*) which is more appropriate and which was extolled by the Buddhas, the Pratyeka-buddhas and the Śrāvakas: Like an imperishable promissory note, so is debt as well as action. It is fourfold in terms of realms and indeterminate in terms of primal nature."

According to this, karma is imperishable like a promissory note. One's debt (*ṛṇa*) remains effective at least as long as the promissory note lasts. Even though there is no continuity of karma (and, it in this case, borrowing), that is, it does not continue in any subtle or substantial way, the responsibility for that karma cannot be denied once that karma is performed. The Buddha, the early Buddhists, and Nāgārjuna were not prepared to say that the promissory note one signs is unreal and therefore to be ignored. The responsibility and commitment remains long after the document is signed (maybe even if the document were to be lost or destroyed).

The idea that one is responsible for one's own actions has been emphasized by the Buddha. A statement in the *Dhammapada* reads: "Neither in the sky nor in the middle of the ocean nor having entered into a cleft of the mountains is there a place on earth seen remaining where a person would be released from his evil actions."[97] The existence and the popularity of a similar statement among the Buddhists who preserved their literature in Sanskrit has already been referred to. There is little doubt that Nāgārjuna was aware of this statement. This conception of the imperishable nature of karma thus turns out to be an important conception in Nāgārjuna, primarily because he was not prepared to accept the notion of substance (*svabhāva*) or self (*ātman*) to explain this process nor was he willing to deny the effectiveness of karma with the denial of substance or self. As such Inada's statement that Nāgārjuna "with equal force condemns any idea of an indestructible continuing action (*avipraṇāśa*)" is surprising.[98] Neither the Buddha nor Nāgārjuna nor even Vasubandu (who compiled the *Karmasiddhiprakraṇa*) were saying that karma *itself* remains indestructible. *Avipraṇāśa-karma* or the imperishable action refers to the responsibility a person has for any karma that he performs and how that karma will, depending upon circumstances, bear fruit (*phala*). The simple notion of human responsibility is what is upheld here, not the metaphysical notion of the fruit or result that lies hidden and gradually attains maturity, as was implied in the question raised by the Buddhist metaphysician.

Therefore, without any hesitation Nāgārjuna attributes the conception of the imperishable (*avipraṇāśa*) karma to the Buddha himself: "Emptiness, however, is not annihilation; life-process is also not permanence; imperishability is of action—such is the doctrine taught by the Buddha." (XVII.34)

The most significant assertion here is that the rejection of permanence and annihilation and the acceptance of emptiness and *saṃsāra* (or the life-process) do not imply the rejection of the relationship between action (*karma*) and consequence (*phala*). The imperishable nature (*avipraṇāśa-dharma*) of action merely implies the possibility of action giving rise to consequences, and this need not involve the notion of an underlying permanent substance in action.

The three verses that follow are critical of the conception of karma that is based on the recognition of self-nature. Such a conception, as explained at XVII.24, conflicts with all the accepted conventions (*vyavahāra*) and would imply the denial of merit and demerit (*puṇya-pāpa*) and such other distinctions (*pravibhāga*).

Action (*karma*), looked upon as something substantial (*svābhāvika*), not only implies the production of a result (*vipāka*), which is already existing in mature form (*vipakva*)(XVII.25), but also goes against the admitted purity or impurity of action. If action has its own nature, then defilement (*kleśa*) also will have its own nature and how these two natures could come together will never be satisfactorily explained (XVII.26–27).

Moving on to XVII.29 without keeping the above definition of action (*karma*) in mind, it is easy to assume that Nāgārjuna rejects action as something dependently arisen and, therefore, there is neither action nor agent. On the contrary, verse 29 simply rejects the possibility of an action being dependently arisen, if that action were to be substantial (*svābhāvika*).

Thus the denial of action (*karma*), agent (*kartṛ*), and consequence (*phala*), as well as of one who experiences the consequences (*bhoktṛ*), comparing them to created forms (*nirmitakākāra*) or to mirages and imaginary entities, needs to be understood *only as referring to the substantial conceptions* of these phenomena and does not represent an unqualified denial of such phenomena (*dharma*).

18. *Self (ātman)*. The examination of self nature (*svabhāva*) was undertaken by Nāgārjuna after a detailed analysis of all factors of experience (*dharma*), such as aggregates, spheres, and elements. The subjects coming under the two previous chapters (XVI-XVII) pertained to bondage and freedom, action and consequence. Therefore, a close scrutiny of the notion of a personal self (*ātman*) and all other concepts associated with it, such as selfishness, identity, or pride, was considered to be relevant. Hence the subject-matter of Chapter XVIII.

The conception of a permanent and eternal self (*ātman*) arose in relation to the conception of the psychophysical personality (*nāmarūpa*). The untenability of the former has already been alluded to in Chapters VIII-XI. In the present chapter, however, a further question in relation to the notion of self needs to be examined, and that pertains to the manner in which the notion of self (*ātman*) leads to bondage (*bandhana*).

Nāgārjuna begins this chapter with the assertion that if the self (*ātman*) is identical with the aggregates (*skandha*), then it will be subject to arising and ceasing (*utpādavyayabhāg*). If it is different from the aggregates, then it will not have the characteristics of the aggregates. Having raised such questions regarding the existence of the self, Nāgārjuna proceeds to show that it is the belief in a *permanent* and *eternal* self that gives rise to notions of possession (*ātmīya*). Absence of possessiveness (*nirmama*) and of pride (*nirahaṃkāra*) are, therefore, the inevitable consequences of the appeasement (*śama*) of that belief in an eternal self (XVIII.2). For similar reasons, the belief that there is a *person* who is without selfishness and pride is also not appropriate (XVIII.3).

The use of the *iti*-formula at XVIII.4 as *aham-iti* and *mama-iti* is important in that it implies the denial of "theories" pertaining to "oneself" (*aham*) as well as "self-possession" (*mama*), rather than the simple reflexive uses of these terms. When such metaphysical views are abandoned, grasping (*upādāna*) as well as rebirth (*janma*) are avoided. The cessation of the defilements of action (*karma-kleśa*) is then declared to be release (*mokṣa*). The *vikalpa* that leads to such defilements of action is, therefore, not any and every form of conceptualization, as some of the translations seem to suggest, but only the discrimination or thought of substantial (*svābhāvika*) entities such as 'I' (*aham*), rejected at the beginning of this chapter, and substantial events like action (*karma*) and effect (*phala*), criticized in the previous chapter. The belief in such substantial entities and events gives rise to the feeling of "possession" as "this is mine" (*mama*), which in turn produces obsessions (*prapañca*). Such obsessions can be prevented by the perception of emptiness (*śūnyatā*) relating to the notion of "self" (*ātman*) referred to above. To speak of "emptiness" apart from this context is to make it not only "nihilistic" (*uccheda*, XVIII.20) but also absolutistic and hence a metaphysical "view" (*dṛṣṭi*, XVIII.8).

A superficial glance at XVIII.6 may leave the impression that Nāgārjuna viewed truth or reality as being beyond conceptualization. However, a more careful consideration of the contents, especially in the light of the teachings of the Buddha as embodied in the "discourses" would indicate that this is not the case. Nāgārjuna seems to have been fully cognisant of the Buddha's use of the term "self" (Pali, *atta*; Sk. *ātman*) to explain individuality, and his attempt to reject a metaphysical entity when he spoke of "no-self" (Pali, *anatta*, Sk. *anātman*). This does not involve two languages: a provisional or ordinary and philosophical.[99] It is a question of two definitions. If the "self" is defined as a permanent and substantial entity, the Buddha was ready to negate it with his conception of "no-self" (*anātman*). If it was not defined as such, he had no difficulty in utilizing that conception in his discourses. Nāgārjuna's understanding of the Buddha's intentions is clearly demonstrated in the first line of XVIII.6, when he said: "The Buddha's have made known the conception of self and taught the doctrine of no-self." When, in the second line, Nāgārjuna maintained: "They have not spoken of something (*kaścit*) as the self or as the non-self," he was certainly denying the conceptions of self-nature (*svabhāva*) and other-nature (*parabhāva*) of phenomena admitted by the Sarvāstivādins and the Sautrāntikas respectively.

With the above statement Nāgārjuna could have concluded his chapter on the "self" (*ātman*). However, there was one more significant issue to be resolved. Up to this point he was discussing an embodied self, a self associated with a psychophysical personality. The question regarding the self that is freed from the psychophysical personality also had to be examined, for it was the belief of the substantialists that when a person attains freedom his permanent and eternal self, dissociated from the psychophysical personality, continues to exist after death. The two verses that follow (XVIII.7–8), therefore, are intended to explain the Buddha's view regarding the nature of a person when he attains *parinirvāṇa*.

What happens to the freed person *at* death was clearly expressed by the Buddha. He ceases to exist, is not reborn, his birth has waned (*khiṇā jāti*), and there is no further existence for him.[100] Yet, if someone were to ask him the question as to whether that person exists in some form after death (*param maraṇā*), the Buddha was not willing to say anything, primarily because there was no epistemological basis on which any predication can be made.[101] With verses 7 and 8, Nāgārjuna is attempting to state this very same idea. "When the realm of thought has ceased, that which is to be designated also has ceased."

"Realm of thought" (*cittagocara*) that has ceased (*nivṛtta*) can refer to the person who is freed (Pali *parinibbuta*, Sk. *pari-nirvṛta*) without his thought being re-established (*appatiṭṭhitena cittena*).[102] The difficulties that would arise if someone were to ask the further question as to what happens to him when his thought process has ceased or is not re-established is then explained. "That which is to be designated has also ceased." This is identical with the Buddha's statement: "That by which one should speak of him does not exist for him" (*yena naṃ vajju taṃ tassa n' atthi*).[103] Indeed, the term *dharmatā* is used in the verse to refer to the nature of the freed one who has passed away. It is not possible to assert whether he has arisen (*utpanna*) after death or whether he has ceased to exist (*niruddha*) after death.

One of the epithets by which the "enlightened one" (*buddha*) came to be described is *tathāgata*, meaning "one who has thus gone." This term gave rise to much controversy probably because of the metaphysical implications of the term "thus" (*tathā*). And it is interesting to note that in the early discourses whenever the question regarding the nature of the freed one after death is raised the term used to refer to him is *tathāgata*.

The term *tathā* ("thus" or "such") involves the epistemological problem of "reality," as opposed to *no tathā* ("not thus"). Hence the secondary derivative *taccha* (Sk. *tathya*) came to be used in the sense of what is true or real.[104] It is, therefore, not surprising to see the term *tathāgata* being utilized when ever the question regarding the *destiny* of the freed one is raised,[105] for in the eyes of the ordinary man no other question would be more important than the *ultimate destiny* of the freed one. As mentioned earlier, for epistemological reasons, the Buddha refused to make any assertions, either positive or negative, regarding this problem. Nāgārguna's application of the fourfold negation (*catuṣkoṭi*) to the conception of "suchness" (*tathya*) comes immediately after his discussion of the nature (*dharmatā*) of the freed one who has reached his final destiny. It is the same context in which the Buddha himself applied the fourfold negation. The four-cornered negation is always used by the Buddha to avoid metaphysics, and the destiny of the *tathāgata* was one of those popular metaphysical issues. Nāgārjuna could not have been unaware of the metaphysical assertions of the pre-Buddhist thinkers who assumed that a "freed self" (*ātman*) becomes united with the all-pervading universal self, the reality in everything (*sarvaṃ*). The dangers involved in the Sarvāstivāda conception of substance (*svabhāva*) in everything (*sarvaṃ*) and how such an idea could influence the interpretation of a *tathāgata* or *tathya* was, indeed, evident to Nāgārjuna. Thus, we have two metaphysical issues combined here—one of "everything" (*sarvaṃ*) and the other of *tathya*—and the fourfold negation was the only reasonable solution that Nāgārjuna could provide. To explain the conception of "suchness" (*tathya*) going beyond the context of the problems of "everything" and the "thus gone one" (*tathāgata*) after death would undoubtedly lead to a distortion of the philosophical standpoint of Nāgārjuna.

As mentioned before, the Buddha was not willing to speculate on the nature of the freed one after death (*param-maraṇā*) but that he was willing to speak positively about what happens to him *at* death. In a passage in the *Aṅguttara-nikāya* the Buddha's understanding of this state is succincntly expressed in the following verse: "This is the last body and is the essence of the higher life. In regard to that this perfect knowledge has arisen without depending upon another." (*Asekhañāṇaṃ uppannaṃ antimo yaṃ samussayo, yo sāro brahmacariyassa tasmiṃ aparapaccayā.*)[106] This realization is elsewhere explained in a stock passage: "Birth has been eliminated, the higher life has been lived, done is what needs to be done and there is not another of this [life]."[107]

This is the highest realization that one can attain and is referred to in the discourses as *aññā*.[108] It is the result of the moral perfection one attains by being freed from the three poisons: greed, hatred, and confusion. It is final nirvana, and may justly be called the ultimate moral truth about the world (see p. 15 above). As such it is to be realized by oneself and is not a state to be known by depending upon another (*aparapaccayā*).

When, therefore, concluding the discussion of the freed one after death, Nāgārjuna proceeded to speak of *tattva* ("reality"), he was not referring to an "ultimate truth" *per se* but to the realization and attainment of freedom from birth. Hence he asserts that the knowledge of this truth is not dependent on another (*aparapratyaya*). It is peaceful (*śānta*), unobsessed by obsessions (*aprapañcita*), and, hence, non-discriminative (*nirvikalpa*) and non-contradictory (*anānārtha*). *Nirvikalpa* does not necessarily mean the absence of the subject-object discrimination. It means the absence of any discrimination based upon one's likes and dislikes, one's obsessions. Conceptions of identity and difference, permanence and annihiliation are then rejected as being part of the Buddha's teaching. This is because things are recognized as being dependently areisen (*pratītya . . . bhavati*).

The conclusion of the chapter represents Nāgārjuna as one who remains aloof from the so-called Hīnayāna-Mahāyāna conflict. He asserts that in the non-emergence of the Buddhas and the waning of the Śrāvakas, the knowledge of the "truth" continues to be perpetuated by the Pratyeka-buddhas, even without association with the Buddhas. The need to depend primarily upon an unbroken tradition or an uninterrupted line of patriarchs for the perpetuation of the "true doctrine" is discounted here.

19. *Time (kāla)*. In the discussion of the notion of imperishable action (*avipraṇāśa-karma*) discussed above, two more conditions relevant to the fruitioning of karma were mentioned, namely, time (*kāla*) and harmony (*sāmagrī*).

These two topics constitute the subject matter of the next two chapters.

Time was conceived in a more empirical way in the early discourses. Impermanence (*aniccatā*) was explained there in terms of the temporality of events. As mentioned in the analysis of the conditioned (VII), such temporality was understood as arising (*uppāda*), ceasing (*vyaya*), and change of what endures (*ṭhitassa aññathatta*). However, the problems created by the Sarvāstivādins and the Sautrāntikas by their analysis of time and temporality have already been alluded to (see the discussion of the "Conditioned" above). There, the focus was more on the substantiality of events (conceived as *bhāva*) and the difficulties that arise as a result of attempting to place such "existents" (*bhāva*) in the context of temporality. The present chapter is devoted to the conception of time itself, especially time as analysed by the metaphysicians into discrete moments (*kṣaṇa*). Nāgārjuna's analysis brings out the disastrous implications of such a notion of time and could appropriately be compared with an analysis provided by E. R. Clay and enthusiastically adopted by William James in Western philosophy. Examining the ordinary notion of time, Clay says:

> The relation of experience to time has not been profoundly studied. Its objects are given as being of the present, but the part of time referred to by the datum is a very different thing from the conterminous of the past and future which philosophy denotes by the name Present. The present to which the datum refers is really a part of the past—a recent past—delusively given as being a time that intervenes between the past and the future. Let it be named the specious present, and let the past, that is given as being the past, be known as the obvious past. All the notes of a bar of a song seem to the listener to be contained in the present. All the changes of place of meteor seem to the beholder to be contained in the present. At the instance of the termination of such a series, no part of the time measured by them seems to be past. Time, then, considered relative to human apprehension, consists of four parts, viz., the obvious past, the specious present, the real present and the future. Omitting the specious present, it consists of three . . . non-entities—the past, which does not exist, the future which does not exist, and their conterminous, the present; the faculty from which it proceeds lies to us in the fiction of the specious present.[109]

Nāgārjuna's analysis indicates, in a similar way, how a metaphysical notion of time would lead to the abolition of the very notion of time as "specious." Furthermore, the metaphysical notion of time, as propounded by the Sarvāstivādins and the Sautrāntikas, also involved the conception of substantial existence (*bhāva*), the denial of which would result in the denial of that particular conception of time.

20. *Harmony (sāmagrī)*. The analysis of the causal process in terms of discrete momentary events eliminated the possibility of explaining harmony as part and parcel of the events that combine to produce the effect. With such discrete events harmony becomes an attribute. Such a problem was not faced by the Buddha when he explained dependence of events because such events were recognized as related events rather than discrete ones. Thus, the Buddhist metaphysicians were compelled either to accept an immediately contiguous cause (*samanantara-pratyaya*) where each event is caused by an immediately preceding event, or make harmony an attribute of such discrete events so that their assemblage could provide a rationale for the production of the effect. The problem of causation received the foremost attention of Nāgārjuna, as is evident from Chapter I. The difficulties involved in explaining the arising of the fruit or effect (*phala*) on the basis of a metaphysical notion of harmony are further elaborated here. Once again, what is denied is not the arising of the fruit or effect, for that was the central philosophy of Buddhism, but only the manner in which such arising is described by the metaphysicians. Hence Nāgārjuna's conclusion: The effect is not made by the harmony, nor is it made by a non-harmony. "Where can there be harmony without an effect?" (XX.24).

21. *Occurence and dissolution (saṃbhava-vibhava)*. This chapter concludes Nāgārjuna's examination of the nature of the human personality as it gradually evolves or dissolves depending upon one's actions (*karma*). In the "Discourse on the Knowledge of the Beginning" (*Aggañña-suttanta*),[110] the Buddha speaks of the evolution and dissolution not only of the world, but also of the human personality. This discourse was intended primarily to refute the rather static conception of the world and the social order presented in the Indian philosophical and religious traditions. Without committing himself to any notion of an absolute beginning, the Buddha spoke of a period of dissolution (*saṃvaṭṭa*) followed by a long period of evolution (*vivaṭṭa*). In spite of the Buddha's reluctance to get involved in the discussion of such theories, because of the epistemological difficulties, he was compelled to do so by the unfortunate moral and ethical implications of the Indian caste-system. Even though the discussion of the world-systems is rare in the early discourses, the evolution as well as the dissolution of the human personality through long periods of time constituted a popular subject. The process of the evolution and dissolution of the human personality came to be designated *saṃsāra* (life-process) or *bhava*

(becoming) and was contrasted with the Indian notion of life as eternal existence (*atthitā*, Sk. *astitva*).

While the concepts of *atthitā* (existence) and *n' atthitā* (non-existence) were used in the pre-Buddhist literature, the Buddha, realizing the metaphysical implications, avoided them and instead utilized the notion of *bhava* (becoming). No sooner than the Buddha explained the human personality as a process of becoming, the metaphysicians of the traditional schools of Indian philosophy began speaking of *bhāva* (instead of *astitva*) and *abhāva* (instead of *nāstitva*) when speaking about existence and non-existence respectively, two terms which were not popular in the Indian tradition before the Buddha.

The Sarvāstivādins and the Sautrāntikas, who were lured into this substantialist trap as a result of their analysis of the process of becoming (*bhava*) into discrete moments, formulated the notion of a "series of becoming" (*bhava-saṃtati*), instead of the "stream of becoming" (*bhava-sota*) referred to in the early discourses. Buddhaghosa, who introduced these different interpretations into the Thervāda tradition in the South and South East Asian countries (circa. sixth century AD), distinguished between three different notions of the present:

i the specious present (*addhā-paccuppanna*),
ii the momentary present (*khaṇa-paccuppanna*), and
iii the flowing present (*saṃtati-paccuppanna*).[111]

He proceeded to identify these with the different stages in the development of the Buddhist thought, maintaining that the "discourses" (*sutta*) advocated the first, that some other Buddhists (probably the Sautrāntikas) spoke of the second, and that the commentaries accepted the third.

Nāgārjuna, compiling his treatise during the second century AD after the Sarvāstivāda and the Sautrāntika theories had come into prominence, could not have been unaware of these differences. In the present chapter he was therefore criticizing the metaphysical notion of a "series of becoming" (*bhava-saṃtati*), a series of disjointed or disconnected momentary (*kṣaṇika*) existences, rather than the conception of becoming as formulated by the Buddha. Thus, after a criticism of the notion of *bhava-saṃtati*, in the present chapter, Nāgārjuna is able to speak of *bhava* at XXVI.7–8 without rejecting it. He carefully avoids the concepts of *bhāva* and *abhāva* as well as *svabhāva* and *parabhāva* throughout the text. Thus, the denial of *bhava-saṃtati* need not be construed as a denial of *bhava* or *bhava-sota* which occur in the discourses of the Buddha.

The problems discussed so far relate primarily to the nature of the human personality, its survival, and its moral responsibility, and Nāgārjuna's endeavor is to establish its non-substantiality (*pudgala-nairātmya*). The chapters that follow deal with the non-substantiality of the person who has attained freedom.

22. *"Thus Gone One" (tathāgata)*. A host of epithets were used to describe the attainments of the person who was able to understand the nature of human existence and overcome the suffering associated with it. Two of them stand prominent. These were *buddha* or the "enlightened one" and *tathāgata* or the "thus gone one," and even these two terms were used synonymously. The first of these describes the ideal achieved by one who was aspiring for knowledge or understanding, an aspiration clearly expressed in the famous Upaniṣadic statement: "From darkness, lead me to light," (*tamaso māṃ jyotir gamaya*).[112] In the *Upaniṣads*, this enlightenment was nothing short of "omniscience" (*sarvajña*),[119] even though this term was not used in a technical sense. For the Buddha, enlightenment is attained as a result of the realization of the means and limits of knowledge (see the above analysis of the *Kaccāyanagotta-sutta*).

The second epithet, *tathāgata*, led to more misunderstanding and misinterpretation in the Buddhist context. As the term implies, it explains the ultimate goal to be achieved by such enlightenment. It represents an attempt to answer the aspirations of the human beings who were looking for immortality avoiding the endless cycle of births and deaths. In the *Upaniṣads* it is expressed in the statement: "From death, lead me to immortality," (*mṛtyor māṃ amṛtaṃ gamaya*).[113] According to the *Upaniṣads*, the "enlightened one" who understands the nature of the real self (*ātman*), upon the dissolution of the psychophysical personality, is united with the universal ideal self (*brahman*) and thereby enjoys eternal life. The Buddha, who was not willing to admit the existence of such a state, merely maintained that the "enlightened one" (*buddha*) is also freed from continuous becoming (*bhava*). Hence, the *tathāgata* or the "thus gone one" is contrasted with one who is subjected to becoming (*bhava*) or re-becoming (*punabbhava*).

With the attainment of enlightenment and freedom from grasping (*upādāna*), the freed one leads a happy and contented life, while at the same time not longing for a future existence. Enlightenment (*bodhi*) is synonymous with waning of craving (*taṇhakkhaya*). However, the unenlightened person, bound by craving and grasping, not only looks for eternal life beyond the grave (*param maraṇā*), but also expects to see something more mysterious and awe-inspiring (*acchariya-abbhuta*) in the life of a freed one who is alive. It is for this reason that two major questions were raised in relation to the conception of a *tathāgata*. The first is the question as to whether the *tathāgata* is identical or different from the psychophysical personality.[114] The second is the question as to whether the *tathāgata* survives the destruction of the psychophysical personality.[115] This may explain why, in the early discourses, whenever such questions were raised they were raised more in relation to a *tathāgata* than in connection with a *buddha*.

Thus, after a detailed examination of the problems of human existence, problems such as action, moral responsibility, or becoming, it was natural for Nāgārjuna to direct his attention to the questions pertaining to the conception of ultimate goal as envisaged in Buddhism. In doing so, he was compelled to deal, first of all, with the meaning of the concept *tathāgata*.

Nāgārjuna's examination of the *tathāgata* follows the line of analysis found in the early discourses. While early Buddhism confronted problems relating to the conception of *tathāgata* because it was understood in terms of the notion of a permanent and eternal self (*ātman*), Nāgārjuna is here struggling with the same conception as explained in relation to the notion of a real substance (*svabhāva*). Nāgārjuna was not willing to consider the *tathāgata*, conceived in such a metaphysical way, as identical with the aggregates (*skandha*). This was the Sarvāstivāda position which Nāgārjuna was rejecting (XXII.2). Nor was he prepared to accept the alternative suggested by the Sautrāntikas, who emphasized non-identity or difference. The notion of *anātman* (no-self) referred to at XXII.3 is really the conception of "other-nature" (*parabhāva*) that was propounded by the Sautrāntikas. Inada's explanation that "the use of the term *anātman* here is not to be confused with the cardinal Buddhist doctrine by the same term,"[116] therefore needs to be qualified as the "cardinal *early* Buddhist doctrine," for the Sautrāntikas were guilty of propounding a theory of *anātman* which emphasized real *difference*. Nāgārjuna was therefore ready to assert that a *tathāgata* conceived in terms of either "self-nature" (*svabhāva*) or "other-nature" (*parabhāva*) is not evident.

The question whether the *tathāgata* is dependent is taken up next. Its dependence or independence is then rejected primarily because once again it is understood in terms of substantial dependence (*svabhāvata upādānaṃ*) or substantial independence (which is the implication of "other-nature" or *parabhāva*)(XXII.9). Views of *tathāgata* as "empty" (*śūnya*) or "not empty" (*aśūnya*) are considered, and these again are particular *views* (expressed in the *iti*-formula) and are therefore rejected.

How the notion of a living *tathāgata*, conceived of in a rather metaphysical way, leads to the belief in a *tathāgata* after death is explicitly stated by Nāgārjuna at XXII.13. Nāgārjuna's argument is that if the *tathāgata* were to be considered empty in terms of self-nature (*svabhāvataḥ*), any thought of his being existent or non-existent after death (*paraṃ-nirodhāt*) is not appropriate. This, indeed, is the view expressed by the Buddha in the early discourses.[117]

The concluding statement of this chapter is rather significant, especially in view of the nature of the "freed one" (*nibbuta*) or "freedom" (*nibbāna*) as enunciated in the early discourses. We have already pointed out that freedom (*nibbāna*) is a state unconditioned by dispositions (*asankhata*). It is not a state that is uncaused (*appaṭiccasamuppanna*). The *tathāgata* is, therefore, unconditioned by dispositions but not in-dependent. Elsewhere Nāgārjuna insists that there is nothing in the world that is in-dependent (XXIV.19). The *tathāgata* is, therefore, like the universe (*jagat*) wherein the principle of dependence (*pratītyasamutpāda*) functions. He has no self (*ātman*) or substance (*svabhāva*), as it is in the case of the universe (*jagat*).

23. *Confusions (viparyāsa)*. The reasons for the misunderstandings that prevail regarding the nature of the enlightened one (*buddha*) or the "thus gone one" (*tathāgata*) as well as anything that takes place in the universe (*jagat*) are then taken up for examination. Once again the nucleus of the chapter can be traced back to the early discourses.

A discussion of the four types of confusions (*vipallāsa*) relating to perceptions (*saññā*), thought (*citta*), and views (*diṭṭhi*) is met with in the *Anguttara-nikāya*.[118] The basic confusions relating to these three different functions are given as follows:

1. Perceiving, thinking and viewing what is impermanent as permanent.
2. Perceiving, thinking and viewing what is not suffering as suffering.
3. Perceiving, thinking and viewing what is non-substantial as being substantial.
4. Perceiving, thinking and viewing what is impure as pure.

The first three of these, in that particular order, are generally referred to as the three characteristics (*lakkhaṇa*) of human existence, that is, impermanence (*anicca*), suffering (*dukkha*), and non-substantiality (*anatta*). Nāgārjuna has already dealt with these concepts at length (see Chapters II, XII and XVIII). Hence, he begins his analysis with the last, namely, the pure (*śubha*) and impure (*aśubha*). These indeed are value judgments made by the human beings and serve as the foundation of the religious and spiritual life. However, in the eyes of the substantialist philosophers, these were ultimate qualities, each having its own nature (*svabhāva*). With the first two verses, Nāgārjuna sets the tone of his criticism of these qualities, which allows him to move on to other types of confusions subsequently. While the interplay between the qualities of *śubha* and *aśubha* are mentioned in verse 11, Nāgārjuna's refutation of the ultimate reality of these qualities is based initially upon his recognition of the dependent arising of both.

The notions purity and impurity, like any other entities, have no ultimate substantial standing. They are based upon lust (*rāga*), hatred (*dveṣa*), and confusion (*moha*), which in turn are the products of thought or conceptualization (*saṃkalpa*). The cessation of lust, hatred, and confusion is generally equated with "freedom" (*nirvāṇa*). Hence, it is generally assumed that *nirvaṇa* is beyond *any* conceptualization or thought. This seems to be the manner in which the notion of a "non-conceptual" and ultimate reality (*paramārtha*) came to be attributed to Nāgārjuna and, hence, to all Mādhyamika philosophy.

Early Buddhism refers to two forms of thought or conceptualization (*saṃkappa*), the more comprehensive and, therefore, right thought or conceptualization (*sammā-saṃkappa*) and the more restricted and, therefore, wrong thought (*micchā-saṃkappa*). This is in no way different from what Nāgārjuna discussed in Chapter XVII (12–13), where he distinguished thoughts (*kalpanā*) that are proper (*yojyate*) from those that are inappropriate (*nopapadyate*).

In many instances, "thoughts" (*saṃkalpa*) and "dispositions" (*saṃskāra*), two terms that are semantically related, function in similar ways. This is attested to by Nāgārjuna's treatment of them. We have already noted how he characterized "dispositions" as "confusions" (*mṛṣā*)(XIII.1 – 2). This definition was, in fact, attributed to the Buddha himself. In the present context, speaking of "confusions" (*viparyāsa*), Nāgārjuna introduces the notion of *saṃkalpa* and proceeds to define it in terms of its consequences, namely, the generation of lust, etc.

A careful analysis of the notions of *saṃkalpa* and *saṃskāra* in relation to freedom or *nirvāṇa* may clarify an important epistemological problem, both in early Buddhism and in Nāgārjuna. We have already referred to the function of dispositions (*saṅkhāra*) in the context of early Buddhism. They cannot be eliminated except at death, and are, therefore, to be appeased (*samatha, upasama*). This process of appeasement is to be achieved by not clinging on to any of the past dispositions when one has to deal with the problem of understanding any situation. Hence, *nibbāna* came to be designated *asaṅkhata*.

When speaking of the thoughts or concepts (*saṃkalpa*), however, we are presented with two types, the right and the wrong. The right ones are to be cultivated and the wrong ones eliminated, a process not recommended in relation to dispositions. This dichotomy between right and wrong thoughts could have unsatisfactory implications. Right thoughts may be taken as pointing to true events or phenomena, while the wrong ones may indicate the absence of such events or phenomena. This, indeed, was the substantialist trap which both the Buddha and Nāgārjuna were attempting to avoid. Therefore, without taking right thoughts in the sense of absolutely true ideas corresponding to ultimate facts, that is, as having substance or self-nature (*svabhāva*), Nāgārjuna wants them to be treated as empty (*śūnya*), not in the sense of absolute non-existence (*abhāva*) but in a more pragmatic sense of being able to produce consequences. Thus, while wrong thoughts (*mithyā saṃkalpa*) are productive of lust (*rāga*), hatred (*dveṣa*), and confusion (*moha*), right thoughts (*samyak saṃkalpa*) give rise to freedom from lust (*vairāgya*), compassion (*karuṇā, adveṣa*), and knowledge (*prajñā*).

The entire chapter on "confusion" (*viparyāśa*), is therefore, devoted, not to an outright rejection of the simple discriminations of purity and impurity, etc., but to a vehement criticism of such discriminations based upon the notions of absolute existence (*astitva*) and absolute non-existence (*nāstitva*).

24. *Truth* (*satya*). Thus we are led to the most important discussions in Nāgārjuna, namely, the conception of the four noble truths (*ārya satya*). The contents of this chapters have generated much discussion as well as controverty during the centuries that followed its compilation. At the same time, this chapter, more than any other, will serve as a glowing testimony to the fact that Nāgārjuna was simply restating the ideas expressed by the Buddha in the early discourses, rather than bringing about a Copernican revolution in Buddhist thought.

In the early discourses, the four noble truths were meant to explain the nature of human existence, both in bondage and in freedom, avoiding the extremes of permanent existence (*atthitā*) and nihilistic non-existence (*n' atthitā*). The difficulties encountered by the Buddha in making this view of existence intelligible to the substantialist thinkers of India are evident from the kind of criticism they levelled against the Buddha. Very often they criticized him as a nihilist (*n 'atthikavāda, ucchedavāda*), insisting that he advocated the annihilation and destruction of the conscious being (*sato sattassa ucchedaṃ vināsaṃ paññapeti*).[119] This was not because the Buddha denied the existence of conscious human beings, but because he was not willing to accept an eternal and immutable self (*ātman*) in them. For he often insisted that a conscious human being is empty (*suñña*) of a permanent and eternal self (*atta*) as well as anything pertaining to or belonging to a self (*attaniya*).[120] The denial of such a self or substantiality was not only in relation to a human personality but also in connection with any experienced phenomena (*sabbe dhammā anattā*).[121]

Nārārjuna was placed in an identical situation as a result of his rejection of the Sarvāstivāda conception of self-nature (*svabhāva*) and the Sautrāntika theory of other-nature (*parabhāva*). The theory of non-substantiality (*anātman*) or emptiness (*śūnyatā*) that he attempted to explain in the previous chapters was not palatable to the substantialist philosophers who raised the objection discussed in the first six verse of the present chapter.

In the first instance, these substantialists, who understood emptiness as "nothingness," assumed that emptiness leads to a denial of the four noble truths, including a denial of the noble fruits (*ārya-phalāni*). These noble fruits are elsewhere referred to as fruits of the ascetic life (*samanathasa* = *śrāmaṇyārtha*,[122] *sāmaññaphala*[123]). Secondly, they felt that it also leads to a denial of the fruits (*phala*) of ordinary human life (*laukika*), including fruits of all the ordinary moral and social conventions (*saṃvyavahāra*) such as good and bad (*dharma-adharma*) (XXIV.6).

Underlying this two-fold criticism there seems to be a basic assumption. Whereas in the early discourses the four noble truths could account for the fruits of ordinary human existence (i.e., of the path, *magga*) as well as the fruits of the higher life (i.e., freedom or *nibbāna*), it seems that when the above criticism of emptiness by the substantialists of the Buddhist tradition was presented, the four noble truths were looked upon as referring primarily to the higher life. Hence the need to present an additional criticism that emptiness contradicts even the worldly (*laukikān*).

Nāgārjuna's attempt here is to collapse these two issues into one and treat them under one rubric, namely dependent arising (*pratītyasamutpāda*) (XXIV.40), which is the central philosophy of Buddhism.

For this reason, having made the initial remark that his critics were not conversant with the use or purpose of emptiness and, therefore, are troubled by both emptiness and its meaning (XXIV.7), Nāgārjuna immediately proceeds to explain the two truths, instead of the four truths.

Nāgārjuna sees the Buddha as expounding two truths:

1. the truth of worldly convention (*loka-saṃvṛti*), and
2. the truth in terms of ultimate fruit (*paramārthataḥ*).

Nāgārjuna had already devoted twenty one chapters (I-XXI) to the explication of the first of these truths. Causality, space, time, motion, the human personality, action, consequence, good and bad—all of these have been dealt with at length. Explanations of these in terms of absolute existence or nihilistic non-existence were rejected in favor of dependence (*pratītyasamutpāda*) and, therefore, of emptiness (*śūnyatā*). *Artha* or fruit of existence, whether that be good or bad, was recognized. Attempts on the part of the metaphysicians who wanted to perceive with absolute certainty how a cause produces an effect were abandoned, since such attempts led to the recognition of unacceptable entities such as self (*ātman*) or substance (*svabhāva*). The abandoning of such attempts did not lead Nāgārjuna on to the other extreme of denying any connection between cause and effect, action and consequence. The element of uncertainty involved in the cause-effect relationship made him more cautious than either the Sarvāstivādins or the Sautrāntikas, and hence he was more defensive and negative in his descriptions. Yet in no way did he want to abandon that principle of explanation, Chapter XVII on "The Examination of Action and Consequence" (*Karma-phala-parīkṣā*) being the most illustrative example.

The fact that a human being, having understood the nature and functioning of phenomena (*dharmāḥ*), attempts to achieve various desired results (*artha*) by manipulating such phenomena, was well known to Nāgārjuna when he spoke of both *saṃskāras* and *saṃkalpas*. However, the possibility of achieving ultimate freedom (*nirvāṇa*) or the ultimate fruit of existence (*paramārtha*)(sometimes referred to by the Theravāda tradition as *agga-phala*, Sk. *agra-phala*[124]), has now been questioned by his opponents. Again, without falling into the extremes of existence and non-existence and recognizing the emptiness of all dependently arisen phenomena, Nāgārjuna had to explain the fruits (*artha*) as well as the ultimate fruit (*paramārtha*) of existence. In speaking of these two truths, if he had assumed that the latter transcended the former, he would be presenting the ideas attributed to the so-called Mahāyāna, rather than quoting the early discourses or referring to the teachings of the Buddhas, Pratyeka-buddhas and the Śrāvakas. This, however, is not the case, for his explanation of *artha* as well as *paramārtha* is couched in the same language, and that was the language of dependence and emptiness. Hence his famous dictum: "Without relying upon convention, the ultimate fruit is not taught. Without understanding the ultimate fruit, freedom is not attained" (XXIV.10).

Artha as well as *paramārtha are truths (satya)*. The former is not presented as an un-truth (*a-satya*) in relation to the latter, as it would be in an absolutistic tradition. Neither is the former sublated by the latter. There is no indication whatsoever that these are two truths with different standing as higher and lower.

The fruits of ordinary human existence (*artha*), understood in terms of permanent existence (*svabhāva*) conflicted with everything in experience: "If you perceive the existence of the existence in terms of self-nature, then you will also perceive these a non-conditions" (XXIV.16). This would lead to a denial of all phenomena such as effect (*kārya*), cause (*kāraṇa*), agent (*kartṛ*), doing (*karaṇa*), action (*kriyā*) as well as arising (*utpāda*), ceasing (*nirodha*), and fruit (*phala*) (XXIV.17). This compelled him to make the most famous of his staements: "We state that whatever is dependent arising, that is emptiness. That is dependent upon convention. That itself is the middle path" (XXIV.18). Everything is placed in one basket, the basket of "dependent arising" (*pratītyasamutpāda*). "A thing that is not dependently arisen is not evident. For that reason, a thing that is non-empty is, indeed, not evident (ibid.19).

With that analysis, Nāgārjuna was ready to defend the four noble truths, reconciling it with his conception of emptiness (ibid. 20-21). "Whoever perceives dependent arising also perceives suffering, its arising, its ceasing and the path [leading to its ceasing]," (ibid 40).

Buddha's statement in the *Majjhima-nikāya*: "He who perceives dependent arising also perceives the *dhamma*," could not have received better confirmation from a disciple who was removed from the Buddha by at least six centuries.

25. *Freedom* (*nivāna*). This is undoubtedly the most significant chapter in the book. The interpretation of the contents of this chapter by Stcherbatsky[125] has dominated the Western understanding of Madhyamika thought for a considerable period of time. Elsewhere, we have disagreed with Stcherbatsky's interpretation of early Buddhism, allowing him his interpretation of Mādhyamika philosophy. Since Stcherbatsky's perception of Nāgārjuna was colored by his understanding of early Buddhism, the rejection of the latter should mean the rejection of the former too, if we are to consider Nagarjuna's philosophy as a continuation of the ideas of early Buddhism. Without devoting much time to an examination of Stcherbatsky's views at this point, we will present the contents of Chapter XXV in the light of the analysis of Nāgārjuna's ideas that we have already presented.

Other modern scholars have rejected Stcherbatsky's ideas and have presented views about nirvana that do not appear to accord with what Nāgārjuna has said in the previous chapterse. One of these is the view presented by Inada that nirvana represents the "uncreated realm" (*asamskrta*).[126] The view that nirvana, as *asaṃskṛta*, belongs to the "uncreated realm," a view which is popular with both the so-called Theravāda and Mahāyāna interpreters (especially of the modern world), may lose its tenability if the contents of this chapter are analysed in the light of what went before rather than in isolation.

The attempt to explain Nāgārjuna's conception as one that is found in the Mahāyāna tradition is based upon a complete misreading of Chapters XVI-XXI of the *Kārikās* that deal with the notion of the human personality, human behavior, and moral responsibility. Such a misreading compels Inada to reject the value of the two chapters (XXVI-XXVII) that follow the chapter on nirvana (XXV), saying: "With the discussion of Nirvana in the last chapter the treatment from the standpoint of Mahāyāna had basically come to a close. In this chapter and the final one to follow, Nāgārjuna goes into the analysis of the Hīnayāna doctrines."[127]

Our analysis of the *Kārikās* so far did not reveal any specific Mahāyāna doctrine presented by Nāgārjuna that may be contrasted with the so-called Hīnayāna, and we have therefore no reason to look at Nāgāruna's conception of nirvana as that of Mahāyāna or reject the last two chapters of the treatise as being representative of the Hīnayāna doctrines. In fact, to assume that such an outstanding philosopher as Nāgārjuna, who presented the world with such a beautifully executed philosophical classic, could simply add two chapters utterly irrelevant to the basic theme of his work does not contribute either to the understanding of his philosophy or an appreciation of his genius.

Nagarjuna begins his analysis of nirvana anticipating the same kind of objection that the substantialist raised against reconciling "emptiness" with the four noble truths. "If all this is empty, there exists neither arising nor ceasing. [As such] through the relinquishing or ceasing of what does one expect freedom?" (XXV.1).

It is necessary to keep in mind here the conception of a thing (*dharma*) that the substantialist envisaged, which was the main subject of scrutiny on the part of Nāgārjuna. The substantialist had difficulty with the conception of emptiness (*śūnyatā*) primarily because an existent or phenomena (*dharma*) for him was one that possessed self-nature (*svabhāva*). As emphasized earlier, if not for that assertion of the substantialist, Nāgārjuna had no reason or provocation to compose the present treatise. This is clearly evident from Nāgārjuna's immediate response to the substantialist: "If all this is non-empty, there exists neither arising nor ceasing. Through the relinquishing and ceasing of what does one expect freedom?" (ibid. 2).

For Nāgārjuna, to say that something is not empty (*aśūnya*) means that it has substantial existence (*svabhāva*) during the past, present and future, and if so it would be meaningless to speak of its arising and ceasing. This would certainly render "freedom" impossible.

Once again, keeping the substantialist view in mind, would it be possible to speak of "freedom" (*nirvāṇa*) as the relinquishing of something that is substantial and the attainment of something completely new or different. This was another important assertion of the substantialist. For him, "freedom" represented a totally different *state* of existence (*astitva*), an existence that is not only permanent and eternal but also perfectly blissful and happy. Freedom or *nirvāṇa* thus turns out to be a metaphysical notion, like the Hindu *brahman*, uncaused, uncreated and, therefore, beyond all spatial and temporal determination. Considering these two views, namely,

1. the substantialist conception of ordinary existence, and
2. the substantialist notion of freedom,

Nāgārjuna proceeds to define freedom (*nirvāṇa*). "Unabandoned and unachieved, uninterrupted and impermanent, unextinguished and non-arisen—this is called freedom" (ibid. 3).

Here are three sets of negations, and unless we are careful in analysing these three as *sets*, it is possible to arrive at conclusions not intended by Nāgārjuna himself. The following analysis of the sets will be made not only on the basis of the conception of *nirvāṇa* presented in early Buddhism but also in the light of the substantialist views that Nāgārjuna was confronted with.

1. *Unabandoned and unachieved* (*aprahīṇam asamprāptam*): It (*nirvāṇa*) is neither casting off nor reaching. These two activities are complementary, and hence to be taken together. Casting off something and reaching for something completely different represents the substantialist or absolutist way of explaining freedom (XVI.10). The attainment of freedom from the three poisons of lust (*rāga*), hatred (*dveṣa*), and confusion (*moha*) by a person who is understood as "being in a process of becoming" (*bhava*) conditioned by various factors (not merely the three poisons) need not be explained in terms of the dual function of casting off and reaching. While on the one hand, one may be casting off the three poisons and not everything, on the other hand there is nothing that is reached for. If there were to be seomthing to be reached for, that would again be a *source* of bondage rather than freedom.
2. *Uninterrupted and impermanent* (*anuçchinnam aśāśvatam*): It is neither interrupted nor eternal. These again are complementary. Cutting off something completely and attaining a state of permanent existence is once again part of the substantialist conception of freedom. As explained in relation to the previous characteristics, a person who has attained freedom certainly cuts off the three poisons. However, this does not mean that "what is distinguishable is also separable" (Humean explanation of distinction). In the Buddhist context, a human being who has eliminated the three poisons, that is, the Buddha or the *arhant*, still continues to be a human being with a body as well as the associated feelings, perceptions, dispositions, and consciousness, and this continuation is on the basis of "dependent arising" (*paṭiccasamuppāda*). Separation of "buddhahood" from that psychophysical personality led to all the metaphysical issues that the Buddha as well as Nāgārjuna were trying to deal with (see Chapter XXII on "The Examination of *Tathāgata*). Hence the state of Buddhahood, if such a terminology can be

used in any meaningful sense, did not signify either a complete interruption or eternality.

3. *Non-ceased and non-arisen* (*aniruddham anutpannam*): It is neither ceased nor arisen. Considering this pair of complementary characteristics independently and in isolation from everything that has so far been said by Nāgārjuna, it would be very easy to assume that nirvana, in his view, transcends all descriptions and characterization. However, if what has been said about arising and ceasing, especially in the chapters on "The Examination of Causality" (Chapter I) as well as in "The Examination of Dispositions" (Chapter VII) were to be taken seriously, one would refrain from such generalizations. Instead, the conceptions of arising and ceasing, as well as the arisen and the ceased, would be placed in the context of a substantialist view of either exitence (*astitva*) or non-existence (*nāstitva*).

   Just as much as ordinary existence (*bhava*) and its fruits (*artha*) cannot be defined utilizing the substantialist conceptions of arising and ceasing, even so existence (*bhava*) and its ultimate fruit (*paramārtha*) cannot be explained on the basis of a similar conceptual framework.

This, indeed is what Nāgārjuna wants to emphasize in the verse that follows (XXV.4) where he takes up the notion of *bhāva* (= *svabhāva*): "Freedom is not an existent. [If it were,] it would follow that it has the characteristics of old age and death. Indeed, there is no existent without old age and death."

A substantialist speaking about the characteristics of the existent will have to maintain that the existent, by its own nature, is invariably associated with old age and death. This would mean that no one will be able to attain freedom, unless he becomes a different sort of existent, an existent that is totally different from what he is. This, indeed, is the absolutist's notion of freedom. It is a total freedom that has nothing to do with ordinary human existence characterized by old age and death. And for the Buddha as well as for Nāgārjuna freedom makes no sense in such a context.

On the contrary, if the existent (*bhāva*) is defined as freedom (*nirvāṇa*), and an existent by definition is "dispositionally determined" (*saṃskṛta*), freedom itself would be "dispositionally determined" (*nirvaṇam saṃskṛtaṃ bhavet*). However, there is no existent that is not dispositionally determined (*na asaṃskṛto hi vidyate bhāvaḥ*). Therefore, freedom could not be an existent.

Having expressed his view that nirvana cannot be understood as an existent (*bhāva*) in a substantialist sense, Nāgārjuna, utilizing the argument from relativity he used in Chapter I to refute "other-nature" (*parabhāva*), proceeds to reject the view that nirvana is a non-existent (*abhāva*).

Most of the confusion regarding the contents of this chapter can be cleared up and the relationship between early Buddhist and Nāgārjunean conceptions of freedom can be established by a careful examination of the following two verses:

> Whatever is of the nature of coming and going, that occurs contingently or dependently. However, freedom is indicated as non-contingent and independent.
>
> The teacher has spoken of relinquishing of both becoming and other-becoming. Therefore, it is proper to assume that freedom is neither existence nor non-existence (XXV.9-10).

Nāgārjuna is here reiterating the extremely important distinction made by the Buddha between *bhava* and *bhāva*. Discussing the contents of Chapter XXI ("The Examination of Evolution and Dissolution"), it was pointed out that in the early discourses the term *bhava* (becoming) was utilized by the Buddha to explain the human life process. Human life as a wandering (*saṃsāra*) was characterized by two motivations or cravings (*taṇhā*), the first of which is craving for continued becoming (*bhava-taṇhā*) or survival (*punabbhava*). This is one of the most dominant motivations for action. When continued becoming, with its attendant suffering or frustrations, fails to satisfy a man, he desires to "become something else" (*vi-bhava*), the attainment of permanent and eternal happiness in heaven or in the state of *brahman* being only one of them. According to the Buddha this process of becoming something else, i.e., the dissolution of the present existence and the attainment of a permanent state of existence is another form of craving (*vibhava-taṇhā*), which, instead of leading on to the desired form of existence, contributes to further becoming (*punabbhava*).

After having rejected the conception of self (*ātman*) understood as permanent existence (*atthitā. astitva*), the Buddha used the term *bhava* to explain the process of becoming. The metaphysicans, as pointed out before, immediately brought back the notion of *ātman* or *astitva* into the Buddhist doctrine when they began speculating on *bhāva*, two species of which were "self-nature" (*svabhāva*) and "other-nature" (*parabhāva*). Nāgārjuna seems to have been well aware of the Buddh'as discourse on becoming (*bhava*) and other-becoming (*vibhava*). He realized that this was the life-process or the wandering (*saṃsāra*) that the Buddha spoke of. In addition, he was also aware that, while encouraging the people to abandon both becoming and other-becoming, the Buddha did not present a permanent and eternal life (*bhāva*, *astitva*) or complete annihilation (*abhāva, nāstitva*) as "freedom" (*nirvāṇa*). This awareness is succinctly presented in XXV.10 quoted above.

If Nāgārjuna's analysis of *bhava-vibhava* and *bhāva-abhāva* is compatible with the Buddha's own analysis of *bhava-vibhava* and *atthitā-n 'atthitā* (*astitva-nāstitva*), Nāgārjuna will be confonted with the same set of problems that the Buddha faced in explaining freedom. Thus, after rejecting the explanation of freedom in terms of *bhāva-abhāva* or a combination or denial of both (XXIV.11-16), in the next two verses Nāgārjuna refuses to use such terminology to explain the freedom attained by the enlightened one, either while he is still alive (*tiṣṭhamāna = sopādisesa-nibbāna*) or when he passes away (*paraṃ nirodhād = anupādisesa-nibbāna*) (XXV.17-18).

This leads Nāgārjuna to make a remark which elicited two polar interpretations:

> The life-process has nothing that distinguishes it from freedom. Freedom has nothing that distinguishes it from the life-process.
>
> Whatever is the extremity of freedom and the extremity of the life-process, between them not even the subtlest something is evident (XXV.19-20).

The two polar interpretations to which these statements led are as follows: The adherents and sympathizers of Mahāyāna has interpreted these statements as implying essential identity of saṃsāra and nirvana, which they recognize as a uniquely Mahāyāna view of nirvana that goes beyond even the Buddha's own explanations. The so-called Theravādins for whom such identification is rather unpalatable have condemned it by saying that this represents a complete aberration of the salient teachings of the Buddha as represented in the early discourses. However, a careful and sympathetic examination of these two statements, placing them specifically in the context in which they were made, would certainly eliminate such conflicting views and lead to a better understanding of both the Buddha and Nāgārjuna. In order to do so, it would be necessary to examine two of the key terms that occur in these two verses, namely, *viśeṣaṇa* and *koṭi*.

These two terms are better understood in the philosophical background in which Nāgārjuna was writing. Though the background in which the Buddha presented his views about nirvana was not as sophisticaed, it was not different. The distinction made by the essentialists of the pre-Buddhist tradition between ordinary human existence (*saṃsāra*) and the state of freedom (*nirvāṇa*) led them to two contradictory conclusions. First, a person has to completely abandon one in order to reach the other. It was not only attachment to the senses or the objects of sense that had to be abandoned, but the senses or the objects of sense themselves. Freedom was thus reached on the basis of a non-sensuous insight, and the "freed one" (*nibbuta*) is one who has developed a form of knowing that transcends all forms of sensory perception, including the duality of subject and object. This was the state of *nirvāṇa* enjoyed by the "freed one" as long as his body, together with the senses lasted. However, when that psychophysical personality is destroyed at death, the "freed one" enters into the state of eternal and blissful life (*brahman*). Secondly, since such an absolute distinction between *saṃsāra* and *nirvāṇa* could not explain how one could reach a state that is qualitatively distinct, the essentialists also had to believe that underlying *saṃsāra* is the reality (*ātman*) that reaches *nirvāṇa*.

On the one hand, there is a point at which a transition is made from bondage to freedom, a transition from one state of existence to something that is completely and absolutely different, so much so that the one has nothing to do with the other. On the other hand, there is a subtle personality (*ātman*) that continued from the time of the origin of existence and which lay concealed within the psychophysical personality.

With the development of metaphysical speculations in Buddhism, it was not surprizing to see two similar conclusions reached by these metaphysicians, especially the Sautrāntikas. On the one hand, the Sautrāntikas emphasized distinctions (*viśeṣaṇa*) in order to reject a permanent and eternal substance (*svabhāva*). Yet, when the need arose for an explanation of the identity of bondage and freedom, they insisted upon a "seed of release" (*mokṣa-bīja*) (see annotation of XXV.19-20). Thus, the first of these two verses (19) is intended to reject the Sautrāntika notion of distinction (*viśeṣaṇa*), while the second (20) purports to deny their conception of "the seed of release", which is not at all different from the Sarvāstivāda conception of substance (*svabhāva*).

Before and during Nāgārjuna's day, traditional Indian philosophy was also dominated by two similar essentialist enterprises, namely, determining identity (*sārūpya*) and differences (*viśeṣaṇa*). The speculations of the Sāṅkhya school concentrated on the problem of identity. The possible influence of this school on the Sarvāstivāda theories has already been noted elsewhere.[128] The Vaiśeṣika school, as its name implies, focussed on the distinctions (viśe*ṣaṇa*) in the hope that such a process would eventually lead to the discovery of the nature of ultimate reality. Some of the speculations of the Sautrāntika school reflect this trend. The notions of self-nature (*svabhāva*) and other-nature (*parabhāva*) were the direct results of such an essentialist search.

Thus, when Nāgārjuna says: "The life-process has nothing that distinguishes it from freedom. Freedom has nothing that distinguishes it from the life-process" (XXV.19), to assume that he was presenting an *identity* of *saṃsāra* and *nirvāṇa* would be too hasty a conclusion. In fact, such an assumption would undermine all the attempts he made to refute the notion of identity in the preceding chapters. Instead, Nāgārjuna's attempt in this chapter is focussed on a denial of any ultimate substance, a *dharma*, that would make either *saṃsāra* or *nirvāṇa*, either bondage or freedom a unique entity and this, indeed, is what is emphasized in the concluding verse: "The Buddha did not teach the appeasement of all objects, the appeasement of obsessions and the peaceful as something to someone at some place," (XXV.24).

The method of criticism adopted here is in no way different from that he utilized in Chapter I in his rejection of the metaphysical theories of causality. In that chapter, there was no denial of a cause (*pratyaya*) or an effect (*artha*) and the arising of the latter depending upon the former, so long as these two events and their mutual dependence is *not* explained on the basis of a theory of self-nature or other-nature. Similarly, in the present chapter, there is no denial of the four noble truths that include the fruit and the ultimate fruit (*paramārtha*), so long as these are not conceived of in the form of unique entities (*bhāva*, *svabhāva*), which indeed was the way in which the Sarvāstivādins and the Sautrāntikas defined *dharma*. The concluding verse of this chapter is not properly explained except in the background of these two definitions, namely, the Sarvāstivāda definition of *dharma* as "that which upholds the unique and general characteristics" (*sva-sāmānya-lakṣaṇa-dhāraṇāt dharmaḥ*)[129] and the Sautrāntika definition that refers only to "unique characteristics" (*sva-lakṣaṇa*).[130]

26. ***Human personality and its survival*** (*dvādasāṅga*). Any reader who has ploughed his way through the preceding chapters of Nāgārjuna will certainly be baffled by the contents of Chapter XXVI on the "Examination of the Twelve Factors" (*Dvādasāṅga-parīkṣā*). By the time he completed reading the first twenty-five chapters, wherein the conception of "emptiness" (*śūnyatā*) occurs in almost every other verse, he would be imbued with that concept to such an extent that it would become a dogma, a *dṛṣṭi*, rather than a mere method of analysis. Therefore, Chapter XXVI would make no sense at all. Thus he would get the impression that it merely deals with the Hīnayāna doctrine, having no relevance to the basic teachings of Nāgārjuna and, therefore, of Mahāyāna. This is confirmed by the fact that there is no negative comment made anywhere in the chapter and no mention of the famous doctrine of emptiness. Another person can come to a more drastic conclusion. He may assume that this chapter is like an "illegitimate child" and could not be the work of Nāgārjuna.

Contrary to all these widely held opinions, we tend to look upon this and following chapter as the actual conclusion of this most valuable treatise. They are integral parts of the work, and without them one gets only a distorted view of Nāgārjuna's thoughts.

It was mentioned earlier that the only discourse that Nāgārjuna mentions by name is the *Kātyāyanāvavāda*, and the significance of this fact cannot be overemphasized. Here the Buddha was responding to the question raised by Kaccāyana as to what "right view" (*sammā-diṭṭhi*) is, compared with "wrong view" (*micchā-diṭṭhi*). Nāgārjuna has devoted most of his energy trying to clarify what "wrong views" are and occasionally spoke of "right views" (see analysis of chapter XVII). If he had concluded his treatise with Chapter XXV, he would have read only a section of the Buddha's discourse to Kaccāyana and ignored the Buddha's own conclusion in that discourse. The two extreme views of existence and non-existence were rejected by the Buddha, not because he had no views to propound, but because he had a better or more appropriate one to offer. And this appropriate view is explained in the conclusion to that discourse.

The appropriate view is the middle position specified as dependent arising, which is intended as an explanation of how a human being, conditioned by various factors, attempts to become this or that and wanders along in a ceaseless process of births and deaths. The theory of personality consisting of the twelve factors explaining such becoming thus turns out to be the philosophical middle position, and the noble eightfold path (*magga*), avoiding the two extremes of behavior, represents the practical middle path intended to achieve the cessation of that process of becoming (*bhava*) and suffering (*dukkha*).

If the *Kātyāyanāvavāda* served as the foundation of Nāgārjuna's philosophy, and there does not seem to be any doubt about it, it would have been impossible for him to overlook the conclusion of that discourse. This indeed is the rationale for a whole chapter on the concept of a person explained in terms of the twelvefold formula of causation.

Part IV (Conclusion)

27. *Views (diṭṭhi)*. Buddha's denial of a permanent and eternal self (*ātman*) and his explanation of the human personality and its survival of death in terms of the doctrine of dependent arising have remained unpalatable to most philosophers ever since he presented them. Veridical memories of past existences being connected with present experience as a result of meditation, as in the case of the Buddha and many other ascetics, and sometimes without any such practice or effort,[131] have received a two-fold interpretation in the hands of these philosophers. Some have assumed the existence of a permanent and eternal self or substratum to account for such phenomena, even in the absence

of so-called empirical evidence (empiricism as understood by the Buddha?) to support the belief in a permanent and eternal self. These are the eternalists (*sassata-vādin*). Others have rejected not only the belief in a permanent and eternal self but also the veridical, though sporadic, memories as mere hallucinations of deranged minds. These are the annihilationists (*uccheda-vādin*). These two views have prevailed in the world until the present day, just as similar views regarding the relationship between cause and effect have survived. The reasons for the prevalence of such views were explained briefly by the Buddha in the *Kaccāyanagott-sutta* when he spoke of inclinations (*upāya*), grasping (*upādāna*), and involvement (*abhinivesa*) on the part of the human beings. More detailed explanations were given in other discourses. Whether there were to be veridical memories of past lives or not, the Buddha recognized that human beings were prone to ask three types of questions regarding existence:[132]

1. "Did I exist in the past or not?" (*Ahosiṃ nu kho atītam addhānaṃ, na nu kho ahosiṃ atītam addhānaṃ*). This, according to the Buddha, pertains to the prior end of existence (*pubbanta*), and is prompted by a desire to know the first beginnig of things, including oneself.
2. "Will I exist in the future or not?" (*Bhavissāmi nu kho anāgataṃ addhānaṃ, na nu kho bhavissāmi anāgataṃ addhānaṃ*). This pertains to the future and is prompted by a desire to know the final end of things, including one's own destiny.
3. "Do I exist in the present, or do I not exist in the present?" (*Ahaṃ nu kho asmi, no nu kho asmi*). This pertains to the status of one's present existence.

The Buddha felt that such speculations led to a wide variety of views (*diṭṭhi*), sixty-two as specified in the *Brahmajāla-suttanta*,[133] of which permanent existence (*atthitā*, *sassata-diṭṭhi*) and annihilation (*n'atthitā*, *uccheda-diṭṭhi*) are foremost. Even though the Buddha recognized veridical memories of past existences, yet because of the absence of any empirical evidence to support the hypothesis of a permanent and eternal substratum as well as the difficulties involved in predicting future events with absolute certainty, the Buddha questioned his disciples as to whether it is appropriate for them to "brood over the past" (*pubbantaṃ paṭidhāveyyatha*) or long for the future (*aparāntaṃ ādhāveyyātha*) or be unnecessarily skeptical about the present (*paccuppannaṃ addhānaṃ ajjhattaṃ kathaṃkathī assatha*). He advised them that instead, with the resources available, they should try to understand things as they have come to be (*yathābhūtaṃ*) and work out freedom from suffering. Getting enamoured of any view, whether it is appropriate or inappropriate, would lead to further bondage and suffering. Hence the Buddha's advice to his disciples: "Without grasping on to a view, being endowed with proper perception and morality, and having restrained one's greed for pleasures of sense, one avoids a future birth."[134]

It is significant to note that Nāgārjuna's final chapter on "Views" (*diṭṭhi*) deals with the same issues. He begins his chapter with a reference to the three epistemological inquiries of human beings in relation to the past, present, and future, which give rise to various views on the nature of man and the universe. The first three verses present in identical terms the Buddha's own explanation of these views as stated in the passage from the *Majjhima-nikāya* quoted above. These inquiries and graspings (*upādāna*) are then understood as the reason for the variety of views discussed in verses 4-28. As the notes on these verses would indicate, these twenty-five verses deal with the variety of views discussed by the Buddha in the *Brahmajāla-suttanta*, thus providing undeniable evidence that Nāgārjuna had access to most of the discourses of the Buddha that came to be preserved in the Nikāyas and the Āgamas, and that he was merely restating the original message of the Buddha rather than providing a philosophical justification of a sectarian view.

The variety of wrong views (*micchā-diṭṭhi*) was rejected by the Buddha primarily on pragmatic grounds, that is, because they do not lead to freedom and happiness.[135] They neither bring about worldly fruits (*attha*) nor they contribute to the ultimate fruit (*paramattha*), i.e., freedom and happiness. Instead they lead to dogmatism, conflict, and suffering. The "middle position" as the right view (*sammā-diṭṭhi*), whether it be dependent arising (*paṭiccasamuppāda*) or non-substantiality (*anatta*), or as Nāgārjuna puts it, "absence of self-nature" (*niḥsvabhāva*) or emptiness (*śūnyatā*), leads to worldly fruits as well as the ultimate fruit. However, if that right view were to become another dogma, it would certainly contribute to conflict and suffering, thereby losing its pragmatic value. In other words, a right view is one for which there cannot be grasping, for if one were to grasp it it would turn out to be a closed view not an open one. This explains why Nāgārjuna concludes his chapter on "views," and along with it his famous treatise, with a salutation to the Buddha, a salutation that clearly reflects his knowledge of the Buddha's attitude towards dogmative views (as embodied in the verse quoted previously):

> I reverently bow to Gautama who, out of compassion, has taught
> the true doctrine for the relinquishing of all views. (XXVII.30)

NĀGĀRJUNA'S PHILOSOPHICAL ENTERPRISE

The above analysis of the contents of Nāgārjuna's *Kārikā* and the annotation of individual verses that follow provide ample evidence to support the view that his primary objective was to reject the substantialist or essentialist thought that emerged in the Buddhist philosophical tradition as a result of the speculations of the Sarvāstivādins and the Sautrāntikas. The fact that he depended upon the teachings embodied in the early discourses, or the fact that the *Kārikā* is here looked upon as a grand commentary on the *Kaccāyanagotta-sutta*, in no way minimize his contribution to the history of Buddhist thought. What is most significant is the manner in which he proceeded to examine the subtle and complex metaphysical issues that blinded the Sarvāstivādins and the Sautrāntikas in a background in which speculative philosophy had reached a high watermark, both among the Buddhists and the traditional Indian philosophers. Nāgārjuna probed into almost every aspect of their speculations, whether relating to epistemology, ontology, moral philosophy, or philosophy of language. He linked disjointed concepts and dissolved the hardened and the solidified. Concepts of identity and difference, substance and quality, self-nature and other-nature, permanence and annihilation, even in their most subtle and imperceptible forms, never escaped his penetrating intellect. It seems as if he had read the Buddhist discourses, manuals, and commentaries, examining every sentence, every word, and every syllable. Even if one cannot discover any tangible evidence to provide that he was a "freed one", a *nirvṛta*, the *Kārikā*, indeed, bears ample testimony to his supreme intellectual stature.

Epistemological Investigations

Nāgārjuna was an empiricist *par excellence*. However, the fundamental metaphysical assertion of most rationalists, and even the empiricists during his day, was the *cogito*, the *ātman* that sees itself before it comes to perceive anything else. Nāgārjuna had no hesitation in demolishing this metaphysical idea at the very outset. "Seeing oneself" (*svātmānaṃ darśanaṃ*) is rejected, not on the basis of any dialectical argument, but simply on the grounds of its non-availability (III.2). Comparable to the manner in which David Hume refused to accept the notion of a *cogito*, Nāgārjuna proceeds to show that the so-called process of "seeing oneself" is no more than "the arising of consciousness depending upon the eye and visible form" (*cakṣu-rūpe pratītyaivam ukto vijñāna-saṃbhavaḥ*), III.7), that is, a perception of some color, shape, etc. However, Nāgārjuna differs from Hume in not recognizing these perceptions as momentary and discrete impressions on the basis of which we construct our world-view. Momentariness, along with its philosophically unacceptable consequences, was rejected, especially in his treatment of "motion" (*gatāgata*, II) and "time" (*kāla*, XIX).

That Nāgārjuna was rejecting sense experience *in favor of* a special intuition is not at all evident from his treatment of sense experience in Chapter III. His relentless criticism of a metaphysical *cogito* does not mean that he was evading the problem. On the contrary, he was quoting a statement from the Buddha to show what a non-metaphysical description of sense experience could be. That description in terms of "dependence" is further elaborated in Chapter XXVI where he presented a quite positive explanation of the human personality as well as its experiences.

Indeed, if "emptiness" (*śūnyatā*) were to be an "ultimate reality," there was no reason why Nāgārjuna should not have devoted at least one chapter of his work solely to explicate this conception and provide information regarding its epistemological basis. At least a chapter on "wisdom" (*jñāna*), explaining how it penetrates into the ineffable ultimate truth, abolishing all linguistic conventions in the process, would have established the basic philosophical standpoint attributed to the Mahayana schools by most classical and modern scholars. No such attempt is made in the *Kārikā*. On the contrary, the term that he most frequently uses is *paśyati*, meaning "perceives." He uses it in the same sense in which the Buddha utilized it in the "Discourse to Kātyāyana." Often what he claims not to perceive (*na paśyati*) is self-nature or substance (*svabhāva*) or permanent existence (*bhāva*, *astitva*). What he claims to perceive (*paśyati*) is dependently arisen phenomena as well as dependent arising. Such perceptions are not presented as the results of a special intuition, but primarily of the absence of ignorance (*avidyā*) or confusion (*mṛṣā*) created by one's dispositions or inclinations for the extremes of substantial existence and nihilistic non-existence.

Picking up the most important epistemological theme from the Buddha's discourse to Kātyāyana, Nāgārjuna is insisting that when one perceives through widsom (*jñana*) the arising and ceasing of phenomena, one abandons the two metaphysical explanations of that experience. Indeed, the theme that is emphasized is not the *perception* of a non-arising and non-ceasing ultimate truth, but rather the *non-perception* of a metaphysical entity that is non-arising and non-ceasing. Thus, for Nāgārjuna, sense experience, explained as a process of dependence, serves as the foundation of human knowledge. Concentrating his attention on this foundation of human knowledge and understanding, Nāgārjuna not only leaves out any discussion of special intuitions not related to sense experience, but also avoids any reference to the so-called "extraordinary perceptions" (*abhijñā*), probably because such perceptions had by this time come to be considered absolutely independent of sensory experience, even though this was not the way in which the Buddha perceived them.[136] Nāgārjuna may have been aware that, even according to the Buddha, human beings whose six sensory faculties are not functioning properly could not develop such perceptions. For example, in the early discourses, one cannot come across any reference to someone who is blind by birth developing "clairvoyance" (***dibba-cakkhu***) or one who is deaf evolving the capacity for "clairaudience"' (***dibba-sota***).

Furthermore, Nāgārjuna seems to have directed his attention more to the fundamental problems that generated metaphysical theories. And the problem of sense experience, indeed, was at the very top of that list.

As reiterated in the above analysis of the ***Kārikā*** as well as in the annotation of the text that follows, the empiricist Nāgārjuna continued to insist upon evidence from experience for any idea before it is accepted. The repeated us of the phrasses: ***na vidyata*** (meaning "not evident," "not known," "not perceived," etc.) and ***nopalabhyate*** (implying "not obtained" or "not available") bears ample testimony to his predominantly empiricist attitude. In the absence of any positive evidence that Nāgārjuna rejected sense experience and accepted a higher "intuition," there is no reason to doubt that he was calling for ***evidence*** that is provided by sense experience. In fact, whenever the phrase ***na upapadyate*** ("is not proper," "not appropriate") is used to describe a situation, it would often follow a statement implying that it is not evident (***na vidyata***). This means that rational or logical arguments attempting to draw implications need to be strongly grounded on empirically verified permises. A thesis had to be first found fault with before its antithesis is faulted. "Self-nature is not evident" (***na hi svabhāvo . . . vidyate***), not because "other-nature" (***parabhāva***) is not evident, as would seem to be the case if Nāgārjuna were to merely utilize the method of ***reductio ad absurdum*** (***prasaṅga***). Self-nature (***svabhāva***) is not evident, because it is not available in experience. It is only after such a straightforward empirical statement that Nāgārjuna proceeds to reject "other-nature" (***parabhāva***), for this latter would make no sense without the conception of "self-nature." Indeed, it is the unknowability of self-nature (***avidyamāne svabhāve***) that destroys the very conception of other-nature (I.3), not simply the relativity of the two differentiated concepts.

Ontology

Just as much as the assertion of a *cogito* led to the belief in a substantial agent, a ***pudgala***, the lop-sided attempt to dissolve that concept insisting that it is dependent upon the elements of experience (***dharma***) led to a substantialist view releating to the objective world. The conception of a person was replaced by a substantial world. The Buddha had spoken of obsession (*prapañca*) as the reason for such world-views. Hence his emphasis on the "appeasement of obsessions" (*prapañcopaśama*) as a means of overcoming metaphysics. Looking at the philosophical background in which the objective world had replaced the *cogito* as an ultimate reality, Nāgārjuna was more specific in insisting upon the "appeasement of the object" (*draṣṭavyopaśama*) as a means to attaining true knowledge (V.8).

In fact, the Sarvāstivādins and Sautrāntikas, while denying the substantiality of the human person (*pudgala*), had moved to the other extreme of admitting the substantiality of elements (*dharma*). This problem being foremost in Nāgārjuna's mind, he devoted the second part of his treatise to its refutation. In this case, he realized that even critical philosophy had fallen prey to the ordinary human search for security and absolute certainty when philosophers, compelled to give up something that provided them with some sort of certainty (and in this case the *cogito*), were clinging like leeches to an objective world as an ultimate reality.

If Nāgārjuna were to be an empiricist like the Buddha, he could not confine himself to a world of abstract ideas. He knew that the Buddha was a "verificationist" (*ehipassika*) and that this involved concrete "identification" (to use a term popular in modern philosophy).[137] Thus, the conception of a person begins with an identifiable and re-identifiable "form" (*rūpa*). While the Buddha recognized the possibility of experiencing formless (*arūpa*) states, it is not very clear whether he had accepted "formless" persons. However, unlike some modern philosophers who would consider the "body" or material form to be fundamental and, therefore, ultimately real, leaving all other constituents as being secondary, the Buddha would merely look upon the "body" as a necessary but not sufficient part of the human person. For him, feeling (*vedanā*), perception (*saññā*), dispositions (*saṅkhāra*), and consciousness (*viññāṇa*) were as important as the material body in making any identification or re-identification. Thus, the elimination of the *cogito* by explaining it as something that is dependently arisen (*paṭiccasamuppanna*) did not mean the recognition of the ultimate reality of these conditions upon which it depended. Hence the Buddha's famous dictum: "All things are non-substantial" (*sabbe dhammā anattā*).

For this reason, Nāgārjuna's first major enterprise in the *Kārikā* is to establish the non-substantiality of the elements (*dharma-nairātmya*). This called for a critique of the Sarvāstivāda conception of substance (*svabhāva*). As mentioned earlier, the epistemological method by which he tried to achieve this was "appeal to experience". In other words, he was calling for *identification* of substance, which none of his opponents were able to do.

However, Nāgārjuna believed that an identification of an event can be made on the basis of "fruit" or "effect" (*artha*), for, according to him, in the absence of a fruit, one cannot speak of a condition or non-condition (I.14). This is a pragmatic theory of truth or reality. However, if his substantialist opponents were to insist that the substance can be identified through its fruit or effect, Nāgārjuna's immediate response is that the fruit or effect is dependent upon a condition (or a set of conditions), whereas substance is not. The definition of substance (*svabhāva*) as "having its own (*svo*) existence (*bhāvo*)" stood in the way of Nāgārjuna accepting his opponent's explanation. "How can a substance be conditioned?" (*svabhāvaḥ kṛtako nāma bhaviṣyati punaḥ katham*, XV.2) grumbled Nāgārjuna. For him, the conception of a "dependent substance" was no more than a self-contradiction (XV.1).

Having criticized the substantialist theory of elements (*dharma*), Nāgārjuna had to return once again to the conception of a person, even though he had begun his treatment of the non-substantiality of elements by rejecting a substantialist conception of a person (Chapter III). The reason for this is not far to seek. The Sautrāntikas, who had themselves rejected the Sarvāstivāda conception of substance (*svabhāva*), were surreptitiously introducing a subtle personality (*pudgala*) to account for human behavior, moral responsibility, bondage, and freedom. Chapters XVI-XXVI were, therefore, devoted to the explanation of the human personality without falling into the substantialist trap.

Unlike some of his predecessors and most of his modern day admirers, Nāgārjuna was indeed cognisant of the possible dangers involved in a "non-substantialist discourse." He was aware that the idea of non-substantiality could eliminate even the empirical conception of a person (*pudgala*) and of elements (*dharma*) and enthrone itself as the ultimate truth or reality. Hence his rather bold declaration: "Those who are possessed of the view of emptiness are said to be incorrigible." (XIII.8)

An absolutistic view of emptiness would certainly contradict his empiricist method that calls for identification as a test of truth or reality. "Non-substantiality" (*nairātmya*) or "emptiness" (*śūnyatā*), taken in themselves, would be as abstract and unidentifiable as a substance (*svabhāva*). Indeed, as pointed out earlier, the notion of a substance was rejected because it could not be identified with anything in experience. Therefore, there was no excuse whatsoever for replacing "substance" with an equally undefinable or unidentifiable conception of "emptiness" or "nothingness." "Emptiness" (*śūnyatā*) distinguished from "the empty" (*śūnya*), "non-substantiality" (*nairātmya*) separated from "the non-substantial" (*nairātmya-dharma*) or "dependent arising" (*pratītyasamutpāda*) differenciated from "the dependently arisen" (*pratītyasamutpanna-dharma*) would be as unidentifiable and therefore nonsensical as any other metaphysical conception that Nāgārjuna was endeavoring to refute.

Thus, for Nāgārjuna, emptiness (*śūnyatā*) was *no more* than what is implied in the statement: "All this is empty" (*sarvam idaṃ śūnyam*). The statement, "All this is empty," is not identical with the statement, "All is empty," (*sarvaṃ śūnyam*). In fact, as pointed out in the annotation, nowhere in the *Kārikā* can one come across an absolute statement such as "All is empty." It is indeed significant that even when making a universalized statement Nāgārjuna retains the demonstrative "this" (*idaṃ*) in order to eliminate the absolutist sting.

The question whether one can speak of "emptiness" (*śūnyatā*) of "emptiness" (*śūnyatā*) is often raised in discussions of Nāgārjuna's "middle way." For example, one could maintain that "emptiness" itself is an identifiable particular on the basis of which a universal "emptiness" could be identified. The language utlized by Nāgārjuna does not permit such a flight into the realm of the Absolute. His conception of "the empty" (*śūnya*) is a particular. Yet this particular is not equivalent to a particular "emptiness" (*śūnyatā*) abstracted from a concrete situation. To move from "the empty" to "emptiness" is an altogether different process. The former is grounded in an experienced situation of an event with a characteristic, while the later begins with a characteristic *sans* the event.

This careful avoidance of any absolutism or substantialism in relation to the conception of "dependent arising" (*pratītyasamutpāda*) as well as "emptiness" (*śūnyatā*) was declared by Nāgārjuna as the "middle path" (*pratipat saiva madhyamā*, XXIV.18). That "emptiness" is a "dependent convention" (*upadāya prajñapti*), for it is dependent upon and, therefore, identifiable in terms of, "the empty" (*śūnya*). Nāgārjuna asserts that "emptiness" so identified would eliminate any dogmatism or obsession (*adhilaya*) and, along with it, any erroneous views (*doṣa-prasaṅga*, XXIV.13).

This, undoubtedly, is a beautiful restoration of the Buddha's conception of "non-substantiality" (*anatta*). However, the modern interpretation of Nāgārjuna seems to move in a totally different directon. Modern scholars, favoring an interpretation by Candrakīti made known to them by T. R. V. Murti, insist that Nāgārjuna had no thesis of his own (*svapakṣa*) to present. This Vedantic interpretation presents Nāgārjuna as a critical or analytical philosopher whose sole funciton was to criticize or analyse (*vigraha*) views presented by others without having to recognize or uphold a view of his own. Such an interpretation has led to two more related theories being attributed to Nāgārjuna. The first is the admission of the inadequacy of conceptual thinking, and therefore of language, to express the ultimate truth. The second is the attribution of a concept of ultimate truth in the form of "absolute emptiness" or "absolute nothingness" inexpressible through ordinary human linguistic apparatus. Thus, we are led to one of the most troublesome questions relating to Nāgārjuna's philosophical enterprise.

In the annotation of the dedicatory verses of the *Kārikā*, we have suggested a different reading which would make it possible for Nāgārjuna to make the claim that he is presenting a right view (*samyag-dṛṣṭi*) when refuting the inappropriate views advocated by his opponents. Furthermore, Nāgārjuna clearly indicates that philosophical enterprise consists not only of analysis (*vigraha*) but also explanation (*vyākhyāna*) (IV.9). This would provide legitimation for the most positive explanation of the Buddha's view in Chapter XXVI, in addition to other positive statements made by Nāgārjuna elsewhere (e.g., Chapter XVII).

However, the two most troublesome questions regarding ultimate reality and the inadequcy of language still remain, primarily because of the manner in which the Vedantic scholars interpreted three related terms utilized by Nāgārjuna. These are *pramārtha*, *nirvikalpa*, and *saṃvṛti*.

For most scholars who have been nurtured in a predominantly substantialist philosophical or religious tradition, *paramārtha* means "ultimate reality," *nirvikalpa* implied "the non-conceptual," and *saṃvṛti* stood for "language." In understanding these three terms in this manner, did modern translators and interpreters impose their own substantialist outlook on Nāgārjuna's thought? The first test of the validity of such translations would be a comparison of the implications of these three translations with the Buddha's own conceptions of "dependent arising" (*pratītyasamutpada*) and "non-substantiality" (*anātman*), all of which Nāgārjuna accepted with reverence.

Philosophy of Language

The term *saṃvṛti* (Pali, *sammuti*) was never used in the early discourses to refer exclusively to language. Analysing the Buddha's philosophy on the basis of the early discourses, it was pointed out that *sammuti*, *vohāra*, and *paññatti* were terms used to refer to any convention, not merely linguistic convention. The specific terms used by the Buddha to refer to language are *nirutti* (etymology) and *adhivacana* (definition or semantics). Nāgārjuna's use of the term *abhidheya*, meaning "that which is to be designated," (XVIII.7) would provide us with a term that he may have used if he had a need for referring to language. Such a term would be *adhidhāna* and would not be semantically much different from the term *adhivacana* used by the Buddha.

However, for Nāgārjuna, the *abhidheya* or "that which is to be designated" ceases with the cessation of *citta-gocara* ("the ojbect of thought"). Thus, anything that is not the object of thought, that is non-conceptual (*nirvikalpa*), is also not describable. If so, Nāgārjuna had no reason to compose more than four hundred verses trying to explain the indescribable. It would be a fruitless attempt on the part of any philosopher, let alone one who is extolled as an "enlightened one" (*buddha*).

If Nāgārjuna was trying to explain something and in that process was utilizing language, he would be dealing with the conceptual or the object of thought (*citta-gocara*). Accordingly, anything that is conceptual would also be the object of thought, and the non-conceptual (*nirvikalpa*) could not be an object of thought. A truth that cannot be thought of, let alone one that cannot be spoken of, would be as metaphysical as the conception of *ātman* in the Brahmanical speculations. *Nirvikalpa* would, therefore, mean something else. In the course of the analysis of the *Kārikā*, it was pointed out that Nāgārjuna was critical of a specific form of discrimination, a discrimination that produced polarities in human thinking. These consisted of existence and non-existence, substance and quality, self-nature and other-nature, permanence and annihilation. In such a context, *nirvikalpa* would refer to polar discriminations, not any and every form of discrimination.

This leads us to one of the most controversial discriminations that the metaphysicians of the Buddhist tradition as well as their counterparts of other substantialist traditions made with regard to bondage and freedom. Chapter XXV of the *Kārikā* is devoted to an analysis of this metaphysical issue. In Chapter XXIV, when Nāgārjuna spoke of *saṃvṛti* and *vyavahāra* on the one hand and *paramārtha* on the other, he was paving his way for a discussion of the discrimination between bondage and freedom.

Nāgārjuna, who provided every indication that he had read the early discourses, could not have been unaware that the Buddha used the terms *sammuti* and *vohāra* (*vyavahāra*) more often in the sense of moral conventions. These moral conventions pertained to good (*dharma*) and bad (*adharma*). Thus, whenever he used the term *vyavahāra*, Nāgārjuna was referring to the moral conventions of good and bad (*dharma-adharma*) (XXIV.36) or merit and demerit (*puṇya-pāpa*) (XVII.24). These moral conventions are accepted not because they are mere conventions agreed upon by consensus but because they work. They are pragmatically grounded. They produce fruits or consequences (*artha*). Such conventions provide a basis for ideal conventions referred to as *paramārtha* ("highest fruit or consequence"). Yet, to safeguard the ideal from becoming a mere ideal and not a fact, Nāgārjuna insists upon the dependence of the ideal on the concrete. A quotation from William James, even though extensive, seems to be relevant here.

> If the ethical philosopher were only asking after the best *imaginable* system of goods he would indeed have an easy task; for all demands as such are *prima facie* respectable, and the best simply imaginary world would be one in which *every* demand was gratified as soon as made. Such a world would, however, have to have a physical constitution entirely different from that of the one which

we inhabit. It would need not only space, but a time, of *n*-dimensions, to include all the acts and experiences incompatible with one another here below, which would then go on in conjunction—such as spending our money, yet growing rich; taking a holiday, yet getting ahead with our work; shooting and fishing, yet doing no hurt to the beasts; gaining no end of experience, yet keeping our youthful freshness of heart; and the like. There can be no question that such a system of things, however brought about, would be the absolutely ideal system; and that if a philosopher could create universes *a priori*, and provide all the mechanical conditions, that is the sort of universe which he should unhesitatingly create.

But this world of ours is made on an entirely different pattern, and the casuistic question is here most tragically practical. The actually possible in this world is vastly narrower than all that is demanded; and there is always a *pinch* between the ideal and the actual which can only be got through by leaving part of the ideal behind.[138]

In a similar way, Nāgārjuna, following the pragmatic teachings of the Buddha, could not divorce *paramārtha* from *saṃvṛti* (i.e., the ultimate fruit from the fruit of everyday life of a human being). Just as much as "emptiness" is based upon "the empty," even so *paramārtha* had to be based upon the *saṃvṛti*. Without any reference to the concrete concepts of good, any notion of ultimate or ideal good would be not only meaningless but also "fruitless" (*an-artha*) and terribly harmful (as proven by many such instances in the history of mankind). Thus, for Nāgārjuna, ultimate good is not one that transcends ordinary notions of good, but merely an extension of the so-called goodness recognized in everyday life (*vyavahāra*).

The sharp dichotomy between the ordinary notion of good and the ideal good is thus broken down. It is significant to note that when speaking of two truths Nāgārjuna utilized the terms *saṃvṛti* and *paramārtha*. Yet, when he proceeded to explain their relationship, he utilized the term *vyavahāra*, thereby establishing the synonymity of *saṃvṛti* and *vyavahāra*. The fact that Nāgārjuna was not prepared to create an unbridgeable chasm between *saṃvṛti* or *vyavahāra* on the one hand and *paramārtha* on the other is clearly expressed in his famous statement that without the former the latter is not expressed (*vyavahāram anāśritya paramārtho na deśyate*, XXIV.10).

Similarly, without understanding the ultimate fruit, freedom is not obtained (*paramārtham anāgamya nirvāṇaṃ nādhigamyate*, ibid.). This would mean that freedom (*nirvāṇa*) itself is not something to be sharply distinguished from *saṃsāra* or ordinary human life, even though they are not identical. Freedom would not be absolute freedom that has nothing to do with *human life*. It is no more than the absence of certain constraints (such as greed, hatred, and confusion) in the life of a human being. It is, therefore, the life of an ordinary human being that is gradually transformed, through the cultivation of moral precepts, into one of moral perfection. This transformation (rather than transcendence) is what is implied by ***nirvāṇa***.

Moral Philosophy

The moral life that leads to the transformation of the human personality is clearly explained by Nāgārjuna in Chapter XVII. The absolutistic interpretation of Nāgārjuna's conception of "emptiness" constrained many of his modern admirers from discussing his views regarding karma and survival, even though these were part and parcel of the Buddha's teachings. The discussion of karma and survival in the *Kārikā* was thus considered to be "Hīnayānistic," having nothing to do with the so-called Mahāyāna. As such, the Buddha's own views regarding these issues turn out to be "Hīnayānistic" or, at least, were intended for those low-witted disciples who surrounded him.

Contrary to this view, our analysis of the contents of Chapter XVII, placed in the background in which Nāgārjuna lived, shows that he was more positive than his modern day disciples in his treatment of karma and survival. Nāgārjuna's major endeavor in this chapter is to rescue the Budda's discourse on moral responsibility from the havoc created by the substantialist thinkers who assumed karma to be either substantial or performed by a substantial agent. His was not an attempt to dissolve the conception of karma in favor of an absolutistic notion of "emptiness."

Indeed, the chapter begins with a reference to the Supreme Sage (***paramarṣi***) whose doctrine he was about to expound. Speaking of the morally good life, Nāgārjuna uses the term ***dharma***, instead of karma, and this may have confounded the modern interpreters. The term ***dharma***, as explained earlier in the discussion of the Buddha's philosophy, was used both in an ontological sense and in an ethical context. Nāgārjuna himself followed this practice, as indicated in the annotation of the *Kārikā* (see XXIV.36). Thus, in the present context too, ***dharma*** means good karma and these are identified as (i) self-restraint, and (ii) benefitting others. Nāgārjuna's selection of these two types of action as the foundation of moral behavior is significant. They are an echo of the Buddha's own first sermon to the world that advocated a middle path between two extremes of self-indulgence and self-mortification. The "Middle Way" (***mādhyamika***) philosopher ***par excellence*** could not have ignored the ethical middle path of the Buddha. He knew the implications of that first sermon. Self-restraint, but not self-mortification or self-immolation, constitutes one of the foundations of moral life. In this regard, Nāgārjuna was not advocating the extremist form of behavior sometimes extolled as the ideal of a *bodhisattva* both in the Theravāda and in the Mahāyāna. Self-restraint is a necessary prerequisite for any altruistic activity, which is the second of the virtues extolled by Nāgārjuna as a "friendly way" (*maitraṃ dharmaṃ*).

The implications of the moral life recommended here should not go unnoticed. In spite of the exceedingly popular theme emerging among the Buddhists during Nāgārjuna's day that emphasized extreme altruism, Nāgārjuna seems to be playing a rather moderate tune recognizing the Buddha's own words in the *Dhammapada* (166): "One should not neglect one's own welfare through excessive altruism. Having understood one's own welfare, one should be devoted to true welfare."

A reader of the early discourses cannot but be impressed by the ideal of human behavior advocated by the Buddha. The noblest person according to the Buddha is one who avoids suffering for himself as well as others (*attabyābādha, parabyābādha*).[139] Thus, a noble action should be one that contributes to one's own happiness as well as the happiness of others. This involves the recognition that, while abandoning a belief in a metaphysical self, one has to cultivate compassion for one's own person. At the same time such compassion should be extended to others as well. Nāgārjuna seems to have picked up this theme well when, unlike many Buddhist writers of his day, he emphasised that self-restraint and benefitting others are both acts of friendliness (*maitram*). He was simply insisting: "Be a friend to yourself and be a friend to others." This would certainly be opposed to the ideal that calls for complete and unqualified self-sacrifice, including self-immolation. Thus Nāgārjuna, the founder of the "Middle Way" (*Mādhyamika*) school, could not have recommended a more sober moral life than one which avoids the two extremes of destroying onself and destroying others.

These two friendly ways are recommended by Nāgārjuna because they are fruitful not only in the present life (*iha*) but also in an after-life (*pretya*). There could be no doubt that here he was recognizing the possibility of human survival. The *samsāra* or "life-process" referred to at XXIV.10 need not be confined to this present life alone. On the contrary, it refers to the continuity of the life-process through several births and deaths, referred to as *punabbhava* in the early discourses. That continuity, along with its attendant suffering, is to be eliminated by the development of wisdom (*jñāna*) which for Nāgārjuna consists in the avoidance of all metaphysical views (*dṛṣṭi*).

Knowledge Leading To Freedom

Knowledge that leads to freedom is not omniscience (*sarvajñatā*). Nowhere in the *Kārikā* does Nāgārjuna refer to omniscience, even though it was a popular theme among the Theravādins and the Mahāyānists. In the absence of omniscience, what form of knowledge could lead man from bondage to freedom? Nāgārjuna refers to "a wise one" (*vidvān*) who, through his perception of the nature of truth (*tattva-darśanāt*), does not accumulate dispositions (*saṃskāra*) that lead to wandering (*saṃsāra*)(XXVI.10). Thus, for Nāgārjuna, as it was with the Buddha, the problem lies in the accumulation and pursuit of one's dispositions. Yet without following the dispositions a human being is unable to deal with the rather complex and excessive sensory input. The "big blooming buzzing confusion" of experience has to be faced without the aid of omniscience. The task is rendered extremely difficult because the dispositional tendencies that are a necessary means of dealing with such experience also lead to extremes, especially when these dispositions are dominated by one's likes and dislikes. When they are dominated by likes and dislikes, they produce perspectives on the basis of which one looks at the world, two of these being eternalism and annihilationism. In order to adopt a middle path avoiding these two extremes, one needs to eliminate the likes and dislikes and thereby appease one's dispositions. A person who has achieved the state of the appeasement of dispositions (*saṃskāropaśama*) (and this would include the appeasement of the object of perception (*draṣṭavyopaśama*), whether that object be the *cogito* or the real external world) is said to have attained enlightenment and freedom. Such a person is enlightened because he comes to perceive things as they have come to be (*yathābhūtajñāna* = *tattvadarśana*), and he is free because he does not adhere to any dogmatic view that rules out other possibilities. The difference between a metaphysical view criticized by the Buddha as well as Nāgārjuna and the "middle position" (*madhyamāpratipat*) accepted by both is that the former is a closed view while the latter is an open one. An open view does not subscribe to an absolute discrimination as either/or. The very idea of openness imiplies non-grasping (*anupādāna*). Thus, when both the Buddha and Nāgārjuna emphasized the renunciation of all views (*sarva-dṛṣṭi-prahāṇa*), they were insisting upon abandoning all forms of dogmatism with regard to views. For them, non-attachment to views does not necessarily mean having "no-views."

Inappropriate rendering of Sanskrit terms into English seems to have contributed in some measure toward the myth that Nāgārjuna had no view to express.[140] The passage often quoted in support of this myth occurs in Nāgārjuna's *Vigrahavyāvartanī* (29): "If I would make any commitment whatever, from that I would incur such error. On the contrary, I do not have a commitment. Therefore, there is no error on my part."

The term that occurs here is *pratijñā*, which has been translated as a simple proposition or statement. It is much more than a simple proposition or statement. It is a commitment and should be contrasted with *vyākhyāna*, "explanation," (IV.9). While avoiding the former, Nāgārjuna continued to resort to the latter (see also XVII.13, etc.). As such, it would be highly inappropriate to compare Nāgārjuna's philosophical method with that of Ludwig Wittgenstein, for example by quoting him as follows: "Philosophy simply puts everything before us, and neither explains nor deduces anything.—Since everything lies open to view, there is nothing to explain."[141] In fact, this quotation misrepresents Wittgenstein's own approach to metaphysics. The most important part of the statement has been omitted. It reads: "For what is hidden, for example, is of no interest to us." If this crucial statement is retained, then Wittgenstein's thought can certainly be compared with Nāgārjuna's or even the Buddha's. This omitted part of the statement makes it abundantly clear that what Wittgenstein was not willing to explain is "what is hidden," and this "something" is, indeed, comparable to what Nāgārjuna was referring to as *kiṃcit* or *kaścit*, that is, the hidden substance in phenomena. Neither "the empty" (*śūnya*) nor "emptiness" (*śūnyatā*), neither "the dependently arisen" (*pratītyasamutpanna*) nor "dependent arising" (*pratītyasamutpāda*) represent a hidden something which Nāgārjuna was reluctant to *explain*. On the contrary, if it can be shown that Wittgenstein did not provide any *explanation* of experience, or did not attempt to *formulate* in linguistic terms what a true experience is, as opposed to a confused one, then he could certainly be enlightened by the language of "emptiness" or of "dependence" adopted by the Buddha and Nāgārjuna.

NOTES

1. *S* 2.16–17; *Tsa* 12.19 (*Taishō* 2.85c).
2. *S* 5.420–424; *Tsa* 15.17 (*Taishō* 2.103c).
3. For a detailed historical study of the *Kathāvatthu*, see S. N. Dube, *Cross Currents in Early Buddhism*, New Delhi: Manohar, 1980. The study of this work will be greatly facilitated by the recent PTS publication of a more carefully edited version of Buddhaghosa's commentary by N. A. Jayawickrema.
4. *Lung-shu-p'u-sa-ch'uan*, Taisho 2047.
5. Kenneth K. Inada, *Nāgārjuna. A Translation of his Mūlamadhyamakakārikā with an Introductory Essay*, Tokyo: The Hokuseido Press, 1970, p.3.
6. *DhsA* 76.
7. *Sdmp* p.43 ff.
8. *Vin* 2.241; see innumerable references to the Chabbaggiya as miscreants whose conduct was responsible for the formulation of many a rule of discipline.
9. *Kp* 105.
10. *Sdmp* p.45; see also *MKV* p.306.
11. T. R. V. Murti, *Central Philosophy of Buddhism*, London: Allen & Unwin, 1960, pp.49–50.
12. Mark Siderits, book review in *Journal of Indian Philosophy*, 8 (1980):192.
13. A. K. Warder, *Indian Buddhism*, Delhi: Motilal Banarsidass, 1970, p.376.
14. *Kārikā* XV.7.
15. *S* 2.17.
16. *Tsa* 12.19 (*Taishō* 2.85c).
17. *Kp* 60–61.
18. Ibid., 56.
19. See Whalen Lai, "Chinese Buddhist causation theories: An analysis of the sinitic Mahāyāna understanding of *Pratītyasamutpada*," *Philosophy East and West*, 27 (1977):241–264.
20. Richard H. Robinson, *Early Mādhyamika in India and China*, Madison: University of Wisconsin, 1967, pp.83–88.
21. *Rg-veda* x.90; also *Bṛhadāraṇyaka Upaniṣad* 1.4.11–13.
22. See David J. Kalupahana, *Causality. The Central Philosophy of Buddhism*, Honolulu: The University Press of Hawaii, 1975, p.39.
23. *S* 2.17. Cf. *Tsa* 12.19 (*Taishō* 2.85c).
24. *D* 1.12 ff.; *Ch'ang* 14.1 (*Taishō* 1.88b ff.). For a detailed treatment of these views, see K. N. Jayatilleke, *Early Buddhist Theory of Knowledge*, London: Allen & Unwin, 1963, pp.23–168.
25. *Ud* 1.
26. *D* 1.58–59; *Ch'ang* 17.1 (*Taishō* 1.107a).

27. *Ud* 80.
28. *M* 1.262–264; *S* 2.28, 70, 96; *Ud* 2; *Tsa* 10.7 (*Taishō* 2.67a); 14.16 (*Taishō* 2.100a), etc. See Kalupahana, *Causality*, p.90.
29. *S* 2.18; *Tsa* 12.20 (*Taishō* 2.86a); see also Kalupahana, *Causality*, p.5–6.
30. Ibid.
31. Ibid.
32. *S* 2.25; 3.3–4; *Tsa* 12.14 (*Taishō* 2.84b).
33. Ibid. Also *M* 1.167, 324, 325.
34. *M* 1.415–417; *Chung* 3.4 (*Taishō* 1.436a ff.).
35. *Thag* 304.
36. *M* 1.395; also 3.237.
37. *Sn* 68.
38. See Kalupahana, *Causality*, pp.177–183.
39. *M* 1.160–175; *Chung* 56.1 (*Taishō* 1.775c ff.).
40. *MKV* pp.264, 492.
41. Ibid., p.374.
42. *D* 1.202 (where all four terms *sāmaññā, nirutti, vohāra* and *paññatti* are used as synonyms); *Sn* 897.
43. *Sn* 897.
44. Ibid., 903.
45. Ibid., 897.
46. *S* 3.70–73; *Tsa* 10.5 (*Taishō* 2.65c-66a).
47. *M* 3.230; *Chung* 43.5 (*Taishō* 1.701a f.).
48. *M* 1.395; 3.237.
49. Inada, *Nāgārjuna*, p.6.
50. See Kalupahana, *Causality*, pp.148–149.
51. Ibid. pp.149–150.
52. *Sakv* p.11.
53. Kalupahana, *Causality*, pp.152–153.
54. See Jiryo Masuda, "Origin and Doctrines of Early Indian Buddhist Schools," (A translation of the Hsuan-Chwang Version of Vasumitra's Treatise), *Asia Major* 2 (1925):17.
55. T. I. Stcherbatsky, *The Central Conception of Buddhism and the Meaning of the Term 'Dharma,'* London: Royal Asiatic Society, 1923, pp.37–38; *Buddhist Logic*, Leningrad: Academy of Sciences of The USSR, 1930, I.4–5.
56. Jayawickrema, *Kathāvatthuppakaraṇa-aṭṭhakathā, London: PTS, 1979, p.xv.*
57. *Kvu*, p.1 ff.
58. Ibid. p.115 ff.
59. Ibid. p.456 ff.
60. See Hajime Nakamura, *Indian Buddhism*, Osaka: Kansai University of Foreign Studies, 1980, p.159.
61. *Kp* 52.

62. *Kārikā* XVII.13; XVIII.12.

63. Marvin Sprung, *The Lucid Exposition of the Middle Way. The Essential Chapters from the Prasannapadā of Candrakīrti*, Boulder: Prajna Press, 1979.

64. *Central Philosophy of Buddhism*, p.134.

65. Translated into French by E. Lamotte, in *Melanges Chinois et Bouddhique*, iv (1935–1936).

66. *MKV* pp.324, 390.

67. See Kalupahana, "The Buddhist Conception of Time and Temporality," in *PEW*, 24 (1974):181–191.

68. Ibid.

69. *The Principles of Psychology*, New York: Henry Holt, vol. I, 1908, p.609.

70. *Bṛhadarāṇyaka Upaniṣad* 1.4.11–14.

71. See Swami Satprakashananda, *Methods of Knowledge. According to Advaita Vedānta*, London: Allen & Unwin, 1965, pp. 41 ff.

72. *Nāgārjuna*, p.54.

73. *M* 2.87.

74. *Ak* 2.62d.

75. *MKV* p.135.

76. *S* 3.38; *Tseng* 12.15 (*Taishō* 2.607C).

77. *Sakv* p.174.

78. *S* 3.36; *Tsa* 2.25 (*Taishō* 2.14a); *S* 3.103; *Tsa* 2.26 (*Taishō* 2.14b–15a).

79. *Ud* 80.

80. *Sn* 916.

81. See J. A. B. Van Buitenen, "Studies in Saṅkhya," *Journal of the American Oriental Society*, 76 (1956):153–157.

82. See, for example, the Āgama version at *Tsa* 34.1 (*Taishō* 2.214b).

83. *S* 2.18 ff.; *Tsa* 12.20 (*Taishō* 2.86a).

84. *Dhp* 165.

85. Ibid. 278.

86. *Sn* 886.

87. *Some Problems of Philosophy*, Cambridge, Mass.: Harvard University Press, 1979, p.33.

88. *M* 1.482.

89. See *Sn* 796–803.

90. *M* 1.111–112; *Chung* 28.3 (*Taishō* 1.604b).

91. Inada, *Nāgārjuna*, p.148.

92. *M* 1.111–112; *Chung* 28.3 (*Taishō* 1.604b).

93. *M* 3.19; *S* 3.103; *Tsa* 2.26 (*Taishō* 2.15a).

94. Inada, p.102.

95. Ibid., pp.104–105.

96. *A* 3.415; *Chung* 27.5 (*Taishō* 1.600a).

97. *Dhp* 127.

98. Inada, *Nāgārjuna*, p.104.

99. Donald Mitchell, "Buddhist theories of causation—commentary," in *PEW*, 25 (1975):102.
100. *M* 1.184; *Chung* 36.2 (*Taishō* 1.658a).
101. *Sn* 1076.
102. *S* 1.120; *Tsa* 39.11 (*Taishō* 2.286a).
103. *Sn* 1076.
104. *M* 1.395; also 3.237; *Chung* 43.5 (*Taishō* 1.703c).
105. *M* 1.426; *Chung* 60.6 (*Taishō* 1.804a-b); *M* 1.483ff.
106. *S* 3.83.
107. *M* 1.184; *Tsa* 39.11 (*Taishō* 2.286a).
108. See Kalupahana, "Aññā," in *Encyclopaedia of Buddhism*, ed. G. P. Malalasekera, Colombo: Government of Ceylon, 1961, 1.693–696.
109. James, *The Principles of Psychology*, vol. I, p. 609.
110. *D* 3.80 ff.; *Ch'ang* 6.1 (*Taishō* 1.36b).
111. *DhsA* p.421; see Kalupahana, "Schools of Buddhism in Early Ceylon," *The Ceylon Journal of the Humanities*, Peradeniya: University of Ceylon, 1 (1970):159–190.
112. *Bṛhadarāṇyaka Upaniṣad* 1.3.28.
113. Ibid.
114. *S* 3.110; *Tsa* 5.2 (*Taishō* 2.31a-b).
115. Ibid.
116. Inada, *Nāgārjuna*, p.132.
117. *S* 3.110; *Tsa* 5.2 (*Taishō* 2.31a-b).
118. *A* 2.52.
119. *M* 1.140.
120. *S* 3.54; *Tsa* 9.4 (*Taishō* 2.56b).
121. *M* 1.228; *S* 3.133; 4.401; *A* 1.286; *Thag* 678; *Dhp* 297; *Tsa* 10.7 (*Taishō* 2.66b–67a); *Tseng* 32.4 (*Taishō* 2.668c).
122. *The Gāndhārī Dharmapada*, ed. J. Brough, London: Oxford University Press, 1962, 190, (also see p.240).
123. *D* 1.51; *Ch'ang* 17.1 (*Taishō* 1.107a ff.).
124. *Petavatthu*, ed. Minayeff, London: PTS, 1888, 57; *Apadāna*, ed. M. E. Lilley, London: PTS, 1925–1927, 395.
125. *The Conception of Buddhist Nirvāna*, Leningrad: Academy of Sciences of the USSR, 1927.
126. Inada, *Nāgārjuna*, p.153.
127. Ibid., p. 160.
128. Kalupahana, *Causality*, p.150.
129. *Sakv* p.12.
130. See Poussin, *L'Abhidharmakośa*, 4.140.
131. See Ian Stevenson, *Twenty Cases Suggestive of Reincarnation*, second revised and enlarged edition, Charlottesville: University Press of Virginia, 1974.
132. *M* 3.94–99; *Tsa* 2.25 (*Taishō* 2.13c–14a).

133. *D* 1.12 ff.
134. *Sn* 152.
135. *D* 1.191 ff.
136. Kalupahana, ***Buddhist Philosophy. A Historical Analysis***, Honolulu: The University Press of Hawaii, 1976, pp.21–23.
137. P. F. Strawson, ***Individuals***, New York: Doubleday, 1963, pp.2 ff.
138. "The Moral Philosophers and the Moral Life," in ***Essays in Pragmatism***, ed. A. Castell, New York: Hafner, 1948, pp.77–78.
139. *M* 1.89–90, 369–370, etc.; *Chung* 25.2 (*Taishō* 1.586a).
140. See Chris Gudmunsen, ***Wittgenstein and Buddhism***, London: Harper & Row, 1977, p.44.
141. ***Philosophical Investigations***, tr. G. E. M. Anscombe, New York: Macmillan, 1958, 126, as quoted by Gudmunsen.

Sanskrit Text, Translation and Annotation

DEDICATORY VERSES

Anirodham anutpādam anucchedam aśāśvatam,
anekārtham anānārtham anāgamam anirgamam,
yaḥ pratītyasamutpādam prapañcopaśamam śivam,
desayāmāsa sambuddhaḥ tam vande vandatām varam.

I salute him, the fully enlightened, the best of speakers, who preached the non-ceasing and the non-arising, the non-annihilation and the non-permanence, the non-identity and the non-difference, the non-appearance and the non-disappearance, the dependent arising, the appeasement of obsessions and the auspicious.

Madhyamakavṛttiḥ, ed. L. de la Vallee Poussin [abbreviated *MKV(P)*],p.11; ed. P.L. Vaidya, [abbreviated *MKV(V)*,p.4.

These introductory verses appear to be equivocal and therefore could account for most of the conflicting views in the two major Mādhyamika traditions: (1) those of the Prāsaṅgikas, represented by Candrakīrti and attributed by him to the earlier Mādhyamika philosophers like Aryadeva and Buddhapālita, who recognized no views and merely utilized the *reductio ad absurdum* method to refute the views of their opponents; and (2) those of the Svātantrikas, represented by Bhāvaviveka, who admitted a positive thesis on the basis of which they criticized the opponents' views. In these verses, the contents of the Buddha's discourse are all referred to in the accusative case as *anirodham, anutpādam, anucchedam, aśāśvatam anekārtham, anānārtham, anāgamam, anirgamam, pratītyasamutpādam, prapañcopaśamam, śivam* without giving any indication as to whether they refer to one doctrine or several.

Modern interpreters of Nāgārjuna, probably following Candrakīrti, whose commentary, the *Prasannapadā*, is the only one available in its original Sanskrit, have assumed that all these terms refer to one doctrine, namely, dependent arising (*parītyasamutpāda*). However, as will be shown below, it is also possible to explain these verses as referring to several different concepts in the Buddha's philosophy, thus providing justification for the standpoint of the 'positivists' (*svātantrika*) of the Mādhyamika tradition.

1. *Prāsaṅgika interpretation.* Candrakīrti's comments on these verses show very definitely how he moves from a *svātantrika* interpretation to a *prāsaṅgika* one. He begins his treatise, the *Prasannapadā*, by emphasizing the significance

of dependent arising (*pratītyasamutpāda*). Accepting both the general or distributive meaning and the particular usage of the term, he explains dependent arising as "the arising of things contingent upon causes and conditions" (*hetupratyayāpekṣo bhāvānām utpādaḥ pratītyasamutpādaḥ*, p.5), contrasting it with the definition offered by those who accepted a theory of momentariness (*kṣaṇika-vāda*). According to the latter dependent arising means "the arising of those that are repeatedly destroyed," (*prati prati ityānāṃ vināśināṃ samutpāda iti*, loc. cit.). In fact, Candrakīrti seems to defend some sort of "radical empiricism" when he raises the question: "How can one maintain that there is arising of that which has reached [another] without obtaining a relation?" (*Katham anenaiva prāpteḥ sambhava ita yuktyanupādānena*, p.9). He continues to emphasize Nāgarjuna's view that "whatever that has arisen reaching such and such, that is not arisen in terms of self-nature" (*tat tat prāpya samutpannaṃ notpannaṃ tat svabhāvataḥ*, pp. 9, 10). This certainly means that the negations in the dedicatory verse are intended to deny that things are arisen through self-nature (*svabhāvataḥ*) and there seems to be no implication that they are applicable to dependent arising itself.

However, a change of perspective appears when Candrakīrti proceeds to explain the principle of dependent arising (*pratītyasamutpāda*). Instead of taking dependent arising as the positive middle position of the Buddha, Candrakīrti applies the negations to dependent arising itself, as if the negations are presented as adjectives qualifying dependent arising. Hence his statement: "The entire treatise [i.e. the *Kārika*] purports to establish the absence of cessation, etc. *of* dependent arising," (*nirodhādayo na santi pratītyasamutpādasya*, p. 11).

This leads Candrakīrti to a position of "no-views" which is then identified with the "appeasement of obsessions" (*prapañcopaśama*) or freedom (*nirvāṇa*), thereby emphasizing its transcendence. Quotations from Nāgārjuna as well as Aryadeva are presented as justification for this identification of "dependent arising" and "appeasement of obsessions" (p. 16), even though Nāgārjuna seems to distinguish between utilizing right views (such as dependent arising) without grasping on to them as the absolute truth. With this interpretation of the negations, the dependent arising and freedom, Candrakīrti then moves on to the contents of Nāgārjuna's first chapter on the examination of "conditions" (*pratyaya*) and involves himself in a lengthy discussion of the Prāsaṅgika and Svātantrika standpoints.

2. *Svātantrika interpretation*. It is possible to interpret these eleven characterizations as expressing three major aspects of the Buddha's discourse:

a) The eight negations may be taken as a refutation of the false views (*mithyā-dṛṣṭi*), primarily the theories of substantial existence (*astitva*) and nihilistic non-existence (*nāstitva*), that is, the non-ceasing (*anirodhaṃ*) of a substantial entity and the non-arising (*anutpādaṃ*) of a non-existent entity. Indeed, the non-ceased (*aniruddhaṃ*) and non-arisen (*anutpannaṃ*) are equivalent to the non-empty (*aśūnya*), a term used to refer to substance (*svabhāva*) (XX.17). Hence these negations appear in couplets and could be considered as another way of presenting the non-substantiality (*anātman*) not only of phenomena but also of those views. They are non-substantial in the sense that they are not absolute, as they were assumed to be by their proponents.

b) "Dependent arising" (*pratītyasamutpāda*) would then stand for the middle position, which is the right view (*samyag-dṛṣṭi*) on the basis of which the wrong views are criticized. "Dependent arising" is considered to be the right view, not because it is an absolute truth, but because it allows for possible explanations of phenomena not permitted by theories of absolute existence and nihilistic non-existence.

c) "The appeasement of obsessions" (*prapañcopaśama*) and "the auspicious" (*śiva*) would be the result of adopting the middle position. This is freedom or nirvana.

Interpreted as such, these verses refer to a positive core of the Buddha's teachings, alongside of the negative aspect which was intended as a rejection of the heretical views. Such an interpretation would leave dependent arising as the position from which the Buddha rejected the metaphysical or absolute views and this would support the Svātantrika understanding of Nāgārjuna. If the analysis of Nāgārjuna's philosophy is undertaken in the light of the "Discourse to Kātyāyana," as is done in the Introduction to the present work, the above interpretation of the dedicatory verses may appear to be more in conformity with the Buddha's own teachings. Such an interpretation would present the *Kārikas* as a compact and well-organized composition and eliminate the need to prune portions of the text as being irrelevant or inessential to the main theme.

CHAPTER ONE
Examination of Conditions
(Pratyaya-parīkṣā)

1. *Na svato nāpi parato na dvābhyāṃ nāpy ahetutaḥ,*
utpannā jātu vidyante bhāvāḥ kvacana kecana.

No existents whatsoever are evident anywhere that are arisen from themselves, from another, from both, or from a non-cause.

MKV(P) p.12; *MKV(V)* p.4.

The four types of events referred to here are comparable to those mentioned by the Buddha at *S* 2.19–20, namely, *sayaṃkataṃ paraṃkataṃ, sayaṃkatañ ca paraṃkatañ ca*, and *asayaṃkāramaparaṃkāram adhiccasamuppannaṃ.* Instead of the term *utpanna* (arisen), which occurs only in the last phrase, here we find the occurrence of the term *kata* (Sk. *kṛta*), "done," primarily because in the *Upaniṣads*, which served as background to the Buddha's teaching, the substantial self (*ātman*) was looked upon more as a "personal agent," than as a substantial principle (*svabhāva, prakṛti*, etc.). With the sophistication in philosophical thinking in the later Indian schools, the "personal agent" was gradually replaced by an "impersonal substance" (*svabhāva*). The Sarvāstivādins, who came to accept a conception of substance while at the sametime rejecting a "personal agent" (*pudgala*), failed to notice the similarity if not the identity of their implications. In this verse, Nāgārjuna presents his negative thesis, which in the dedicatory verse he expressed with the eight negations. It is the thesis that he undertakes to prove in the first twenty-five chapters. He has not provided any arguments yet, except saying that these four kinds of events are not evident. Probably he felt that these events needed further explanation before he proceeds to refute them.

However, Candrakīrti is all too impatient. His commentary on this verse is more than one tenth of his entire work (almost 65 pages), and it is a stupendous commentary filled with lot of metaphysical trivia and diatribes, mostly directed at Bhāvaviveka and the Svātantrika tradition. After assuming that Nāgārjuna had "no position" (see note on the dedicatory verses) with which to criticize these four theories, Candrakīrti settles down to justify the *reductio ad absurdum* by which the inherent contradictions in a thesis are exposed. He realizes that self-causation (*svata-utpatti*) is based on the belief in a permanent and eternal self or substance (*svabhāva*). Quoting Buddhapālita, he maintains: '"Things are not arisen from self," because such arising is meaningless, (*tad ut-padavaiyarthyāt*, p.14).' For, there is no purpose in the arising of things that are already existent. This certainly is Nāgārjuna's criticism of a substantialist notion of a "condition" (*pratyaya*) at I.6. However, in the present verse and at I.3, Nāgārjuna appears to use the argument from empiricism to deny the substantialist view.

Thus, while Nāgārjuna was saying that substance is not evident (*na vidyate*) and, therefore, inappropriate (*na yujyate*), Candrakīrti was maintaining that substance is not appropriate (*na yujyate*) and, therefore, not evident (*na vidyate*). This indeed is the difference between empiricism and rationalism, a difference that is soon to lead to the conflict between the Svātantrikas and the Prāsangikas.

2. *Catvāraḥ pratyayā hetuś cālambanam anantaram,*
tathaivādhipateyaṃ ca pratyayo nāsti pañcamaḥ.

There are only four conditions, namely, primary condition, objectively supporting condition, immediately contiguous condition, and dominant condition. A fifth condition does not exist.

MKV(P) p.76; *MKV(V)* p.26.

Candrakīrti's comments on this verse have misled almost everyone who analysed the contents of this chapter. He could not have been unaware that the theory of four conditions (*pratyaya*) was presented for the first time by the Ābhidharmikas. However, he failed to distinguish the Ābhidharma theory (see *AK* 2.61-62) from those of the interpreters of the Abhidharma, namely, the Sarvāstivādins (like Vasumitra) and the Sautrāntikas (see *Akb* pp.98-100). He simply assumed that the theory of conditions represents an instance of external causation. Hence his statement: "Therefore, since things arise from those that are external, there is arising from another" (*tasmād ebhyaḥ parabhūtebhyo bhāvānām utpattir asti parata-utpattir iti*, p.77).

In the first place, such an interpretation would leave a rather tainted image of Nāgārjuna as an unsystematic philosopher, for having spoken of four causal theories beginning with self-causation (*svata-utpatti*), Nāgārjuna is here represented as elaborating upon the second, namely, external causation (*parata-utpatti*), ignoring self-causation altogether.

Secondly, while the four causal theories mentioned in I.1 are categorically denied by Nāgārjuna, no such denial is made of the four theories of conditions (*pratyaya*). Thus, unlike Candrakīrti, Nāgārjuna seems to have accepted the Ābhidharmika theory of four conditions, without characterizing it either as self-causation or as external causation. After stating the Abhidharma theory, Nāgārjuna then proceeds to analyse the views of the *interpreters* of Abhidharma, and, as the verse that immediately follows (I.3) seems to indicate, he found that these are the ones who produced theories of self-causation (*svata-utpatti*) and external causation (*parata-utpatti*) out of the Abhidharma theory of conditions (*pratyaya*).

3. *Na hi svabhāvo bhāvānām pratyayādiṣu vidyate,*
avidyamāne svabhāve parabhāvo na vidyate.

The self-nature of existents is not evident in the conditions, etc. In the absence of self-nature, other-nature too is not evident.

MKV(P) p.78; *MKV(V)* p. 26.

These indeed are the most significant statements of Nāgārjuna in the present chapter. The first statement is not a simple but an *emphatic denial* (*na hi*) of the view that the substance or self-nature (*svabhāva*) of an existent is found in the condition (*pratyaya*). Since the theory of conditions is primarily a Buddhist theory, and since among the Buddhist schools the first to advocate a theory of substance (*svabhāva, dravya*) at this early stage was the Sarvāstivāda school, there can be little disagreement that Nāgārjuna's statement represents a outright rejection of the Sarvāstivāda interpretation of the conditions.

This denial needs to be carefully analysed. In the first place, as noted earlier, the phrase used to express the denial is *na vidyate* ("is not evident") and not *na yujyate* ("not proper") or *na upapadyate* ("not appropriate"). Hence the denial should be empirically grounded. Secondly, there is no outright denial of the "conditions" (*pratyaya*) but only of self-nature (*svabhāva*). Neither the Buddha nor the early Ābhidharmikas assumed that identity, defined as permanent substance or self-nature, is a necessary condition for the explanation of conditions or of dependence (*pratītyasamutpāda*).

When no such absolute identity is *perceived*, is it the case that absolute difference is *perceived*? This would be the case *only if* the perceptions are confined to the two extremes (*anta*), not otherwise. In the "Discourse to Kātyāyana," the Buddha maintains that he will teach a "middle position" without approaching (*upagamma*) the two extremes of existence and non-existence. This means that he was providing an explanation of existence without relying upon this particular form of explanation. And that middle position allows for an explanation of experience or perception of arising and ceasing in terms of dependence. It is indeed a similar view of existence and non-existence that Nāgārjuna is denying, without, at the same time, denying the doctrine of conditions (*pratyaya*) or of dependence (*pratītyasamutpāda*).

4. *Kriyā na pratyayavatī nāpratyayavatī kriyā,*
pratyayā nākriyāvantaḥ kriyāvantaś ca santy uta.

Activity is not constituted of conditions nor is it not non-constituted of conditions. Conditions are neither constituted nor non-constituted of activity.

MKV(P) pp.79-81; *MKV(V)* pp.26-27. The former reads *santy atu*, which is corrected in the latter as *santy uta*.

The term *kriyā*, used in philosophical discourse, can convey two meanings. First, it can refer to an inherent activity, a power or potentiality (*śakti*) in something to produce an effect (*artha*). Activity would then be an embodiment of a condition (*kriyā pratyayavatī*) or a condition would be an embodiment of activity (*pratyayā kriyāvantaḥ*). In either case, the activity or the condition is said to produce the effect (*artha*). This, once again, is the substantialist interpretation of causation. If the philosophical explanation of experience is confined to the two alternatives, then the contrasting view would be that activity is not an embodiment of a condition (*apratyayavatī kriyā*) or that a condition is not an embodiment of activity (*pratyayā akriyāvantaḥ*). And Nāgārjuna says no to both extremes.

The denial of the above extremes does not mean the denial of a second meaning that can be attributed to both *kriyā* and *pratyaya*, namely, the pragmatic view which defines both in terms of the effect (*artha*). Nāgārjuna was not unaware of such an explanation of activity, for in the Buddhist context *kriyā* is generally identified with *arthakriyā* (*-kāritra*) or simply *kāritra*.

5. *Utpadyate pratītyemān iti 'me pratyayāḥ kila,*
yāvan notpadyata ime tāvan nāpratyayāḥ katham.

These are conditions, because depending upon them these [others] arise. So long as these [others] do not arise, why are they not non-conditions?

MKV(P) p.81; *MKV(V)* p.28.

The first line of this verse presents a definition of a condition (*pratyaya*) that would satisfy the pragmatic sense referred to earlier and therefore would be acceptable to the early Buddhist as well as Nāgārjuna. However, Nāgārjuna wants to make sure that there are no metaphysical interpretations of this definition of condition. Would someone assume that for this statement to be true the dependence has to be invariable and eternal? In fact, the Sarvāstivāda notion of self-nature, in terms of which they defined a condition, implied such eternalism. In spite of the Sarvāstivāda assertion, no such guarantee can be given on empirical grounds. If so, it is appropriate to ask the question as to whether the so-called condition has to be called a non-condition so long as the effect does not arise. This means that it is inappropriate to say that a condition is such by its own nature (*svabhāva*). Instead, it becomes a condition depending upon the arising of the effect.

6. *Naivāsato naiva sataḥ pratyayo 'rthasya yujyate,*
asataḥ pratyayaḥ kasya sataś ca pratyayena kiṃ.

A condition of an effect that is either non-existent or existent is not proper. Of what non-existent [effect] is a condition? Of what use is a condition of the existent [effect]?

MKV(P) p.82; *MKV(V)* p.28.

Here the condition (*pratyaya*) is examined in relation to the effect (*artha*). Even though the criticism up to now has been directed on the metaphysical notion of a substantial condition, and not on a pragmatic definition understood in relation to the effect, the present verse is intended to clarify the nature of the effect. The question is: In terms of what kind of effect should a condition be defined? An existent effect or a non-existent effect? An effect existent in terms of self-nature needs no support for its arising and, as such, a condition would be meaningless. An effect that is non-existent in the sense of being absolutely different from the condition will not be related in any way to a condition.

7. *Na san nāsan na sad asan dharmo nirvartate yadā,*
kathaṃ nirvartako hetur evaṃ sati hi yujyate.

Since a thing that is existent or non-existent or both existent and non-existent is not produced, how pertinent in that context would a producing cause be?

MKV(P) p.83; *MKV(V)* p.28.

This is an examination of the first of the four conditions referred to in I.2, namely, a primary condition (*hetu-pratyaya*). After examining the nature of a condition (*pratyaya*) and the effect (*artha*) or the causally arisen phenomena (*pratītyasamutpanna dharma*), in this and the next three verses Nāgārjuna is directing his attention to the four specific conditions formulated by the Ābhidharmikas.

In defining the primary condition, the Abhidharma refers to five of the six causes (*hetu*)(*AK* 2.61). They are (1) a "co-operative cause" (*sahabhū-hetu*) or factors that work together in producing another; (2) the "complementary cause" (*sabhāga-hetu*), which is a cause helping other causes of its kind; (3) the "associated cause" (*saṃprayuktaka-hetu*); (4) the "all pervading cause" (*sarvatrage-hetu*) and (5) the "fruitioning cause" (*vipāka-hetu*). However, the interpreters of the Abhidharma defined a primary condition (*hetu-pratyaya*) as a producing (*nirvartaka*) or a root cause (*mūlaṭhena hetu upakarākaṭṭhena paccayo*, *Vism* p.533). Nāgārjuna, in the hope of clarifying the implications of this definition, raises the question as to whether this condition is supposed to give rise to an existent (*sat*) phenomena or a non-existent (*asat*) phenomena or something that is both existent and non-existent (*sad asat*). The early Ābhidharmikas do not seem to have involved themselves in such speculations regarding the absolute identity or absolute difference between a çondition and its effect; hence this criticism of Nāgārjuna applies only to the later interpreters of the Abhidharma conception of a primary condition.

8. *Anālambana evāyaṃ san dharma upadiśyate,*
   athānālambane dharme kutu ālambanaṃ punaḥ.

A thing that exists is indicated as being without objective support. When a thing is without objective support, for what purpose is an objective support?

MKV(P) p.84; *MKV(V)* p.29.

The Abhidharma defines the objectively supporting condition as all "phenomena" (*sarvadharmāḥ*) (*AK* 2.61). It was intended to explain the occurrence of all ideas of experience. Buddhism recognized external objects as conditions for the arising of ideas of experience (in contrast to the ideas of imagination). For example, it is admitted that "depending upon eye and visible form arises visual consciousness" (*cakkhuñ ca paṭicca rūpe ca uppajjati cakkhuviññāṇaṃ*, *M* 1.111-112), and these serve as conditions for the ideas of perceptual experience.

During the Abhidharma period these various conditions as well as the ideas of experience came to be categorized into mind (*citta*), mental concomitants (*caitta, cetasika*), and material form (*rūpa*), even though they were not sharply distinguished into substantially different entities as mind and matter. Yet those who defined these categories ultimatley ended up recognizing mental substances and material substances, the mental substances have the capacity to perceive their own mental concomitants (*caitta*), even though these concomitants are conditioned by materially constituted objects. The mental substances thus became the subject, the mental concomitants the contents of perception and the material form the objective condition. Such speculation not only led to the belief in a *cogito*, thinking of its own subject-matter (*caitta*) carrying with it all the metaphysical implications, but also raised the question as to the need for an external object (*ālambana*) as a support for the concomitants. While the question regarding the *cogito* is taken up by Nāgārjuna in Chapter III, the need for an external objective support is raised in the present verse.

Thus, it is recognized by Candrakīrti that the question regarding objective support is raised by Nāgārjuna because those whose views he was criticizing admitted a *cogito* (*athaivam anālambane dharme svātmanā prasiddhe kim asyālambanayogena parikalpitena*, (P) 84; (V) 29) This is similar to the refutation of a "material object" by the Western philosopher George Berkeley. If the object appears to the perceiving mind in its own form (i.e. in the form of a mental impression) (*svātmanā prasiddhe*), there is no need for an objective support (*ālambana*). If it does not appear to be the perceiving mind in its own form, it will never be perceived, since the perceiving mind and the material object are of completely different natures (*parātman*?). This is indeed not a rejection of the notion of an objective support (*ālambana-pratyaya*) *per se*, but an object that is conceptualized in a metaphysical way, that is, as an object constituted of a material substance distinguished from a mental substance.

9. *Anutpanneṣu dharmeṣu nirodho nopapadyate,*
nānantaram ato yuktaṃ niruddhe pratyayaś ca kaḥ.

When things are not arisen [from conditions], cessation is not appropriate. When [a thing has] ceased, what is [it that serves as] a condition? Therefore, an immediate condition is not proper.

MKV(P) p.85; *MKV(V)* p.29.

The immediately contiguous condition (*samanantara-pratyaya*) was first formulated by the Ābhidharmikas in order to account for certain kinds of relations implied in the Buddha's statements such as: "In this way, monks there is the immediate (*anantara*) waning of defilements,"' (*S* 3.58). The Ābhidharmikas, therefore, specified the relation as one among mind and mental concomitants (*cittacaittā acaramā uppannāḥ samanantarāḥ*, *AK* 2.62). With the acceptance of a theory of moments (*kṣaṇa*), the interpreters of the Abhidharma were faced with several questions: Does this relation obtain among events of a similar nature (*svajāti*)? How can the emergence of dissimilar events be explained?

(*Akb* pp.65-66). The problems are not different from those that are associated with the conception of a series (similar to the problems faced by empiricists like David Hume). The question as to how one momentary event can give rise to another or how one series could pave the way for a different series was discussed, in relation to the problem of knowledge, especially the knowledge of the future. Some of the interpreters of the Adhidharma recognized an unimaginable range of comprehension on the part of the Buddha (*acintyo hi buddhānāṃ buddhiviṣaya iti, Akb* p.66), which was probably a view advocated by the Sarvāstivādins, who admitted the possibility of knowing the existence of everything (*sarvam asti*) belonging to the past, the present and the future. The Sautrāntikas, who refused to accept such a position, maintained that the Buddha follows 'signs' (*naimittako*) and that even in the absence of direct perception of future events (*na sākṣātkārī*) he is able to predict them on the basis of "intention" (*icchāmatrena*, ibid.).

Nāgārjuna, realizing the difficulties inherent in such speculations, raises questions regarding the very conception of 'arising' in such a context. Neither the momentary events, nor the substances that were posited to account for the continuity of series of such events, according to Nāgārjuna, can be described as "arisen" (*utpanna*). If they are not arisen (*anutpanna*), their cessation is also inconceivable. If they were to cease momentarily, they could not serve as conditions (*pratyaya*).

10. *Bhāvānāṃ niḥsvabhāvānāṃ na sattā vidyate yataḥ,*
satīdam asmin bhavatīty etan naivopapadyate.

Since the existence of existents devoid of self-nature is not evident, the statement: "When that exists, this comes to be," will not be appropriate.

MKV(P) p.86; *MKV(V)* p.30.

The notion of dominance was understood in a very general and broad way in the early discourses. For example, oneself (*atta*), the world (*loka*), and righteousness (*dhamma*) were considered dominant conditions (*ādhipateyya*) in the matter of refining one's moral life (*A* 1.147-150). The Ābhidharmikas defined the dominant condition as an active cause (*kāraṇa-hetu*) and this differed from the other five causes (see note on I.7) because of the dominant effect of this cause. Dominance, of course, can be of different sorts. For example, a seed may be a dominant cause of the sprout, just as much as water is. The Ābhidharmikas reserved the notion of dominant condition (or active cause) to explain the latter kind of relationship, namely, that between water and the sprout. Hence it was defined as something "other than itself" (*svato 'nye, AK* 2.50). However, this distinction between self and other came to be "reified" to such an extreme that the later interpreters of the Abhidharma were left with the notions of self-nature (*svabhāva*) and other-nature (*parabhāva*). It became almost impossible to speak of 'this' and 'that' without getting involved in a discussion of self-nature and other-nature. Therefore, when the Buddha's formulation of the general causal principle as: "When that exists, this comes to be," (*asmin satīdaṃ bhavati*) came up for discussion, the metaphysicians were quick to interpret *sat* (occurring in the locative absolute construction *asmin sati*) as substantial existence of the two entities referred to by *asmin* (that) and *idam* (this).

Here too Candrakīrti, in spite of his leanings towards "no views," presents dependent arising as a position from which to criticize self-nature or self-existence (*svabhāva*). He argues: "Because existents are dependently arisen and, therefore, without self-nature, how can that statement: 'When that (exists),' be intended as an active cause?'" (*Bhāvānāṃ pratītyasamutpannatvāt svabhāvābhave kutas tad yad asminn iti kāraṇatvena vyapadiśyate*, (P) 87; (V) 30). Nāgārjuna's criticism, therefore, leaves the Buddha's general formula of causation untouched, for it was not the Buddha's intention to reify either "this" or "that."

11. *Na ca vyasta-samasteṣu pratyayeṣv asti tat phalaṃ,*
pratyayebhyaḥ kathaṃ tac ca bhaven na pratyayeṣu yat.

The effect does not exist in the conditions that are separated or combined. Therefore, how can that which is not found in the conditions come to be from the conditions?

MKV(P) p.87; *MKV(V)* p.30.

Once again, the question raised in the second line: "How can that which is not found in the conditions come to be from the conditions?" is grounded on the assertion or premise mentioned in the first line. What is denied in the first line is that the effect is found *in* the causal conditions taken either separately or together. It does not mean a denial of the statement that the effect comes to be

depending upon a condition or a group of conditions. In other words, it is a rejection of the essentialist method of looking for the effect even before it comes to be. A truly empiricist approach would not be concerned with such an enterprize.

12. *Athāsad api tat tebhyaḥ pratyayebhyaḥ pravartate,*
    apratyayebhyo 'pi kasmān nābhipravartate phalam.

If that effect, being non-existent [in the conditions] were to proceed from the conditions, why does it not proceed from non-conditions?

MKV(P) pp.87-88; *MKV(V)* p.30.

So far, most of the arguments were directed against self-causation and the substantial existence of the effect in the condition that gives rise to it. The present verse is a direct refutation of the view that the effect is different from the condition, that is, the basic premise of the theory of external causation. As implied by Nāgārjuna, in such a context, the term "condition" loses its meaning, for if the cause and effect were sharply distinguished, one could maintain that anything can come out of anything. It is in, fact, the contrary of the substantialist view: "Nothing comes out of nothing."

13. *Phalaṃ ca pratyayamayaṃ pratyayāś cāsvayammayāḥ,*
    phalam asvamayebhyo yat tat pratyayamayaṃ kathaṃ.

The effect is made of conditions, but the conditions are themselves not self-made. How can that effect made of conditions [arise] from what is not self-made?

MKV(P) p.88; *MKV(V)* p.30.

The first line of this verse contains two assertions. First of these is that "the effect is made of causal conditions" (***phalaṃ pratyayamayaṃ***), which is already negated at I.4 (***kriyā na pratyayavatī***) where the term ***kriyā*** is equivalent in meaning to the term *phalaṃ* in the present context. So does the term *pratyayavatī* convey the same meaning as *pratyayamayaṃ*. It is a statement asserting the identity between the condition and the effect. However, the next statement implies difference between the conditions that give rise to the effect and those other conditions that produce the conditions themselves, for the former are not "self-made" (*asvayammayāḥ*). This, therefore, is a theory that attempts to accommodate both identity and difference in the causal process, and Nāgārjuna sees this as a self-contradiction. It is indeed a refutation of the third theory of causation negated at I.1, namely, causation through both self and other (*dvābhyāṃ*).

14. *Tasmān na pratyayamayaṃ nāpratyayamayaṃ phalaṃ,*
saṃvidyate phalābhāvāt pratyayāpratyayāḥ kutaḥ.

An effect made either of conditions or of non-conditions is, therefore, not evident. Because of the absence of the effect, where could conditions or non-conditions be evident?

MKV(P) p.89; *MKV(V)* p.31.

Thus, the identity of condition and effect (*pratyayamayaṃ phalaṃ*), as implied in the identity theory of causation, as well as the difference between condition and effect (*apratyayamayaṃ phalaṃ*), as envisaged in the non-identity theory of causation, are both not evident (*na saṃvidyate*). The second statement is, indeed, the final conclusion of Nāgārjuna in this immensely significant chapter. A superficial interpretation of this statement is bound to leave the impression, generally popular among the interpreters of Nāgārjuna, that he rejected any form of causation, including the arising of an effect *depending* upon a cause or condition or a group of such causes or conditions (*pratītyasamutpāda*). Hence, Nāgārjuna is perceived as a trancendentalist who recognized an "absolute" beyond all linguistic expression. (Following the prevalent interpretation, the present author himself has taken that position, see *Buddhist Philosophy*, pp.129-141). A more careful contextual analysis would reveal that the effect (*phala*) Nāgārjuna was referring to in this verse, as well as in the entire chapter, is one that is identical with the cause or different from it. It is only an effect understood in such a manner, as clearly indicated in the present statement, that he was categorically denying. If no such effect is seen, why speak of a condition (*pratyaya*) that is identical with an effect, or a non-condition (*a-pratyaya*) that is different from the effect?

CHAPTER TWO

Examination of The Moved and the Not-moved *(Gatāgata-parīkṣā)*

1. *Gataṃ na gamyate tavād agataṃ naiva gamyate,*
gatāgatavinirmuktaṃ gamyamānaṃ na gamyate.

What has been moved, in the first instance, is not being moved. What has not been moved is also not being moved. Separated from what has been moved and has not been moved, present moving is not known.

MKV(P) p.92; *MKV(V)* p.33.

The positive statement: "What has moved is being moved" (*gataṃ gamyate*) does, indeed, carry the implication of a permanent substantial entity, an entity with which movement was associated in the past and which is also presently moving. Nāgārjuna's negative statement is, therefore, a denial of such an entity. Yet, this denial may be interpreted as involving the opposite view, namely, that an entity that was previously not associated with movement is at present moving, that is, the entity that is presently moving is completely different from the previous entity.

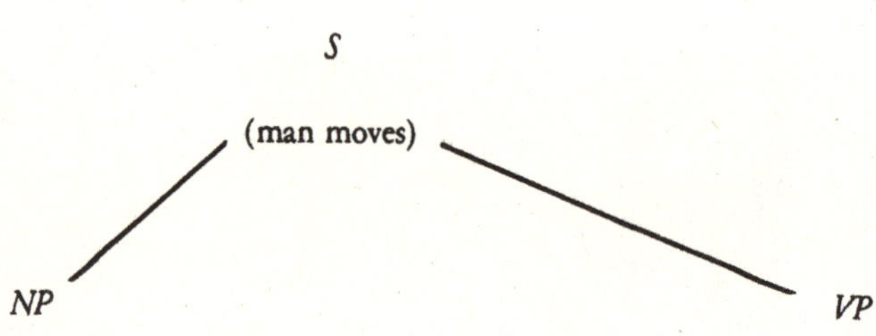

i. (moving) man	moves
ii. (non-moving) man	moves
iii. (moving and non-moving) man	moves

If the two positive assertions: (i) "What has moved *is being moved*" and (ii) "What has not moved *is being moved*," are accepted, then we have a present moving which is with and without prior movement. This is in a way self-contradictory. It is like saying that "a first cause is both caused and uncaused," or that "a mover is both moved and unmoved." Nāgārjuna would appear as a transcendentalist if he had assumed the "present moving" (*gamyamāna*) which has the characteristic of both "moved and not-moved." The substantialist perspective was thus contributory to *three* views, all of which were not acceptable.

2. *Ceṣṭā yatra gatis tatra gamyamāne ca sā yataḥ,*
na gate nāgate ceṣṭā gamyamāne gatis tataḥ.

Where there is movement, there is motion. For which reason movement is in the present moving, and not either in the moved or in the not moved, for that reason motion is available in the present moving.

MKV(P) p.93; *MKV(V)* p.33.

If a Cartesian perspective were to generate metaphysical views such as those presented by the Sarvastivadins, one way of eliminating such metaphysics is by adopting the "Humean" perspective that emphasizes the "immediate present," without any reference to the past or the future. However, such an unrelated or independent static present may once again lead to a substantialist reductionism. The only way to get rid of such "essentialist" perspectives, both of the rationalists and of some of the empiricists, is by adopting a more "phenomenological" explanation where, instead of a "present," one speaks of "presencing." If so, present movement (*gamyamāna*) could simply mean "motion" (*gati, ceṣṭa*) which is not found either in the past or the future. Having rejected the substantialist implications of the Sarvāstivāda in the previous verse, Nāgārjuna is here speculating on the meaning of the alternative views of the Sautrantikas, who wrestled with the problems of atomic discreteness as well as the experienced continuity, only to reject them in the verse that follows.

3. *Gamyamānasya gamanaṃ kathaṃ nāmopapatsyate,*
gamyamānam hy agamanaṃ yadā naivopapadyate.

How appropriate would be the movement of the present moving? For, the non-movement in the present moving is certainly not appropriate.

MKV(P) p.94; *MKV(V)* p.34.

As pointed out earlier, the statement "Man moves," can have two possible metaphysical "deep structures." The same could be said of the assertion, "The present moving moves."

S

present moving moves (= man moves)

NP *VP*

(i) non-moving (= non-moving man) moves (involves non-movement, *(agamana)*.

(ii) moving (= moving man) moves (involves two movements, (*dvigamana*).

After observing these two metaphysical implications of the statement: "movement of the presnt moving," (*gamyamānasya gamanaṃ*), Nāgārjuna seems to take up the first alternative for examination and maintains that a present movement, conceived in such a manner, is indeed a non-movement (*gamyamanaṃ hy agamanaṃ*).

The Tibetan versions (text as well as commentaries) seem to preserve this original reading [see *MKV(P)* p. 94, note 2] as do all the Chinese translations (see Inada, pp.44-45), including Kumārajīva's. As such, the available reading in the Sanskrit version as *gamyamāne dvi-gamanaṃ* could prove to be a scribal error. This assumption is further strengthened by the fact that II.44 that follows provides a criticism of the *first* metaphysical assumption, while II.5 take the *second* metaphysical assumption for criticism.

4. *Gamyamānasya gamanaṃ yasya tasya prasajyate,*
ṛter gater gamyamānaṃ gamyamānaṃ hi gamyate.

For him who asserts the movement of the present moving, it follows that there could be present moving without motion. [However,] the present moving, indeed, means being moved [i.e., the present moving, indeed, takes place].

MKV(P) p.95; *MKV(V)* p.43.

In asserting the statement: "The movement of the present moving," one is compelled to assume that present moving is independent of motion and that the latter is something attributed (*ādheyabhūtaṃ*) to the former. In that case, the present moving should be without motion. However, Nāgārjuna seems to be ready to assume that "the present moving indeed takes place" (*gamyamānaṃ hi gamyate*) without allowing for such metaphysical implicatons.

5. *Gamyamānasya gamane prasaktaṃ gamana-dvayaṃ,*
yena tad gamyamānaṃ ca yac cātra gamanaṃ punaḥ.

A two-fold movement is implied in the movement of the present moving: that by which there comes to be present moving and, again, the movement itself.

MKV(P) p.95; *MKV(V)* p.34.

This verse takes up the second metaphysical implication mentioned in the analysis of II 3, namely, "the movement of the present moving" involves two forms of movement (*dvi-gamanaṃ*). The first is the movement through designation (*vyapadeśa*) and the other is the movement in itself (*adhikaraṇabhūta*). This seems to be the distinction between the phenomenal designation and the "thing-in-itself." Further metaphysical implications of this understanding are presented in the next verse.

6. *Dvau gantārau prasajyete prasakte gamana-dvaye,*
gantāraṃ hi tiraskṛtya gamanaṃ nopapadyate.

If two movements are allowed, it would follow that there would be two movers. For, separated from a mover, a movement is not appropriate.

(MVP(P) p.96; *MKV(V)* p.35.

The assumption of two movements, as explained in the previous verse, will imply two movers (*dvau gantārau*). Here, then, is a basic assertion of Nāgārjuna with regard to language, namely, that one cannot speak of, say, movement, in a vacuum, but only in relation to something that is moving (*gantṛ*). This is the non-substantialist approach in Buddhism which refuses to recognize a sharp dichotomy between substance (*svabhāva*) and attribute (*lakṣaṇa*), a dichotomy that has become an inalienable part of the essentialist traditions in Indian philosophy that are in pursuit of a truly real or ultimate entity.

7. *Gantāraṃ cet tiraskṛtya gamanaṃ nopapadyate,*
gamane 'sati gantā 'tha kuta eva bhaviṣyati.

If it is thought that a movement separated from a mover is not appropriate, then, when no movement exists, how could there be a mover?

MKV(P) p.97; *MKV(V)* p.35.

This represents a simple refutation of the esse ıtialist view involving substance and attribute. If there were to be no movement separated from the mover, then in the absence of the movement there could be no mover. The emphasis here is on the term *tiraskṛtya* (separated). When there is no such separation and where the movement is dependent upon (*pratītya*) the mover and *vice versa*, Nāgārjuna sees no difficulty.

8. *Gantā na gacchati tāvad agantā naiva gacchati,*
anyo gantur agantuś ca kas tṛtīyo hi gacchati.

As much as a mover does not move, a non-mover too does not move. Other than a mover and a non-mover, what third party moves?

MKV(P) p.97; *MKV(V)* p.35.

Nāgārjuna's analysis now moves from the present movement to the present mover. The possible metaphysical implications he perceived in the statement "present moving moves," are not very different from those that may be involved in the assertion that a "present mover moves" (*gantā gacchati*). Yet, the question raised is in a slightly different context from that embodied in II.1 which refers to the past, that is, the moved or the one who has moved (*gata*), whereas the present verse relates to a present mover (*gantā*). It shows that metaphysical interpretations can arise not only regarding the past and the future but also in relation to the present.

9. *Gantā tāvad gacchatīti katham evopapatsyate,*
gamanena vinā gantā yadā naivopapadyate.

Indeed, how appropriate will be the view that a mover moves? For, a mover without movement is certainly not appropriate.

MKV(P) p.98; *MKV(V)* p.36.

This again is a positive assertion of Nāgārjuna, who would be willing to speak of a movement in a mover, without having to assume that there are two entities involved here, namely, a mover and a movement. For him, the mover and movement are dependent or contingent; one cannot speak of the one without implying the other. The statement, "A mover without movement is certainly not appropriate," is the ultimate refutation of a substantialist assumption that there can be a real entity about whom or which certain attributes can be predicated, the entity and the attributes being completely different.

10. *Pakṣo gantā gacchatīti yasya tasya prasajyate,*
gamanena vinā gantā gantur gamanam icchataḥ.

For him who entertains the view: "A mover moves," and who looks for the movement of a mover, it follows that there is a mover without movement.

(*MKV(P)* p.98; *MKV(V)* p.36.

A mover without movement is an entity without an attribute. For the essentialist tradition, an entity is an entity "in itself" without any attributes, of which attributes are predicated. An "entity-in-itself" thus becomes indefinable and indescribable. Nāgārjuna has no interest in such speculations. No predication is meaningful without the predicated. These are mutually dependent (*pratītya*) and not independent (*a-pratītya*).

11. *Gamane dve prasajyete gantā yady uta gacchati,*
ganteti cocyate yena gantā san yac ca gacchati.

If a mover were to move, then it would follow that there will be two movements; one in virtue of which he is spoken of as a mover, and the other in terms of which an existing mover is said to move.

MKV(P) p.99; *MKV(V)* p.36.

This is the converse of II.5. The statement: "A mover moves" would imply two movements: the first is a mover by designation (*vyapadeśa*) and the second, the really existent (*sad*) mover or "the mover-in-itself." Whether Nāgārjuna is prepared to maintain that all designations are so wild in their implications or whether such is the case with only some of them needs to be carefully examined, as in the case of concepts of causal dependence.

12. *Gate nārabhyate gantuṃ gantaṃ nārabhyate 'gate,*
nārabhyate gamyamāne gantum ārabhyate kuha.

Movement is not begun in the moved, nor is it begun in the not moved. Neither is it initiated in the present moving. Wherein is then movement initiated?

MKV(P) p.100; *MKV(V)* p.36.

Nāgārjuna now moves on to the question regarding the origin of movement, a question that has left a trail of metaphysical speculations from the very early period of philosophical thinking. Metaphysical speculations regarding time, leading to a theory of existence analysed in terms of discrete momentary events into the past, present and future, coupled with the problem of explaining the origin of each moment, a senario created by the Abhidharma interpreters, provided Nāgārjuna with the opportunity to utilize a method comparable to Zeno's paradoxes in order to expose the meaninglessness of such metaphysics.

13. *Na pūrvaṃ gamanārambhād gamyamānaṃ na vā gataṃ,*
yatrārabhyeta gamanaṃ agate gamanaṃ kutaḥ.

Prior to the commencement of movement, there is neither the present moving or the moved from which movement is initiated. How could there be a movement in the not moved?

MKV(P) p.100; *MKV(V)* p.37.

Agate gamanaṃ kutaḥ ("How could there be movement in the not moved?") seems to be the refutation of the idea of an "unmoved mover" at a microcosmic or phenomenal level. The interpreters of the Abhidharma were probably aware of the Buddha's reluctance to discuss the absolute origin of the universe. Yet their way of handling the Abhidharma analysis, especially their understanding of change as momentary destruction *(kṣaṇa-bhaṅga)*, left them sometimes with four discrete moments (i.e. origin, stasis, decay, and destruction recognized by the Sarvāstivādins), sometimes with three (i.e., origin, stasis, and destruction, as in the case of the Theravādins) and sometimes with two (i.e., origin and destruction, as it was the case with the Sautraāntikas). In all these instances, each preceding moment had to account for the succeeding moment that is different.

14. *Gataṃ kiṃ gamyamānaṃ kim agataṃ kiṃ vikaplyate.*
adṛśyamāna ārambhe gamanasyaiva sarvathā.

When the commencement of movement is not being perceived in any

way, what is it that is discriminated as the moved, the present moving, or the not moved?

MKV(P) p.101; *MKV(V)* p.37.

Unless the metaphysics referred to above is kept in mind, it would be easy to assume that this verse represents a refutation of ***any form of discrimination*** of events as past, present, or future. On the contrary, what is being emphasized here is that the commencement of movement, as explained in the previous verses, is not perceived at all anywhere (***sarvathā***). As such, a question is raised regarding the validity of discriminations or thoughts regarding the past, present, and future, which are based upon that particular conception of the commencement of movement (***gamanasya ārambha***). Nāgārjuna is ***not*** claiming that there is only one way in which commencement of movement can be explained; he is merely refuting the metaphysical explanation of movement and its commencement.

15. ***Gantā na tiṣṭhati tāvad agantā naiva tiṣṭhati,***
anyo gantur agantuś ca kas tṛtīyo 'tha tiṣṭhati.

As much as a mover is not stationary, so is a non-mover not stationary. Other than a mover and a non-mover, what third party is stationary?

MKV(P) p.101; MKV(V) p.37.

To say that a mover is stationary (***gantā tiṣṭhati***) is self-contradictory. To maintain that a non-mover is stationary (***agantā tiṣṭhati***) is tautological. Looking for something or someone (***svabhāva, pudgala***) to which/whom the characteristics of motion and stasis can be attributed, one merely ends up conceiving of a "hare's horn" (***śaśa-viṣāṇa***) or "crow's teeth" (***kāka-danta***). Such is the essentialist enterprise. This certainly does not mean the rejection of the empirical notion of relativity or dependence of motion on stasis and ***vice versa***, as in the case of short and long. It is indeed a simple refutation of the view that there are independent entities to which the characteristics of motion and stasis can be attributed.

16. *Gantā tāvat tiṣṭhatīti katham evopapatsyate,*
gamanena vinā gantā yadā naivopapadyate.

How appropriate would it be [to say]: "A mover, at the moment, is statonary"? For, a mover without movement is not appropriate.

MKV(P) p.102; *MKV(V)* p.38.

The argument in the previous verse is made very clear by the present. Empirically, a "mover" without motion is inconceivable, just as a pure entity (*svabhāva*) without function or characteristics is empirically meaningless. As such, the statement: "A mover, at the moment, is stationary," can be made assuming that the entity that previously possessed the characteristic of motion (*gamana*) has now abandoned it in order to assume a different characteristic, namely, stasis. The Sarvāstivāda theory of *prāpti* and *aprāpti* was formulated to explain such "possession" and "non-possession" after they assumed the metaphysical notion of a substance or "pure being" (*svabhāva*) (see Poussin, *AK* ii.36).

17. *Na tiṣṭhati gamyamānan na gatān nāgatād api,*
gamanaṃ saṃpravṛttiś ca nivṛttiś ca gateḥ samā.

One does not come to be stationary because one is either moving, or has moved, or has not moved. Movement, commencement and cessation (of movement) are all comparable to motion.

MKV(P) p.102-103; *MKV(V)* p.38.

The substance/attribute distinction openly endorsed by the metaphysicians cannot account for "stasis" in terms of motion, whether that motion relates to the past, present or future. According to their analysis, stasis is distinct from motion and therefore is independent. So are concepts of commencement and cessation.

18. *Yad eva gamanaṃ gantā sa eveti na yujyate,*
anya eva punar gantā gater iti na yujate.

The view that movement is identical with the mover is not proper. The view that the mover is different from motion is also not proper.

MKV(P) p.104; *MKV(v)* p.39.

Having distinguished substance and attribute, the metaphysicians attempt to solve the resultant philosophical issues either by assuming identity (*sa eva*) on the basis of an eternal substance (*svabhāva*), thereby rendering the attribute (*lakṣaṇa*) an ephimeral or impermanent come-and-go entity, as the Sarvastivadins did, or by emphasizing difference (*anya eva*), thereby denying the substance and accepting fleeting and momentary flashes of attributes without any real connections, as the Sautrāntikas did. For Nāgārjuna, both are inappropriate views. The two verse that follow provide specific reasons for the rejection of these two views.

19. *Yad eva gamanaṃ gantā sa eva hi bhaved yadi,*
ekībhāvaḥ prasajyeta kartuḥ karmaṇa eva ca.

If movement were to be identical with the mover, it would follow that there is identity of agent and action.

MKV(P) p.104; *MKV(V)* p. 39.

Identity (*ekībhāva*) with regard to agent and action is here presented as a necessary implication of considering the mover and motion to be the same. The non-absolutism in Nāgārjuna's way of thinking would leave the agent meaningless independent of action and *vice versa*. Nāgārjuna will have no difficulty in speaking of either an agent or an action in an analytical way without reaching the extremist position of recognizing distinct entities. For him, analysis (*vigraha*) was meaningful and practical so long as the limits of such analysis are observed.

20. *Anya eva punar gantā gater yadi vikalpyate,*
gamanaṃ syād ṛter gantur gantā syād gamanād ṛte.

If the discrimination is made that the mover is different from motion, then there would be movement without a mover, and mover without movement.

MKV(P) p.105; *MKV(V)* p.39.

This verse specifically lays down the limits to which Nāgārjuna was prepared to go with his analytical method. That is, the analysis should not be carried out to such an extent that leaves "motion" without a "mover" or a mover without "motion." Empirical explanation does not allow for such "pure entities" completely independent of each other.

21. *Ekībhāvena vā siddhir nānābhāvena vā yayoḥ,*
na vidyate tayoḥ siddhiḥ kathan nu khalu vidyate.

Whose establishment is not evident either through identity or through difference, how is their establishment evident at all?

MKV(P) p.105; MKV(V) p.39.

Here again, Nāgārjuna is examining the concepts of substance and attribute. For him, these are not established either through identity or through difference. The question then is: "How is their establishment evident at all?" The rejection of the substance/attribute distinction as admitted by the Sarvāstivādins and the Sautrāntikas does not mean the rejection of all conceptualizations or discriminations (*vikalpa*). It is this particular form of conceptualization that is being questioned, not any form of conceptualization.

22. *Gatyā yāyocyate gantā gatiṃ tāṃ sa na gacchati,*
yasmān na gati-pūrvo 'sti kaścit kiṃcidd hi gacchati.

Whatever motion in terms of which a mover is spoken of, he does not move by that motion. Because he does not exist prior to motion, who or what is it that moves?

MKV(P) pp.105-106; *MKV(V)* p.40.

It is possible for one to speak of a mover depending upon motion. However, when that mover is distinguished from motion, then we are left with a pure entity or person (*svabhāva, pudgala*) to which or whom the motion is attributed and, in that case, the entity or person should precede movement. Such an entity or person is not evident in experience. Hence the statement: "He does not move by that motion."

23. *Gatyā yāyocyate gantā tato 'nyaṃ sa na gacchati,*
gati dve nopapadyete yasmāt eke pragacchati.

Whatever motion in terms of which a mover is spoken of, he does not carry out a motion that is completely different from it. A two-fold motion is not appropriate, since it is only one person that moves.

MKV(P) p.106; *MKV(V)* p.40.

The distinction between the "mover" and "motion" also does not mean that the "mover" carries out a motion that is different from himself. If such a distinction is recognized, then, as explained earlier, there would be two movements, the movement as a result of which one comes to be called "mover" and the movement itself. No such dual motion is found, nor are there two movers corresponding to the twofold motion. The *fact* is that it is only one person that moves.

24. *Sadbhūto gamanaṃ gantā triprakāraṃ na gacchati,*
nāsadbhūto 'pi gamanaṃ triprakāraṃ sa gacchati,

25. *gamanaṃ sadasadbhūtaṃ triprakāraṃ na gacchati,*
tasmād gatiś ca gantā ca gantavyaṃ ca na vidyate.

An existent mover does not carry out the movement in any of the three ways. Neither does a non-existent mover carry out the movement in any of the three ways. Nor does a person carry out a movement, both existent and non-existent, in any of the three ways. Therefore, neither motion, nor the mover, nor the space to be moved is evident.

MKV(P) p.107; *MKV(V)* p.40.

The conclusion is very specifically stated in these two verses. It is not any kind of mover or movement that is rejected as being impossible. It is the really or substantially or independently existent (*sad*) mover or movement that is rejected. This is a criticism of eternalism (*śāśvata-vāda*). The opposite view, namely, a non-real, non-substantial and non-independent existence (*asad*) was the kind of impermanence advocated in annihilationism (*uccheda-vāda*) which, in the Buddhist context, is commensurate with momentary destruction (*kṣaṇa-bhaṅga*), rather than the impermanence (*anitya*) advocated by the Buddha on the basis of "dependent arising" (*pratītyasamutpāda*). The combination of the two metaphysical views of existence and non-existence does not lead to a happy synthesis. Change and impermanence understood in this metaphysical way do not contribute toward a reasonable and empirical explanation of the motion, the mover, or even the space moved.

CHAPTER THREE

Examination of the Faculty of Eye
(Cakṣur-indriya-parīkṣā)

1. *Darśanaṃ śravaṇaṃ ghrāṇaṃ rasanaṃ sparśanaṃ manaḥ,*
indriyāṇi ṣaḍ eteṣāṃ draṣṭavyādīni gocaraḥ.

Seeing, hearing, smelling, tasting, touching, and mind are the six faculties. Their spheres consist of the object of seeing, etc.

MKV(P) p.113; *MKV(V)* p.43.

Although the traditional Adhidharma classification lists the "aggregates" (*skandha*) , "spheres" (*āyatana*), and "elements" (*dhātu*) in that order, for Nāgārjuna, the epistemology, the faculties (included under spheres) were more important, primarily because of the current controversies surrounding the concept of existence (*dharma*). Furthermore, even in the discussion of faculties, Nāgārjuna was not so much interested in the faculties *per se*, for there was not much controversy regarding the eye, etc. No school doubted the existence of these faculties. The controversies were centered more on the function of the faculties, that is, with regard to seeing, hearing, smelling, tasing, touch, and thinking. For this reason, after providing a title for the chapter as "Examination of the Faculties" (*Indriya-parīkṣā*), Nāgārjuna immediately moves on to an analysis of the more complicated issues relating to their functions. Hence the reference to seeing, hearing, etc., especially as means of identification of events (see, e.g., P. F. Strawson, *Individuals*, New York: Doubleday, 1963, pp.35 ff.) that is so important for an empiricist like Nāgārjuna. Even among these various faculties and their functions, the most important epistemological issues were connected with seeing. Hence Nāgārjuna's interest in the problem of seeing or visual perception. Note that the term *manaḥ* is used here to refer to the function, even though *manana* would be more appropriate in the context. This may have been done to preserve the metre.

2. *Svam ātmānaṃ darśanaṃ hi tat tam eva na paśyati,*
na paśyati yad ātmānaṃ kathaṃ drakṣyati tat parān.

Seeing does not perceive itself, its own form. How can that which does not perceive itself, see others?

MKV(P) p.113; *MKV(V)* p.43.

Nāgārjuna was clearly aware of the major controversy raging among the adherents of the various "essentialist" schools regarding the problem of perception. In their search for certainty, these essentialist schools assumed that in any act of perception the "most clear and distinct" is the perception of "oneself." (see *Bṛhadāraṇyaka Upaniṣad* 1.4.1). "I think, therefore, I am" (*cogito ergo sum*) was the premise with which the essentialist thinkers of pre-Buddhist India began their exposition of perception. The Buddha was himself aware of the difficulties involved in such an assumption when he advised his disciples not to follow such speculations (*mantā asmīti sabbaṃ uparundhe, Sn* 916). While the Buddha was willing to recognize consciousness or "self-consciousness" (*viññāṇa, vijñana*) as an important constituent of the human personality as well as its experiences, he was not willing to assume a metaphysical substratum such as the "self" or "I" as being the object of such awareness. He was clearly aware that this latter epistemological method was the source of most obsessive conceptions (*mūlaṃ papancasaṅkhāya*, ibid.). However, the later Buddhist metaphysicians, innocently unaware of the implications of such a method, seem to have been led in that direction, thereby dragging themselves into the quagmire of *svabhāva*-metaphysics from which they could not easily get out. The result was the description of perception in the *Vibhāṣāprabhāvṛtti* (p.32):

> *The substance called the eye is of the nature of that which sees*. In it is produced an action of seeing, when its power is awakened on account of the emergence of the totality of its causes and conditions. The eye does not apprehend independently of consciousness (*vijñāna*), nor does eye-consciousness know the object unsupported by the active eye. Eye as well as eye-consciousness, with the help of accessories such as light, cooperate simultaneously toward bringing the perception of an object. The object, the eye, the eye-consciousness, and the light, cooperate simultaneously toward bringing the perception of an object. The object, the eye, the eye-consciousness, and the light, all manifest their power, i.e., become active and flash forth simultaneously. The object appears, the eye sees, and the eye-conscoiusness knows it. This is called the direct knowledge of an object. [Emphasis mine]

Reading through the present chapter of Nāgārjuna, one can hardly miss the target of his criticism if one were to keep in mind the above passage of the

Vibhāṣāprabhāvṛtti. These problems will be discussed in their contexts. However, before taking up the metaphysical issues involved in the above sort of description, Nāgārjuna needed to eliminate the very source of such metaphysics, namely, the *cogito*. For Nāgārjuna, the method by which one arrives at the *cogito* not only leads to the belief in a "*sva ātman*", but also the sharp dichotomy between "self" (*sva ātman*) and "other" (*para ātman*). Therefore, having stated positively that there is no "seeing of oneself" (*svam ātmānaṃ darśanaṃ*), Nāgārjuna raises question as to the possibility of "seeing an other" (*paraṃ*). Thus, the dichotomy between self and other in a more metaphysical form is not only ethically unacceptable, but also epistemologically unfounded.

3. *Na paryāpto 'gnidṛṣṭānto darśanasya prasiddhaye,*
sa darśanaḥ sa pratyukto gamyamānagatāgataiḥ.

The example of fire is not adequate for the establishment of seeing. That [fire] together with seeing are refuted by [a refutation of] the present moving, the moved and the not moved.

MKV(P) p.114; *MKV(V)* p.43.

While those who accepted the *cogito* assumed that seeing oneself precedes any act of seeing, their opponents seem to have used the example of the fire to maintain that, like fire which burns everything but itself, seeing perceives everything else but itself.

The theory of moments (*kṣaṇa*) that led to metaphysics in the sphere of causation (Chapter I) and change (Chapter II) did not leave the problem of perception untouched. Indeed, it was the problem of perception that was most affected by a theory of moments, as is evident from the variety of contradictory theories of perception presented by the Sarvāstivādins, the Sautrāntikas and the Theravādins (see Kalupahana, ***Buddhist Philosophy***, pp.97-107).

Being aware of this fact, Nāgārjuna takes the easy route of referring to his previous refutation of change (Chapter II). Hence Candrakīrti's composition of a verse comparable to II.1: What has been seen is not being seen; what has not been seen is also not being seen. Apart from the seen and the not seen, the present seeing is also not seen."

The same can be said of that which is burnt (*dagdhvaṃ*), etc. This is what

Nāgārjuna means when he says: "That [fire] together with seeing are refuted by [a refutation of] the present moving, the moved and the not moved."

4. *Nāpaśyamānaṃ bhavati yadā kiṃcana darśanaṃ,*
darśanaṃ paśyatīty evaṃ katham etat tu yujyate.

When some form of seeing that is not perceiving does not exist, how pertinent is the view that seeing perceives?

MKV(P) p.115; MKV(V) p.44.

The essentialist definition of "seeing" as possessing the "nature of seeing" (*darśana-svabhāva*) is tantamount to saying that "seeing always sees." This, indeed, is the statement with which the Sarvāstivāda (specifically Vaibhāṣika) began its description of perception, as indicated by the quotation referred to in the note to III.2. In other words, it is not possible to recognize any form of seeing that is "not presently perceiving" (*na apaśyamānaṃ*), or there cannot be a "non-seeing perception." If such be the definition, Nāgārjuna raises a question regarding the appropriateness of the statements, "Seeing perceives."

5. *Paśyati darśanaṃ naiva naiva paśyaty adarśanaṃ,*
vyākhyāto darśanenaiva draṣṭā cāpy upagamyatāṃ.

Seeing does not perceive, nor does non-seeing perceive. One should admit that a seer is explained by [the analysis of] seeing itself.

MKV(P) pp.115-117; *MKV(V)* p.44.

After explaining the difficulties involved in the statement, "Seeing perceives," here Nāgārjuna insists that it is not possible to assert that "non-seeing perceives." Just as much as a substantial event like "seeing" cannot be appropriately explained, even so a substantial entity like a "seer" (*draṣṭṛ*) also cannot be established. The rejection of the latter follows from the refutation of the former. This point is further elaborated in the following verse.

6. *Tiraskṛtya draṣṭā nāsty atiraskṛtya ca darśanam,*
draṣṭavyaṃ darśanaṃ caiva draṣṭary asati te kutaḥ.

A seer does not exist either separated or not separated from seeing. When a seer does not exist, whence can there be seeing and the object of seeing?

MKV(P) pp.117-118; *MKV(V)* p.45.

The metaphysical views discussed previously lead to two different conceptions of a "seer" (*draṣṭṛ*), namely, (i) a seer associated with seeing (a seeing seer), which is based on a theory of identity, and (ii) a seer dissociated from seeing (a non-seeing seer), which emphasizes difference. Having denied both, Nāgārjuna raises the question: "In the absence of a seer, whence can there be seeing and the object of seeing?" This question is raised not by a dogmatic philosopher, but by a critical epistemology. It is simply asking the question, "Just because you have come up with an unacceptable definition of a 'seer', are we going to ignore the fact that there is seeing and also the objects of such seeing? If there were to be no seer, how can you account for the perception of objects?" In other words, Nāgārjuna, in the way he formulates his question, is asserting that seeing and the objects of seeing are mutually dependent upon a seer. This assertion leads Nāgārjuna directly to the statement of the Buddha in the early discourses.

7. *Pratītya matā-pitarau yathoktaḥ putra-saṃbhavaḥ,*
cakṣu-rūpe pratītyaivam ukto vijñāna-saṃbhavaḥ.

Just as the birth of a son is said to be dependent upon the mother and the father, even so, the arising of [visual] consciousness is said to be dependent upon eye and material form.

MKV(P) p.118; *MKV(V)* p.45.

Being a competent and insightful philosopher, Nāgārjuna immediately perceives the difference between the Buddha's analysis and those of his "substantialist" protagonists. Abandoning the misleading terminology of the substantialist, Nāgārjuna adopts the Buddha's own terminology to explain the process of perception: "Depending upon the eye and visible form arises visual consciousness," (*Cakkhuñ ca paṭicca rūpe ca uppajjati cakkhu-viññāṇaṃ*) (*M* 1.111).

Even though the three terms used here correspond to the terms used by the substantialists—*cakkhu* stands for *darśana*, *rūpa* for *draṣṭavya*, and *draṣṭṛ* for *vijñāna*—the description itself is different. Here the explanation of visual perception does not begin with the assertion of the *cogito* in order to end with the perception of the external object, which was one of Nāgārjuna's criticism of the substantialist view. Neither is perception defined in a more substantialist way as in the quotation from the Sarvāstivādins which says: "The substance called the eye is of the nature of that which sees," (see note III.2). No metaphysical jargon is introduced here at all. Without getting involved in the substantialist terminology and concepts, the present statement of perception is based entirely on the principle of dependence (*pratītyasamutpāda*). Thus, visual consciousness is said to be dependent upon the eye (= faculty) and visible form (= object). Such an explanation immediately eliminates the conception of a substance (*svabhāva*, *ātman*) and replaces it with a principle of "dependence" (*pratītyasamutpāda*). In order to illustrate this process of perception, Nāgārjuna utilizes the example of the birth of a son depending upon the mother and father

It would, therefore, be unfair to think that an illustrious Buddhist philosopher like Nāgārjuna failed to see the important philosophical differences between the Buddha's explanation of the causality of perception and that presented by the metaphysicians. This verse, therefore, embodies another of the more appropriate views (*kalpanā yātra yojyate*, see XVII.13) that Nāgārjuna has been elsewhere attributing to the Buddhas, the Srāvakas, and the Pratyeka-buddhas.

8. *Draṣṭavya-darśanābhāvād vijñānādi-catuṣṭayam,*
nāstīty upādānādīni bhaviṣyanti punaḥ katham.

If it is the view that the four factors, beginning with consciousness, do not

exist, because of the absence of seeing and the object of seeing, how then can there be grasping?

MKV(P) p.119; *MKV(V)* pp.45-46.

Candrakīrti's negativist approach creates a problem in regard to the interpretation of this verse. The use of the *iti*-formula needs to be carefully handled if we are to avoid a gross misinterpretation of Nāgārjuna's thoughts at this point. Nāgārjuna has already refuted the metaphysical views pertaining to seeing and seer. However, at III.6, he was asserting that one cannot speak of seeing and the seen without a seer. It is possible that someone may insist: "If there were to be no seeing (*darśana, cakṣu*) and the seen (*draṣṭavya, rūpa*), *then* the four factors [namely, feeling (*vedanā*), perception (*saṃjñā*), dispositions (*saṃskārāḥ*) and consciousness (*vijñānaṃ*), which constitute the psychic part of the psychophysical personality and hence the equivalent of *draṣṭṛ*] are also nonexistent (*nāsti*)." The *iti*-formula converts this to a view or a statement someone could express. If so, Nāgārjuna's counter-question would be: "How then can there be grasping?" Surprisingly, Candrakīrti interprets Nāgārjuna's question as implying a denial of grasping (*na santy upādānādīnīty arthaḥ*). However, if the statement preceding *iti* is understood as the view of the opponent, then Nāgārjuna's answer is: "How can you explain grasping?" In other words, Nāgārjuna seems to be saying: "Grasping exists, for that is what is eliminated at the moment of enlightenment and freedom (*anupādā-vimukti*). Grasping is dependent upon consciousness (*vijñāna*) which is, in turn, dependent upon the eye and visible form. Any other explanation of perception is unacceptable to me."

Such an explanation is in perfect conformity with the contents of the two preceding verses both of which represent positive statements of Nāgārjuna.

9. *Vyākhyātaṃ śravaṇaṃ ghrāṇaṃ rasanaṃ sparśanaṃ manaḥ,*
darśanenaiva jānīyāc chrotṛ-śrotavyakādi ca.

What has been explained as hearing, smelling, tasting, touching, and mind, as well as the hearer, the sound, etc. should be known in the same way as seeing.

MKV(P) p.120; *MKV(V)* p.46.

Thus, after pointing out the inappropriatness of certain metaphysical views pertaining to visual perception and having stated the Buddha's own explanation of perception in terms of "dependent arising" (*pratītyasamutpada*), Nāgārjuna concludes that the other five faculties and their objects should be understood in the same way as "seeing." This indeed is a very positive explanation of sensory experience and a faithful representation of the Buddha's teaching as embodied in the "discourses."

CHAPTER FOUR
Examination of Aggregates
(Skandha-parīkṣā)

1. *Rūpa-kāraṇa-nirmuktaṃ na rūpam upalabhyate,*
rūpeṇāpi na nirmuktaṃ dṛśyate rūpa-kāraṇam.

Material form, distinct from the cause of material form, is not obtained. Similarly, a cause of material form, distinct from material form, is also not seen.

MKV(P) p.123; *MKV(V)* p.48.

From among the five aggregates (*skandha*), Nāgārjuna selects material form (*rūpa*), and not one of the explicitly psychological aggregates such as feeling, perception, disposition, or consciousness. The reason is clear. He has already examined the process of perception and, therefore, needs to analyse the object of perception, rather than perception itself.

In the discourses, material from (*rūpa*) was analysed into the four great elements (*cattāro mahābhūtā*) and the elements derived from these four (*catunnaṃ mahābhūtānaṃ upādāya rūpaṃ*) (*M* 2.87). In their attempt to determine what these derived elements were, the Ābhidharmikas scanned all the discourses looking for any element (*dharma*) that would be predominantly material and compiled varying lists. As a result of speculation on these different lists, there came to be a distinction between gross matter (*sthūla-rūpa*) and subtle matter (*sūkṣma-rūpa*). Yet, it was assumed that the four great elements constituted the foundation of all forms of matter.

When the question regarding the nature of the four great elements was raised, the Buddha maintained that these consist of hardness and rigidity (*kakkhalaṃ kharigataṃ*) which is earth (*paṭhavi*), watery element (*āpogata*) which is water (*āpo*), the fiery element (*tejogataṃ*) which is fire (*tejo*), and the airy (*vāyogataṃ*) which is air (*vāyo*) (*M* 1.421 ff.). This explains the manner in which they are experienced. However, the interpreters of the Abhidharma began to define them as "the four elements that support self-nature as well as derived form" (*svalakṣaṇopādāyarūpadhāraṇād dhātavaḥ*, *Akb* p.8). An almost identical definition was gradually being offered for the conception of dharma (*svasāmānyalakṣaṇadhāraṇād dharmaḥ, Sakv* p. 12) where *svalakṣaṇa* refers to self-nature or substance and *sāmānyalakṣaṇa* to "general characteristics" or "quality," the latter corresponding in some way to the derived elements. These ideas appeared in the Theravāda tradition only in the Abhidhamma commentaries and the later manuals and sub-commentaries (e.g., *sabhāva-sāmañña-lakkhaṇaṃ dhāretīti dhammā, Abhvt* p.11). Thus, with the Sarvāstivāda speculation, two new categories were emerging—substance and charcteristics—which ultimately involved a one-way relationship. The substances serve as the cause (*kāraṇa*) of characteristics, but not *vice versa.*

Even though these speculations are recorded in treatises composed long after Nāgārjuna, they did not originate with such treatises but were prevalent during his day or even before, as is evident from a careful reading of the *Kārikā*. It is the above mentioned substantialist view of material form (*rūpa*) that is criticized in the present verse. For Nāgārjuna (as well as for the Buddha), material form distinct from the cause of material form (*rūpa-kāraṇa = mahābhūta*) is not acceptable. Similarly, a cause of material form distinct from material form is also not experienced. Here there is no denial of material form, but only a rejection of the idea that there is an invisible ground of material form.

2. *Rūpa-kāraṇa-nirmukte rūpe rūpaṃ prasajyate,*
āhetukaṃ na cāsty arthaḥ kaścid āhetukaḥ kvacit.

When material form is [considered to be] distinct from the cause of material form, it follows that material form is without a cause. Nowhere is there any effect (*arthaḥ*) without a cause.

MKV(P) p.123; *MKV(V)* p.48.

It is the sharp distinction between material form and its assumed cause that was posing an epistemological problem for Nāgārjuna. In fact, evidence from a later Theravāda sub-commentary seems to indicate that a school with Sautrāntika leanings was trying to eliminate the distinction between these two ideas. Referring to the definition of *dhamma* mentioned in relation to IV.1. it is said: "There is no *dhamma* over and above the nature of supporting," [*na ca dhāriyamāna-sabhāvā añño dhammo nāma atthi, DhsT* p.21; see also my article, "Schools of Buddhism in Early Ceylon," in *The Ceylon Journal of the*

Humanities, Peradeniya 1 (1970):78], a view that resembles the one presented by George Berkeley during modern times.

Nāgārjuna seems to be unwilling to accept such a solution. Considering the philosophical issues a philosopher like Berkeley had to face, one can understand Nāgārjuna's unwillingness to subscribe to such a view. Without allowing the experienced elements (*dharma*) to hang loose, Nāgārjuna was interested in providing a causal explanation. Therefore, following the Buddha's explanation of "dependent arising", Nāgārjuna boldly asserts: "Nowhere is there any effect without a cause," (see also XXIV.19, *apratītyasamutpanno dharmaḥ kaścin na vidyate*).

3. *Rūpeṇa tu vinirmuktaṃ yadi syād rupa-kāraṇaṃ,*
akāryakaṃ kāraṇaṃ syāt nāsti akāryaṃ ca kāraṇaṃ.

If there were to be a cause of material form distinct from material form, there would then be a cause without an effect. There certainly is no in-effect-ive cause.

MKV(P) p.124; *MKV(V)* p.48.

The statement in the previous verse: "Nowhere is there an effect without a cause," (*na cāsti arthaḥ kaścid āhetukaḥ kvacit*) could lead to the belief in an invisible ultimate cause (like substance, or even God) that is eternal. While the characteristics, perceived qualities, etc. could be looked upon as the experienced, yet variable, effects, their ultimate ground would be the substance, eternally existing even when it is not producing the effects. Realizing that such a view could emerge from his previous assertion, Nāgārjuna immediately proceeds to nip it in the bud when he insists: "There is no in-effect-ive cause."

Thus, IV.2 and 3, in combination should provide the interpreters of Nāgārjuna with the clearest evidence that he was upholding the theory of "dependent arising" (*pratītyasamutpāda*) in the form in which it was formulated by the Buddha in the early discourses.

4. *Rūpe saty eva rūpasya kāraṇaṃ nopapadyate,*
rūpe 'saty eva rūpasya kāraṇaṃ nopapadyate.

When a material form exists, a cause of material form is not appropriate. When a material form does not exist, a cause of material form is also not appropriate.

MKV(P) p.124; *MKV(V)* p.48.

Here Nāgārjuna is reverting back to the criticisms he made of the Sarvāstivāda and Sautrāntika views in Chapter I. The first is the identity theory of causation and the second, the non-identity theory, and these criticisms are here applied to the causality of material form (*rūpa*).

5. *Niṣkāraṇaṃ punā rūpaṃ naiva naivopapadyate,*
tasmāt rūpa-gatān kāṃścin na vikalpān vikalpayet.

Furthermore, a material form without a cause is absolutely inappropriate. Therefore, one should not discriminatively think of anything confined to material form.

MKV(P) p.125; *MKV(V)* p.29.

A theory of an uncaused event, as reiterated, was clearly unacceptable to Nāgārjuna. Indeed, it is emphasized by the repetition of the negation, *naiva*. Not accepting the epistemology that is generally and indiscriminately attributed to Nāgārjuna, we have avoided translating the term *vikalpa* either as "conceptualization" or "conceptual construction" or even "discrimination," (see Introduction). The importance of the term *rūpagatān* cannot be over-emphasized. The comments on the previous verses show to what extent speculation "confined" strictly to material form (*rūpa*) led to all kinds of weird philosophical theories. The analysis of material form should be undertaken in relation to various other issues, especially language and epistemology. In the last few verses, Nāgārjuna was engaged precisely in such an enterprise. Hence his advice in the present verse. The suffix *-gata* is better understood in the meaning in which it occurs in phrases like *kāya-gata* ("confined to the body"), *hasta-gata* ("confined to the hand"), etc.

6. *Na kāraṇasya sadṛśaṃ kāryam ity upapadyate,*
na kāraṇasyāsadṛśam kāryam ity upapadyate.

The view that the effect is identical with the cause is not appropriate. The view that the effect is not identical with the cause is also not appropriate.

MKV(P) p.125; *MKV(V)* p.49.

Unlike IV.4 which states the inappropriateness of identity and non-identity theories of causation applied specifically to the subject matter under discussion, namely, material form (*rūpa*), the present verse emphasizes the inappropriateness of identity and non-identity theories in general.

7. *Vedanā-citta-saṃjñānām saṃskārāṇāṃ ca sarvaśaḥ,*
sarveṣām eva bhāvānāṃ rūpeṇaiva samaḥ kramaḥ.

The method of treatment of all existents such as feeling, thought, perception and dispositions is in every way similar to that of material form.

MKV(P) p.126; *MKV(V)* p.49.

The previous comments on the contents of this chapter would indicate that Nāgārjuna did not deny the reality of material form but only the method of explaining it. A similar treatment is requested of the other aggregates too. Note the use of the term *bhāva* in the present context, which prompts Inada to render it as "existential actions" (compared with its usage at I.3 which Inada translated as "entities").

8. *Vigrahe yaḥ parihāraṃ kṛte śūnyatayā vadet,*
sarvaṃ tasyāparihṛtaṃ samaṃ sādhyana jāyate.

When an analysis is made in terms of emptiness, whosoever were to ad-

dress a refutation, all that is left unrefuted by him will be equal to what is yet to be proved.

9. *Vyākhyāne ya upālambhaṃ kṛte śūnyatayā vadet,*
sarvaṃ tasyānupālabdhaṃ samaṃ sādhyena jāyate.

When an explanation in terms of emptiness is given, whosoever were to address a censure, all that is left uncensured by him will be equal to what is yet to be proved.

MKV(P) p.127; *MKV(V)* pp.49-50.

These two subtle and cryptic verses can best be understood in the context in which they appear. They are placed at the end of an extremely important analysis of the metaphysics relating to material form (*rūpa*). As such they should be considered the conclusion of that analysis.

The basic theme of the chapter has been the rejection of any metaphysical substance (*svabhāva*) as the cause of material form (*rūpa-kāraṇa*). Indeed, there was no rejection of the cause of material form, only the criticism of the view that this cause is an invisible permanent entity distinct from the perceived material form. This criticism if referred to at IV.8 as "an analysis in terms of emptiness" (*śūnyatayā vigrahe kṛte*). Interestingly, the term "emptiness" (*śūnyatā*) never occurred in that analysis. The analysis was made on the basis of mutual "dependence" of material form (*rūpa*) and the cause of material form (*rūpa-kāraṇa*). Thus, material form and the cause are empty of substance because they are mutually dependent. At this stage, if someone were to present a refutation of Nāgārjuna's view, that refutation would be intended as a refutation of the "mutual dependence" of the material form and its cause. However, such a refutation does not automatically prove the validity of the metaphysical idea, namely, *svabhāva* that is being rejected by Nāgārjuna on the basis of "dependence." The argument in favor of dependence is experience. Hence, the person presenting a refutation of this idea should be in a position not only to negate "mutual dependence" but also provide evidence for the establishment of a metaphysical substance (*svabhāva*). This has not yet been achieved. Thus, according to Nāgārjuna, what still remains to be proved (*sādhya*) is the thesis regarding "substance" rather than "mutual dependence."

These two verses are very significant in that they seem to admit that the Mādhyamikas have a positive thesis, namely, "dependent arising" which is accepted on the basis of experience. The "emptiness" (*śūnyatā*) they advocate is simply a challenge for the metaphysician to prove his own metaphysics.

The two verses are identical except for the use of the two pairs of terms, *vigraha* and *parihāra* in the former, and *vyākhyāna* and *upālambha* in the latter. As is well known, Nāgārjuna is also the author of a treatise called *Vigraha-vyāvartanī*. The term *vigraha* means "analysis." On the basis of this work, modern interpreters of Nāgārjuna have assumed that he was merely an analytical philosopher whose enterprise was confined solely to "analysis" (*vigraha*) of opposing views utilizing the conception of "emptiness" (*śūnyatā*). However, IV.9, cast in the same mould as IV.8, raises doubts about the validity of such an interpretation of the character of Nāgārjuna's philosophical method. The use of the term *vyākhyāna* meaning "explanation" seems to indicate that, in addition to "analysis in terms of emptiness," Nāgārjuna was also providing an "explanation." That explanation is once again said to be based upon emptiness (*śūnyatayā vyākhyāne kṛte*). But as mentioned above, the term "emptiness" did not occur at all in the chapter. Instead the explanation was provided on the basis of "dependent arising" (*pratītyasamutpāda*). "Emptiness" being the counterpart of "dependent arising," "explanation in terms of dependent arising" would, therefore, be the same as "explanation in terms of emptiness."

Thus, Nāgārjuna, even when presenting his positive theory of "dependent arising," need not worry about someone censuring him, for the theory of "dependence", like "emptiness," was intended to reject the metaphysics of substance, and the responsibility once again falls on his opponent to prove his own substance-metaphysics.

CHAPTER FIVE
The Examination of Elements *(Dhātu-parīkṣā)*

1. *Nākāśaṃ vidyate kiṃcit pūrvam ākāśa-lakṣaṇāt,*
   alakṣaṇaṃ prasajyeta syāt pūrvaṃ yadi lakṣaṇāt.

No space is evident prior to the spatial characteristics. If it exists prior to the characteristics, then it would follow that it is without characteristics.

MKV(P) p.129; *MKV(V)* p.51.

As pointed out earlier, the categories of aggregates, spheres, and elements constituted an important part of the Buddha's teachings as well as of the Abhidharma analysis (III.1). This early classification was intended to account for the human personality (*skandha*), its experience (12 *āyatanas* = 6 *indriyas* and 6 *viṣayas*) and finally the elements to which this whole experience can be analysed (18 elements = 6 *āyatanas*, 6 *viṣayas* and 6 forms of consciousness). However, Nāgārjuna does not take them in that particular order. This is because of the problems created by the interpreters of the Abhidharma. They were more concerned with defining each one of the elements in each of the categories without considering them in the light of other elements within the category to which it belongs or in terms of other categories outside of themselves. This led to a wide range of metaphysical speculations. For example, one of the elements (*dhātu*) that caused much misunderstanding and led to many metaphysical ideas is the conception of "space" (*ākāśa*). Although "space" is not an item included among either the aggregates, spheres or elements (in the earlier classification), it indeed was part of an analysis of the human personality comparable to the analysis into five aggregates (*skandha*). The counterpart of the *skandha*-classification is the explanation of the human personality in terms of six elements (*cha-dhātu* or *ṣaḍ dhātu*), one of which was "space" (*ākāśa*) (*M* 3.239). At *S* 2.150, the Buddha specifically recognized the interdependence of material form and "the sphere of space" (*Yāyaṃ . . . ākāsañcāyatanadhātu ayaṃ dhātu rūpaṃ paṭicca paññāyati*). However, the Buddhist metaphysicians, treating each one of the categories and items independently, assumed that "space" is "unconditioned" (*asaṃskṛtaṃ*, *Akb* p.3), the latter being understood as "independence" (see *Sakv* p.174; *DhsA* p.193). Thus, space came to possess the unique nature of "non-obstruction" (*anāvaraṇa-svabhāvam ākāśaṃ*) where material form finds its locale (*yatra rūpasya gatiḥ*, *Akb* p.3).

This, indeed, was a very absolutistic conception of space, a conception that muddled up the entire Buddhist epistemology. It posed the most significant challenge for Nāgārjuna. In order to eliminate such metaphysics, Nāgārjuna adopted the ingenious method of analysing the source of knowledge (i.e., seeing, *darśana*, Chapter III), the object of knowledge (i.e., material form, *rūpa*, Chapter IV) and its locale (i.e, space, *ākāśa*, Chapter V) and this he did on the pretext of examining the Buddha's own categories of aggregates, spheres and elements (*skandha-āyatana-dhātu*). Thus, the present chapter on the examination of elements comes to be devoted not to the traditional category of elements, but rather to the conception of space, highlighting its relativity, especially to material form, discussed in the previous chapter. With these three chapters, Nāgārjuna was thus able to give a rather comprehensive account of the problem of knowledge.

Here there is no denial of space, but only the rejection of a particular way of understanding or conceiving it. If space were to be understood as the ultimately real pure entity, a substance to which various characteristics are attributed, in which case space precedes the characteristics, then Nāgārjuna finds no epistemological justification for it. This is a criticism of the first aspect of the metaphysical explanation of space referred to above, namely, that space has the character of non-obstructon (*anāvaraṇa-svabhāva*). The obstruction, in this case, refers to material form (i.e., *pratigha*).

2. *Alakṣaṇo na kaścic ca bhāvaḥ saṃvidyate kvacit,*
asaty alakṣaṇe bhāve kramatāṃ kuha lakṣaṇaṃ.

An existent that is without characteristics is nowhere evident. When an existent without characteristics does not exist, where can characteristics appear?

MKV(P) pp.129-130; MKV(V) p.51.

The denial of pure "space" at V.1 is here extended to all elements or entities (*bhāva*). The question that follows next is: If there were to be no pure entity or a *tabula rasa*, then one also cannot account for adventitious elements through which something comes to be known. This represents the second aspect of the metaphysical definition mentioned earlier, namely, the "unobstructed space" serving as the locale for the appearance of material form (*yatra rūpasya gatiḥ* = *rūpasya kramatāṃ*).

3. *Nālakṣaṇe lakṣaṇasya pravṛttir na salakṣaṇe,*
salakṣaṇālakṣaṇābhyāṃ nāpy anyatra pravartate.

The occurrence of a characteristic does not take place either in something without characteristic or in something with characteristic. Nor does it proceed from something other than those with or without characteristic.

MKV(P) p.130; *MKV(V)* p.51.

Here again, it seems inappropriate to assume that Nāgārjuna was denying either space or material form, but only the manner in which they were explained by the metaphysicians. It is the sharp dichotomy between a thing and its properties that cannot account for either of them. The substantialist mode of speaking about entities (*bhāva*) leads to two extremist views, namely, identity or difference. The second statement rejects the view that the problem of identity and difference can be solved by transcending both. The reasoning seems to be that, rather than attempting to solve the problem of identity and difference by following the method of transcendence, it is more appropriatge not to create such a sharp distinction in the first place.

4. *Lakṣaṇāsaṃpravṛttau ca na lakṣyam upapadyate,*
lakṣyasyānupapattau ca lakṣaṇasyāpy asaṃbhavaḥ.

When the characteristic does not occur, the characterized is not appropriate. In the absence of the characterized, there is no occurrence of the characteristic.

MKV(P) p.131; *MKV(V)* p.52.

The relativity of concepts, or more specifically the contextual meaning of concepts, is here underscored. Definitions may be useful in clarifying the meaning of terms. Yet these meanings are not derived independently; they occur in contexts and, as such, any reference to substance and attribute should not be taken to imply distinct or pure referents. What are denied here are not the concepts of the characterized or of the characteristics, but merely their independent existence.

5. *Tasmān na vidyate lakṣyaṃ lakṣaṇaṃ naiva vidyate,*
lakṣya-lakṣana-nirmukto naiva bhāvo'pi vidyate.

Therefore, the characterized is not evidenct. Neither is the characteristic evident. Distinct from the characterized and the characteristic, an existent is certainly not evident.

MKV(P) pp.131-132; *MKV(V)* p.52

This is not a blanket denial of the characterized and the characteristic. Rather it is a denial of these two elements as explained at V.4, namely, as substance and attribute constituting independent entities. Therefore, one cannot find any event, any entity, any existence that is separated from the characterized and the characteristic. An existent separated from the characterized as well as the characteristic could turn out to be a "pure entity," an idea clearly unacceptable to Nāgārjuna.

6. *Avidyamāne bhāve ca kasyābhāvo bhaviṣyati,*
bhāvābhāva-vidharmā ca bhāvābhāvam avaiti kaḥ.

When an existent is not evident, whose non-existence can there be? Who could comprehend the distinct things: existent and non-existent as well as existence and non-existence?

MKV(P) p.132; *MKV(V)* pp.52-53.

Here again, if we are to understand "existent" (*bhāva*) without taking into consideration the sort of "existent" referred to at V.5, we would be left with a universal statement regarding all "existents" (*bhāva*). Yet, it is not meant to be taken that way. The "existent" referred to here is already defined at V.5. It is an "existent" that is separated from either the characterised or the characteristic or both. It is a "pure existent." Such a pure existent could then be contrasted with a pure non-existent, and it is this sharp distinction or dichotomy that is being questioned by Nāgārjuna. Indeed, it is significant to note the use of the term *vi-dharma* (whose occurrence in any other text is not known to the present author) in the sense of "distinct things."

7. *Tasmān na bhāvo nābhāvo na lakṣyaṃ nāpi lakṣaṇaṃ,*
ākāśaṃ ākāśa-samā dhātavaḥ pañca ye pare.

Therefore, there is neither an existent nor a non-existent, neither the characterized nor the characteristic, neither space nor the other five elements similar to space.

MKV(P) p.134; *MKV(V)* p.53.

Thus, neither existence nor non-existence, the characterized nor the characteristic as envisaged by the metaphysicians exist. The five elements—earth, water, fire, air and consciousness, which together with space constitute the personality (*cha-dhaturoyaṃ puriso*)—do not exist if these elements are conceived of in the same way as space. This does not mean that the way in which the metaphysicians conceive of the six elements is the *only* way in which they can be understood and explained.

8. *Astivaṃ ye tu paśyanti nāstitvaṃ cālpabuddhayaḥ,*
bhāvānāṃ te na paśyanti draṣṭavyopaśamaṃ śivaṃ.

Those who are of little intelligence, who perceive the existence as well as

the non-existence of existents, do not perceive the appeasement of the object, the auspicious.

MKV(P) p.135; *MKV(V)* p. 54.

The "appeasement of the object" (***drasṭavyopaśama***) is, no doubt, a synonym for the "appeasement of dispositions" (***saṃskāropaśama***) or the "appeasement of obsessions" (***prapañcopaśama***). It is indeed not the elimination of the object (***drasṭavya-kṣaya***), implying the abandoning of both subject and object. It is merely the appeasement of the object. What is implied by the appeasement of the object is its non-reification. The conception of the non-existence of the object will emerge only if its existence is understood in a substantial way. Existence (***astitva***) and non-existence (***nāstitva***) are correlative. Assertion or denial of one involves the assertion or denial of the other respectively. Asserting existence in a metaphysical way one is led to the denial of existence. Denying existence in the same way one is led to the assertion of non-existence. Instead of eliminating both existence and non-existence and looking for a transcendent reality, a reality that is beyond both existence and non-existence, it is possible to appease, calm, or pacify one's dispositions (***saṃskāra***) or obsessions (***prapañca***). Dispositions or obsessions, when followed to their positive extreme, lead to the belief in a permanent existence (***astitva***); when completely negated they contribute toward the belief in non-existence (***nāstitva***). Hence the emphasis on their appeasement rather than their promotion or elimination.

CHAPTER SIX
The Examination of Lust and the Lustful
(Rāga-rakta-parīkṣā)

1. *Rāgād yadi bhavet pūrvaṃ rakto rāga-tiraskṛtaḥ,*
   taṃ pratīya bhaved rāgo rakte rāge rāgo bhavet sati.

If a lustful one, separated from lust, were to exist prior to lust, then depending upon him there will be lust. Lust exists when there is a lustful one.

MKV(P) p.138; *MKV(V)* p.55.

So far Nāgārjuna was considering the basic elements (*dharma*) involved in an explanation of the problem of perception, namely, the "faculties" (*indriya*), the "aggregates" (*skandha*), and "elements" (*dhātu*). However, the analysis of perceptual experience, and therefore of the elements (*dharma*) involved in such experience, is not confined to these. In the Buddhist view, lust (*rāga*) is an important constituent of perception, primarily because in Buddhism the analysis of perception was not undertaken for its own sake, but for the sake of discovering the cause of bondage and freedom.

We have already referred to the confusions created by Candrakīrti, especially in regard to the interpretation of the most crucial Chapter I where he fails to recognize the significance even of the order in which Nāgārjuna takes up the variety of ideas for examination, let alone the ideas themselves.

Another unfortunate misinterpretation emerges when Candrakīrti assumes that every initial verse in every chapter represents a statement of the opponent's view which is to be repudiated. While this may be true in some chapters, there is no need to universalize it. There is no reason why Nāgārjuna could not take up his or the Buddha's views first and then go on to repudiate what are considered to be inappropriate ideas.

In the Buddha's own analysis of perception, obsessions (*prapañca*) appears in a personality that is already smeared with lust. The Buddha consistently avoided any speculation regarding absolute origins. As such, he was not willing to assume *either* a pure personality, a *tabula rasa* which comes to be defiled by adventitious elements (see *A* 1.254) *or* the existence of an element called lust (*rāga*) in the external world independent of a conscious person who generates lust on the basis of external objects (see *S* 1.22). For him, objects can be classified as pleasurable (*śubha*), loathsome (*aśubha*), or neutral only in relation to a perceiving individual who is *prone* to make such distinctions. A person who is prone to make such distinctions is one who is either dominated by lust (*rāga*) or aversion (*dosa*) or indifference.

Thus, Nāgārjuna is able to assert that if any object were to cause any lust (*rāga*), then there must be a lustful one (*rakta*), not simply a "pure person" who is untained by lust. For him, there is no difficulty in speaking of lust, so long as that lust is not distinguished as an entity which is then supposed to infect a person who is pure and undefiled by lust. It is the same sort of relation that is exemplified by a compassionate one (*maitra*) and the recipient of compassion (*upagrāhaka*), a very apt example given by Candrakīrti to illustrate the conception of "otherness' ' (*paratva*), but which has been misunderstood by many a translator [*MKV(P)*p.78; Sprung, *Lucid Exposition*, p.66, who was probably following Stcherbatsky's earlier translation]. There is no sense in speaking of a compassionate one or even compassion in a vacuum. A compassionate one or compassion becomes meaningful only in the context of people who are recipients of such compassion. The same sort of relationship exists among the lustful (*rakta*), lust (*rāga*), and the objects that generate lust in the individuals.

The present verse, therefore, is a clear statement of Nāgārjuna's own position, not the statement of an opponent that is to be rejected.

2. *Rakte 'sati punā rāgaḥ kuta eva bhaviṣyati,*
sati vāsati vā rāge rakte 'py eṣa samaḥ kramaḥ.

When a lustful one does not exist, whence can there be lust? Whether lust exists or not, the method (of analysis) even of the lustful one would be comparable.

MKV(P) pp.138-139; *MKV(V)* p.55.

Thus, Nāgārjuna raises the question as to how there could be lust in the absence of a lustful one. This avoids the theory of a *tabula rasa* and the adventitious impressions. Let alone the existence or the non-existence of lust, even the lustful one has to be analysed in terms of dependence, not in terms of pure entities having their own self-nature (*svabhāva*).

3. *Sahaiva puna udbhūtir na yuktā rāga-raktayoḥ,*
bhavetāṃ rāga-raktau hi nirapekṣau parasparaṃ.

Again, the simultaneous occurrences of lust and the lustful one is not proper. Lust and the lustful one would then be mutually non-contingent.

MKV(P) p.139; *MKV(V)* p.56.

To conceive of lust or the lustful one in vacuity and then proceeding to explain their simultaneous arising (*sahaiva udbhūtir*) is not the purpose of "dependent arising." In such a case, what is found is independent existence of lust as well as the lustful one, each having its own nature. This, once again, represents Nāgārjuna's rejection of the substance/attribute relationship. "Cow-ness" implies the fact of having "four legs;" the latter is not an independent attribute of the former. The dangers inherent in carrying out the analytical process initiated by the Buddha to its extreme is here indicated. Analysis is useful in eliminating metaphysics, but useless when its leads to further metaphysics.

4. *Naikatve sahabhāvo 'sti na tenaiva hi tat saha,*
pṛthaktve sahabhāvo 'tha kuta eva bhaviṣyati.

In identity, there is no co-existence. That which is associated does not arise together. In discreteness, how can there be co-existence?

MKV(P) pp.139-140; *MKV(V)* p.56.

The philosophical problems created by an over-extended analytical process cannot be resolved by either a conception of identity or of discreteness. The relationship of co-existence (*sahabhāva*) cannot be established once the analysis leads to a sharp dichotomy between substance and attribute.

5. *Ekatve sahabhāvaś cet syāt sahāyaṃ vināpi saḥ,*
pṛthaktve sahabhāvaś cet syāt sahāyaṃ vināpi saḥ.

If, in identity, there were to be co-existence, it could occur even without association. If, in discreteness, there were to be co-existence, it could occur even without association.

MKV(P) p.140; *MKV(V)* p.55

The Sarvāstivāda conception of identity in terms of substantial existence (*svabhāva*), each substance being a part of a larger and more pervading substance (like Plato's "forms") did not need a conception of association. Co-existence comes to be overshadowed by identity (just as much as the three Platonic forms—truth, beauty, and goodness—could be found in a more comprehensive form, i.e., Good). The Sautrāntika analysis of reality into discrete momentary entities (comparable to the Humean impressions) led to an explanation of co-existence in terms of "associaiton." In fact, such co-existence did not need any "association." Things could co-exist even without association. Thus, association is not a viable solution to problems either of identity or of discreteness.

6. *Pṛthaktve sahabhāvaś ca yadi kiṃ rāga-raktayoḥ,*
   siddhaḥ pṛthak-pṛthag-bhāvaḥ sahabhāvo yatas tayoḥ.

If there were to be co-existence in discreteness, is it the case that lust and the lustful one are completely separated, as a result of which their co-existence is also established.

MKV(P) p.140; *MKV(V)* p.56.

The problem of "association" arises more with the conception of "discreteness," than with the notion of identity. "Association" was not much of a concern for the Sarvāstivādins. However, it was indeed a major problem for the Sautrāntikas. Hence their emphasis on the conception of "immediate contiguity" (*samanantara*). For Hume, with a similar atomic analysis of experience, "association" was the glue that bound together the discrete impressions. The present question of Nāgārjuna was a challenge to that Sautrāntika (/Humean) theory of the "ideas of association."

7. *Siddhaḥ pṛthak-pṛthag-bhāvo yadi vā rāga-raktayoḥ,*
sahabhāvaṃ kim arthaṃ tu parikalpayase tayoḥ.

If complete separation between lust and the lustful one is established, for what purpose do you conceive of their co-existence?

MKV(P) p.141; *MKV(V)* p.56.

The usefulness of appealing to co-existence after analysing events into discrete entities is here questioned. Nāgārjuna's approach here is to resolve the very idea that gave rise to the problem rather than solving it, namely, to avoid creating sharp distinctions instead of trying to find solutions to problems generated by such distinctions.

8. *Pṛthag na siddhyatīty evaṃ sahabhāvaṃ vikāṅkṣasi,*
sahabhāva-prasiddhy arthaṃ pṛthaktvaṃ bhūya icchasi.

You fancy co-existence assuming that the discrete is not established. You, again, look for discreteness for the purpose of establishing co-existence.

MKV(P) p.141; *MKV(V)* p.57.

No better explanation of the dilemma of an analytical philosopher who recognizes discreteness can be found than in the present statement of Nāgārjuna. The vicious circle in which one gets involved when, after analysing things into discrete entities, one tries to put things together is clearly explained here.

9. *Pṛthag-bhāvāprasiddheś ca sahabhāvo na siddhyati,*
katamasmin pṛthag-bhāve sahabhāvaṃ satīcchasi.

When discreteness is not established, co-existence is not established. In

the presence of what kind of discreteness would you expect co-existence.

MKV(P) p.142 *MKV(V)* p.57.

Nāgārjuna's question here is specifically on the nature of discreteness. If discreteness is absolute, then association of co-existent entities is not acceptable. If there is no such discreteness, then there is no need for co-existence, for the lack of complete discreteness implies "dependence" (*pratītyasamutpāda*). Hence, the question pertains to the *kind* of discreteness envisaged.

10. *Evaṃ raktena rāgasya siddhir na saha nāsaha,*
rāgavat sarvadharmāṇāṃ siddhir na saha nāsaha.

Thus, with or without the lustful one, there is no establishment of lust. Like lust, there is no establishment of anything with or without [accompaniments].

MKV(P) p.142; *MKV(V)* p.57.

On the basis of the *kind* of discreteness referred to above, one cannot explain either the association or the non-association of lust and the lustful one. Avoid the sharp distinction, the problems are not there to solve. The same can be said in regard to all phenomena (*dharma*). For this reason, neither absolute identity nor absolute discreteness can establish the nature of phenomena.

CHAPTER SEVEN
The Examination of the Conditioned *(Saṃskṛta-parīkṣā)*

1. *Yadi saṃskṛta utpādas tatra yuktā tri-lakṣaṇī,*
athāsaṃskṛta utpādaḥ kathaṃ saṃskṛta-lakṣaṇam.

If arising is conditioned, therein three characteristics are proper. If arising is unconditioned, how can there be characteristics of the conditioned?

MKV(P) pp.145-146; *MKV(V)* p.59

The examinaiton of the "conditioned" (*saṃskṛta*) coming immediately after the analysis of lust (*rāga*) and the lustful one (*rakta*) brings out another important aspect of the Buddha's conception of the pragmatic meaning of truth, a conception that Nāgarjuna seems to be clearly aware of.

Lust, as pointed out earlier, is one of the most important elements in the Buddha's analysis of experience. Lust is operative in the perceptual process especially in the formation of ideas derived from experience. Having rejected "omniscience" (*sarvajñatva*) as a source of knowledge, the Buddha depended primarily on sense experience. However, for him, sense experience was a "big, blooming, buzzing confusion." One way of dealing with this confusing mass of sense data is by concentrating upon items that are of interest to the individual and then forming ideas. Such selection is generally based upon one's interest. This is the significance of "dispositions" (*saṃskāra* = compounding of ideas). For the Buddha, one's conception of truth is invariably bound up with such dispositions. Therefore, all ideas are "dispositionally conditioned" (*saṃskṛta*). The Buddha's final statement before his death: "Dispositions are subject to change" (*vayadhammā saṅkhārā, D* 2.156), therefore, is an assertion that, since ideas are impermanent, there can be no absolute truth.

However, the above conception of the "dispositionally conditioned" (*saṃskṛta*) was to undergo a radical change at the hands of the Buddhist metaphysicians. Nāgārjuna's examination of *saṃskṛta* becomes meaningful only in the background of that change of perspective. His was, indeed, an attempt to reject the Sarvāstivāda and Sautrāntika interpretations of *saṃskṛta* (and this would apply to the ideas that came to be accepted by the later Theravādins) and to revert back to the original teachings of the Buddha.

Once again, the Sarvāstivāda school was responsible for initiating this change of perspective. In the early discourses, the term *saṃskṛta* is used along with the term *pratītyasamutpanna*, but not as synonyms (*S* 3.96, 103). While the former implied "the dispositionally conditioned," the latter was used in the more comprehensive meaning of "the dependent." Thus, all dispositionally conditioned phenomena are dependent, but not all dependent phenomena are dispositionally conditioned. The equation of *saṃskṛta* and *pratītyasamutpanna* occurs for the first time in the interpretation of the Abhidharma. It was this latter tradition that Vasubandhu was recording when he said: "Those that are made by the conditions having come together are called the *saṃskṛtas*" (*sametya sambhūya pratyayaiḥ kṛtā iti saṃskṛtāḥ*, *Akb* p.4; see also *AA* 2.252, *paccayehi samāgantvā katassa*). The Sarvāstivādins seem to have understood the concept of *saṃskṛta* as a mere refutation of the belief in the production of an event by a single cause (*eka-pratyaya-janitam*, ibid.). Yaśomitra, commenting upon this statement, goes on to say that *saṃskṛta* and *pratītyasamutpanna* are, therefore, synonyms (*Sakv* pp.171-172), thereby obliterating the semantic difference between "made" (*kṛta*) and "arisen" (*utpanna*).

This erroneous simple equation was to lead to further complications, especially in understanding the Buddha's characterization of *nirvāṇa* as *asaṃskṛta*. Even though the early discourses presented *nirvāṇa* as an *asaṃskṛta*, it was never considered to be an *apratītyasamutpanna* ("independent"). For early Buddhism, both *saṃskṛta* and *asaṃskṛta* are *pratītyasamutpanna*. However, the Sarvāstivāda equation led to the equation of their negations as well. *Asaṃskṛta* seems to have been understood in the sense of *apratītyasamutpanna*. To what extent their perspective was dominated by an adherence to the notion of self-nature (*svabhāva*), for which they gave no causal explanation at all other than merely maintaining that it is permanent, remains a surmise.

It is this Sarvāstivāda conception of *saṃskṛta* as being identical with *pratītyasamutpanna* that is being criticized at VII.1. Nāgārjuna, as indicated in the first line of this verse, had no difficulty in assuming that the *saṃskṛta* is characterized by arising, change, and ceasing. This indeed was a statement attributed to the Buddha in the early discourses, where it is said: "Monks, there are these three characteristics of the dispositionally conditioned. The arising of that which is dispositionally conditioned is evident. Its cessation is also evident. Change of what has come to endure is also evident," (*A* 1.152). Yet if, as explained by the Sarvastivadins, *saṃskṛta* is identical with *pratītyasamutpanna* (the latter also accounting for arising, change and ceasing), then one cannot speak of these three characteristics in the context of the *asaṃskṛta*.

It may be of interest to note that it is not only *nirvāṇa* that came to be included in the category of *asaṃskṛta* by these metaphysicians. They also admitted "space" (*ākāśa*) as an *asaṃskṛta*. The implications of that view was examined by Nāgārjuna in Chapter V.

2. *Utpādādyas trayo vyastā nālaṃ lakṣaṇa-karmaṇi,*
saṃskṛtasya samastāḥ syur ekatra katham ekadā.

When the triad consisting of arising, etc. are discrete, they are not adequate to function as characteristics of the conditioned. If they were to be combined, how can they be in the same place at the same time?

MKV(P) p.146; *MKV(V)* p.59.

Further objections to the Sarvāstivāda and Sautrāntika theories relating to the characteristics of the conditioned are raised here. The discreteness of the three characteristics, as envisaged by these two schools, would not allow them to function as the characteristics of the conditioned. The Sarvāstivāda theory of an underlying substance, which comes to be superficially characterized by the three (or four) moments, as well as the Sautrāntika theory that each moment is inherent in the previous one in the form of potentiality or seed (*śakti, bīja*), were the direct results of such a perspective. Furthermore, if these characteristics were distinct in relation to both time and space, they could not occur in any one *saṃskṛta* at the same time.

3. *Utpāda-sthiti-bhaṅgānām anyat saṃskṛta-lakṣaṇam,*
asti ced anavasthaivaṃ nāsti cet te na saṃskṛtaḥ.

If there were to be a characteristic of the conditioned other than arising, duration, and destruction, there would be infinite regress. If there were to be no such [characteristics], these would not be conditioned.

MKV(P) p.147; *MKV(V)* p.60.

If arising, stasis, and ceasing are three distinct events, then each one of these will require further characteristics of arising, stasis, and ceasing to account for themselves. Thus, the moment of arising will need three further characteristics of arising, stasis, and ceasing before it could give rise to the next moment, namely, stasis. The same applies to stasis and ceasing. This will lead to infinite regress (*anavasthā*). On the contrary, if each of these moments do not possess further characteristics, then they cannot be defined as the conditioned.

4. *Utpādotpāda utpādo mulotpādasya kevalaṃ,*
utpādotpādam utpādo maulo janayate panaḥ.

The arising of arising is exclusively the arising of primary arising. Again, the primary arising produces the arising of arising.

MKV(P) p.149; *MKV(V)* p.60.

In order to avoid infinite regress, one may assume that the arising of arising is the primary arising (*mūla-utpada*), and that this latter again causes the arising of arising. Such mutual action on the part of primary arising and arising of arising could eliminate infinite regress.

5. *Utpādotpāda utpādo mūlotpādasya te yadi,*
maulenājanitas taṃ te sa kathaṃ janayiṣyati.

If arising of arising is the primary arising, not being produced by the primary, how can it [the former] produce that [the latter]?

MKV(P) p.150; *MKV(V)* p.61.

The question raised here by Nāgārjuna pertains to active causation. The substantialist (Sarvastivada) view of causation, which assumes the essence of the effect to be already latent in the cause, does not permit mutual dependence of cause and effect. In such a case, the cause-effect relationship would be a one-way relationship. Nāgārjuna perceives that the interdependence utilized in VII.4 in order to avoid infinite regress would not be appropriate in the context of a substantialist theory of causation.

6. *Sa te maulena janito maulaṃ janayate yadi,*
maulaḥ sa tenājanitas tam utpādayate kathaṃ.

If, produced by the primary, it produces the primary, how can that primary, not produced by it, produce it?

MKV(P) p.150; *MKV(V)* p.61.

Here again, Nāgārjuna refuses to recognize the mutual dependence of cause and effect in the context of an active or substantialist theory of causation.

7. *Ayam utpadyamānas te kāmam utpādayed imaṃ,*
yadīmam utpādayitum ajātaḥ śaknuyād ayaṃ.

This, while arising, if it may so desire, produce that, so that it, being not yet born, will be able to produce that.

MKV(P) p.150; *MKV(V)* p.61.

At this point Nāgārjuna proceeds to state the Sautrāntika theory of causation, which is described very succinctly by Vasubandhu (*Akb* pp.76-77). The Sautrāntikas believed that the Buddha's discourse on the three characteristics of existence—arising (*utpāda*), change of what has endured (*sthitasyānyathātva*), and ceasing (*vyaya*)—was intended for the foolish people who are blinded by ignorance (*avidyāndhabālāḥ*). According to them, the recognition of such characteristics involves the belief in the substantial existence (*astitva*) of the "conditioned" (*saṃskṛta*) (see ibid., p.77). However, these three characteristics are not part of reality which consists of momentary (*kṣaṇika*) events. Such momentary events or impressions coming one after another in rapid succession (*pūrvasya purvasyottarakṣaṇasyānubandhaḥ*) produces the appearance of "change of what has endured" (*sthityānyathātva*), whereas it is merely a series of events (*pravāha*) resembling one another (*avisadṛśa*). In such a context, arising is merely the immedidate arising from a state of non-existence (*pratikṣaṇam abhūtvā bhāva utpādaḥ*). A moment thus comes to be from nowhere and ceases immediately. (Here one is naturally reminded of the Humean version of causal relations.)

In the present verse, Nāgārjuna is providing his own description of the Sautrāntika theory of change. As this theory is based upon the recognition of momentariness (*kṣaṇikatva*), Nāgārjuna insists that the preceding event has to produce the succeeding event (in the series of similar events) even before the former is born, for the former does not endure in order to produce the latter. In other words, if there were to be any causal connection between two momentary events, the moment that serves as the cause should be ready to generate the effect before it passes away, that is, even before it is born.

8. *Pradīpaḥ sva-parātmānau saṃprakāśayitā yathā,*
utpādaḥ svaparātmānav ubhāv utpādayet tathā.

As a light illuminates itself as well as others, so does arising produce both itself and others.

MKV(P) p.151; *MKV(V)* p.62.

Here, a metaphor is utilized to explain the Sautrāntika version of the causal theory. The thrust of the argument is that it is not necessary for an event to endure before it can produce some other effect. A lamp or light does not have to remain for a while before it could illuminate itself as well as others. This is the same argument used by the Sautrāntikas and other idealistic schools to justify the existence of a *cogito* discussed above (see also Masaaki Hattori, *Dignaga On Perception*, Cambridge: Harvard University Press, 1968, p. 101). The Sautrāntikas feared that any conception of duration or statis (*sthiti*) will lead to the unacceptable view of substance (*svabhāva*).

9. *Pardīpe nāndhakāro 'sti yatra cāsau pratiṣṭhitaḥ,*
kiṃ prakāśayati dīpaḥ prakāśo hi tamo-vadhaḥ.

There exists no darkness either in the light or in whatever place it is situated. What does light illuminate? For, illumination is indeed the destruction of darkness.

MKV(P) p.151; *MKV(V)* p.62.

Nāgārjuna's criticism of the Sautrāntika theory begins here. In order to get rid of the metaphysics associated with the Sautrānika theory of change and causation, Nāgārjuna begins by questioning the *meaning* of the term "illumination" (*prakāśa*). For him, light (*āloka*) and darkness (*andhakāra*) are relative ideas. This same idea is expressed by the Buddha at *S* 2.150, where it is said: "This so-called element of light is known through its dependence upon darkness" (*yāyaṃ . . . ābhādhātu ayaṃ dhātu andhakāraṃ paṭicca paññāyati*; see also Nāgārjuna's discussion in his *Ratnāvalī* [*Ratnāvalī of Nāgārjuna*, ed. G. Tucci, *Journal of the Royal Asiatic Society*, London, 1934, 1936, 1.48]). The relatonship here is by way of contrast; the absence of one means the presence of the other. Thus, "illumination" is synonymous with the "destruction of darkness" (*tamo-vadhaḥ*), one is not produced by the other in any substantial way.

10. *Katham utpadyamānena pradīpena tamo hataṃ,*
notpadyamāno hi tamaḥ pradīpaḥ prāpnute yadā.

How can darkness be destroyed by the emergent light, when the emerging light, indeed, does not teach darkness?

MKV(P) p.152; *MKV(V)* p.62.

The example of light and darkness used to illustrate the causal relationship between two momentary events is here shown to be inappropriate, as it eventually leads to a rather substantialist notion of light reaching up to darkness in order to destroy it.

11. *Aprāpyaiva pradīpena yadi vā nihataṃ tamaḥ,*
iha-stahaḥ sarva-loka-sthaṃ sa tamo nihaniṣyati.

On the contrary, if darkness is destroyed by light without reaching it, then that [light] remaining here will destroy the darkness present in all the worlds.

MKV(P) p.153; *MKV(V)* p.62.

The contrary of the substantialist view referred to at VII.10 is here shown to lead to further confusion. If light can destroy darkness without reaching it, the implication would be that any spark of light anywhere can destroy the darkness present in the entire universe.

12. *Pradīpaḥ sva-parātmānau samprakāśayate yadi,*
tamo 'pi svaparātmānau chādayiṣyaty asaṃśayam.

If light were to illminate both itself and others, then certainly darkness too will conceal itself and others.

MKV(P) p.154; *MKV(V)* p.63.

Taking the argument of the substantialist at VII.8 that light illuminates itself as well as others, Nāgārjuna is here showing that the same could be said of darkness too, which would invalidate the meaningfulness of the very example used by the substantialist.

13. *Anutpanno 'yam utpādaḥ svātmānaṃ janayet kathaṃ,*
athotpanno janayate jāte kiṃ janyate punaḥ.

How can this non-arisen arising produce itself? If it is the arisen that produces, then being born, what is it that is produced again?

MKV(P) p.157; *MKV(V)* p.64.

The principle adopted at I.6 in criticizing the identity and non-identity theories of causation is here applied to reject the notion of a self-creating arising. The metaphysical assumptions associated with the Sautrāntika theory of momentary arising is laid bare by an examination of the so-called "deep structures."

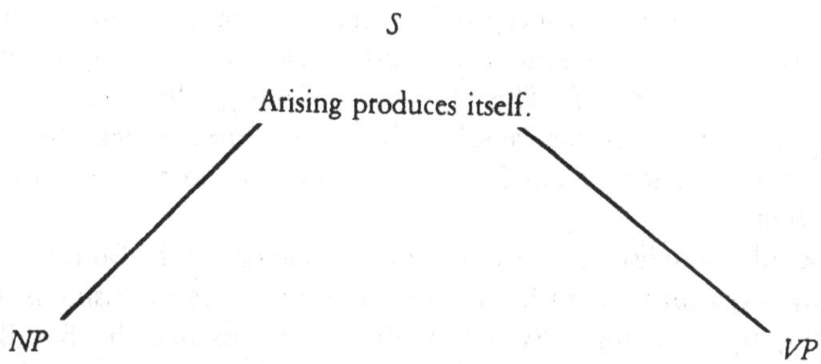

i. (non-arisen) arising — produces itself

ii. (arisen) arising — produces itself

The first alternative is impossible. The second is meaningless.

14. *Notpadyamānaṃ notpannaṃ nānutpannaṃ kathaṃcana,*
utpadyate tathākhyātaṃ gamyamāna-gatāgataiḥ.

Neither the present arising, nor the arisen, nor the non-arisen, is being arisen in any way. This has already been explained by means of [the concepts of] present moving, the moved and the not yet moved.

MKV(P) p.157; *MKV(V)* p.64.

The analysis of present arising (***utpadyamāna***), the arisen (***utpanna***), and the non-arisen (***anutpanna***) conceived of in metaphysical terms compares well with the analysis of motion in Chapter II.

15. *Utpadyamānam utpattāv idaṃ na kramate yadā,*
katham utpadyamānaṃ tu parītyotpattim ucyate.

When this present arising does not proceed from within arising, indeed, how can the present arising be spoken of as dependent arising?

MKV(P) p.158; *MKV(V)* p.65.

The first line utilizes the conceptual apparatus of the substantialists in speaking of the effect (i.e., the present arising, ***utpadyamāna***) as issuing out of the cause (i.e., the arising, ***utpatti***). This is a theory of self-production. As indicated in I.7, Nāgārjuna rejects this causal explanation as meaningless, for there is actually no production of anything new in such a context. It is mere self-reproduction.

If the substantialist were to adopt the terminology of the Buddha (utilized so often by Nāgārjuna), then he could say that the "present arising is dependent (***pratītya***) upon arising." Even though this sounds like the Buddha's (and, therefore, Nāgārjuna's) formulation of the causal principle, yet Nāgārjuna is not willing to recognize it. This is because dependent arising does not simply mean the reproduction of the same thing. In the present case, it is an explanation of the present arising (***utpadyamāna***) on the basis of arising (***utpatti***), which is simply tautological with no new information provided. "Dependent arising" accounts for the arising of something new or different, even though such newness or difference is not emphasized to the complete neglect of the relationship of dependence.

The present verse is indicative of the manner in which the Sautrāntikas, while trying to explain causation in terms of "association" of discrete momentary entities, were eventually led to a substantialist conception causation. Either they had to accept self-causation or remain satisfied with mere self-reproduction, the latter providing no explanation of creativity at all. "Dependent arising," on the contrary, accounts for creativity without falling into the substantialist trap.

16. ***Partītya yad yad bhavati tat tac chāntaṃ svabhāvataḥ,***
tasmād utpadyamānaṃ ca śāntam utpattir eva ca.

Whatever that comes to be dependently, that is inherently peaceful. Therefore, that which is presently arising as well as arising itself are peaceful.

MKV(P) p.159-160; *MKV(V)* p.66.

This singularly important statement in the present chapter comes after VII.15 where Nāgārjuna refused to recognize a form of "dependent arising" that also carries the implication of self-causation (*svata-utpatti*). The notion of dependent arising (*pratītya bhavati* = *pratītyasamutpāda*) is simply free from any idea of self-causation involving substance or self nature (*svabhāvataḥ śātaṃ*) and, in that sense, is "inherently peaceful." It does not contribute to the notion of "self" (*ātman, svabhāva*) or "other" (*para*) and, as a result, does not generate lust (*rāga*) or hatred (*dveṣa*), attachment or aversion. It is the more appropriate view regarding the present arising (*utpadyamāna*) as well as arising (*utpatti*) and constitutes an understanding (*jñāna*) or wisdom (*prajñā*) that brings about freedom (*vimukti, nirvāṇa*). It is indeed not a negation of arising (*utpada, utpatti*), but simply a non-substantialist way of perceiving such phenomena.

17. *Yadī kaścid anutpanno bhāvaḥ saṃvidyate kvacit,*
utpadyeta sa kiṃ tasmin bhāva utpadyate 'sati.

If a certain non-arisen existent is evident somewhere, then that would arise. When such a thing does not exist, how can an existent arise?

MKV(P) p.160; *MKV(V)* p.66.

Here Nāgārjuna seems to be setting up the Sarvāstivāda theory of identity against the Sautrāntika view of non-identity. The identity theory of causation recognizes an entity (*bhāva*), permanent and eternal, lying concealed somewhere (*kvacit*), and therefore not yet arisen (*anutpanna*). If such a thing were to exist, then it could be said to arise. However, if such a thing were to be non-existent (*tasmin asati*), how can one say that a thing or entity arises? This is, once again, a criticism of the Sautrāntika theory of the arising of a non-existing entity (*abhūtvā bhāva utpāda, Akb* p.77; see also Kalupahana, *Causality*, p. 151). Here, Nāgārjuna is maintaining that the Sarvāstivāda theory of causation, though excessively metaphysical, may be intelligible in some way, but that the Sautrāntika theory of the arising of a non-existent entity makes no sense at all.

18. *Utpadyamānam utpādo yadi cotpādayaty ayaṃ,*
utpādayet tam utpādam utpādaḥ katamaḥ punaḥ.

If arising were to produce this present arising, which arising would again produce that arising of that arising?

MKV(P) p.161; *MKV(P)* p.66.

Infinite regress becomes a necessary corollary of the Sautrantika theory of momentary events. As mentioned earlier, the Sautrāntikas were compelled to assume the notion of potentiality (*śakti, bīja*) in order to avoid such infinite regress. Nāgārjuna was not ready to accept that solution.

19. *Anya utpādayaty enaṃ yady utpādo 'navasthitiḥ,*
athānutpāda utpannaḥ sarvam utpadyate tathā.

If this arising were to produce another, arising would turn out to be infinite regression. If the non-airising is arisen, then it will produce everything in this manner.

MKV(P) p.162; *MKV(V)* p.67.

Not only does the Sautrāntika theory lead to infinite regress (*anavasthā*), it also contributes to the chaotic view that anything can come out of anything, which is the opposite of the Sarvāstivāda view that nothing comes out of nothing. Causal uniformity has no place whatsoever in the Sautrāntika scheme of things. This is another point of comparison between the Sautrāntika and Humean views of causation.

20. *Sataś ca tāvad utpattir asataś ca na yujyate,*
na sataś cāsataś ceti pūrvam evopapāditaṃ.

As such, neither the arising of an existent nor the arising of a non-existent is proper. Even so is the arising of that which is both existent and non-existent, and this has been previously explained.

MKV(P) p.162; *MKV(V)* p.67.

Neither the identity theory of causation nor the non-identity theory nor even a combination of these two will appropriately account for all the issues relating to causation. This idea continues to be emphasized by Nāgārjuna.

21. *Nirudhyamānasyotpattir na bhāvasyopapadyate,*
yaś cānirudhyamānas tu sa bhāvo nopapadyate.

The arising of an existent that is ceasing is not appropriate. Whatever existent that is non-arising, that existent too is not appropriate.

MKV(P) p.163; *MKV(V)* p.67.

The theory discussed at VII.20 was the arising of a non-existent entity. The discussion now moves on to the question regarding the arising of an event that is ceasing. The Abhidharma interpreters recognized two types of causes (*hetu*) that provide a foundation for the causal efficacy of an event that is ceasing (*nirudhyamāne kāritraṃ dvau hetū kurutaḥ, AK* ii.63; *AKB* p.100; also see definition of *kāritra* at *AD* 321; *Adv* p.281). Nāgārjuna is reluctant to accept even the fact that an existent that is on its way to ceasing can arise. In other words, cessation and arising cannot be described as events taking place in relation to the same entity. Or more specifically, a changing substance is unacceptable to Nāgārjuna. Similarly, one cannot speak of an entity that is not ceasing (*anirudhyamāna*).

22. *Na sthita-bhāvas tiṣṭhaty asthita-bhāvo na tiṣṭhati,*
na tiṣṭhati tiṣṭhamānaḥ ko 'nutpannaś ca tiṣṭhati.

An existent that has endured is not stationary, nor is an existent that has not endured. The presently enduring is not stationary. What non-arisen can stay?

MKV(P) p.164; *MKV(V)* p.68.

The Sarvāstivādins (especially the Vaibhāṣikas) argued that unless "stasis" *(sthiti)* of an entity (*dharma*) is not recognized, it causal efficacy also cannot be admitted (*Adv* p.109). This is contrary to the view (referred to in VII.21) expressed by the Sautrāntikas, namely, that an entity, when it is ceasing, can generate causal efficiency. Thus, while the Sautrāntikas refused to recognize a moment of stasis fearing that it would lead to a belief in substance, the Sarvāstivādins insisted upon admitting such a static moment.

As such, the Sarvāstivādins can maintain that a static moment endures (*sthita-bhāvaḥ tiṣṭhati*), primarily because they assumed that stasis has its own nature (*svabhāva*). If there was no such nature, then phenomena could not endure. Here again, we have the distinction between a phenomenon and its static nature. What Nāgārjuna is denying here is not that a phenomenon can endure, but that a static nature can endure (*asthita-bhāvaḥ tiṣṭhati*)? This would appear to be self-contradictory to Nāgārjuna. To say that "presently enduring is enduring" (*tiṣṭhamānaḥ tiṣṭhati*) would be tautological.

All the above mentioned views would pertain to something that has already arisen. Finally, Nāgārjuna insists that we cannot speak of a non-arisen entity as having stasis.

23. *Sthitir nirudhyamānasya na bhāvasyopapadyate,*
yaś cānirudhyamānas tu sa bhāvo nopapadyate.

Duration of an existent that is ceasing is not appropriate. Whatever existent that is non-ceasing is also not appropriate.

MKV(P) p.164; *MKV(V)* p.68.

While the Sautrāntikas (as mentioned earlier) recognized causal efficiency in a phenomenon at the moment of its arising (*utpāda*), and as such they did not have to accept a static moment, the Sarvāstivādins argued that without a static moment a phenomenon cannot generate any causal efficiency (*yadi hi dharmasya sthitir na syāt, tasyātmanyavasthitasya hetvākhyāḥ śaktiprabhavaviśeṣo na syāt, Adv* p.105). A moment of stasis is to be followed by decay (*jarā*) and destruction (*vyaya*). If the Sarvāstivādins were not happy about recognizing causal efficiency of a phenomenon at the moment of its arising, the moment being such a minute instant of time, they will be compelled to admit such causal efficiency in a static moment as it begins to disappear (*nirudhyamāna*). Nāgārjuna's argument here is, therefore, directed agains the Sarvāstivādins when he says: "The duration of an existent that is presently ceasing is not appropriate." However, someone may assume that Nāgārjuna's criticism of the Sarvāstivāda theory of stasis would mean that he is compelled to accept the contrary view, namely, that there is a phenomenon that is not ceasing (*anirudhyamāna*). This latter view he rejects in the second line.

24. *Jarā-maraṇa-dharmeṣu sarva-bhāveṣu sarvadā,*
tiṣṭhanti katame bhāvā ye jarā-maraṇaṃ vinā.

When all existents are always of the nature of decay and death, which existents that are without decay and death can stay?

MKV(P) p.165; *MKV(V)* p.68.

This is a simple rejection of any metaphysical idea pertaining to the real stasis (*sthiti*) of phenomena. This rejection is based upon the empirical notions of decay and death (*jarā-maraṇa*) emphasized by the Buddha himself.

The interpreters of the Abhidharma seem to have experienced difficulty in reconciling the Buddha's description of the "dispositionally conditioned" (*saṃskṛta*) as having three characteristics (*trīṇi lakṣaṇāni*) (*A* 1.152; *Tseng* 12.5 [*Taishō* 2.607c]) with their own theories of momentariness. While the Sarvāstivādins recognized a fourth moment (*caturtham atra vaktavyaṃ syāt, Akb* p.75), splitting up "change of what has remained" (*ṭhitassa aññathatta*) into two moments as stasis (*sthiti*) and decay (*anyathātva, jarā*), the Sautrāntikas admitted only two moments rejecting both stasis and decay. The Theravādins accepted a theory of three moments, once again omitting decay.

The need for recognizing stasis on the part of the Sarvāstivādins and its denial by the Sautrāntikas is discussed at length by Vasubandhu (*Akb* pp.75-76). Both schools assumed (and this is the case with the later Theravādins too) that the Buddha's definition of the "dispositionally conditioned" in terms of three characteristics (as arising, decay or change of what has remained, and ceasing) is for the sake of the unenlightened (*vineyajanārthaṃ*). They argued that it is for this reason that the Buddha utilized the term "appears" (*paññāyati, prajñāyate*) when speaking of these three characteristics. However, this is not the case with the Abhidharma theory of moments (*na tu kṣaṇasya*).

The interpreters of the Abhidharma (hardly realizing that the Abhidharma did not have a theory of moments) were making a distinction between the "discourses" (*sūtra*) and Abhidharma, comparable to the distinction made in the *Saddharmapuṇḍarīka* between the Āgama and Mahāyāna discourses. They assumed that the Abhidharma analysis (i.e., in terms of moments) is for those who really understand the "meaning" (*arthajña*), not for those who merely go after the "texts" (*granthajña*). Thus came to be established the definition of Abhidharma as containing "taintless wisdom" (*prañā 'malā sānucarā 'bhidharmaḥ, AK* i.21).

Nāgārjuna seems to have remained undaunted by such claims on the part of the Buddhist metaphysicians. He was probably aware that all three metaphysical views presented by the Sarvāstivādans, the Sautrāntikas and the later Theravādins (the last was probably not known to him) were incompatible with the Buddha's own conception of change explained in terms of decay and death (*jarā-maraṇa*). Therefore, he perceives no existents (*bhāva*) that are free from decay and death.

25. *Sthityanyayā sthiteḥ sthānaṃ tayaiva ca na yujyate,*
utpādasya yathotpādo nātmanā na parātmanā.

The endurance of an enduring thing based on the endurance of itself or of another is not proper. It is like the absence of arising of arising, either from itself or from another.

MKV(P) p.165; *MKV(V)* p.68.

If stasis (*sthiti*) were to be a distinct event, then the metaphysicians who needed to explain such an event in terms of causality will have to maintain that it could occur either depending upon itself (= self-causation, *svatotpatti*) or based upon another (external causation, *parata utpatti*). Both are not appropriate. This is similar to the criticism made of arising at VII.18-19.

26. *Nirudhyate nāniruddhaṃ na niruddhaṃ nirudhyate,*
tathāpi nirudhyamānaṃ kim ajātaṃ nirudhyate.

That which has not ceased does not cease. That which has ceased also does

not cease. Even so is that which is ceasing. Is it the unborn that ceases?

MKV(P) p.167; *MKV(V)* p.69.

After analysing the metaphysical concepts of arising (*utpāda*) and stasis (*sthiti*), Nāgārjuna settles down to an examination of the problem of cessation or destruction (*nirodha, vyaya*). This criticism follows the method adopted at II.1, excepting the final question: "Is it the unborn that ceases?" If cessation were to be understood in the sense of momentary cessation, it cannot be explained. However, if one were to accept a permanent and eternal substance (*svabhāva*) which would, at the same time, be unborn (*ajāta*), as the Sarvāstivādins did, then that certainly cannot cease to exist.

27. *Sthitasya tāvad bhāvasya nirodho nopapadyate,*
nāsthitasyāpi bhāvasya nirodha upapadyate.

The cessation of an existent that has endured is not appropriate. The cessation of an existent that has not endured is also not appropriate.

MKV(P) p.168; *MKV(V)* p.70.

As mentioned earlier, the Buddha's discourse pertains to "change of what has remained" (*ṭhitassa aññathatta*), where "what has remained" (*ṭhita*) would not imply something that has remained static without any change, but rather "what has become" (*bhūta, bhūtvā*). What has become can then cease to exist. Thus, "change of what has remained" (namely, something that has undergone a process of change or transformation—*vipariṇāma*) can come to an end. Hence, it is meaningful to speak of cessation (*vaya*) after "change of what has remained" (*ṭhitassa aññathatta*).

However, this is not the case with stasis (*sthiti*) as explained by the metaphysicians, primarily because such stasis was distinguished from change (*anyathātva*). As such, stasis implied that something remains static, without change, for a while and then without any cause or reason it would suddenly start changing or would cease to exist. This is the implication of the theory referred to in the first line which is not acceptable to Nāgārjuna.

The second line implies the equally metaphysical and unacceptable view of the Sautrāntikas who argued that an event ceases immediately upon arising without remaining even for one moment (*kṣaṇikasya hi dharmasya vinā sthityā vyayo bhavet, Akb* p.77).

28. *Tayaivāvasthayāvasthā na hi saiva nirudhyate,*
anyayāvasthayāvasthā na cānyaiva nirudhyate.

Indeed, a certain state [of existence] does not cease from a state identical with its own. Nor does a state [of existence] cease from another state different from its own.

MKV(P) p.169; *MKV(V)* p.70.

The principles of self-causation (*svata-utpatti*) and external causation (*parata-utpatti*), rejected in Chapter I, may have to be adopted in order to explain cessation itself (*nirodha*), if the latter were to be understood in the way the Sarvāstivādins and the Sautrāntikas conceived of it. Either cessation will have to occur on its own, or on the basis of another. Such discussions were rampant during the scholastic period in Indian philosophy (especially with the domination of the doctrine of momentariness) when it was argued as to whether destruction is inherent in birth or whether it is brought about by external causes or conditions (see *Adv* pp.106-108). Nāgārjuna's rejection applies to both views.

29. *Yadaiva sarva-dharmāṇām utpādo nopapadyate,*
tadaiva sarva-dharmāṇāṃ nirodho nopapadyate.

Indeed, when the arising of all things is not appropriate, then the cessation of all things is also not appropriate.

MKV(P) p.169; *MKV(V)* p.70.

Note that the term ***sarva*** **(all) is used as an adjective of** ***dharma*****, but not** ***utpāda*** **(arising). This means that Nāgārjuna is not rejecting all forms of arising (*****sarva-utpāda*****) as being unsatisfactory. Rather, he is critical of utilizing the conception** of arising (*utpāda*), discussed previously, to any or all phenomena (*dharma*). If arising in a metaphysical sense cannot be applied to all phenomena, then cessaton (*nirodha*) too, similarly conceived, is inapplicable.

30. *Sataś ca tāvad bhāvasya nirodho nopapadyate,*
ekatve na hi bhāvaś ca nābhāvaś copapadyate.

Furthermore, the cessation of a real existent is not appropriate. Indeed, in the context of identity, neither existence nor non-existence is appropriate.

31. *Asato 'pi na bhāvasya nirodha upapadyate,*
na dvitīyasya śirasaḥ chedanaṃ vidyate yathā.

The cessation of an unreal existent is also not appropriate, just as a second beheading [of a person] is not evident.

MKV(P) pp.169-170; *MKV(V)* pp.70-71.

Nāgārjuna's criticism so far has been confined to arising, stasis and ceasing metaphysically conceived as events in themselves. In the present contexts, he returns to the criticism of the cessation of real existents (*sataḥ bhāvasya*), similar to the criticism of the real existents in Chapter I. Neither existence or non-existence, nor a combination of both, are acceptable to him.

32. *Na svātmanā nirodho 'sti nirodho na parātmanā,*
utpādasya yathotpādo nātmanā na parātmanā.

There is no cessation by itself or by another entity, just as the arising of arising is neither by itself nor by another.

MKV(P) p.171; *MKV(V)* p.71.

This is the final criticism of the identity and non-identity theories as applied to the idea of cessation (*nirodha*). It is comparable to the criticism of arising (*utpāda*) presented at VII.12.

33. *Utpāda-sthiti-bhaṅgānām asidher nāsti saṃskṛtam,*
saṃskṛtasyāprasiddhau ca kathaṃ setsyaty asaṃskṛtam.

With the non-establishment of arising, duration and destruction, the conditioned does not exist. With the non-establishment of the conditioned, how could there be the unconditioned?

MKV(P) p.176; *MKV(V)* p.73.

Arising (*utpāda*), stasis (*sthiti*), and destruction (*bhaṅga*), as explained by the metaphysicians, would not establish their conception of the "conditioned" (*saṃskṛta*). If the "conditioned", so conceived, is not established, indeed there cannot be a similarly formulated conception of the "unconditioned" (*asaṃskṛta*).

One very significant fact that cannot escape a careful scrutiny of the contents of this entire chapter is that, while Nāgārjuna has specifically criticized the three kinds of events (arising, stasis, and ceasing), he has made no criticism whatsoever of decay (*jarā*). In fact, at VII.24, decay and death (*jarā-maraṇa*) were used as arguments for the rejection of stasis (*sthiti*). In short, the Buddha's own conceptions of arising (*uppāda*), ceasing (*vaya, nirodha*), change of what has remained (*ṭhitassa aññathatta*), decay (*jarā*), impermanence (*anicattā*) have been left intact. These have no room for a substantial entity (an *ātman*, a *svabhāva*) and are indeed compatible with the Buddha's famous doctrine of non-substantiality (*anatta*). There could be no reason why a philosopher of Nāgārjuna's calibre could not distinguish the empirical nature of the Buddha's analysis of the "characteristics of the dispositionally conditioned" (*saṅkhatassa saṅkhata-lakkhaṇāni*) from the metaphysical character of the ideas expressed by the interpreters of the Abhidharma.

34. *Yathā mayā yathā svapno gandharva-nagaraṃ yathā,*
tathotpādas tathā sthānaṃ tathā bhaṅga udāhṛtam.

As an illusion, a dream, a city of the *gandharvas*, so have arising, endurance and destruction been exemplified.

MKV(P) p.177; *MKV(V)* p.73.

If the analysis of the contents of the present chapter is correct, then there could be no question that the illusory character as exemplified by "dream" and "the city of the *gandharvas*" is appplicable only to the metaphysical ideas of arising, stasis and ceasing as presented by the interpreters of the Abhidharma, and not to any one of the concepts of arising, ceasing, decay, change, and impermanence formulated by the Buddha and accepted by Nāgārjuna himself.

The Buddha utilized the similies of foam (*pheṇa*), bubble (*bubbula*), mirage (*marīci*), trunk of a plantain tree (*kadalī*), and illusion (*māyā*) in order to illustrate the non-substantiality of the five aggregates (*S* 3.142). Nāgārjuna is here using comparable similies for the same purpose. A careless applicaton of these similies to explain all forms of ideas, whether substantialist or non-substantialist, has given rise to enormous misunderstandings relating to the Buddhist doctrine.

CHAPTER EIGHT
Examination of Action and the Agent
(Karma-kāraka--parīkṣā)

1. *Sadbhūtaḥ kārakaḥ karma sadbhūtaṃ na karoty ayaṃ,*
kārako nāpy asadbhūtaḥ karmasadbhūtam īhate.

This really existent agent does not perform a really existent action. Neither is it intended that a really non-existent agent performs a really non-existent action.

MKV(P) p.180; *MKV(V)* p.75.

The examination of the "dispositionally conditioned" (*saṃskṛta*) naturally led Nāgārjuna to another major philosophical problem that has been the subject of much misunderstanding among the Buddhists as well as the non-Buddhists, namely, the doctrine of karma.

In the early discourses, karma and *saṃskāra* (and, therefore, *saṃskṛta*) are mutually related. While karmas are said to form *saṃskāras* (see *M* 2.121), *saṃskāras* themselves are determinants of karma. The Buddha who denied an eternal soul or self (*ātman*) was often confronted by skeptics who raised the question as to how karmas performed by a "no-self" can affect a person (*anatta-katāni kammāni kaṃ* (*kataṃ*) *attānaṃ phusissanti*, *M* 3.119; *S* 3.103). This is not, however, the problem of moral responsibility (*karma-phala*), which Nāgārjuna takes up later in Chapter XVII. The present problem relates mostly to the nature of an action and an agent (*karma-kāraka*). When this latter question was raised in the discourses, very often it is said that there is no substantial agent who is the author of actions. What is generally understood as a substantial being (*satta*) or person (*puggala*) is nothing more than a "lump of dispositions" (*saṅkhāra-puñja*, *S* 1.134), which is another name for the five aggregates (*khandha*), each receiving its form conditioned by the *saṅkhāras* (*S* 3.87; *Tsa* 2.14 [*Taishō* 2.11c]). Neither the "lump of dispositions" nor the aggregates were considered to be substantial, that is, having a reality of their own. The "dispositions" (*saṅkhāra*), which are acquired by the person and, therefore, impermanent, are also responsible for conditioning that personality. Thus, according to early Buddhism, neither the person nor the aggregates (one of which is disposition, *saṅkhāra*) have any substantial reality. In the first place, the dispositions themselves are impermanent (*vayadhammā saṅkhārā, D* 2.156) and, secondly, all phenomena, including all persons or aggregates, are non-substantial (*sabbe dhammā anattā, M* 2.228; *S* 3.133; 4.401; *A* 1.286; *Tsa* 10.7 [*Taishō* 2.668]).

Yet, when the canonical Abhidharma texts rejected a real self or soul (*atta*) and listed the various physical and psychological factors that go to constitute the human personality, the interpreters of these physical and psychological factors transgressed the limits of speculation and admitted the real existence of these various factors. Thus came to be the theory of the substantiality of elements propounded by the Sarvāstivādins.

Therefore, in his attempt to establish the non-substantiality of all elements (*dharma-nairātmya*), Nāgārjuna was compelled to examine the concepts of action (*karma*) as well as the agent of such action (*kāraka*) in the present section of his treatise (leaving the question regarding moral responsiblity for a detailed discussion at a later and more appropriate time). As explained previously, Nāgārjuna realized that the concepts of substantial existence (*sat, astitva*) as well as absolute non-existence (*asat, nāstitva*) were two extremes to be avoided in any discussion of action and agent.

2. *Sadbhūtasya kriyā nāsti karma ca syād akartṛkam,*
sadbhūtasya kriyā nāsti kartā ca syād akarmakaḥ.

A really existent entity has no activity. Therefore, acton would be without an agent. A really existent entity has no activity. Therefore, even an agent would be without action.

MKV(P) p.181; *MKV(V)* p.75.

This is an extremely interesting analysis of the implications as well as the consequences of admitting a really existing entity (*sadbhūta*), a soul or a self (*ātman, pudgala*) or even a substance (*svabhāva*). The concept of a self (*ātman*) as envisaged in the substantialist traditions, like the *Upaniṣads*, is one of pure entity, permanent and eternal, unaffected by the changes taking place in the phenomenal world. It is beyond all forms of duality and multiplicity. The concept of substance, even though rarely defined as a "pure entity," yet partakes of all other characteristics, namely, permanence, eternality, non-duality, and non-multiplicity. This means that any activity, any change in quality, in quantity, in character, or in form would be merely superficial. The real or the essential is eternal. Such implications of the Sarvāstivāda theory of substance (*svabhāva*) were noted earlier (see Chapter I). If the cause and effect were to be identical in essence, then their difference becomes superficial. A cause becomes un-productive and would be like a tree stump that remains motionless (*vañjha kūṭaṭṭha, D* 1.14, 56; *S* 3.211; *M* 1.517; *avicalita-nityatva*, see Kalupahana, *Causality*, p. 28).

Hence Nāgārjuna's statement: "A really existing entity is without activity." This assertion leads to two rather disastrous consequences, especially for the doctrine of karma; either an action (*karma*) will be rendered agent-less (*a-kartṛka*) or an agent (*kartṛ*) would be action-less (*a-karmaka*).

3. *Karoti yady asadbhūto 'sadbhūtaṃ karma kārakaḥ,*
ahetukaṃ bhavet karma kartā cāhetuko bhavet.

If a non-existent agent were to perform a non-existent action, the action would be without a cause, and the agent too would be without a cause.

MKV(P) p.182; *MKV(V)* pp.75-76.

If one were to accept the view which is contrary to the one mentioned at VIII.2, that is, a non-existent entity performing a non-existent action, then both agent (*kartṛ*) and action (*karma*) would be rendered cause-less (*a-hetuka*).

VIII.2-3 thus turn out to be a clear warning against the universal and indiscriminate application of the examples of "illusion" (*māyā*), "dream" (*svapna*) and the "city of the *gandharvas*" (*gandharva-nagara*), especially in the matter of explaining "emptiness" (*śūnyatā*) at VII.34 and elsewhere.

4. *Hetāv asati kāryaṃ ca kāraṇaṃ ca na vidyate,*
tad abhāve kriyā kartā karaṇaṃ ca na vidyate.

When a cause does not exist, both the effect and the sufficient condition

are not evident. When these are non-existent, activity, agent and performance of action are also not evident.

MKV(P) p.182; *MKV(V)* p.76.

Further implications of the denial of a cause at VIII.3 are highlighted here. Not only would it negate an effect (*kārya*) or a sufficient condition (*kāraṇa*), it would also lead to the abandoning of activity, agent as well as action, none of which is acceptable to Nāgārjuna.

5. *Dharmādharmau na vidyete kriyādīnām asaṃbhave,*
dharme cāsaty adharme ca phalṃ tajjaṃ na vidyate.

With the non-occurrence of activity, etc., good and bad are also not evident. When both good and bad do not exist, a fruit arising from these would also not be evident.

MKV(P) p.183; *MKV(V)* pp.76-77.

Inada's rendering of this verse clearly indicates his faithful adherence to the transcendentalist interpretation of Nāgārjuna offered by previous interpreters like Stcherbatsky, Murti, Conze, and most of the Japanese scholars. In spite of Kumārajīva's very clear rendering into Chinese, Inada translates *dharma* and *adharma* as factors and non-factors respectively (p.73). While it is true that the term *dharma* is used in the Buddhist texts, both in an ontological sense (referring to "phenomena") and in a more ethical sense (meaning "good"), there is no evidence at all that the negative term *a-dharma* was ever used in the former sense. A careful examination of the contexts in which it occurs provides sufficient evidence that the term meant "bad" and, hence synonymous with *akusala*. Furthermore, of all the terms used to refer to an effect, the term *phala* occurring in this verse is invariably used in the sense of "fruit," having a moral connotation.

The present verse, therefore, provides unmistakable evidence that Nāgārjuna was upholding the moral philosophy advocated by the Buddha in his first discourse—the *Dhammacappavattana-sutta*—which lays down a middle path between the two extremes, which in its turn is based upon the philosophical middle position presented in the "*Discourse to Kātyāyana*."

The belief in substantial existence or eternalism (*atthitā, sassata*) leads to self-denial (*atta-kilamathānuyoga*) and the idea of nihilistic non-existence or annihilationism (*n'atthitā, uccheda*) contributes to self-indulgence (*kāma-sukhallikānuyoga*) (see Introduction). Verses VIII.3-4 refer to the substantialist and annihilationist views of karma, both of which lead to the abandoning of a moral life (including moral responsibility) as understood by the Buddha. Having spoken of *artha* (effect, fruit, consequence) in relation to *pratyaya* (cause, condition) in Chapter I, Nāgārjuna is here addressing himself to the question regarding the "fruit of action" (*karma-phala*), a detailed treatment of this problem being reserved for a later occasion (Chapter XVII). In the present chapter, Nāgārjuna's intention is to explain the non-substantiality of the "agent" and the "action," rather than settle the question of moral responsiblity. However, he could not help referring to the "fruits of action," primarily because the metaphysical notions of "agent" and "action" contributed to their very denial.

6. *Phale 'sati na mokṣāya na svargāyopapadyate,*
mārgaḥ sarva-kriyāṇāṃ ca nairarthakyaṃ prasajyate.

When the fruit does not exist, the path of release or of heaven is not appropriate. This would imply the futility of all activity.

MKV(P) pp.183-184; *MKV(V)* p.77.

Not only is Nāgārjuna interested in the "ultimate fruit" (*paramārtha*), i.e., freedom from suffering (*mokṣa*), he is also concerned with the fruits (*artha, phala*) that actions can generate as human beings proceed along the moral path (*mārga*) gradually leading to that "ultimate fruit." Hence his interest in "heaven" (*svarga*), so often discussed in the "discourses" as the "fruits" enjoyed by the "wayfarer." As far as Nāgārjuna is concerned, human actions are rendered "fruitless" or "meaningless" (*nir-artha*), if one were to adhere to either a theory of eternalism or of annihilationism.

7. *Kārakaḥ sad-asad-bhūtaḥ sad asat kurute na tat,*
paraspara-viruddhaṃ hi saccāsacc-aikataḥ kutaḥ.

An agent who is both existent and non-existent does not perform an action that is both existent and non-existent, for they are self-contradictory. Where can existence and non-existence co-exist?

MKV(P) p.185; *MKV(V)* p.77.

After criticizing the substantialist as well as the annihilationist views relating to agent and action, Nāgārjuna examines the theory that attempts to combine them. This follows the criticism at I.13. For Nāgārjuna, contradictory predicates such as existence (*sat*) and non-existence (*asat*) cannot be applied to the same thing.

8. *Satā ca kriyate nāsan nāsatā kriyate ca sat,*
kartrā sarve prasajyante doṣās tatra ta eva hi.

A non-existent action is not performed by a presently existing agent. Nor is an existent action performed by a presently non-existent agent. Indeed, if that were to be the case, all errors relating to the agents [mentioned earlier] would follow.

MKV(P) p.185; *MKV(V)* p.78.

Existence (*sat*) and non-existence (*asat*) applied to the agent and action will produce some other alternative theories than those mentioned earlier, e.g.:

i. A presently existent agent (*santa)* performs a non-existent (*asat*) action, and
ii. a presently non-existent agent (*asanta*) performs an existent (*sat*) action.

Here, the agent is described by means of a *present participle (santa)*.

9. *Nāsadbhūtaṃ na sadbhūtaḥ sad-asad-bhūtam eva vā,*
karoti kārakaḥ karma pūrvoktair eva hetubhiḥ.

For reasons stated above, an agent who has come to be existent does not perform an action that is non-existent or both existent and non-existent.

10. *Nāsadbhūto 'pi sadbhūtaṃ sad-asad-bhūtam eva vā,*
karoti kārakaḥ karma pūrvoktair eva hetubhiḥ.

For reasons stated above, an agent who has come to be non-existent does not perform an action that is existent or both existent and non-existent.

11. *Karoti sad-asad-bhūto na san nāsac ca kārakaḥ,*
karma tat tu vijānīyāt pūrvoktair eva hetubhiḥ.

An agent that has come to be both existent and non-existent does not perform an action that exists and does not exist. This too should be understood in terms of the reasons adduced above.

MKV(P) pp.186-187; *MKV(V)* p.78-79.

While VIII.8 utilized the present participle to refer to the agent, the present verses employ the past participle: (i) an agent who has come to be existent (*sadbhūta*); (ii) an agent who has come to be non-existent (*asadbhūta*), and (iii) an agent who has come to be both existent and non-existent (*sadasadbhūta*).

VIII.10 is not found in the Chinese version.

12. *Pratītya kārakaḥ karma taṃ pratītya ca kārakaṃ,*
karma pravartate nānyat paśyāmaḥ siddhi-kāraṇam.

An agent proceeds depending upon action and action proceeds depending upon the agent. We do not perceive any other way of establishing [them].

MKV(P) p.189; *MKV(V)* p.79.

After criticizing the metaphysical interpretations of agent (*kāraka*) and action (*karma*), Nāgārjuna gives a positive description of both in terms of the principle of "dependent arising" (*pratītyasamutpāda*). Indeed, a more positive assertion such as, "We do not perceive any other way of establishing [them]" (*nānyat siddhi-kāraṇaṃ paśyāmaḥ*), is rarely met with in the *Kārikās*.

13. *Evaṃ vidyād upādānaṃ vyutsargād iti karmaṇaḥ,*
kartuś ca karma-kartṛbhyāṃ śeṣān bhāvān vibhāvayet.

Following this method of the rejection of agent and action, one should understand grasping. The remaining existents should be critically examined in terms of the concepts of action and agent.

MKV(P) pp.189-190; *MKV(V)* p.80.

Nāgārjuna began the chapter with the problem of grasping (*upādānā*). If he were to accept the substantialist notions of agent and action, he could not explain grasping. During the course of this chapter, he was able to analyse the metaphysical (and, therefore, unacceptable) implications of the substantialist views such as the denial of moral responsibility and freedom. The abandoning (*vyutsarga*) refers to the giving up of such metaphysical views. After giving up such metaphysical views, he presented an alternative view, namely, dependent arising of both agent and action (VIII.12). Such a view allows for a satisfactory explanations of "grasping" (*upādāna*). A life with reduced grasping contributes to worldly fruits such as the attainment of "heavenly" bliss. The complete elimination of grasping culminates in perfect freedom (*mokṣa*) or the ultimate fruit.

This does not mean that Nāgārjuna has no conception of an agent or an action or moral responsibility or freedom. It is merely the renunciation of wrong views and the adoption of more appropriate explanations of these phenomena. Such explanations, Nāgārjuna concludes, should be extended to all phenomena.

CHAPTER NINE
Examination of the Prior Entity
(Pūrva-parīkṣā)

1. *Darśana-śravaṇādīni vedanādīni cāpy atha,*
bhavanti yasya prāg ebhyaḥ so 'stīty eke vadanty uta.

"For whomsoever there exists seeing, hearing, etc., and feeling, etc., he exists prior to these." So do some declare.

2. *Kathaṃ hy avidyamānasya darśanādi bhaviṣyati,*
bhāvasya tasmāt prāg ebhyaḥ so 'sti bhāvo vyavasthitaḥ.

How can there be seeing, etc. of an existent who is not evident? Therefore, it is determined that, prior to these things, such an existent is.

MKV(P) p.192; MKV(V) p.81.

While the previous chapter is devoted to the refutation of the Cartesian enterprise adopted later on by some of the Buddhist metaphysicians, the present chapter seems to be taking up specifically the Kantian project, namely, the assumption of a primordial condition for all forms of knowledge, including the *cogito*. Hence the question regarding prior existence (*pūrva*).

He could not have been unaware of the Buddha's attitude toward the problem of the past (*pubbanta*). For a radical empiricist like the Buddha, knowledge of the past (*atītaṃse ñāṇa*) is as important as any other knowledge (*D* 3.275). Indeed, knowledge of "dependent arising" (*paṭiccasamuppāda*) is invariably based upon such knowledge. Yet, when the pursuit of that knowledge is attempted beyond its limits, that is, when one tries to achieve absolute certainty with regard to such knowledge, one ends up in speculations regarding the past (*pubbantānudiṭṭhi*) rather than knowledge (*ñāṇa*). The *Brahmajāla-suttanta* refers to a whole host of metaphysical views presented by those who were involved in such speculations (*D* 1.13 ff., *pubbanta-kappikā* = *pūrvānta-kalpikā*).

Nāgārjuna was thus convinced that the concepts of the *cogito*, the *ātman* or *svabhāva* were formulated by the metaphysicians who were attempting to know the past with certainty. No other explanation would satisfy their yearning for certainty regarding the past. Permanent self, eternal substance, pre-existing *cogito*, a transcendental unity of apperception—these could account for any breaks or interruptions in human experience as well as their continuity. The symbolism of the charioteer (*Kaṭha Upaniṣad* 3.3-6) as well as the example of the two birds, one enjoying the fruit, the other watching (*Muṇḍaka Upaniṣad* 3.1.1), adopted so enthusiastically by the Brahmanical thinkers, were gradually making inroads into Buddhist philosophical thinking. The Sammitīyas (if not identical with, at least related to the Sautrantika school) were accused of permitting such a belief into the Buddhist fold. So says Candarkīrti. Yet, Sarvāstivāda, with its *svabhāva*-metaphysics is no less culpable of this deviation than the Sammitīyas with their *pudgala*-metaphysics or even the later Theravadins with the *bhavaṅga*-metaphysics. Nāgārjuna begins the present chapter with a statement, not only of this theory, but also of the rationalizations of those who formulated such a theory.

3. *Darśana-śravaṇādibhyo vedanādībhya eva ca,*
yaḥ prāg vyavasthito bhāvaḥ kena prajñapyate 'tha saḥ.

Whatever existent is determined as existing prior to seeing, hearing, etc., and also feeling, etc., by what means is he [it] made known?

MKV(P) p.193; *MKV(V)* p.81.

As usual, Nāgārjuna's first objection against positing such an entity that exists prior to the experiences such as seeing, hearing, etc. as well as feeling, etc., is epistemological. This objection should serve as warning against those who believe that Nāgārjuna recognizes a special intuitive non-sensuous experience through which the so-called "ultimate reality" (*paramārtha*?) is known. In fact, this question on the part of Nāgārjuna is a clear indication of the fact that he was quite aware of the sort of empiricism advocated by the Buddha, especially in his "Discourse on Everything (*Sabba-sutta*, *S* 4.15; see also Kalupahana, "A Buddhist tract on empiricism," in *PEW* 19 (1969):65-67).

4. *Vināpi darśanādīni yadi cāsau vyavasthitaḥ,*
amūny api bhaviṣyanti vinā tena na saṃśayaḥ.

If he is determined as existing even without seeing, etc., undoubtedly even these [i.e., seeing, etc.] will exist without him.

MKV(P) p.193; *MKV(V)* p.81.

After questioning the empirical validity of such an assumption, Nāgārjuna is here raising a logical objection. If a prior existing entity can be determined without depending upon its experiences such as seeing, then it should also be logically possible that such experiences as seeing can be determined without a prior entity. Indeed, this logical conclusion seems to be so strong that Nāgārjuna is willing to use the term *asaṃśaya* ("without doubt") to describe it.

5. *Ajyate kenacit kaścit kiṃcit kenacid ajyate,*
kutaḥ kiṃcid vinā kaścit kiṃcit kaṃcid vinā kutaḥ.

Someone is made known by something. Something is made known by someone. How could there be someone without something and something without someone?

MKV(P) p.194; *MKV(V)* p.81

Here then is Nāgārjuna's method of explaining (*vyākhyāna*) the relationship between substance and attribute. It is a relation of dependence and neither the substance nor the attribute can be understood properly if they were to be conceived of as independent entities, each having its own nature.

6. *Sarvebhyo darśanādibhyaḥ kaścit pūrvo na vidyate,*
ajyate darśanādīnām anyena punar anyadā.

Someone is not evident prior to all of seeing, etc. Again, on different occasions, one could be made known by things different from seeing, etc.

MKV(P) p.194; *MKV(V)* p.82.

While rejecting the view that there is an entity prior to all forms of experiences such as seeing, Nāgārjuna is, at the same time, trying to avoid the other extreme of assuming two different entities when the experiences are different. Avoiding a metaphysical notion of identity does not mean that one is invariably committed to an equally metaphysical notion of difference. Just as much as identity can be explained on the basis of an empirical notion of dependence, Nāgārjuna seems to assert that difference can and need to be accounted for on an empirical basis.

7. *Sarvebhyo darśanādibhyo yadi pūrvo na vidyate,*
ekaikasmāt kathaṃ pūrvo darśanādeḥ sa vidyate.

If someone existing prior to all of seeing, etc. is not evident, how can someone existing prior to each of seeing, etc. be evident.

MKV(P) p.195; *MKV(V)* p.82.

It seems that here Nāgārjuna is referring to an interesting assumption underlying an identity theory. The notion of self (*ātman*) or substance (*svabhāva*) would generally be presented in order to account for the continuity in a large number of dissimilar experiences. Taking that premise, Nāgārjuna is arguing that if it is not possible to discover someone or entity that pre-exists all forms of different experiences, then such a person or entity would not be available even in the case of individual experiential situations. A momentary *cogito* would be as impossible as a permanent and eternal self (*ātman*).

8. *Draṣṭā sa eva sa śrotā sa eva yadi vedakaḥ,*
ekaikasmād bhavet pūrvaṃ evaṃ caitan na yujyate.

If a seer is, at the same time, a hearer and feeler, then someone would exist prior to each one [of the functions]. But this is not proper.

MKV(P) p.195; *MKV(V)* pp.82-83.

Only if the seer, hearer, and experiencer are absolutely identical, then he will pre-exist each individual experiential situation. Nāgārjuna rightly denies any such absolute identity. He was probably assuming that even in the act of seeing the same object at different times, there cannot be absolute identity, let alone in the acts of seeing different objects. The reason is not that human experiences or even the objects of experience change every moment, but that the circumstances under which such experiences take place could vary. (For a discussion of the perceptual flux, see William James, *Some Problems of Philosophy*, Cambridge, Massachusetts: Harvard University Press, 1979, pp.31-32.)

9. *Draṣṭānya eva śrotānyo vedako 'nyaḥ punar yadi,*
sati syād draṣṭari śrotā bahutvaṃ cātmanāṃ bhavet.

If seer and hearer and feeler are different, then, when there is a seer, there also would be a hearer, and as such there would be a plurality of selves.

MKV(P) pp.196-197; *MKV(V)* p.83.

If absolute identity is not a possibility, absolute difference also would be impossible, for in that case within each stream of experience there would be plurality of distinct selves or entities corresponding to the different experiences.

10. *Darśana-śravaṇādīni vedanādīni cāpy atha,*
bhavanti yebhyas teṣv eṣa bhūteṣv api na vidyate.

It [i.e., the self] is not evident in the elements from which seeing, hearing, etc., and feeling, etc. come to be.

MKV(P) p.179; *MKV(V)* p.83.

In the Chapter V on the "elements" (*dhātu*), Nāgārjuna examined the theories presented by the metaphysicians relating to the physical foundations of human experiences such as seeing, hearing, etc. Even though the Abhidharma classified the first five sensory organs as well as their objects under the category of derived matter (*upādā rūpa*), there was no indication that this involved the assertion of any self or substance in the individual elements that go to constitute these sensory organs and objects. The interpreters of the Abhidharma, as reiterated earlier, were responsible for such metaphysics. Nāgārjuna is here going back to the analysis in the discourses as well as in the Abhidharma where, not only in the combination of aggregates or elements, but also in each individual element, there is no recognition of such a metaphysical self or substance (see also Chapter IV).

11. *Darśana-śravaṇādīni vedanādīni cāpy atha,*
na vidyate ced yasya sa na vidyunta imāny api.

If he, to whom belongs seeing, hearing, etc. and feeling, etc., is not evident, then even these would not be evident.

MKV(P) p.198; *MKV(V)* p.84.

Nāgārjuna starts with the negation of an opponent's view that there is a prior entity to which the experiences such as seeing and hearing belongs. The implication of the opponent's view is that the experiences of seeing, etc. are independent elements appropriated by an equally independent prior entity. As such, for Nāgārjuna, it is not merely the prior entity that is unacceptable, but also the experiences themselves as conceived of by the opponent. This, therefore, is not a simple denial of any and all forms of description of experience. Rather, it is a particular type of discrimination resorted to by the metaphysician that is rejected.

12. *Prāk ca yo darśanādibhyaḥ sāmpratam cordhvam eva ca,*
na vidyate 'sti nāstīti nivṛttās tatra kalpanā.

Wherein someone prior to, simultaneous with or posterior to, seeing, etc. is not evident, therein thoughts of existence and non-existence are also renounced.

MKV(P) p.199; *MKV(V)* p.84.

The existence of an independent entity in the experiential process, whether it be prior to experience, simultaneous with it, or posterior to it, is rejected by Nāgārjuna. This does not mean that he was willing to accept the independent occurrence of impressions coming one after another in rapid succession with no causal connectoins, as the Sautrāntikas believed. In these particular contexts (*tatra*), Nāgārjuna is ready to abandon the thoughts (*kalpanā*) of existence and non-existence (*asti nāstīti*) in the way they were understood by the metaphysicians.

CHAPTER TEN
Examination of Fire and Fuel
(Agnīndhana-parīkṣā)

1. *Yad indhanaṃ sa ced agnir ekatvaṃ kartṛ-karmaṇoḥ,*
anyaś ced indhanād agnir indhanād apy ṛte bhavet.

If fire were to be fuel, then there would be identity of agent and action. If fire were to be different from fuel, then it would exist even without the fuel.

MKV(P) p.202; *MKV(V)* p.86.

Chapter IX, as pointed out, was devoted to an examination of the *cause* or *foundation* of the speculations that eventually led to the belief in metaphysical notions such as "self" (*ātman*) or "substance" (*svabhāva*). Such speculations pertained to the "past" (*pūrva*). Why should that analysis be followed by an examination of the metaphor of "fire and fuel" (*agnīndhana*)? What is its relevance?

Only a glance at the controversies going on during Nāgārjuna's day can provide justification for this chapter. Once again, Vasubandhu comes to our assistance. In his *Abhidharmakośa-bhāṣya*, he was recording a controversy among the Buddhists that was continued for centuries before him. And that controversy could not have escaped the attention of Nāgārjuna.

The ninth chapter of the *Abhidharmakośa* is an appendix (*Akb* pp.461-479; translated into English by T. I. Stcherbatsky, *The Soul Theory of the Buddhists,* in the *Bulleting de l'Academie des Sciences de Russie*, Petrograd, 1920, reprinted 1970, Bharatiya Vidya Prakasan, Varanasi). It deals with the controversial views of the Vātsīputriyas (considered to be the same as the Arya-Sammitīyas, see *Sakv* p.699) who propounded the view that there is a "real person" (*santaṃ pudgalaṃ*). In the discussion that follows, the Vātsīputriyas are made to admit that this "person" is neither a substance (*dravya*), like material form (*rūpa*), etc., nor a mere designation (*prajñapti*), a mere name like "milk" (*kṣīra*), this latter being nothing more than an aggregate of substances (*dravya*). When the Sautrāntika Vasubandhu pressed his questions as to whether the person is real or nominal, the Vātsīputriyas fell back upon the metaphor of "fire and fuel" (*agnīndhana*) in order to illustrate their point of aview (*Akb* p.461). This metaphor is then discussed at length and seems to have been *the* most important means by which the Vātsīputriyas attempted to justify their conception of a "person."

Therefore, it is understandable why Nāgārjuna, after dealing with the question regarding a substantial agent (*kāraka*, Chapter VIII) and also the motivation for such a theory (namely, the desire to trace one's identity to the past, *pūrva*, Chapter IX), would settle down to an examination of a singularly important metaphor used by the substantialists to justify their conception of an agent.

It may be necessary to keep in mind that Vasubandhu, who wrote the *Abhidharmakośa*, was a Sautrāntika who believed that a "person" (*pudgala*) is a mere designation (*prajñapti*) without any reality. Hence his agreement with the nominalist position (*Akb* p.461, *atha prajñaptiḥ, vayam apy evaṃ brūmaḥ*). The substantialist position (*dravya-vāda*) was therefore identified with the Sarvāstivāda view. Even though the Sarvāstivādins did not actually propound a substantialist theory of a person, their conception of substance (*svabhāva*) could not escape such implications (see *Sakv* p.362, *svabhāvata ity ātmataḥ*).

However, even if by implication, the Sarvāstivāda theory were to be identified with the substantialist view of a person (*pudgala*), what sort of conception were the Vātsīputriyas upholding? They were looking for a middle position between substantialism (*dravya*) and nominalism (*prajñapti*). The discussion in terms of the metaphor of "fire and fuel" was, therefore, intended to overcome such duality.

The argument follows thus: "Without fuel, there would be no designation of fire. Yet, fire cannot be designated as something different from fuel, nor as something identical," (*Akb* p.462, *Na hi vinendhanenāgniḥ prajñapyate, na cānya indhanād agniḥ śakyate prajñapayituṃ nāpy ananyaḥ*). Similarly, a person is neither identical nor different from the aggregates. (If we are to accept the negative interpretation of the Nāgārjunian dialectic, as is often presented by most modern scholars, the Mādhyamika position would be no different from that of the Vātsīputriyas as described above.)

When the question was raised as to which of the six sense organs provide knowledge of the "person," the Vātsīputriyas answered: "By means of all six," (*ṣaḍbhir api*, *Akb* p.463). They argued: "A 'person' is recognized depending upon visually cognized material form (*cakṣur-vijñeyāni rūpāṇi*). As such a person should be declared as being visually cognizable and visually not cognizable; it is neither material form nor not material form."

These and other arguments seem to indicate that the Vātsīputriyas were following a dialectical method at arriving at a higher synthesis by avoiding the dichotomies of thesis and antithesis. This, unfortunately, is the view attributed to Nāgārjuna. The contents of the present chapter needs to be carefully evaluated in the light of the Vātsīputriya conception of a person.

When the Vātsīputriyas maintained that fire and fuel are neither identical nor different, they were actually admitting both. For them, both fire and fuel are each constituted of four substances (*ubhayam aṣṭa-dharmakaṃ*), the only difference is that in the case of fire the heat element (*uṣṇam*) predominates, whereas in the fuel it is latent. In this way, they are both identical or non-different. Yet they are different in terms of the difference in time (*bhinnakālatvāt*). Thus, the negative description of the Vātsīputriyas is not meant as a negation of metaphysical views, as it was in the case of Nāgārjuna (see above, commentary on the dedicatory verses), but an assertion of both identity and difference in order to arrive at a higher synthesis. No such move is found in Nāgārjuna when he criticizes the identity of fire and fuel in the above verse. For him identity of fire and fuel means identity of agent and action. If they were different, then each could be independent.

2. *Nitya-pradīpta eva syād apradīpana-hetukaḥ,*
punar ārambha-vaiyarthyam evaṃ cākarmakaḥ sati.

A burning without a cause would be eternally aflame. Furthermore, its commencement will be rendered meaningless [useless]. When that happens, it will be without a function.

MKV(P) p.203; *MKV(V)* p.86.

The identity of fire and fuel recognized by the Vātsīputriyas (as explained in terms of the eight elements, *aṣṭa-dharmaka*, see above) would lead to the view that both fire and fuel are burning all the time (*nitya-pradīpta*), for the caloric element (*uṣṇa*) is found in both, the difference being quantitative rather than qualitative. This further leads to the denial of the empirical fact of starting a fire. If fire and fuel are always burning, then fire would be deprived of any specific function. Indeed, the Buddha's use of the metaphor of the fire at *M* 1.487 is non-substantialist in implication He wanted to show that just as fire is not stored up anywhere when it is extinguished, even so a "freed one" (*tathāgata*) does not exist in eternal bliss after death (*param maraṇā*). Nāgārjuna's criticism of the metaphor of "fire and fuel" seems to follow closely the Buddha's own explanation of the phenomenon of fire.

3. *paratra nirapekṣatvād apradīpana-hetukaḥ,*
punar ārambha-vaiyarthyaṃ nitya-pradīptaḥ prasajyate.

A burning without a cause, because it is not contingent on another and, therefore, eternally aflame, would imply the meaninglessness of its commencement.

MKV(P) p.203; *MKV(V)* p.86.

A substantialist view of fire makes it independent of other elements or things. Hence, all the implications mentioned at X.2 will follow from such a view.

4. *Tatraitasmād idhyamānam indhanaṃ bhavatīti cet,*
kenedhyatām indhanaṃ, tat tāvan matram idaṃ yadā.

Herein, if it is assumed that fuel is the present burning and, therefore, that [i.e., buring] is merely this [i.e., fuel], by what is fuel being burnt?

MKV(P) p.204; *MKV(V)* p.87.

The substantialist point of view expressed at X.2 is further analysed here. If fuel already has the caloric element (*uṣṇa*) and, therefore, is already burning (*idhyamāna*), one could not only raise the question as to when it started burning but also inquire as to what it is that brings about that burning.

5. *Anyo na prāpsyate 'prāpto na dhakṣyaty adahan punaḥ,*
na nirvāsyaty anirvāṇaḥ sthāsyate vā svaliṅgavān.

[Fuel] that is different is not reached; the unreached is not ignited. Furthermore, that which is not ignited does not cease. That which does not cease remains, like one that has its own mark.

MKV(P) p.205; *MKV(V)* p.87.

If it is assumed that fire and fuel are different, a further series of questions arise. Difference in the present case implies absolute distinction or independence. As such, one entity cannot reach up to another. Fire cannot reach the fuel. When fire cannot reach the fuel, it cannot burn. That which does not burn remains for ever and does not cease. This explains the vicious circle the metaphysical speculations can lead to.

6. *Anya evendhanād agnir indhanaṃ prāpnuyād yadi,*
strī saṃprāpnoti puruṣaṃ puruṣaś ca striyaṃ yathā.

If fire is different from fuel it would reach the fuel, just as a woman would reach for a man and a man for a woman.

MKV(P) p.206; *MKV(V)* p.88.

If fire and fuel were considered to be different yet complementary, then Nāgārjuna is willing to allow some sort of mutual relationship. He perceives such a relationship bewteen a man and a woman.

Unfortunately, here again we have a negative interpretation from Candrakīrti. Without taking much trouble to examine the import of the metaphor of "man and woman" used by Nāgārjuna, Candrakīrti assumes that the relationship exemplified by it is meaningless (*dṛṣṭānta-vaiyarthyaṃ*). On the contrary, Nāgārjuna is throwing the gauntlet at his opponent asking him to show that the sort of relationship that exists between a man and a woman can also be obtained between fire and fuel *as the opponent has conceived of them*.

Indeed, there could not be much difficulty in understanding the empirical relationship between a man and a woman. Because of their complementarity, they are attracted to each other. Such a relationship is clearly expressed by the Buddha in the first two discourses in the *Aṅguttara-nikāya* (1.1-2). Yet the Buddha never attempted to go beyond that empirical relationship to inquire as to how it all happened. Such an inquiry was undoubtedly the foundation of the speculations recorded in the *Upaniṣads*. Describing the origin of the universe from a single unitary "self" (*ātman*), the *Bṛhadāraṇyaka Upaniṣad* (I.4.3-4) says:

> He, verily, had no delight. Therefore he who is alone has no delight. He desired a second. He became as large as a woman and a man in close embrace. He caused that self to fall into two parts.

From that arose husband and wife. . . . He became united with her. From that human beings were produced.

She thought, "How can he unite with me after having produced me from himself?" Well, let me hide myself. She became a cow, the other became a bull and was united with her and from that cows were born. . . . Thus, indeed, he produced everything whatever exists in pairs, down to the ants.

This is the sort of answer that emerges from an inquiry that is not only directed at understanding the absolute origin of things, but also their substantiality. The metaphor of the fire and fuel were utilized by the Vātsīputriyas, not merely to understand the relationship between two empirical events, but also to justify the conception of a prior existent "person" (*pudgala*), no different from the pre-existent "self" (*ātman*) assumed in the *Upaniṣads*, which is clearly expresed in the metaphor of "man and woman."

Perceptive Nāgārjuna was thus aware of the motivations of those who presented the metaphor. In the present verse he was therefore allowing the possibility of fire and fuel having a complementary relationship. However, if any other implication is drawn from such a relationship, Nāgārjuna was ready to expose its untenability. This he does in the verses that follow.

7. *Anya evendhanād agnir indhanaṃ kāman āpnuyāt,*
agnīndhane yadi syātām anyonyena tiraskṛte.

The fire that is different from fuel may reach the fuel only if fire and fuel were to exist mutually separated.

MKV(P) p.206; *MKV(V)* p.88.

Here again, Nāgārjuna is qualifying the sort of relationship that may obtain between fire and fuel if they are attracted to one another. One of the first conditions would be that they are separate. Without such separation it would be meaningless to speak of one reaching for the other. It is an attempt to destroy the belief in a mysterious underlying unity, any substantial connection. Nāgārjuna is willing to allow for the empirical differences and the relationship of dependence among such events. However, he is not prepared to leave any room for any speculation about underlying substances (*svabhāva*).

8. *Yadīndhanam apekṣyāgnir apekṣyāgniṃ yadīndhanaṃ,*
katarat pūrva-niṣpannaṃ yad apekṣyāgnir indhanaṃ.

If fire is contingent upon fuel and fuel upon fire, which of them is pre-accomplished so that fire could be contingent upon fuel?

MKV(P) p.207; *MKV(V)* p.88.

The motivation of the substantialists who were utilizing the metaphors of "fire and fuel" (*agnīndhana*) as well as "woman and man" (*strī-puruṣa*), as exlained at X.6, are brought to the forefront here. Let fire and fuel be related by way of contingence (*apekṣā*). Nāgārjuna has no objection to it and this is clearly indicated by the manner in which Candrakīrti himself utilizes this particular conception of contingence on numerous occasionions (see *MKV(P)* pp.67, 189, 200, 202, 345, 492, 527). In the present case, Nāgārjuna is not rejecting the mutual contingence (*parasparāpekṣā*) of phenomena, but only the inquiry relating to the pre-accomplishment or prior existence (*pūrva-niṣpanna*) of any one of them. Chapter IX made it abundantly clear that speculations regarding the prior entity led to most metaphysical speculations. Having raised the question as to which one of these two things—fire and fuel—is prior, a question that a substantialist cannot resist asking, Nāgārjuna proceeds to analyse the possible answers and explain their unsatisfactory implications.

9. *Yadīndhanam apekṣyāgnir agneḥ siddhasya sādhanaṃ,*
evaṃ satīndhanaṃ cāpi bhaviṣyati niragnikaṃ.

If fire were to be contingent upon fuel, there would be proof of fire that is already proved [to exist]. When that is the case, even fuel would exist without fire.

MKV(P) p.207; *MKV(V)* pp.88-89.

Frustrating any attempt on the part of the substantialist, Nāgārjuna insists that if fuel were to be the prior entity (*pūrva-niṣpanna*), and that fire is contingent upon it, then what is to be established is already established. In other words, the substantialist interpretations of contingence (*parasparāpekṣā*) would mean that fire is already existent in the fuel, which is itself the prior entity. If it is already existent in the fuel, then the implication is that it will need no fuel for its real existence. If so, fire and fuel could not be mutually contingent and one can conceive of fuel without fire (*nir-agnikaṃ*).

10. *Yo 'pekṣya sidhyate bhāvas tam evāpekṣya sidhyati,*
yadi yo 'pekṣitavyaḥ sa sidhyatāṃ kam apekṣya kaḥ.

MKV(P) p.208; *MKV(V)* p.89.

If events are to be truly contingent, then they should be mutually contingent or dependent. If any one of two mutually contingent entities is to be found in a substantial or essential way in the other, then the notion of contingence is nullified. One becomes the essential and the other the superficial. The problem then would be: which depends upon what? The Vātsīputriyas, as mentioned earlier, were not looking for means of dissolving identity and difference. They are struggling to retain both identity and difference, and then move on to a higher synthesis. Nāgārjuna's attempt here is not to allow the metaphysician the very concepts of identity and difference, which they were going to utilize as a springboard for leaping toward the notion of a metaphysical "person" (*pudgala*).

11. *Yo 'pekṣya sidhyate bhāvaḥ so 'siddho 'pekṣate kathaṃ,*
athāpy apekṣate siddhaḥ tv apekṣāsya na yujyate.

Whatever existent that is established through contingence, how can that, if it is not yet established, be contingent? Even so [how can] that which is already established be contingent? For, its contingence is not proper.

MKV(P) p.209; *MKV(V)* p.89.

X.10 refers to the fire that is already established (*siddha*), that is, something that is really existent (*sad-bhūta*). If one were to move to the other extreme and speak about events that are not established (*asiddha*), that is, those that are really non-existent (*asad-bhūta*), how can such events be contingent (*apekṣya sidhyate*)?

Thus, neither the already established (*siddha*) nor the unestablished (*asiddha*) can be related by way of mutual contingence. Contingence (*apekṣā*) is not established in this substantialist way.

12. *Apekṣyendhanam agnir na nānapekṣyāgnir indhanaṃ,*
apekṣyendhanam agniṃ na nānapekṣyāgnim indhanaṃ.

Fire is not contingent upon fuel; fire is not non-contingent upon fuel.
Fuel is not contingent upon fire; fuel is not non-contingent upon fire.

MKV(P) p.209; *MKV(V)* pp.88-90.

If the ideas expressed in the present verse were to be examined independent of what went before, it would be easy to leap to the conclusion that Nāgārjuna is here expressing the "inexpressible"; that the negations such as "non-ceasing" (*anirodhaṃ*) and "non-arising" (*anutpādaṃ*) were supposed to clear the way for the "non-conceptual," "non-dual" ultimate reality (*paramārtha*?). On the contrary, if these thoughts are placed in their proper context, namely, the metaphysical explanations of "mutal contingence" (*parasparāpekṣā*), then these negative statements can be understood as outright rejections of such metaphysical explanations. As is evident from several quotations from Candrakīrti himself (see X.7), "contingence" (*apekṣā*) can be explained in a non-metaphysical or empirical way, just as much as the notion of cause or condition (*pratyaya*) or the idea of motion (*gati*) can be elucidated without falling into the quagmire of metaphysics (see Chapters I,II).

13. *Agacchaty anyato nāgnir indhane 'gnir na vidyate,*
atrendhane śeṣam uktaṃ gamyamāna-gatāgataiḥ.

Fire does not come out of something different nor is fire seen to be in the fuel. Herein, with regard to fuel, the rest is stated as in the case of present moving, the moved and the not moved.

MVK(P) pp.210-211; *MKV(V)* p.90.

After dealing with the metaphysical interpretations of "contingence" (***apekṣā***) assumed between fire and fuel, Nāgārjuna returns to the more familiar substantialist theories of self-causation (***svata utpatti***) and external causation (***parata utpatti***). Fire is not inherent in the fuel nor does it issue out of something external. If any further explanations are to be provided which are themselves founded upon such substantialist ideas, all such explanations can be analysed in terms of the methods adopted in Chapter II dealing with motion (***gati***).

14. ***Indhanaṃ punar agnir na nāgnir anyatra cendhanāt,***
nāgnir indhanavān nāgnav indhanāni na teṣu saḥ.

Furthermore, fuel is not fire. Apart from fuel there is no fire. Fire is not possessed of fuel. Fuel is not in the fire, nor is it [i.e., fire] in them.

MKV(P) p.211; *MKV(V)* p.91.

The refutation of all metaphysical formulations of the notion of identity as applied to fire and fuel is presented here. This is done in terms of the analytical methods followed in Chapter I.

15. ***Agnīndhanābhyāṃ vyākhyātā ātmopādānayoḥ kramaḥ,***
sarvo niravaśeṣena sārdhaṃ ghaṭa-paṭādibhiḥ.

Through the examples of fire and fuel, together with the examples of pot, cloth, etc. every method of analysis of the self and grasping have been explained without exception.

MKV(P) pp.212-213; *MKV(V)* pp.91-92.

The metaphysical interpretations of "self" (*ātman*) and "grasping" (*upādāna*) are exposed here, especially in relation to the metaphor of fire and fuel (*agnīndhana*). Does this mean that there could be non-metaphysical explanations of both "self" and "grasping?" The answer would be in the positive, especially in vew of what Nāgārjuna has said in reference to "grasping" and the "one who grasps" (*upādātṛ*) or the action and the agent (*karma-kāraka*).

This analysis is not confined to the metaphor of "fire and fuel" alone. It applies to all other metaphors used during this period of speculation, such as "clay and the pot," and "thread and the cloth."

16. *Atmanaś ca satattvaṃ ye bhāvānāṃ ca pṛthak pṛthak,*
nirdiśanti na tān manye śāsanasyārtha-kovidān.

Those who posit the substantiality of the self as well as of discrete existents—these I do not consider to be experts in the meaning of the [Buddha's] message.

MKV(P) p.214; *MKV(V)* p.92.

Here then is a clear and unequivocal assertion on the part of Nāgārjuna. Those who assert the ***substantial existence*** (*satattvam*), whether that be of a monistic "self" (*ātman*) or of distinct entities (*pṛthak pṛthak bhāvānāṃ*) are not conversant with the teachings of the Buddha. When Nāgārjuna makes that assertion with the statement: "[I] do not consider" ([*ahaṃ*] *na manye*), what sort of self was he recognizing? It certainly could not be anything like what he was refuting. The answer to this question will be provided later.

CHAPTER ELEVEN
Examination of the Prior and Posterior Extremities *(Pūrvāparakoṭi-parīkṣā)*

1. *Pūrvā prajñāyate koṭir nety uvāca mahāmuniḥ,*
saṃsāro 'navarāgro hi nāsty ādir nāpi paścimaḥ.

The Great Sage has stated that the prior end is not known. The life-process is without beginning and end. There is neither a beginning nor an end.

MKV(P) p.219; *MKV(V)* p.95.

The criticism of the "self" (*ātman*) as a substantial entity continued in the last few chapters brings up more related issues for discussion. If there is no such entity, how can the life process consisting of repeated births and deaths be explained?

Rebirth or rebecoming (*punabbhava*) was an important element in the Buddhist doctrine, even though the Buddha was concerned more with the problems of the present life than of the past. As mentioned earlier (see commentary on IX.1-2), for the Buddha, the knowledge of the past (*atītaṃse ñāṇa*) was an important means of understanding the present. Yet he did not encourage speculation regarding the past as he feared that this would eventually lead to all sorts of metaphysical views. For this reason, he remained aloof from speculating on the absolute origin of things. That aloofness is clearly implied in his statement: "Inconceivable is the beginning of this life-process. The prior end is not evident," (*Anamataggo 'yaṃ . . . saṃsāro pubbākoṭi na paññāyati, S* 2.178, 193; 3.144.151). There is here no denial of the prior end or the first beginning of things, but only of its conceivability or perceptibility. However, with the problems that emerged during the scholastic period in the matter of explaining any form of origin (*utpāda*), not merely of the first beginning (*pūrvā koṭi*), some Buddhists were compelled to deny outright any form of beginning. While the Sarvāstivāda conception of substance left no room for origin and cessation, the Sautrāntikas had difficulties explaining the origin and cessation of momentary events. The difficulties involved in providing an explanation seems to have led the metaphysicians to assume the absence of a prior end, rather than of its inconceivability. Hence the term *anamatagga* ("inconceivable is the beginning") came to be replaced by *anavarāgra* ("without end and beginning"). As such, Nāgārjuna proceeds with the examination of the view current during his day, only to revert back to the Buddha's own approach to this problem in the end. Candrakīrti, confining himself to the literary tradition of his day and influenced by a transcendentalist approach in his interpretation of Nāgārjuna, does not seem to recognize the above mentioned change taking place in the Buddhist conception of the life-process (*saṃsāra*).

2. *Naivāgraṃ nāvaraṃ yasya tasya madhyaṃ kuto bhavet,*
tasmān nātropapadyante pūrvāpara-saha-kramāḥ.

How could there be the middle of that which has neither a beginning nor an end? Therefore, the methods of (distinguishing) the prior, the posterior or both together (i.e., the middle) are not appropriate.

MKV(P) pp.220-221; *MKV(V)* p.96.

Starting with the current assumption that there is neither a prior nor a posterior end, Nāgārjuna raises the question as to how, in the absence of these two extremities, one can speak of a "middle" (*madhya*). He then proceeds to apply this criticism to the conception of the life-process (*saṃsāra*) as understood and interpreted by the metaphysicians.

3. *Pūrvaṃ jātir yadi bhavej jarā-maraṇam uttaraṃ,*
nir-jarā-maraṇā jātir bhavej jāyeta cāmṛtaḥ.

If birth were to come first and decay and death were to follow, then birth would be without decay and death, and an immortal would thus emerge.

MKV(P) p.221; *MKV(V)* p.96.

The difficulties created by the Sarvāstivādins and the Sautrāntikas in the matter of explaining causal continuity have been discussed at length. The linear view of the causal process broken up into discrete events, one following the other, left these events without any possible relations. If the same model were to be used in explaining events such as birth (*jāti*) decay-death (*jarā-maraṇa*), then the implication would be that birth has nothing to do with decay-death. There is no necessary connection between them. If this argument were to be carried to its conclusion, then it could be maintained that there is immortality (*amṛta*), for there could be something that continues without decay-death. Here, Nāgārjuna is not insisting that decay-death should be inherent in birth. Rather, he is exposing the difficulties confronted by the metaphysicians who upheld a linear view of the causal process.

4. *Paścāj jātir yadi bhavej jarā-maraṇam āditaḥ,*
ahetukam ajātasya syāj jarā-maraṇaṃ kathaṃ.

If birth were to be posterior and decay-death anterior, then the latter would be without a cause. How could there be decay-death of one who is not born?

MKV(P) p.222; *MKV(V)* p.97.

Placing birth after decay-death in this linear view of the life-process, the logical conclusion is inevitable that birth cannot relate itself to anything prior and, therefore, is uncaused. If birth cannot be explained, just as much as decay-death could not be accounted for (as stated at XI.3), then we are left with the unborn (*ajāta*). Nāgārjuna considers it inappropriate to speak of decay-death of something/someone who is not born.

5. *Na jarā-maraṇenaiva jātiś ca saha yujyate,*
mriyeta jāyamānaś ca syāc cāhetukatobhayoḥ.

Indeed, decay-death as concomitant of birth is not proper. [In that case,] what is in the process of being born will also be dying and both would be rendered causeless.

MKV(P) p.223; *MKV(V)* p.97.

As mentioned in commentary on XI.4, one way of explaining the problems raised at XI.4-5 would be to assume that decay-death (*jarā-maraṇa*) is inherent in birth (*jāti*). This relationship of inherence would mean that decay-death begins at the same time as birth, and as such it would be appropriate to say that one who is being born is at the same time dying. If so, neither one of them could be the cause of the other. Being uncaused, their occurrence would be rather spontaneous.

6. *Yatra na prabhavanty ete pūrvāpara-saha-kramāḥ,*
prapañcayanti tāṃ jātiṃ taj jarā-maraṇaṃ ca kiṃ.

Wherever such methods of (discriminating) the prior, the posterior and the simultaneous do not arise, why be obsessed by such birth and such decay-death.

MKV(P) p.224; *MKV(V)* p.97.

The speculation that is questioned here is specifically related to the sort of succession discussed previously. It is not every form of reflection that is rejected. Even if the verb *prapañcayanti* were to mean "conceptualizing", as understood by a majority of modern translators of Buddhist texts, in this context, it does not mean the emptying of the mind of all concepts of birth and decay-death. It is the particular form of conceptualization mentioned in the previous statements as well as the earlier verses that is to be avoided.

7. *Kāryaṃ ca kāraṇaṃ caiva lakṣyaṃ lakṣaṇam eva ca,*
vedanā vedakaś caiva santy arthā ye ca kecana.

Effect and cause as well as characterized and characteristic, together with feeling and feeler or whatever fruits there are,

8. *Pūrva na vidyate koṭiḥ saṃsārasya na kevalaṃ,*
sarveṣām api bhāvānāṃ pūrvā koṭī na vidyate.

the prior end of these is not evident. Of the entire life-process as well as of all existents, the prior end is not evident.

MKV(P) p.224; MKV(V) p.98.

It is not suprizing to see Nāgārjuna concluding his analysis of extremities (*koṭi*) of events, whether they be of cause and effect, or the characterized and the characteristic, of experiences, of the life-process, and even of all existents (*bhāva*), with the assertion that they are not evident (*na vidyate*). He does not maintain that these events are *without* extremities.

CHAPTER TWELVE
Examination of Suffering
(Duḥkha-parīkṣā)

1. *Svayaṃ kṛtaṃ para-kṛtaṃ dvābhyāṃ kṛtam ahetukaṃ,*
   duḥkham ity eka icchanti tac ca kāryaṃ na yujyate.

Some assume that suffering is self-caused, caused by another, caused by both or without a cause. [Suffering as] such an effect is indeed not appropriate.

MKV(P) p.227; *MKV(V)* p.100.

The discussion of the life-process (*saṃsāra*) leads Nāgārjuna to an examination of the problem of suffering (*duḥkha*). It seems that when compiling this chapter Nāgārjuna had a copy of the Buddha's discourse to Acela-Kassapa (*S* 2.18-22; *Tsa* 12.20 [*Taishō* 2.86a]) in front of him.

The Buddha's discourse to Acela-Kassapa begins with the four theories of the causation of suffering referred to by Nāgārjuna in almost identical terms. The only difference is with regard to the explanation of the fourth. Where Nāgārjuna has *ahetukaṃ*, the Buddha's discourse refers to *adhiccasamuppannaṃ* (see XII.9 below). Another difference is that while the Buddha's advises Kassapa not to get involved in such speculations, insisting, "Do not [say] so," (*mā h' evaṃ*), Nāgārjuna maintains that these theories are not appropriate.

2. *Svayaṃ kṛtaṃ yadi bhavet pratīya na tato bhavet,*
   skandhān imān amī skandhāḥ saṃbhavanti pratīya hi.

If [suffering were to be] self-caused, then it could not occur dependently. Indeed, depending upon these aggregates, these other aggregates occur.

MKV(P) p.228; *MKV(V)* p.100.

The notion of self-causation of suffering is further elaborated by the Buddha as the view expressed in the statement, "He acts and he [himself] reaps the consequences," (*so karoti so paṭisaṃvediyati*). The Buddha's reason for not accepting such a view is that it leads to the belief in eternalism (*sassataṃ etaṃ pareti*). Nāgārjuna certainly knew that the Buddha was utilizing the conception of dependence (*paṭiccasamuppāda*) to avoid any metaphysical theory of eternalism. This was the basic theme, not only in the discourse to Kaccāyana, but also in the discourse to Acela-Kassapa, where it is once again presented as the middle position between the extremes of eternalism and annihilationism (*S* 2.20). It is, therefore, not surprising to see Nāgārjuna rejecting the conception of self-causation of suffering on the grounds that in such a case suffering would not be dependently arisen (*na pratītya bhavet*).

Furthermore, the eternalism that comes to be embodied in a theory of self-causation of suffering pertains more to the individual self or soul (*ātman*), and not the substance (*svabhāva*). Therefore, Nāgārjuna insists that what is being asserted as a self or soul is nothing other than the arising of a set of aggregates depending upon (*pratītya*) another set of aggregates.

3. *Yady amībhya ime 'nye syur ebhyo vāmī pare yadi,*
bhavet para-kṛtaṃ duḥkhaṃ parair ebhir amī kṛtāḥ.

If from these those that are different were to come to be, or if from those these different [things] were to come to be, then suffering would be caused by another, for these are caused by those that are different.

MKV(P) p.229; *MKV(V)* p.100.

Here we find a definition of "external causation" (*para-kṛta*). Nāgārjuna has already explained the relationship between self-nature or substance (*svabhāva*) and other-nature (*parabhāva*)(see I.3). There he maintained that without self-nature there cannot be other-nature (*avidyamāne svabhāve parabhāvo na vidyate*). In the present verse, Nāgārjuna applies the same principle to explain "causation by another." Thus, we find him utilizing the ablative case (*amībhyaḥ, ebhyaḥ*), expressive of "source" or "origin," in order to explain the arising of something different *from within* something that preceded. In other words, even though the effect is different from the cause, it arises from the cause; that is, external causation is invariably related to self-causation.

It is important to distinguish this statement from that found at XII.2 which, instead of using the ablative case, employs the accusative (*imān skandhān pratītya*) in order to highlight the principle of dependence. Indeed, the very term *idappaccayatā* (*idaṃ-pratyayatā*) utilized by the Buddha to express the principle of dependence is couched in the accusative case (*idaṃ*), instead of the ablative of source.

4. *Sva-pudgala-kṛtaṃ duḥkhaṃ yadi duḥkhaṃ punar vinā,*
sva-pudgalaḥ sa katamo yena duḥkhaṃ svayaṃ kṛtaṃ.

If suffering is caused by one's own person, then that own person can exist without suffering. Who is he by whom suffering is self-caused?

MKV(P) p.230; *MKV(V)* p.101.

As shown before, the Buddhist metaphysicians who adopted a theory of moments had difficulty explaining personal continuity or identity in a more empirical way. They were confronted with the problem of explaining good and bad, suffering and happiness as part of the personal continuity. Thus, the Sarvāstivādins would maintain that suffering, etc. are mere qualities (*lakṣaṇa*) that characterize the substance (*dravya*), or they would, along with the Sautrāntikas, maintain that qualities are appropriated or become part of the stream (*svasaṃtāna-patita, AK* 2.36; *Akb* p.62; Poussin, *L'Abhidharmakośa*, vol. 1. p. 179). Such a perspective inevitably leads to a distinction between the person or the stream of personal identity, on the one hand, and qualities like suffering on the other. What Nāgārjuna is attempting to do in the present verse is to bring out the metaphysical implications of this theory. According to this theory, suffering is something external to the individual. It is an entity having its own reality. It is something caused by a person, as a carpenter would produce a piece of furniture. As such, Nāgārjuna questions the very nature of that person who, being independent of suffering, causes suffering on its own.

5. *Para-pudgalajaṃ duḥkhaṃ yadi yasmai pradīyate,*
pareṇa kṛtvā tad duḥkhaṃ sa duḥkhena vinā kutaḥ.

If suffering were to be produced by one person and given over to another, that suffering is caused by the former. How can the latter be identified without suffering?

MKV(P) p.231; *MKV(V)* p.101.

If one were to accept the separation of suffering from the person who produces it (i.e., the theory criticized at XII.4), then it will lead to difficulties not only for one who adopts self-causation of suffering (*svayaṃ kṛtaṃ duḥkhaṃ*), but also for one who upholds the opposite view, namely, suffering is caused by another (*para-kṛtaṃ duḥkhaṃ*). The latter will have to maintain that suffering is caused by one person and passed on to another. But that other would himself be independent of suffering, in the same way as the person who caused it. The question still remains as to how that person can be identified.

6. *Para-pudgalajaṃ duḥkhaṃ yadi kaḥ para-pudgalaḥ,*
vinā duḥkhena yaḥ kṛtvā parasmai prahiṇoti tat.

If suffering is caused by another person, who is that other person who, himself without suffering, causes it and bestows it on another?

MKV(P) p.231; *MKV(V)* p.101.

This is similar to the arguments presented before. The sharp dichotomy between the agent of suffering and suffering itself prompts Nāgārjuna to question the nature of that other person (*para-pudgala*) who is supposed to be the author of suffering and who passes it on to another.

7. *Svayaṃ kṛtasyāprasiddher duḥkhaṃ para-kṛtaṃ kutaḥ,*
paro hi duḥkhaṃ yat kuryāt tat tasya syāt svayaṃ kṛtaṃ.

With the non-establishment of self-causation, how can there be suffering caused by another? For, indeed, if another were to cause that suffering, in relation to him it would be self-caused.

8. *Na tāvat svakṛtaṃ duḥkhaṃ na hi tenaiva tat kṛtaṃ,*
paro nātmakṛtaś cet syād duḥkhaṃ para-kṛtaṃ kathaṃ.

So long as suffering is not self-caused, it is, indeed, not caused by oneself. If the other were not to do it by himself, how could suffering be caused by another?

MKV(P) p.232; *MKV(V)* pp.101-102.

The implications of XII.3 discussed earlier are stated once more clearly and explicitly in these two verses. If some other person were to cause suffering, then that suffering, in relation to that particular person, would be self-caused. Thus, if one perspectvie is not valid then the other too would be invalidated. This, as pointed out earlier, is the method adopted at I.3 to reject both self-nature (*svabhāva*) and other-nature (*parabhāva*).

9. *Syād ubhābhyāṃ kṛtaṃ duḥkhaṃ syād ekaika-kṛtaṃ yadi,*
parākārāsvayaṃkāraṃ duḥkham ahetukaṃ kutaḥ.

If suffering were to be caused by both, it would be caused by each individually. Whence can there be suffering that is caused neither by another nor by oneself and is without a cause?

MKV(P) p.233; *MKV(V)* p.102.

The third theory of the causation of suffering referred to in the discourse to Acela-Kassapa is a combination of causation by oneself and causation by another (*sayaṃ katañ ca paraṃ katañ ca*). This is understood by Nāgārjuna as causation by each individual (*ekaika-kṛtaṃ*). However, he has already rejected both types of causation.

If suffering were not caused by oneself or another, then according to the Buddha it would "arise one top of another" (*adhiccasamuppanna*). Such arising is contrary to "arising by moving towards or depending upon another" (*paṭiccasamuppanna*). This implies arising without any causal connection. Hence, *adhiccasamuppanna* becomes a synonym for *ahetuka* (cause-less). For Nāgārjuna, there is no such uncaused suffering.

10. *Na kevalaṃ hi duḥkhasya cāturvidyaṃ na vidyate,*
bāhyānām api bhāvānāṃ cāturvidyaṃ na vidyate.

It is not that the fourfold theory applied exclusively to suffering is not evident. The fourfold theory pertaining to other existents too is not evident.

MKV(P) p.233; *MKV(V)* p.102.

Inada's explanation that these are the "four-fold possible views" (*c̄aturvidhyaṃ*) (p.88) seems to leave no room for a fifth view which both the Buddha (in his discourse to Kassapa) and Nāgārjuna (at XII.2) were very clearly and unequivocally upholding, namely, "dependent arising of suffering." Hence his conclusion that these four possible views can equally be applied to demonstrate the *impossibility of asserting* elements of the external world. On the contrary, Nāgārjuna (as well as the Buddha) were merely criticizing the futility of adopting these four *particular* views in explaining suffering as well as other elements in the world of experience. Indeed, Nāgārjuna was clearly aware of the fact that these four are not the only views explicating the causation of suffering. Hence his statement in the very first verse in this chapter, "Some assert" (*eke icchanti*), which means that it is not everyone that asserts such theories.

CHAPTER THIRTEEN
Examination of Action and the Agent *(Saṃskāra-parīkṣā)*

1. *Tan mṛṣā moṣa-dharma yad bhagavān ity abhāṣata,*
   sarve ca moṣa-dharmāṇaḥ saṃskārāḥ tena te mṛṣā.

The Blessed One has said that whatever is of deceptive nature, that is delusion. All things that are of deceptive nature involve dispositions. Therefore, they are delusions.

MKV(P) p.237; *MKV(V)* p.104.

A chapter dealing with dispositions (*saṃskāra*) immediately following an analysis of suffering (*duḥkha*) need not create any confusion. Nor should the fact the the title of this chapter is presented in the Tibetan translation as *tattva*, instead of *saṃskra* (see Inada, p.91), lead to difficulties in understanding it.

There cannot be any doubt that the original chapter was named "Examination of the Dispositions." Even the most cursory glance at the statements of the Buddha in the discourses would reveal the naked fact that he never looked upon all phenomena (*sabbe dhammā*) as "suffering" or "unsatisfactory" (*dukkha*). However, the classical Hindu philosophers who misquoted the Buddhist texts, and some of the modern interpreters who were guided by such philosophers, have been responsible for portraying Buddhism as a pessimistic religion by misinterpreting the Buddha-word, especially the doctrine of "suffering" (see Kalupahana, "The notion of suffering in early Buddhism, compared with some reflections of early Wittgenstein," *PEW* 27 [1977]:423-431.)

The three prominent characteristics, impermanence (*anicca*), suffering (*dukkha*), and non-substantiality (*anatta*) have been recklessly lumped together by these interpreters and applied to all phenomena when the Buddha in innumberable instances (*M* 1.228; *S* 3.133; 4.401; *A* 1.286; *Dhp* 277-279; *Tsa* 10.7 [*Taishō 2.66b-67a]; Tseng* 23.4 [*Taishō* 2.668c] *Ch'ang* 1.1 [*Taishō* 1.9b]) and in every statement he made in regard to these three characteristics, *always* distinguished between *saṅkhāra* and *dhamma.* These three characteristics are always mentioned as follows:

i. "All dispositions are impermanent" (*sabbe saṅkhārā aniccā*).
ii. "All dispositions are suffering" (*sabbe saṅkhārā dukkhā*).
iii. "All phenomena are non-substantial" (*sabbe dhammā anattā*).

In the first place, the clear distinction made by the Buddha between "dispositions" (*saṃskāra*) and "phenomena" (*dharma*) and, secondly, the fact that he specifically referred to the former being subject to suffering, could not have escaped the penetrating and careful eye of Nāgārjuna, a philosopher whose writings have influenced some of the best brains in the East throughout the centuries. If all dispositions were considered by the Buddha to be subject to suffering, then there is no reason to doubt as to why Nāgārjuna should not concentrate his attention on these "dispositions" after his examination of the problem of suffering. Hence the reason for the present chapter.

Why the Tibetan translators should consider this to be an examination of truth (*tattva*) is also not a mystery. They were simply looking at the conclusion of the chapter. Is there any connection between "dispositions" and "truth"?

As pointed out earlier (V.8), the "appeasement of dispositions" (*saṃskāropaśama*) is the ultimate goal of Buddhism. Excessive lust (*rāga*) is supposed to lead to the strengthening or solidification of one's dispositions, which in turn contributes to grasping, not only for the objects of sense pleasure, but also for ideas. The result would be the dogmatic grasping on to absolute truth or truths. The elimination of lust would then mean the elimination of the dispositions too (*saṃskāra-kṣaya*) which would imply virtual death and no motivation for any action or even to continue with one's present life. Thus, the Buddha himself was willing to characterize the death of a "freed one" (*tathāgata*) as the "cessation of dispositions" (*saṅkhārakkaya*) (*Dhp* 383) leading to the cessation of the stream of becoming (*bhava-sota*).

However, while recognizing the waning of lust (*rāgakkhaya*) as the way to freedom, the Buddha did not encourage the complete elimination of dispositions which would mean suicide. It seems that the Buddha did not recognize a one-to-one relationship between the waning of lust and the cessation of dispositions. Hence his emphasis on the appeasement of dispositions while living and the cessation of dispositions at the time of death.

The strengthening of dispositions, as mentioned earlier, leads to dogmatic beliefs. These would pertain to personal immortality, conceived in the form of a belief in an eternal soul or self (*ātman*) or of a universal reality (*loka, brahman*). Any form of eternalism (*śāśvata*) would be the consequence of such strong dispositional tendencies. The opposite of it would be annihilationism (*uccheda*), and it is not difficult to understand why the critics of the Buddha would refer to him as an annihilationist (*ucchedavādī*) upholding the annihilation of really existing sentient being (*M* 1.140). They were probably referring to the Buddha's advocacy of the "cessation of dispositions" (*saṅkhārakkhaya*) at death.

Yet, for the living human being the Buddha was not prescribing the elimination of dispositions. Rather he advocated their appeasement. This view has significant epistemological implications. A living human being needs to act. Action involves understanding. Conduct (*caraṇa*) is preceded by knowledge (*vidyā*). One needs knowledge of oneself as well of the external world. "Omniscience" or knowledge of everything was not available to the Buddha. Hence, neither the absolute origin of things nor the absolute end of things were discussed in Buddhism (see Chapter XI). Any theory that attempts to explain such origins and ends, whether it pertains to an eternal self or soul (*ātman*) or a substance (*svabhāva*), was unacceptable to the Buddha.

Dispositions are invariably associated with the knowledge derived from the senses. The innumerable data provided by the senses cannot easily be handled by the human being. As William James characterized sense experience, it is a "big, blooming, buzzing confusion" (*Some Problems of Philosophy* p.32). Being unable to deal with such confusion, human beings are compelled to be selective. They pick out the things that interest them, leaving out others. In that process, they develop dispositions and these dispositions in turn contributes their share in gaining knowledge of the world. As such, the world of ordered experience is one that is constructed, made, put together (*sam* + √*kṛ*, "to do, to make"), by the human being. This is the pragmatic conception of truth (*tattva*) that is prominent in the Buddha's teaching. The appeasement of dispositions thus contributes to the elimination of dogmatism, of grasping after absolute truth or truths, when all the time human beings are creating truths. If a person is not aware of the process by which he constructs the truths about the world, he will not only be confused but also disappointed. Dispositions can thus turn out to be a great source of confounding and delusion (*mṛṣā*), unless one understands their function in the formulation of truths (*tattva*). The translators of Nāgārjuna's text into Tibetan probably perceived the direction of the argument in this chapter and named it accordingly.

Note that the delusion (*mṛṣā*) is produced, not by all the phenomena (*sarvadharma*) but only by the way in which these phenomena are put together (*saṃskaroti*) for purposes of understanding (see *Websters' Seventh Collegiate Dictionary*, 1965, p. 219 where delusion is defined as "self-deception concerning facts or situations"). That putting together is the function of dispositions (*saṃskāra*). Hence, for Nāgārjuna, as it was for the Buddha, if anything is to contribute toward delusion that would not be all phenomena (*sarve dharmāḥ*), rather it would be all dispositions (*sarve saṃskārāḥ*).

2. *Tan mṛṣā moṣa-dharma yad yadi kiṃ tatra muṣyate,*
etat tūktaṃ bhagavatā śūnyatā-paridīpakam.

If, whatever that is of deceptive nature is delusion, what is it about which there is delusion? That too, namely, that which illuminates emptiness, has been spoken of by the Blessed One.

MKV(P) pp.238-239; *MKV(V)* p.104.

If dispositions cause delusions, what is it about which there are delusions? The answer would be: "The world of experience." The Buddha has spoken of that world too. It is the world that is non-substantial, is empty of any permanent and eternal entity. All delusions arise regarding that world which is dependently arisen and non-substantial, but which is being understood as being either eternal or absolutely unreal.

3. *Bhāvānāṃ niḥsvabhāvatvaṃ anyathā-bhāva-darśanāt,*
asvabhāvo bhāvo nāsti bhāvānāṃ śūnyatā yataḥ.

Because of the perception of change, the absence of self-nature of existents is [recognized]. Because of the emptiness of existents, there is no existent without self-nature.

MKV(P) p.240; *MKV(V)* p.105.

This is a clear statement that truth or reality (*tattva*) (there being no provisional truth and ultimate reality) is neither substantial existence nor nihilistic non-existence. The perception of change or variation (*anyathābhāva*) confirms the non-substantiality of phenomena (*niḥsvabhāva*). This is another way of expressing the idea embodied in the discourse to Kaccāyana that "to him who perceives through right wisdom the cessation of the world as it has come to be, the notion of existence (*atthitā*) in the world does not occur," (*S* 2.17).

Cessation (*nirodha*) or change (*anyathābhāva*) does not imply complete annihilation. Hence Nāgārjuna's view that there is no existent that is without substance (*a-svabhāva*), that is, something that goes into complete oblivion after existing for a while (*bhūtvā prativigacchati*) leaving no trace at all. The discourse to Kaccāyana says that he who perceives arising (*samudaya*) does not hold on to the non-existence of the world. In other words, arising (*samudaya* or *samutpāda*) contradicts nihilistic non-existence (*nāstitā, a-svabhāva*). Nāgārjuna perceives this to be emptiness (*śūnyatā*).

This, then, is the way in which "dependent arising" of phenomena (*pratītyasamutpāda*) becomes a synonym for "emptiness" (*śūnyatā*) or "non-substantiality" (*nairātmya*) which will be further elaborated in Chapter XXIV.

4. *Kasya syād anyathā-bhāvaḥ svabhāvaś cen na vidyate,*
kasya syād anythā-bhāvaḥ svabhāvo yadi vidyate.

Whose change would there be, if self-nature were not evident? Again, whose change would there be, if self-nature were evident.?

MKV(P) p.241; *MKV(V)* p.105.

Nāgārjuna is here contrasting identity and difference. If things are completely different from one another, then there is no reason to speak of the change of things (*anyathābhāva*). If, on the contrary, there were to be a substance (*svabhāva*) which is assumed to be permanent and eternal, it could not change.

5. *Tasyaiva nānyathā-bhāvo nāpy anyasyaiva yujyate,*
yuvā na jīryate yasmād yasmāj jīrṇo na jīryate.

Neither change of something in itself nor of something different is proper. The reason being that a youth does not age nor does an aged person age.

MKV(P) p.241; MKV(V) p.106.

Nāgārjuna continues to emphasize the view that change (*anyathābhāva*) is inexplicable in the context of identity or difference. "Of itself" (*tasya eva*) means "of something that has substantial existence;" "of another" (*anyasya eva*) implies "belonging to something completely different." As mentioned previously

(VII.24), "decay" (*jarā*) was ***not*** rejected by Nāgārjuna. In the present context, what he intends to convey is that such decay makes no sense when applied to explain a person who is metaphysically conceived either as possessing an eternal self or as being different from moment to moment.

6. ***Tasya ced anyathā-bhāvaḥ kṣīram eva bhaved dadhi,***
kṣīrād anyasya kasyacid dadhi-bhāvo bhaviṣyati.

If change were to be of something in itself, then milk itself would be butter. Butter-ness would then be something other than milk.

MKV(P) p.242; *MKV(V)* p.106.

If change were to be applied to something recognized as exisiting in itself, i.e., a substance, then the conception of change would be negated. Here we find the example of milk and butter (*kṣīra-dadhi*) utilized by the Vātsīputriyas, along with the metaphor of "fire and fuel" (*Akb* pp.432-433), to illustrate the relationship between the aggregates and the self. If butter is considered to be substantially the same as milk, then butter-ness will have to belong to something different from milk. Otherwise we will be left with two different substances having the same substantial constitution.

7. ***Yady aśūnyaṃ bhavet kiṃcit syāc chūnyam iti kiṃcana,***
na kiṃcid asty aśūnyaṃ ca kutaḥ śūnyaṃ bhaviṣyati.

If there were to be something non-empty, there would then be something called empty. However, there is nothing that is non-empty. How could there be something empty?

MKV(P) p.245; *MKV(V)* p. 107.

The conception of "emptiness" or "non-substantiality" is intended to eliminate the belief in substance and attribute conceived in a metaphysical sense. However, if "emptiness" itself were to be used in an attributive sense, that is as a characteristic of something substantial, then "emptiness" itself becomes "something" (*kiṃcana*). A substantial thing is a "non-empty-something" (*aśūnyaṃ kiṃcit*). Such a thing does not exist. If so, there cannot be something called "empty" (*śūnyam iti kiṃcana*).

This is the clearest warning from Nāgārjuna against moving towards the metaphysics of "emptiness" (*śūnyatā dṛṣṭi*, see below).

8. *Śūnyatā sarva-dṛṣṭīnāṃ proktā niḥsaraṇaṃ jinaiḥ,*
yeṣāṃ tu śūnyatā-dṛṣṭis tān asādhyān babhāṣire.

The Victorious Ones have announced that emptiness is the relinquishing of all views. Those who are possessed of the view of emptiness are said to be incorrigible.

MKV(P) p.247; *MKV(V)* p.1084.

The inevitable conclusion to be derived from XIII.7 is that the conception of "emptiness" (*śūnyatā*) or "non-substantiality" (*nairātmya*), utilized by the Buddha in order to free oneself from all metaphysical views (*dṛṣṭi*), can turn out to be an equally unsatisfactory view, if its application is to be carried beyond its proper limits. Indeed, Nāgārjuna perceives such activity as leading to worse forms of dogmatism.

CHAPTER FOURTEEN
Examination of Association
(Saṃsarga-parīkṣā)

1. *Draṣṭavyaṃ darśanaṃ draṣṭā trīṇy etāni dviśo dviśaḥ,*
sarvaśaś ca na saṃsargam anyonyena vrajanty uta.

The object of seeing, the seeing and the seer—these three do not function in mutual association either in pairs or all together.

2. *Evaṃ rāgaś ca raktaś ca rañjanīyaṃ ca dṛśyatām,*
traidhena śeṣāḥ kleśāś ca śeṣāṇy āyatanāni ca.

Lust, the lustful as well as the object of lust should be seen in the same way. The remaining defilements as well as the remaining spheres of sense should be seen in the triadic mode.

MKV(P) pp.250-251; *MKV(V)* p.110.

The pragmatic theory of truth, that is, truth as something put together according to human dispositions (*saṃskāra*) depending upon something experienced (*dharma*), is not a very palatable one, especially for some analytical philosopher who wants to carry his analysis to the very extreme. In the present treatment of Nāgārjuna's philosophy, it has been repeatedly pointed out that an extremist analysis left the Buddhist metaphysician with absolutely distinct entities. For him (and this was the position accepted even by a philosopher like Hume), "What is distinguishable is also separable." Of course, these metaphysicians would then proceed to explain events in terms of "composition," of putting different entities together (*saṃskaraṇa*) according to one's dispositions (*saṃskāra*) or, as Hume insisted, in terms of one's imagination. However, they will have to carry the burden of explaining how only certain things can be so put together and not anything and everything. For example, one can insist that it is possible to bring together events such as the eye, color, and visual consciousness together to produce the impression called "perception of color." Yet, one cannot, either in terms of dispositions or according to any imagination, put together the eye, sound, and gustatory consciousness and produce either a visual impression or an auditory impression.

The only way in which such metaphysicians can explain any possible association is by assuming a substantial relation, an inherent nature among those events that are so associated. This is how the analysis of events into absolutely different entities contributed to the recognition of mysterious substances. The Sarvāstivāda notion of substance or self-nature (*svabhāva*) was, therefore, an inevitable answer to such extremist analysis, in the same way as Bertrand Russell's theory of relations, defined as neither mental or physical, was the answer to the Humean analysis.

For such philosophers, a pragmatic theory of truth, where truth is defined as something "made" (*saṃskṛta*), becomes a problem because their analysis has deprived them of any empirical relations in terms of which things can be associated. It is, therefore, not surprizing to see Nāgārjuna taking up the question of association (*saṃsarga*), in order to show that it does not work in the background of the metaphysical assumptions of certain analysts.

Thus it becomes necessary to keep in mind that Nāgārjuna's criticism of association is specifically related to the association of events that were so distinguished that each was assumed to have its own nature (*svabhāva*). He begins this chapter with a reference to the various categories he has already examined at the very outset in this section of the book, namely, seeing (*darśana*), the object of seeing (*draṣṭavya*) and the seer (*draṣṭṛ*) (Chapter III). XIV.2 refers to another set of categories examined in Chapter VI. This application is then extended to all occurrences such as the defilements and faculties.

3. *Anyenānyasya saṃsargaḥ tac cānyatvaṃ na vidyate,*
draṣṭavya-prabhṛtīnāṃ yan na saṃsargaṃ vrajanty ataḥ.

Association is of the mutually different [events]. Such difference is not evident in the objects of seeing, etc. Therefore, they do not function in mutual association.

MKV(P) p.251; *MKV(V)* p.110.

Association, as mentioned above, becomes a philosophical problem only when distinctions or differences are rendered absolute. Nāgārjuna, basing himself on the principle of "dependent arising," insists that such distinctions are not available among objects of seeing, etc. If these are distinguished or differentiated in the way metaphysicians do, then they cannot enjoy mutual harmony or association.

4. *Na ca kevalam anyatvaṃ draṣṭavyāder na vidyate,*
kasyacit kenacit sārdhaṃ nānyatvam upapadyate.

It is not only that the difference with regard to objects of seeing, etc. is not evident; the possibility of something possessing difference jointly with another is also not appropriate.

MKV(P) p.252; *MKV(V)* p.110.

This is an interesting analysis of identity and difference. The dilemma of substance is brought out clearly in this analysis. In order to relate things, differences need to be recognized. Once the differences are recognized as being absolute, each thing is assumed to have its own nature. It becomes a substance different from any other substance. If each substance is different, it cannot have a substance that is shared by another. If it does, the difference breaks down. Either there is difference or there is identity.

5. *Anyad anyat pratītyānyān nānyad anyad ṛte 'nyataḥ,*
yat pratītya ca yat tasmāt tad anyan nopapadyate.

Different things are dependent upon different things. Different things are not without different things. Because something depends upon something, a different thing is not appropriate.

6. *Yady anyad anyad anyasmād anyasmād apy ṛte bhavet,*
tad anyad anyad anyasmād ṛte nāsti ca nasty ataḥ.

If a thing is different from another because it arises from a different thing, then it would exist even without that other thing. However, that

other thing does not exist without the other, and therefore, it does not exist.

7. *Nānyasmin vidyate 'nyatvam ananyasmin na vidyate,*
avidyamāne cānyatve nāsty anyad vā tad eva vā.

A difference is not evident in relation to a different thing. Nor is it not evident in a different thing. When difference is not evident, there is neither difference nor identity.

MKV(P) pp.252-255; *MKV(V)* pp.111-112.

These verses seem to highlight the fact that one cannot speak of dependence so long as one recognizes absolute difference among events. They are a reminder of the detailed treatment of the relation of contingence (*apekṣā*) undertaken previously in relation to the metaphor of "fire and fuel" (Chapter X).

8. *Na tena tasya saṃsargo nānyenānyasya yujyate,*
saṃsṛjyamānaṃ saṃsṛṣṭaṃ saṃsraṣṭā ca na vidyate.

The association of identical things or of different things is not proper. Neither the associating nor the associated nor even the agent of association is evident.

MKV(P) pp.255-256; *MKV(V)* pp.112-13.

Identity and difference assumed by the Buddhist metaphysicians cannot solve the problem of truth, especially its pragmatic version. The only solution available to them is a recognition of the Buddha's "omniscience" (*sarvajñatva*), which they unhesitatingly attributed to him, even without attempting to define what "omnis" (*sarvaṃ*) stood for in the Buddhist context (see commentary on IX.3).

CHAPTER FIFTEEN
Examination of Self-nature
(Svabhāva-parīkṣā)

1. *Na saṃbhavaḥ svabhāvasya yuktaḥ pratyaya-hetubbiḥ,*
hetu-pratyaya-saṃbhūtaḥ svabhāvaḥ kṛtako bhavet.

The occurrence of self-nature through causes and conditions is not proper. Self-nature that has occurred as a result of causes and conditions would be something that is made.

MKV(P) p.259; *MKV(V)* p.114.

Chapter XV is the conclusion to Part II of Nāgārjuna's text. The main thrust of Part II, as explained in the Introduction, is in the direction of clarifying the conception of *dharmas* (in the plural), whether they represented ideas, things, events, or phenomena. As was eviden' from an examination of the preceding twelve chapters, Nāgārjuna's analysis of *dharmas* was intended to eliminate the metaphysical ideas relating to identity and difference (*ekārtha-nānārtha*). In that process, he refuted the metaphysical notions of arising and ceasing (*utpāda-nirodha*), of eternalism and annihilationism (*śāśvata-uccheda*) and of appearance and disappearance (*āgama-nirgama*). These metaphysical notions were the result of assuming a substance or self-nature (*svabhāva*) in phenomena, an assumption that is mutually related by a conception of absolute "otherness" (*parabhāva*).

Self-nature or substance (*svabhāva*) thus being the major issue, it is natural for Nāgārjuna to conclude this section with an examination of this particular conception.

In refuting the conception of substance, Nāgārjuna relies heavily upon the Buddha's own conception of a "middle position," namely, "dependent arising." Because he was here concerned mainly with refuting the metaphysical extremes, Nāgārjuna refers only to that section of his *locus classicus* (i.e., the discurse to Kātyāyana) that deals with the two extremes of existence (*astitva*) and non-existence (*nāstitva*).

In the very first verse, Nāgārjuna states his own pragmatic view of truth as something made (*kṛtaka*) depending upon causes and conditions (*hetu-pratyaya-saṃbhūtaḥ*). Substance or self-nature, if it were to exist, could not escape the principle of dependent arising (*pratītyasamutpāda*).

2. *Svabhāvaḥ kṛtako nāma bhaviṣyati punaḥ katham,*
akṛtrimaḥ svabhāvo hi nirapekṣaḥ paratra ca.

Again, how could there be a self-nature that is made? Indeed, an unmade self-nature is also non-contingent upon another.

MKV(P) pp.260-262; *MKV(V)* pp.114-115.

An artificial substance (*kṛtakaḥ svabhāvaḥ*) is not possible, for by definition a substance is eternal and therefore not subject to arising and ceasing. Anything that is subject to arising and ceasing cannot be a substance and, hence, contrary to dependent arising. It is simply non-contingent (*nirapekṣaḥ*).

3. *Kutaḥ svabhāvasyābhāve para-bhāvo bhaviṣyati,*
svabhāvaḥ para-bhāvasya para-bhāvo hi kathyate.

In the absence of self-nature, whence can there be other-nature? For, self-nature of other-nature is called other-nature.

MKV(P) pp.265-266; *MKV(V)* p.116.

This represents a repetition of the argument used by Nāgārjuna at I.3 and XIV.4 to indicate the relativity of self-nature and other-nature. If one is not acceptable, the other too is not admissible.

4. *Svabhāva-para-bhāvābhyām ṛte bhāvaḥ kutaḥ punaḥ,*
svabhāve para-bhāve vā sati bhāvo hi sidhyati.

Without self-nature and other-nature, whence can there be an existent? For, the existent is established only when there is self-nature or other-nature.

MKV(P) p.266; *MKV(V)* p.116.

This probably could serve as evidence against the belief that Nāgārjuna recognized an ultimate reality beyond both self-nature and other-nature. In the case of the Vātsīputriyas, the "ultimately real" emerges on the basis of an assertion of both identity and difference, (see commentary on X.1, "Fire cannot be designated as something different from the fuel, nor as something identical.") The Japanese Buddhist scholar Y. Ueda perceives a unique logical principle adopted in Mādhyamika logic derived from the metaphor of "fire and fuel." According to him, "There are inherent conditions in each such that their ultimate relatonship into a ***whole*** or ***unity*** entails a mutual denial of each other," (see Inada, p.80, emphasis added). However, Nāgārjuna is here raising the question: "Distinct from self-nature and other-nature, whence can there be an existent?"

Thus, the eight negations are not intended to prove or establish the nature of reality, as it is often and loudly asserted. They are primarily and solely intended to eliminate metaphysical notions, not to characterize either an ultimate reality or dependent arising. Dependent arising is a totally differnt way of expressing the truth or reality.

In the second statement above, Nāgārjuna maintains that ***svabhāva*** and ***parabhāva*** are both dependent upon ***bhāva***. They represent a further bifurcation of ***bhāva***.

5. *Bhāvasya ced aprasiddhir abhāvo naiva sidhyati,*
bhāvasya hy anyathā-bhāvam abhāvaṃ bruvate janāḥ.

When the existent is not established, the non-existent is also not established. It is, indeed, the change of the existent that people generally call the non-existent.

MKV(P) p.267; *MKV(V)*p.117.

While ***svabhāva*** and ***parabhāva*** represent a bifurcation of ***bhāva***, the latter is itself dependent upon *abhāva*. Ordinarily people speak of *abhāva* as change in *bhāva*. The *bhāva - abhāva*, though more comprehensive than the *svabhāva -parabhāva* dichotomy, carries the same implications as the latter. Both involve the metaphysical notions of identity and difference.

Neither the Buddha's conceptions of "dependent arising" (*paṭiccasamuppāda*) and "non-substantiality" (*anatta*) nor Nāgārjuna's views on dependence and emptiness (*śūnyatā*) should be understood as involving or creating the metaphysical notions of identity and difference. In fact, the interpretation of *śūnyatā* by some scholars as an "ultimate reality" has brought about an immediate response from others who characterize it as "nothingness." The dichotomy that ordinary people assume is immediately brought into play here. It was this incorrigibility (*asādhya*) that Nāgārjuna was referring to at XIII.8. Hence, Nāgārjuna's declaration that follows.

6. *Svabhāvaṃ para-bhāvaṃ ca bhāvaṃ cābhāvam eva ca,*
ye paśyanti na paśyanti te tattvaṃ Buddha-śāsane.

Those who perceive self-nature as well as other-nature, existence as well as non-existence, they do not perceive the truth embodied in the Buddha's message.

MKV(P) p.267; *MKV(V)* p.117.

It is not merely self-nature and other-nature that are rejected, but also existence and non-existence. The former pair covers a limited range of explanation, compared to the more comprehensive notions of existence and non-existence.

An empirical definition of existence, as presented by the Buddha, would mean some thing, some event, some phenomenon available to the six senses (see *S* 4.15, *Sabba-sutta*). Such a phenomenon is assumed to have come to be on the basis of conditions (*paṭiccasamuppanna*), to remain for a while showing signs, at the same time, of decay (*ṭhitassa aññathatta*), and then cease to exist (*nirodha, vyaya*), once again depending upon conditions. So that even ordinary unenlightened people would say: "Change of what is existent is non-existence" (*bhāvasya hy anyathābhāvam abhāvaṃ bruvate janāḥ*, XV.5).

However, the metaphysicians can take over from this ordinary man's language, especially with its use of the genetive or possessive case (*bhāvasya*). He will assume that change is something possessed by the existent (*bhāva*) which is always the same. Yet he cannot say the same about non-existence (*abhāva*). The metaphysicians part company here, one dogmatically holding on to a theory of eternal existence (*śāśvata*), the other advocating absolute non-existence, which is annihilationism (*uccheda*).

Another metaphysician who is interested in explaining the empirically felt "selfhood" and "others" will attempt to bifurcate existence (*bhāva*) as self-nature (*svabhāva*) and other-nature (*parabhāva*). When applying this latter dichotomy to the explanation of causality, the metaphysician once again brings the duality of existence and non-existence into play.

Such metaphysics has no place whatsoever in the Buddha's explanation of existence and non-existence. Hence Nāgārjuna's statement that those who adhere to these notions do not understand the truth or reality expressed in the Buddha's message.

7. *Kātyāyanāvavāde cāstīti nāstīti cobhayaṃ,*
pratiṣiddhaṃ bhagavatā bhāvābhāva-vibhāvinā.

In the admonition to Kātyāyana, the two theories [implying] 'exists' and 'does not exist' have been refuted by the Blessed One who is adept in existence as well as in non-existence.

MKV(P) p.269; *MKV(V)* p.117.

This, as mentioned in the Introduction, is the single most important piece of evidence available in the work of Nāgārjuna, which can relate him to the Buddha as presented in the Pali Nikāyas and the Chinese Āgamas. Inada's note on this verse is too brief and vague: "The Sanskrit Kātyāyanāvavāda, either refers to the sutra or the instructions given to Kātyāyama [sic.] by the Buddha," (p.99). This statement of Nāgārjuna deserves much more attention than has ever been accorded to it.

The main theme of the discourse is to expose the untenability of the two metaphysical views of existence (*astitva*) and non-existence (*nāstitva*). This is done by appealing to the empirical notions of arising (*utpāda*) and ceasing (*nirodha*). With the fifteen chapters (including the present), Nāgārjuna has presented an outstanding explanation of how the empirical conceptions of arising and ceasing, of impermanence and change, can profitably be used to expose the futility of metaphysics. Hence, he is satisfied with merely referring to that portion of the "Discourse to Kātyāyana" which deals with the rejection of the two metaphysical extremes. A discussion of the remaining ideas expressed by the Buddha in this discourse, especially the positive description of the human personality as well as its experiences, is reserved for a later occasion.

8. *Yady astitvaṃ prakṛtyā syān na bhaved asya nāstitā,*
prakṛter anyathā-bhāvo na hi jatūpapadyate.

If existence were to be in terms of primal nature, then there would not be its non-existence. A change of primal nature is certainly not appropriate.

MKV(P) p.271; *MKV(V)* pp.118-119.

This and the next three verses seem to constitute a digest of the detailed and meticulous analysis of the two extreme views presented by Nāgārjuna so far.

If existence is understood in the sense of primal nature (*prakṛti*), in the way the Sankhya school did, for, in fact, the Sankhya used the term *svabhāva* to refer to the primal nature, then there cannot be its non-existence. The reason is that change and primal nature or substance are incompatible.

9. *Prakṛtau kasya cāsatyam anyathātvaṃ bhaviṣyati,*
prakṛtau kasya ca satyām anyathātvaṃ bhaviṣyati.

When primal nature is non-existent, whose change would there be? When primal nature is existent, whose change would there be?

MKV(P) p.271-272; *MKV(V)* p.119.

Not only the existence of primal nature, but also its non-existence is incompatible with change. Here primal nature is understood as the substance and change as the attribute. If the substance is not available, the attributes cannot be applied to it. If the substance is present, the attributes become superficial. In brief, the substantialist enterprise consists of reconciling substance and attribute after creating a sharp and irreconciliable distinction between them (see Chapter V).

The above explanation would eliminate the need for assuming that the first line of the verse represents a question raised by an opponent to which Nāgārjuna gives his own reply in the second (see Inada p.99, who follows Candrakīrti's interpretation of this verse.)

10. *Astīti śāśvata-grāho nāstīty uccheda-darśanam,*
tasmād astitva-nāstitve nāśrīyeta vicakṣaṇaḥ.

"Exists' implies grasping after eternalism. "Does not exist" implies the philosophy of annihilation. Therefore, a discerning person should not rely upon either existence or non-existence.

11. *Asti yadd hi svabhāvena na tan nāstīi śāśvatam,*
nāstīdānīm abhūt pūrvam ity ucchedaḥ prasajyate.

"Whatever that exists in terms of self-nature, that is not non-existent" implies eternalism. "It does not exist now, but existed before" implies annihilation.

MKV(P) pp.272-273; *MKV(V)* p.119.

These theories of existence and non-existence are not simple and harmless ones. They contribute to unfortunate consequences. The theory of existence leads to the dogmatic grasping on to the belief in eternalism. The conception of non-existence leads to an equally dangerous view of annihilation, both of which, as will be pointed out later, are damaging to the moral life. Hence, a wise man would not associate himself with such extreme views.

This seems to be a most appropriate conclusion to an analysis that was intended to establish the non-substantiality of all phenomena (*dharma-nairātmya*). Nāgārjuna did not allow any room for the reification of any one single phenomenon that was referred to as being part of human experience.

CHAPTER SIXTEEN
Examination of Bondage and Release (*Bandhana-mokṣa-parīkṣā*)

1. *Saṃskārāḥ saṃsaranti cen na nityāḥ saṃsaranti te,*
saṃsaranti ca nānityāḥ sattve 'py eṣa samaḥ kramaḥ.

If it is assumed that dispositions transmigrate, they would not transmigrate as permanent entities. Neither do they transmigrate as impermanent entities. This method (of analysis) is applicable even in the case of a sentient being.

MKV(P) p.280; *MKV(V)* p.123.

Part Three, according to our analysis, consists of Chapter XVI-XXVI, and is different from Part Two in its treatment of the subject matter, even though the subject matter itself appears to be similar in them. While Part Two was concerned with the analysis of the elements of existence (*dharma*) showing how they are lacking in any substance (*dharma-nairātmya*) and how they are dependently arisen (*partītyasamutpanna*), Part Three is concerned more with the explanation of the human personality (*pudgala*) without falling into metaphysical traps. The human personality, both in bondage and in freedom, is analysed here. The problems of "self" (*ātman*), questions regarding moral responsibility and its associated concepts of time and fruitioning, are discussed first. Moving therefrom, Nāgārjuna takes up the problem of the person who has attained freedom, the question of truths, of freedom itself, trying to deal once again with the metaphysical interpretations, until he reaches Chapter XXVI when he presents the most positive explanation of that human personality.

The present chapter beings with one of the most popularly held misconceptions about the Buddha's teachings pertaining to rebirth (*punabbhava*). Even during the Buddha's day, when he spoke about rebirth being causally conditioned or "dependently arisen" (*paṭiccasamuppanna*), and enumerated several conditions that would contribute to it (*M* 1.265), one of his disciples picked out one among these conditions, namely, consciousness (*viññāṇa*), maintaining that it is "This very same consciousness that transmigrates, not another" (*idam eva viññāṇaṃ sandhāvati saṃsarati anaññaṃ*, *M* 1.256; *Chung* 54.2 [*Taishō* 1.766c]). There certainly were many others, including some of his disciples, who continued to uphold such views throughout the centuries. The widespread prevalence of this view seems to indicate the adamant way in which people believed that for survival to take place there must be a permanent and eternal substance.

The Buddha's answer to these believers in a permanent and eternal self or entity is that any factor that contributes to human survival, whether it is consciousness (*viññaṇa*) or disposition (*saṅkhāra*), or action (*kamma*) or even grasping (*upādāna*), all these are dependently arisen. For the Buddha, continuity can be explained in a more empirical way by following the principle of dependence of impermanent factors of existence, where on leaves an impression on another, thus eliminating the need for assuming a permanent entity.

Nāgārjuna is here referring to two extremes, i.e., permanence (*nitya*) and impermanence (*anitya*), this latter being the momentary destruction (*kṣaṇa-bhaṅga*) advocated by the Buddhist metaphysicians. The former represents the Sarvāstivāda point of view; the latter, the Sautrāntika.

If the dispositions (*saṃskāra*) are presented as being either permanent or impermanent when they transmigrate, and if there is no mention of causal conditioning of these dispositions as well as the other factors, then the theories of eternalism and annihilationism are inevitable. Furthermore, such extreme conclusions are especially unavoidable when one factor or entity is singled out and shown to be *the* factor involved in transmigration.

2. *Pudgalaḥ samsaranti cet skandhāyatanadhātuṣu,*
pañcadhā mṛgyamāṇo 'sau nāsti kaḥ saṃsariṣyati.

It may be assumed that a person transmigrates. Yet, such a person, sought for in the fivefold way in the aggregates, spheres (of sense) and elements, does not exist. Who then will transmigrate?

MKV(P) p.284; *MKV(V)* p.124.

It is interesting to note that in the previous statement Nāgārjuna rejects only the view that dispositions transmigrate. He did not deny the dispositions themselves. However, in the present verse Nāgārjuna maintains that if a transmigrating "person" (*pudgala*) is sought for (*mṛgyamāno*) *in* the aggregates, faculties, and elements (as Nāgārjuna tried to do in the last fifteen chapters) one does not discover him. The "person" referred to here is no ordinary person. This person should possess the same characteristic which, according to the previous verse, made it impossible for the "dispositions" to transmigrate, namely, permanence.

Inada seems to miss the meaning of the term *mṛgyamāṇa* in his translation of this verse.

3. *Upādānād upādānaṃ saṃsaran vibhavo bhavet,*
vibhavaś cānupādānaḥ kaḥ sa kiṃ saṃsariṣyati.

Moving from one form of grasping to another, there would be other-becoming. Who is this person who has ceased to be and is [therefore] non-grasping? Wherein does he transmigrate?

MKV(P) p.284; *MKV(V)* p.124.

Understanding the causal process in a linear way one runs into difficulties in explaining "grasping" (***upādāna***) as a reason, not only for transmigration but also for conceptualizing a person. While grasping was considered an important cause for the unhappiness and suffering (***dukkha***), as also the rebirth of a human being, "non-grasping" (***anupādāna***) was a condition for happiness (***sukha***) in this life and for not being reborn in a future life. In addition, even the very notion of a substantial "self" (***atta***) is supposed to be the result of grasping on to the five aggregates (***upādānakkhandha***).

However, if grasping is singled out and explained in a linear way, then moving from one moment of grasping to another, one will be faced with other-becoming (***vibhava***). To explain this broken or interrupted series of graspings, one needs to assume that there is something to be grasped so that grasping can continue. The aggregates do not continuously provide a foundation for grasping. They arise and cease. With such arising and ceasing, grasping itself would be interrupted. This means that grasping that has come to be non-existent (***vibhava***) would also be non-grasping (***anupādāna***). If so, where is this so-called permanent entity and where does he transmigrate?

4. *Saṃskārāṇāṃ na nirvāṇaṃ kathaṃcid upapadyate,*
sattvasyāpi na nirvāṇaṃ kathaṃcid upapadyate.

The cessation of dispositions is somehow not appropriate. The cessation even of a sentient being is also not appropriate in any way.

MKV(P) p.288; *MKV(V)* p.126.

The Buddha left unanswered the question regarding the nature of a "freed person" (*tathāgata*) after death (*parammaraṇā*). Nāgārjuna will return to this question in his final chapter, "The Examination of Views" (*Dṛṣṭi-parīkṣa*). In the present context, Nāgārjuna is concerned mostly with the living person. The previous verses referred to the metaphysical views regarding a living person in bondage. The present verse is, therefore, devoted to an examination of the metaphysical view pertaining to a living person who has attained freedom. Speaking of that freedom, Nāgārjuna does not want to assume that it is the cessation of dispositions, or of a "person." He was probably aware that the Buddha spoke of the pacification of dispositions (*saṅkhāra-upasama*) in relation to a living person who has attained freedom. He was also aware that the Buddha did not advocate the annihilation of a sentient being (*sattva*, see commentary of XIII.1). Hence his present statement.

5. *Na badhyante na mucyanta udaya-vyaya-dharmiṇaḥ,*
saṃskārāḥ pūrvavat satto badhyate na na mucyate.

Dispositions that are of the nature of uprising and ceasing are neither bound nor released. A sentient being, like the foregoing, is neither bound nor released.

MKV(P) p.290; *MKV(V)* p.127.

According to the substantialist way of thinking, an eternal self or soul (*ātman*) is in bondage because it is bound to various ephemeral factors such as the psycho-physical personality (see. *Bhagavadgītā*, Chapter XIII). Such a self has to break away from its bondage in order to be free. Having rejected a permanent entity like the self, if the Buddhists were to consider the dispositions as the condition for bondage, such dispositions, being of the nature of arising and ceasing, could neither be bound nor freed. In other words, one cannot look at the dispositions through the eyes of the substantialist. The same can be said of a sentient being (*sattva*).

6. *Bandhanaṃ ced upādānaṃ sopādāno na badhyate,*
badhyate nānupādānaḥ kim avastho 'tha badhyate.

If grasping were to be considered a bondage, one who is with grasping is not being bound. Neither is one without grasping being bound. A person in which state is then bound?

MKV(P) 290; *MKV(V)* p.127.

The substance/attribute distinction that emerges from the statement such as "one who is with grasping" (*sa-upādāno*) militates against saying that he is being bound (*badhyate*). In this sense, the attribute is already implicit in the substance and there is no point in piling up another identical attribute on it. If the substance is without attribute (as in the case of *an-upādāna*), then there seems to be no way in which one can attribute an attribute to it. They could always remain independent. These difficulties relating to identity and difference give rise to the question regarding the status of the person who is being bound.

7. *Badhnīyād bandhanaṃ kāmaṃ bandhyāt pūrvaṃ bhaved yadi,*
na cāsti tat śeṣam uktaṃ gamyamāna-gatāgataiḥ.

If it is assumed that bondage exists prior to the binding of that which is to be bound, that does not exist. The rest has been explained by [the analysis of] present moving, the moved and the not moved.

MKV(P) pp.291-292; *MKV(V)* pp.127-128.

If, in answer to the question raised in the previous verse, it is said that bondage exists prior to someone being bound, such bondage, according to Nāgārjuna, does not exist. The analysis in Chapter II as well as in Chapter X can be utilized here to refute the implications of a substantialist view of bondage.

8. *Baddho na mucyate tāvad abaddho naiva mucyate,*
syātāṃ baddhe mucyamāne yugapad-bandha-mokṣaṇe.

One who is bound is not released, nor is one who is not bound freed. When there is releasing of one who is bound, then there would be simultaneous occurrence of bondage and release.

MKV(P) p.293; *MKV(V)* p.128.

One who is substantially bound (*baddha*), i.e., one who has the self-nature (*svabhāva*) of bondage, cannot be freed. Similarly, it is meaningless to speak of someone who is absolutely free (*a-baddha*), i.e., whose self-nature is freedom, as one being freed. If one were to speak of someone who is already bound and is being freed, then bondage and freedom would be simultaneous.

9. *Nirvasyāmy anupādāno nirvāṇaṃ me bhaviṣyati,*
iti yeṣāṃ grahas teṣām upādāna-mahā-grahaḥ.

"Non-grasping, I shall be free. Freedom will then be mine." For whomsoever there is grasping in this manner, that will be a gigantic grasping.

MKV(P) p.295; *MKV(V)* p.129.

Nāgārjuna is here presenting a fundamental idea expressed in the early discourses (see *M* 1.145-151, *Rathavinīta-sutta*) as well as in the Prajñāpāramitā literature, especially the *Vajracchedikā*. It is the idea that one cannot be freed and still cling to freedom, let along bragging about it. However, one need not construe the Buddha's statement at *M* 1.171 (*Ariyapariyesana-sutta*) as an instance of such bragging. That statement was made by the Buddha in response to a question raised by Upaka at a time when the only freed one in the world was the Buddha himself. He was simply describing to Upaka the absence of any one who had attained freedom, in the sense in which the Buddha understood the conception of freedom. Whether the Buddha would make such a statement subsequent to the preaching of the first sermon and the attainment of enlightenment and freedom by his first five disciples is extremely doubtful.

10. *Na nirvāṇa-samāropo na saṃsārāpakarṣaṇam,*
yatra kas tatra saṃsāro nirvāṇaṃ kiṃ vikalpyate.

Wherein there is neither the attribution of freedom nor the elimination of the life-process, what is it that is being discriminated as life-process or as freedom?

MKV(P) p.299; *MKV(V)* p.130.

This concluding verse provides a beautiful summary of the metaphysical views relating to a life of bondage (*saṃsāra*) and freedom (*nirvāṇa*) and can serve as a key to unlocking the mysteries surrounding the chapters to come. The constant debates among modern scholars as to the implications of Nāgārjuna's famous chapter on *Nirvāṇa* (XXV) can easily be eliminated if we are to keep in mind the nature of the theories pertaining to bondage and freedom that Nāgārjuna had to deal with.

Presented in the substantialist mould, freedom becomes an attribution (*samāropa*), while the life-process with its suffering requires elimination (*apakarṣaṇa*). No such freedom or life process is accepted by Nāgārjuna. Such a description was too metaphysical for him.

Attribution and elimination imply the existence of a neutral substance to which freedom can be attributed or strung on to, while bondage in the form of life-process can be wrestled away from. If no neutral substance is recognized, there could be two other ways of explaining freedom and bondage. First, it is possible to say that the substance is inherently free and that it is held in bondage by adventitious elements. Thus, the Upaniṣadic or the Brahmanical notion of "self" which is pure and luminous is understood as something kept in bondage to the psychophysical personality, like a sword kept in its sheath. The originally pure mind (*prakṛti-prabhāsvara-citta*) of the Buddhist metaphysician (see *Laṅkāvatāra*, ed. Nanjio, 1956, p.358) resembles the Upaniṣadic and Brahmanical views of the "self." Secondly, if such an originally pure entity is not acceptable, then it is possible to argue that what is called the life-process (*saṃsāra*) is completely annihilated and a completely new process of freedom is initiated. The former has nothing to do with the latter. Indeed, one cannot ignore the solutions offered by the Buddhist metaphysicians when they came to analyse the personal stream of becoming (*bhava-sota*) into discrete entities. The concepts of "attainment" (*prapti*) and "non-attainment" (*a-prāpti*) provided a solution that is almost identical with those mentioned above. *Nirvāṇa* thus becomes a *prāpti* that fall into the stream (*sva-saṃtāna-patita*) and at that point *saṃsāra* becomes an *a-prāpti*.

As pointed out in the Introduction, the Buddha's conceptions of bondage and freedom (and this would also apply to Nāgārjuna's views) have nothing to do with any one of the alternative explanations mentioned above.

CHAPTER SEVENTEEN
Examination of the Fruit of Action
(Karma-phala-parīkṣā)

1. *Atma-saṃyamakaṃ cetaḥ parānugrāhakaṃ ca yat,*
   maitraṃ sa dharmaḥ tad bījaṃ phalsya pretya ceha ca.

Self-restraint as well as benefitting others – this is the friendly way and it constitutes the seed that bears fruit here as well as in the next life.

MKV(P) p.303; *MKV(V)* p.132.

The present chapter, unlike Chapter VIII, deals with the problem of moral responsibility. It is an attempt to explain the "fruits" (*phala*) reaped as a result of one's actions (*karma*). The doctrine of the fruits of action or moral responsibility is pivotal to any explanation of human life, whether it is in bondage or in freedom. However, in the present chapter, the idea of the accumulation of merit and demerit (*puṇya-pāpa*) (for future benefit) is examined at length, primarily because this particular idea is mostly associated with the life-process (*saṃsāra*) in bondage. The Buddha insisted that such accumulation of merit and demerit is abandoned (*prahīṇa*) by a person who is enjoying freedom (*nirvāṇa*), even though he does not transcend morals or is not unconcerned with questions relating to moral responsibility.

Inada assumes that verses 1-19 represent the popular explanation of karma. This is questionable. In fact, the popular, and therefore, a mistaken view of karma is presented only in verses 6-12. Verse 13, as will be pointed out, refers to a more sophisticated theory of moral responsibility held by the Buddha and his disciples.

The present verse deals with two important virtues – self-restraint and benevolence – and these constitute the friendly way (*maitraṃ dharmaḥ*) which serves as the seed that fruitions here as well as in the future. Inada reads three virtues – self-restraint, kindness towards others and benevolence. On the contrary, *maitraṃ* seems to qualify *dharma*, and Kumārajīva understood it in this latter sense.

2. *Cetanā cetayitvā ca karmoktaṃ parama-ṛṣiṇā,*
tasyānekavidho bhedaḥ karmaṇaḥ parikīrtitaḥ.

The Supreme Ascetic has said that action is volition as well as volitional. Many distinct varieties of that action have also been expounded.

MVK(P) pp.305-306; *MKV(V) p.133.*

At *A* 3.415 (*Chung* 27.5 [*Taishō* 1.600a]), the Buddha identified karma with "volition" and maintained that karma, whether it be bodily, verbal, or mental, is to be recognized as karma if it is volitional (*Cetanā 'haṃ bhikkhave kammaṃ vadāmi. Cetayitvā kammaṃ karoti kāyena vācāya manasā ca*). The emphasis on volition was intended to eliminate the wrong belief that a person is responsible for any and every action he performs, a view that was advocated by the Jaina thinkers of pre-Buddhist India (see Kalupahana, *Causality*, pp.125-126). The distinct varieties of karma referred to here are the one's presented in the canonical Adhidharma, and these are based upon the discussions available in the early discourses.

3. *Tatra yac cetanety uktaṃ karma mānasaṃ smṛtaṃ,*
cetayitvā ca yat tūktaṃ tat tu kāyika-vācikam.

Herein, what is called volition is reminisced as mental action. Whatever is called volitional consists of the bodily and verbal.

MKV(P) p.306; *MKV(V)* p.133.

A difference is noticeable between the Buddha's own explanation of karma in the statement from *Aṅguttara* quoted at XVII.2 and the present description of Nāgārjuna. While *cetanā* or volition is definitely mental, the Buddha seems to assume that not all mental actions are volitional. Hence his statement that all three forms of karma, bodily, verbal and mental, can be determined by volition. However, in the present statement, volition seems to have been identified with mental action, the volitional being confined strictly to bodily and verbal. This latter view may be a reflexion of the Buddha's own statement at *M* 2.25 (*Chung* 47.2 [*Taishō* 1.720]), wherein both bodily and verbal actions are considered to have mind as a basis.

4. *Vāg-viṣpando 'viratayo yāś cāvijñapti-saṃjñitāḥ,*
avijñaptaya evānyāḥ smṛtā viratayas tathā.

5. *Paribhogānvayaṃ puṇyam apuṇyaṃ ca tathāvidhaṃ,*
cetanā ceti saptaite dharmāḥ karmāñjanāḥ smṛtāḥ.

Whatever words and deeds that are associated with delight and designated as non-intimation, and also those others reminisced as non-intimation, but are associated with non-delight; similarly, merit as well as demerit consequent upon enjoyment, and finally, volition – these are reminisced as the seven things that are productive of action.

MKV(P) p.307; *MKV(V)* p.133.

Some of the terms used here to define the various forms of karma appear for the first time in the Abhidharma (see *Akb* iv.1-2; *Akb* pp.162-164; *Adv* pp.118-119). They are absent in the early discourses. However, taken in themselves, they do not seem to create any philopsophical problems. The philosophical problems arose because of the manner in which these actions were ***interpreted***. These interpretations are then taken up for examination by Nāgārjuna in the following verses.

6. *Tiṣṭhaty apāka-kālāc cet karma tan nityatām iyāt,*
niruddhaṃ cen niruddhaṃ sat kiṃ phalaṃ janayiṣyati.

If it is assumed that action remains during the time it is maturing, then it will approach permanence. If it is assumed to have ceased, then having ceased, how can it produce a fruit?

MKV(P) p.311; *MKV(V)* p.134.

This is actually the point at which Nāgārjuna begins his analysis of the metaphysical assumptions. Here he immediately turns on to the theories of identity and difference. The assumption taken up for criticism in the first line needs to be examined carefully. Undoubtedly, it is the problem of ***potential*** existence. Such existence may be understood in various ways. Potentiality may be taken as the existence of conditions that would eventually give rise to some particular event. Nāgārjuna, as may be seen in a moment, does not seem to object to such an explanation. On the contrary, if potentiality is understood in the sense of substantial existence of the particular event (in this case, karma), even when it has not matured or come to fruition, then that assumption leads to eternalism. This latter view is certainly not acceptable to Nāgārjuna. It also leads to the contrary view, that is, if the event is completely absent (and this absence pertains to the very conditions that will eventually give rise to the event), then there will be doubts about the occurrence of the event at all. This is annihilationism. Thus, Nāgārjuna is not denying the fruit of action but only the manner in which it is explained.

7. *Yo 'ṅkura-prabhṛtir bījāt saṃtāno 'bhipravartate,*
tataḥ phalaṃ ṛte bījāt sa ca nābhipravartate.

Whatever series that begins with a sprout proceeds from a seed, and then produces a fruit. However, without a seed, such [a series] would not proceed.

MKV(P) p.312; *MKV(V)* p.135.

The metaphysical assumptions of the Sautrantika doctrine of karma are under review here. The atomistic view of the life-process accepted by the Sautrāntikas compelled them to analyse an event into a series (*saṃtāna*) of moments. Their major difficulty lay in explaining how one series (e.g., a sprout-series) comes to be tied up with another preceding series (e.g., a seed-series), since they are different. If they are radically different, then the sprout-series can occur even in the absence of the seed-series. Nāgārjuna maintains that this does not happen. In other words, he is insisting that philosophers like the Sautrāntikas will have to accept the view that no event can come into being unless there were conditions that give rise to it; in this case it is the seed-series.

8. *Bījāc ca yasmāt saṃtānaḥ saṃtānāc ca phalodbhavaḥ,*
bīja-pūrvaṃ phalaṃ tasmān nocchinnaṃ nāpi śāśvatam.

Since a series arises from a seed and a fruit arises from a series, a fruit that is preceded by a seed is, therefore, neither interrupted nor eternal.

MKV(P) p.313; *MKV(V)* p.135.

In answer to the question raised by Nāgārjuna, a Sautrāntika can respond thus: Instead of conceiving of these as two different series, let us say that a series is produced from a seed. This series then gives rise to the effect (which is the sprout). In that sense, a fruit is preceded by a seed (*bīja-pūrvaṃ phalaṃ*). Understood in this way, one does not fall into either the eternalistic or the annihilationist view.

9. *Yas tasmāc citta-saṃtānaś cetaso 'bhipravartate,*
tataḥ phalaṃ ṛte cittāt sa ca nābhipravartate.

Therefore, whatever thought-series there is, that proceeds from a thought and from that fruit. That thought series would not proceed without a thought.

10. *Cittāc ca yasmāt saṃtānaḥ saṃtānāc ca phalodbhavaḥ,*
karma-pūrvaṃ phalaṃ tasmān nocchinnaṃ nāpi śāśvataṃ.

Since a continuous series arises from thought and from the continuous series the uprising of a fruit, the fruit that is preceded by action is neither interrupted nor eternal.

MKV(P) p.313-314; *MKV(V)* p.135.

The Sautrāntika continues: Similarly, a though series (*citta-saṃtāna*) emerges from a thought (*cetasaḥ*). From that series arises the fruit. Thus, without a thought, the fruit does not come to be. The thought followed by a thought-series thus gives rise to the fruit. The fruit is thus preceded by a thought which is its cause. As such, it is neither permanent nor interrupted.

The causal connection envisaged by the Sautrāntikas above is simple ***antecedence***.

11. *Dharmasya sādhanopāyāḥ śuklāḥ karma-pathā dasa,*
phalaṃ kāmaguṇāḥ pañca dharmasya pretya ceha ca.

The ten pure paths of action are the means of achieving good. The five strands of sense pleasure represent the fruit of good, here as well as in the next life.

MKV(P) p.314; *MKV(V)* p.136.

Following the causal pattern laid down above, namely, antecedence, the Sautrāntika would explain the tenfold path of action (*karma-patha*) as being initiated by volition (*cetanā*) which puts it together (*tathābhisaṃskaraṇāt*, Akb p.248). Volition thus becomes the karma, and the series of actions, bodily and verbal (*kāya-vāk*), determined by that volition, becomes the vehicle of action" (*karmaṇaś ca panthānaḥ, ibid.*). The pure bodily and verbal actions would then be the means by which good is achieved (*dharmasya sādhanopāyāḥ*). The five strands of pleasure to be enjoyed in a "heavenly" life (*svarga*), either here or in the next world, would be the fruit of the good volition. This is the manner in which the Sautrāntikas explained the Buddha's notion of karma and its effect.

12. *Bahavaś ca mahantaś ca doṣāḥ syur api kalpanā,*
yady eṣā tena naivaiṣā kalpanātropapadyate.

If there were to be such a thought, there would be many a great error. Therefore, such a thought is not appropriate here.

MKV(P) p.316; *MKV(V)* p.136

Nāgārjuna is not impressed by such an explanation. He perceives many and substantial errors in such conceptualizations. Hence he considers them to be inappropriate.

Inada's translation, once again, skips an extremely important qualification made by Nāgārjuna. "If conceptualizations are permitted, there will arise many as well as great errors," (p.107). The implication would be that Nāgārjuna rejects all conceptualizations. However, this is not the case. Nāgārjuna is very specific in his reference when he says: *eṣā kalpanā*, "these conceptualizations," where "these" refers to the preceding conceptualizations or explanations. Indeed, it is for this reason that Nāgārjuna can turn around and speak of a more appropriate thought or conceptualization in the next verse.

13. *Imāṃ punaḥ pravakṣyāmi kalpanāṃ yātra yojyate,*
buddhaiḥ pratyeka-buddhaiś ca śrāvakaiś cānuvarṇitam.

Moreover, I shall expound the following thought which is appropriate and which has been extolled by the Buddhas, the self-enlightened ones and the disciples.

MKV(P) p.317; *MKV(V)* p.13.

The present statement by Nāgārjuna should serve as an antidote to most of the misunderstandings that have prevailed so far regarding his views about thought and language. Nāgārjuna is about to explain in no unclear terms a more appropriate thought or conceptualization (*kalpanā*), a right thought (*samyak-saṃkalpa*), a right view or perception (*samyag-dṛṣṭi*) relating to karma and its fruit (*phala*). It is one that is extolled not only by the Buddha, but also by his disciples (*śrāvaka*) and the self-enlightened ones (*pratyeka-buddha*). If Nāgārjuna had recognized a linguistically transcendent truth or reality, he could not have made the above statement.

14. *Pattraṃ yathā 'vipraṇāśas tathā-ṛṇam iva karma ca,*
caturvidho dhātutaḥ sa prakṛtyā 'vyākṛtaś ca saḥ.

Like an imperishable promissory note, so is debt as well as action. It is fourfold in terms of realms and indeterminate in terms of primal nature.

MKV(P) p.317; *MKV(V)* p.137

Here, a debt and karma are compared to an imperishable promissory note. The metaphor is significant and needs to be carefully examined. It is used by Nāgārjuna to illustrate the doctrine of karma as described in one of the most popular and authoritative statements in the Indian Buddhist tradition. Two centuries later, Vasubandhu wrote a whole treatise—*Karmasiddhiprakaraṇa*—attempting to explain this statement. Candrakīrti quotes it twice in his commentary (pp.324,390). The fact that he does not quote it at this point, where it seems to be most relevant, indicates that he was using it to illustrate a completely different point (see below XVII.21). The statement runs thus: "Karmas do not perish even after hundreds of millions of aeons. Reaching the harmony of conditions and the appropriate time, they produce consequences for human beings."

The first statement, taken in isolation, will convey the impression that the Buddhist theory of karma is deterministic in an extreme sense. However, the second statement provides sufficient qualifications to take the determinist sting away. What seems to have compelled Inada to assume that here, "With equal force he condemns any idea of an indestructible continuing action (*avipraṇāśa-karma*) which gives the sense of continuity or transition in man's everyday life and deeds" (*Nāgārjuna,* p.104), is his failure to evaluate the *first* statement in the light of the qualifications provided in the *second* statement. In the present chapter Nāgārjuna is simply explaining the first statement, i.e., "karmas do not perish" (*na praṇaśyanti karmāṇi*). His analysis, at this point, is confined to it. He leaves the second statement to be examined in two other chapters that follow. After examining what an imperishable karma is, Nāgārjuna wants to keep any soul-theory out of the way, and this he does with Chapter XVIII. And from there, he immediately gets down to analyse the contents of the second statement by compiling two chapters: (i) Chapter XIX on the "Examination of Time" (*Kāla-parīkṣā*) and (ii) Chapter XX on the "Examination of Harmony" (*Sāmagrī-parīkṣā*). As such, it would be inappropriate to come to any definite conclusions regarding the contents of this chapter until the three following chapters are carefully examined. However, Nāgārjuna's statement at XVIII.13 that he "will state *this* more appropriate view" (*imaṃ kalpanāṃ pravakṣyāmi yātra yojyate*), which he then attributes to the Buddhas, his disciples, and the Pratyeka-buddhas would certainly seem to indicate that he is presenting an acceptable view, rather than one that should be rejected.

Furthermore, having made such a strong statement indicating that he is presenting "*this*" (*imāṃ*) appropriate view, if Nāgārjuna were to follow it up with a theory that he is condemning, one will need to think twice before considering Nāgārjuna to be a second Buddha.

To return to the metaphor of the promissory note (*patra*) that one signs when borrowing money—this metaphor being Nāgārjuna's own—he is not speaking of a permanent and eternal promissory note, but something that will remain so long as it is not redeemed. As long as a promissory note is preserved, and unless one were to honor one's obligations, one will eventually, depending upon time and conditions, have to face the consequences. The imperishability of the promissory note may also mean that even if the promissory note is destroyed there is an obligation on one's part to honor such an agreement.

If, in order to account for such an obligation, one were to assume a substantial nature (*prakṛti* = *svabhāva*) in that act, Nāgārjuna's reponse is that such a nature is "not determinate" or is "inexplicable" (*avyakṛta*), an answer that the Buddha himself gave when questioned about metaphysical issues (see Chapter XXVII).

Finally, in terms of the realms in which the consequences may be reaped, such actions can be fourfold. Candarkīrti refers to the fourfold realms as (i) the sphere of sensuality (*kāmāvacara*), (ii) the sphere of materiality (*rūpāvacara*), (iii) the sphere of the formless (*arūpāvacara*), and (iv) the state of freedom or absence of influxes (*anāśrava*).

15. *Prahāṇto na praheyo bhāvanā-heya eva vā,*
tasmād avipraṇāśena jāyate karmaṇāṃ phalaṃ.

That [i.e., the imperishable karma] would not be relinquished by simple relinquishing. It is to be relinquished only through cultivation. Thus, through the imperishable arises the fruit of action.

16. *Prahāṇataḥ praheyaḥ syāt karmaṇaḥ saṃkrameṇa vā,*
yadi doṣāḥ prasajyeraṃs tatra karma-vadhāyaḥ.

If it is to be relinquished through simple relinquishing or through the transformation of action, then there would follow a variety of errors such as the destruction of actions.

MKV(P) pp.319-320; *MKV(V)* p.137-138.

When speaking of imperishable karma, naturally the question can be raised as to how it can be gottern rid of. Is it possible to nullify the effect, say, of a bad karma by simply not doing it again (*prahāṇato praheyo*)? The theory of *prāpti* ("attainment") and *aprāpti* ("non-attainment") may imply such a situation.

Preventing the momentary stream of life from appropriating a bad karma would mean the nullification of the effects of all previous karmas. Nāgārjuna perceives this to be a negation of the doctrine of karma (*karma-vadha*). He therefore insists that the abandoning of the fruits of karma can be achieved, not through simple abandonment, but through constant practice (*bhāvanā*), i.e. constant performance or promotion of good actions and the constant avoidance of evil actions (cp. *sabbapāpassa akaraṇaṃ kusalassa upasampadā*, *D* 2.49; *Dhp* 183).

17. *Sarveṣāṃ viṣabhāgānāṃ sabhāgānāṃ ca karmaṇāṃ,*
pratisaṃdhau sadhātūnāṃ eka utpadyate tu saḥ.

Of all these actions, whether dissimilar or similar, belonging to certain realms, only one would arise at the moment of birth [of a being].

MKV(P) p.321; *MKV(V)* p. 138.

Even though this statement of Nāgārjuna is in perfect conformity with the Buddha's own explanation of the doctrine of karma, it may come as a surprise to most Nāgārjunian scholars, especially because it conflicts with most opinions expressed about Nāgārjuna's philosophy. Here is an explanation of rebirth (*punarbhava*) examined in relation to past karma. In the eyes of most scholars, Nāgārjuna could never make a statement like this. Here, karma is presented as the connecting link between two lives. It is one of a myriad of karmas an individual may have performed, whether they be similar or dissimilar. The fact that only one (*eka*) among such actions of a life-time may appear at the time of the conception of a being (*pratisaṃdhi*) and which can influence the new life-process is acknowledged by Nāgārjuna. He could not have been unaware of the statement of the Buddha that consciousness (*viññāṇa* which is inextricably bound up with volitional karma) was a possible connecting link between two lives (*D* 3.105; *Chang* 12.2 [*Taishō* 1.77b]) and also of the emphasis placed by his fellow Buddhists on the last thought of the dying person (*cuti-citta*) as having influence over a new life-process (*paṭisandhi-citta*, see detailed discussion at *VbhA* 155-160). Without falling back upon a metaphysical theory of moments, as some of the Abhidharma interpreters did, Nāgārjuna is here recognizing the dependence of rebirth (*pratisaṃdhi*) on at least one previous karma. It is a similar recognition that made the Buddha declare: "Beings have karma as their own, karma as inheritance, karma as the source, karma as kin. It is karma that distinguishes human beings, for example, as inferior and superior," (*kammassakā . . . sattā kammadāyādā kammayoni kammabandhu, kammaṃ satte vabhajati yadidaṃ hīṇappaṇītatāya*, *M* 3.203; *Chung* 44.1 [*Taishō* 1.704c]). Unfortunately, Buddhaghosa's explanation, though retaining the ideas expressed by the Buddha as well as Nāgārjuna, is marred by a theory of moments (see *VbhA* 156). Just as much as memory is being described by most psychologists as being "owned" without having to assume its permanence, here we find a person's karma being perceived as something "owned" by him.

18. *Karmaṇaḥ karmaṇo dṛṣṭe dharma utpadyate tu saḥ,*
dvi-prakārasya sarvasya vipakve pi ca tiṣṭhati.

That [imperishable] arises in the present life, corresponding to all the actions having dual natures [similar and dissimilar, good and bad, etc.] and stays so even when matured.

MKV(P) p. 321; *MKV(V)* p.138.

A further exploration of the Buddha's doctrine of karma is continued here. The phrase *dṛṣṭe dharme* is a sanskritization of Pali *diṭṭha dhamma*, which itself can be traced back to *dṛṣṭa-janman*, meaning "the present life." The fruitioning of karma into good and bad consequences is admitted here.

19. *Phala-vyatikramād vā sa maraṇād vā nirudhyate,*
anāśravaṃ sāśravaṃ ca vibhāgaṃ tatra lakṣayet.

That [imperishable] ceases as result of the interruption of the fruit or as a result of death. Herein, a distinction between one with influxes and the one without influxes is to be signified.

MKV(P) p.322; *MKV(V)* p.138.

The so-called imperishable action (*avipraṇāśa-karma*) can terminate as a result of two events: (i) the interruption of the fruit (*phala-vyatikrama*), or ((ii) death of the individual. In the case of the latter, it is necessary to remember what was said at XVII.17, i.e., that all actions performed during a lifetime are not continued. Only one of the myriads of actions performed can dominate the last thought moment of a person. This would mean that many other karmas, even though all of them have not matured, may become nullified at the time of death.

20. *Śūnyatā ca na cocchedaḥ saṃsāraś ca na śāśvatam,*
karmaṇo 'vipraṇāśaś ca dharmo buddhena deśitaḥ.

Emptiness, however, is not annihilation; life-process is also not eternal; the imperishability is of action—such is the doctrine taught by the Buddha.

MKV(P) p.322; *MKV(V)* 138.

If what is said before is an appropriate explanation of karma, then Nāgārjuna can maintain that "emptiness" (*śūnyatā*) does not mean "annihilation" (*uccheda*). At the same time he can maintain that the life-process (*saṃsāra*) is not a permanent and eternal (*śāśvata*) process. In such a context, an imperishable action (*avipraṇāśa-karma*) simply means the continuity of that life-process conditioned by karma until some of these karmas bear fruit or are lost on the way, while others like the threads of a web can continue to influence the future life-process. In any case, the entire process is one of dependence—dependence upon a whole composite of factors.

Nāgārjuna has no hesitation in attributing such a doctrine of karma and personal idenity to the Buddha himself and praising it as the Buddha-word, even though the attribution of such a doctrine to Nāgārjuna would be unacceptable to some of the classical and modern followers of Nāgārjuna himself.

21. *Karma notpadyate kasmāt niḥsvābhāvaṃ yatas tataḥ,*
yasmāc ca tad anutpannaṃ na tasmād vipraṇaśyati.

Why does action not arise? Because it is without self-nature. Since it is non-arisen, it does not perish.

MKV(P) pp.323-324; *MKV(V)* p.139.

Having concluded the explanation of the more appropriate view of karma as advocated by the Buddha, Nāgārjuna does not leave the discussion without taking a look at the possible metaphysical interpretations or any misunderstanding of this doctrine. He has already spoken of the arising (*utpāda*) of karma at the moment of rebirth (*pratisaṃdhi*). That arising is understood in relation to the principle of dependent arising (*pratītyasamutpāda*). The imperishability (*avipraṇāśa*) is introduced in order to explain the continuity in the fruitioning of action. It is *not* intended as a justification for the belief in a permanent and eternal substance (*svabhāva*). However, some of the Buddhists did utilize a notion of substance to account for the functioning of karma. It is this particular notion of substance that is taken up for analysis.

If karma is "non-substantial" (*niḥsvabhāva*) in the way the Sautrāntikas understood it, i.e., without any perceivable continuity, but only as something that is continually interrupted, then the arising of such karma cannot be explained. If arising cannot be accounted for in such a metaphysical way, neither can cessation be admitted. Imperishability (*avipraṇāśa*), as explained by Nāgārjuna, becomes the only other alternative.

Unfortunately, Candrakīrti, who favored a rather absolutistic interpretation of Nāgārjuna (see comments on the Dedicatory Verses), utilizes the conception of imperishability in order to deny *any* form of arising. It is because he had such an interpretation in mind that he quotes the famous verse elucidating karma at this point rather than utilizing it when the imperishability was first mentioned by Nāgārjuna at XVII.14. As has been shown already, Nāgārjuna was not critical of any and every form of arising or ceasing. He was only rejecting the metaphysical ideas.

22. *Karma svabhāvataś cet syāc chāśvataṃ syād asaṃśayaṃ,*
akṛtaṃ ca bhavet karma kriyate na hi śāśvataṃ.

If it is assumed that action comes to be from self-nature, it certainly will

be eternal, and action would also be uncaused, for that which is eternal is, indeed, not caused.

MKV(P) p.324; *MKV(V)* p.139.

If the arising of karma cannot be accounted for by following the Sautrāntika method, can it be explained in terms of the Sarvāstivāda conception? Nāgārjuna's answer is negative. He seems to know with great certainty (*asaṃśayaṃ*) that the Sarvāstivāda solution does not work. It implies permanence and as a result karma would appear to be "un-done" or "uncreated" (*akṛta*).

23. *Akṛtābhyāgama-bhayaṃ syāt karmākṛtakaṃ yadi,*
abrahmacarya-vāsaś ca doṣas tatra prasajyate.

If an action were not performed [by the individual], then there would be fear of being confronted by something not performed [by him]. An ignoble life as well as error would follow from this.

MKV(P) p.325; *MKV(V)* p.140.

If actions were to be something not performed, then a person would be haunted by the fear (*bhaya*) or anxiety that he has no hand in the organization of his own life-process. Fears and anxieties, according to Nāgārjuna's view, are one's own creations. Deny one's own responsibility, one does not have to justify a life of moral purity (*brahmacarya-vāsa*). This is a clear and unequivocal assertion of personal responsibility for one's own purity and defilement.

24. *Vyavahārā virudhyante sarva eva na saṃśayaḥ,*
puṇya-pāpa-kṛtor naiva pravibhāgaś ca yujyate.

Undoubtedly, all conventions would then be contradicted. The distinction between the performance of merit and evil will also not be proper.

MKV(P) p.325; *MKV(V)* p.140.

With the rejection of a life of moral purity resulting from the denial of human responsibility for actions, all moral conventions like merit and demerit (*puṇya-pāpa*) would be rendered meaningless. It is interesting to note that Nāgārjuna is not referring to the good-bad (*dharma-adharma* or *kusala-akusala*) distinction, for this latter distinction is different from the former in regard to its value as a convention (*vyavahāra*). This is compatible with the Buddha's own explanation of karma. On pragmatic grounds, the Buddha recognized the merit/demerit distinction. It was helpful in leading the ordinary people toward accepting a moral life. However, the notions of merit and demerit could be harmful in the long run, especially because it involves the idea of accumulation of merit for the sake of future enjoyment and pleasure. Furthermore, it is easily associated with the notions of reward and punishment, a notion that the Buddha was not willing to relate to the doctrine of karma (see *M* 1.373; *Chung* 32.1 [*Taishō* 1.628b]). As such, the Buddha insisted that a morally perfected person would eliminate the desire to accumulate merit or demerit (*puñña-pāpa-pahīṇa, Dhp* 39; *samitāvī pahāya puññapāpaṃ, Sn* 520). Yet, it does not mean that such a person also abandons the good/bad (*kusala-akusala*) distinction which is the very basis of merit and demerit. Indeed, a morally perfect person is expected to promote good, while eliminating evil or unmeritorious actions (see above XVII.1, 17). It may be for this reason that even a later Mahāyāna philosopher like Dogen deemed it appropriate to compile a whole treatise on this subject.

25. *Tad vipakva-vipākaṃ ca punar eva vipakṣyati,*
karma vyavasthitaṃ yasmāt tasmāt svābhāvikaṃ yadi.

If action were to be determined, because it possesses self-nature, then a maturity that has matured will again mature.

MKV(P) p.326; *MKV(V)* p.140.

If an action were to take place without being performed by someone (*akṛtakaṃ*), then it will occur on its own. It will possess its own nature (*svabhāva*). Such a substantial action will have its own consequences (*vipāka*) inherent in it. In that case, what is being described as the fruitioning of karma, namely, a manifestation of its consequences, would merely be a re-fruitioning.

This is the same sort of criticism that Nāgārjuna made of self-causation (*svata-utpatti*) in Chapter I.

26. *Karma kleśātmakam cedam te ca kleśā na tattvataḥ,*
na cet te tattvataḥ kleśāḥ karma syāt tattvataḥ katham.

If this action is associated with defilements, these defilements, in turn, are not found in themselves. If defilements are not in themselves, how could there be an action in itself?

MKV(P) p.236; *MKV(V)* p.140.

The substantialist explanation of karma presented at XVII.25 would lead to the distinction between karma and its quality or attribute. Qualities referred to as defilements (*kleśa*), etc., would be merely incidental. A karma can then make defilement "its own" (*kleśātmaka*) or it can be freed from defilements (*niḥ-kleśika*). Such a substantialist perspective, as mentioned so often by Nāgārjuna, would render the defilements unreal (*na tattvataḥ*), especially because they come and go, arise and pass away, and hence without self-nature. Karma, in such a case would be substantial, and the attributes non-substantial. Nāgārjuna, the empiricist, sees no way in which such a substantial karma, divorced from the attributes, can be identified.

27. *Karma kleśās ca dehānāṃ pratyayāḥ samudāhṛtāḥ,*
karma kleśāś ca te śūnyā yadi deheṣu kā kathā.

Action and defilements are specified as the conditions of the [different] bodies. However, if these actions and defilements are empty, what could be said about the bodies?

MKV(P) p.327; *MKV(V)* p.141.

Here Nāgārjuna moves on to a higher generality. Both karma and defilements are generally considered to be the conditions that determine the individual. As such, karma and defilments become attributes of the personality (*deha*). In the previous verse, Nāgārjuna questioned the substantial reality of both karma and defilments. If they are empty of such reality, what could be said about the personality itself?

28. *Avidyā-nivṛto jantus tṛṣṇā-saṃyojanaś ca saḥ,*
sa bhoktā sa ca na kartur anyo na ca sa eva saḥ.

A sentient being, beclouded by ignorance, is also fettered by craving. As an experiencer, he is neither identical with nor different from the agent.

MKV(P) p.328; *MKV(V)* p.141.

The Buddha's discourse to Acela-Kassapa, the discourse which served as the foundation for Nāgārjuna's treatment of "suffering" (Chapter XII. *Duḥkha-parīkṣā*), rejected the theories of self-causation and external causation of suffering. Rejecting self-causation, the Buddha maintained: "Kassapa, to say that 'a person acts and he himself experiences the consequences,' where self-caused suffering belongs to one who has existed from the beginning, implies eternalism" (*so karoti so paṭisaṃvediyatī ti kho Kassapa ādito sato sayaṃkataṃ dukkhanti iti vadaṃ sassataṃ etaṃ pareti, S* 2.20; *Tsa* 12.20 [*Taishō* 2.86a]). On the contrary, "To say that 'one acts and another experiences the consequences,' where the suffering caused by another belongs to one who has been afflicted with pain, implies annihilationism" (*añño karoti añño paṭisaṃvediyatī ti . . . vedanābhitunnassa sato paraṃkataṃ dukkhanti iti vadaṃ ucchedaṃ etaṃ pareti,* ibid.). It is interesting to note that in the former case, the Buddha refers to the belief in a being who existed from the beginning (*ādito sato*), an idea that is generally considered both by the Buddha and by Nāgārjuna as contributing to a belief in a permanent entity (see Chapter IX on *Pūrva-parīkṣā*).

In the present verse, Nāgārjuna is faithfully following the Buddha's own argument to reject the identity as well as difference between a doer and an experiencer. A person who believes either in identity or in difference is looked upon a someone who is beclouded by ignorance (*avidyā*) and craving (*tṛṣṇā*).

29. *Na pratyaya-samutpannaṃ nāpratyaya-samutthitaṃ,*
asti yasmād idaṃ karma tasmāt kartāpi nāsty ataḥ.

Since this action does not exist as arisen from a condition nor as issuing forth from a non-condition, even an agent does not exist.

MKV(P) p.328; *MKV(V)* p.141.

The causal explanations of karma offered by the metaphysicians, namely, self-causation, external causation, etc., or the non-causal explanations are not acceptable. If karma itself cannot be explained in this way, it would be futile to attempt any such explanations of an agent of karma. Note the use of the term *idaṃ* (this) to refer to karma, similar to the use of the term *eṣā* at XVII.6, thus specifying the type of explanation that is rejected by him. For this reason, we prefer to confine his criticism only to the metaphysical views mentioned in the verses immediately preceding (XVII.21-28), leaving the more appropriate view he mentioned untouched. This seems to be the only way in which one can recognize consistency in Nāgārjuna's statements throughout this chapter.

30. *Karma cen nāsti kartā ca kutaḥ syāt karmajaṃ phalaṃ,*
asaty atha phale bhoktā kuta eva bhaviṣyati.

If both action and agent are non-existent, where could there be the fruit born of action? When there is no fruit, where can there be an experiencer?

MKV(P) p.329; *MKV(V)* p.141.

In the absence of either an aciton or an agent metaphysically conceived, there could be no fruit or consequence born of such action (***karmajam phalam***). Here again, it is not a denial of fruit or consequence born of action, but only of those that are born of ***such*** action as explained previously. If the fruit or consequence is not obtained, its experiencer (***bhoktā***) would also not be appropriate.

31. *Yathā nirmitakaṃ śāstā nirmimīta ṛddhi-sampadā*
nirmito nirmimītānyaṃ sa ca nirmitakaḥ punaḥ,

Just as a teacher, through psycho-kinetic power, were to create a figure, and this created figure were to create another, that in turn would be a created.

32. *Tathā nirmitakāraḥ kartā yat karma tat kṛtaṃ,*
tad yathā nirmitenānyo nirmito nirmitas tathā.

In the same way, an agent is like a created form and his action is like his creation. It is like the created form created by another who is created.

MKV(P) p.330; *MKV(V)* p.142.

One metaphysical view leads to another, that to a further metaphysical view. Such is the unending circle. A metaphysical view is, indeed fabricated by someone. Yet the fact that such a metaphysical view turns out to be empty does not mean that the experience depending upon which the metaphysical view was formulated or the process of conception are themselves non-existent. Experience as well as concept are available. Only that the conception is carried beyond its limits to assume the existence of independent entities, whether they be *ātman* or *svabhāva*. To understand the significance of Nāgārjuna's statement here it would be necesary to take a look at one of the rare statements of the Buddha recorded in the *Sāmaññaphala-suttanta* (*D* 1.76-77). In this passage, which explains the fruit of recluseship, the Buddha refers to two forms of knowledge a contemplative could develop before he directs his attention to the so-called higher forms of knowledge (*abhiññā*). The first is described as follows:

With his mind thus serene, made pure, translucent, cultured, devoid of evil, supple, ready to act, firm and imperturbable, he applies and bends down his mind to that knowledge and insight whereby he grasps the fact: "This body of mine has form, it is built up of the four elements, it springs from mother and father, is continually renewed by so much boiled rice and juicy foods, its very nature is impermanence, it is subject to erosion, abrasion, dissolution, and disintegration; and therein lies this consciousness of mine, too, bound up, on that it does depend.

This represents the Buddha's experience and conception of his own personality. Having stated this, he immediately proceeds to examine whether there is anything beyond this experience and conception. What he describes is no more than the funciton of *manas*, the faculty which is responsible for the formulation of the metaphysical ideas of self (*ātman*) and substance (*svabhāva*). The statement reads:

> With his mind thus serene, . . . firm and imperturbable, he applies and bends down his mind to the calling up of a mental image. He calls up from this body another body, having form, made of mind (*mano-maya*), having all (his own body's) limbs and parts, not deprived of any organ.

This is how *manas* becomes a *sensus communis* surveying the sensory fields of other faculties (*M* 1.295) and maintaining a feeling of identity, which then gets converted to a permanent and eternal *ātman*. Could it not be possible that Nāgārjuna was aware of the above statement of the Buddha? What could be the difference between the creation of a non-existent form through the power of psychokinesis and the generation of a belief in a permanent and eternal self though the activities of *manas*? It seems that human beings, with faculties through which they are able to perceive and conceive, are not the objects of Nāgārjuna's criticism. It is only the manner in which perceptions and conceptions are formulated that is under criticism.

33. *Kleśāḥ karmāṇi dehāś ca kartāraś ca phalāni ca,*
gandharva-nagarākārā marīci-svapna-saṃnibhāḥ.

Defilements, actions and bodies, agents as well as fruits, all these are similar to the cities of the *gandharvas*, are comparable to mirages and dreams.

MKV(P) p.334; *MKV(V)* p.143.

The metaphors used at the end of Chapter VII to illustrate the nature of metaphysical theories pertaining to arising, stasis, and ceasing, are employed here to elucidate the character of similarly conceived theories relating to defilements, actions, personalities, agents, and consequences.

CHAPTER EIGHTEEN
Examination of Self
(Ātma-parīkṣā)

1. *Ātmā skandhā yadi bhaved udaya-vyaya-bhāg bhavet,*
   skandhebhyo 'nyo yadi bhaved bhaved askandha-lakṣaṇaḥ.

If the self were to be identical with the aggregates, it will partake of uprising and ceasing. If it were to be different from the aggregates, it would have the characteristics of the non-aggregates.

MKV(P) p.341; *MKV(V)* p.145.

The conception of an individual self (*ātman*) was previously examined in a variety of contexts. The present analysis was occasioned by a need to explain the life-process as conditioned by human actions (*karma*), the subject matter of the preceding chapter.

The Buddha's analysis of the human personality into five aggregates (*pañcakkhandha*) was intended to show that underlying the empirical factors constituting the human personality there is no permanent and eternal self. The Buddha's view was that these five factors served as the basis for any conceptualization of a self or soul. Hence they are always referred to as aggregates of grasping (*upādānakkhandha*).

Nāgārjuna begins his investigation into the conception of self by raising two questions pertaining to the nature of the self, especially in its relationship to the five aggregates. If the self and the aggregates were identical, then the self would have to partake of the characteristics of the aggregates. These latter being subject to arising and ceasing, the self cannot remain permanent and eternal. On the contrary, if the self and the aggregates were to be different, then the former could not have the same characteristics as the latter. Leaving the argument at that, Nāgārjuna is allowing the readers to come to their own conclusions.

So far Nāgārjuna has not given any indication that he recognizes a special intuitive faculty through which one can see beyond the world of change and impermanence. Indeed, all that he has admitted points to his recognition of sense experiences as the foundation of human knowledge. The impermanent aggregates constitute not only the human personality, but also its experiences. If the self is considered to be different from the aggregates, Nāgārjuna is here implying that it is unknowable, not merely inconceivable, for it will not have any of the characteristics of the aggregates that are all that we know through sense experience.

2. *Ātmany asati cātmīyaṃ kuta eva bhaviṣyati,*
nirmamo nirahaṃkāraḥ samād ātmātmani-nayoḥ.

In the absence of a self, how can there be something that belongs to the self? From the appeasement of the modes of self and self-hood, one abstains from creating the notions of "mine" and "I."

MKV(P) p.345-347; *MKV(V)* pp.147-148.

If a permanent entity does not exist, one cannot assume the existence of anything that belongs to it. The denial of a permanent entity does not mean that Nāgārjuna is committed to a rejection of self-awareness or self-consciousness. The rejection of the latter would undermine the very foundation of his epistemology. As mentioned earlier (see III.17), Nāgārjuna, following the Buddha, recognized consciousness (and this includes self-awareness), not as a pre-existent *cogito*, but as part of the human personality conditioned by factors such as the sense organs and the objects of perception. Self-awareness or self-instinct can be pursued to its extreme limit. The result is the "construction of a self" (*aham* + *kāra*), which eventually leads to the belief in permanence. The other extreme is the complete rejecton of any form of self-awareness, which is tantamount to annihilation.

Without falling into these two extremes, Nāgārjuna is here presenting the Buddha's own "middle way" philosophy when he speaks of the appeasement (*śama*), not the complete eradication, of the "self" (*ātman*) and "whatever that pertains to a self" (*ātmani*). This is perfectly in accord with the "appeasement of dispositions" (*saṃskāropaśama*), the "appeasement of the object" (*draṣṭavyopaśama*), and the "appeasement of obsessions" (*prapañcopaśama*), discussed earlier (see commentary on V.8).

Through the appeasement of the self-instinct one eliminates the metaphysical notions of a self (*ātman*), and through the appeasement of the object (*draṣṭavyopaśama*) one is able to realize the non-substantiality of phenomena and would not cling to them as "one's own" (*ātmani*). These culminate in the absence of selfishness (*nirmama*) and the absence of egoism (*nirahaṃkāra*).

The dual meaning of the term *ahaṃkāra* is worth noting. *Ahaṃkāra* (literally, "I-making") means both ego-centeredness and pride. While the term *ahaṃkāra* has come to be so popular in ordinary language, it is interesting to note that no such term is constructed with the plural of *ahaṃ*, namely, *mayaṃ*, as *mayaṃkāra* ("we-making") would have expressed an idea which is equally unacceptable to the Buddha and Nāgārjuna, for they were not willing to eliminate the notion of oneself (*ahaṃ*) altogether in favor of an equally metaphysical notion of a "social self".

3. *Nirmamo nirahaṃkāro yaś ca so 'pi na vidyate,*
nirmamaṃ nirahaṃkāraṃ yaḥ paśyati na paśyati.

Whosoever is free from selfishness and egoism, he too is not evident. Whoever perceives someone as free from selfishness and egoism, he too does not perceive.

MKV(P) p.348; *MKV(V)* p.148.

Nāgārjuna approvingly spoke of the appeasement of the notion of self and the consequent elimination of selfishness and egoism. However, knowing his contemporaries who were so prone to metaphysical speculations, he was not willing to rest satisfied with such a statement.

As a reminder to those who have not achieved the "appeasement of the notion of self," Nāgārjuna points out that *someone* who is assumed to have gotten rid of egoism and pride is also not available. The constant attempt by the metaphysicians to reify things, entities, persons, etc. was kept in mind by Nāgārjuna whenever he makes any positive assertion.

4. *Memety aham iti kṣīṇe bahirdhādhyātmam eva ca,*
nirudhyata upādānaṃ tat kṣayāj janmanaḥ kṣayaḥ.

When views pertaining to "mine" and "I", whether they are associated

with the internal or the external, have waned, then grasping comes to cease. With the waning of that [grasping], there is waning of birth.

MKV(P) p.349; *MKV(V)* p.149.

The use of the *iti* formula as *mama-iti* and *aham-iti* in the present statement makes it significantly different from the former statement at XVIII.2. In the former statement, Nāgārjuna spoke of *ātman* (self) and *ātmīya* (that which belongs to the self) and emphasized the need to appease such awareness or feeling. In the present verse, he refers to *aham* ("I") and *mama* ("mine") using the *iti*-formula and insists upon their complete elimination (*kṣaya*). Thus, it is not the fact of self-awareness that causes problems for the human beings but the *theorizing* based upon such self-awareness. The *cogito* may thus turn out to be harmless, so long as it is considered to be a product of the sensory process (see III.7), but *ergo sum* is what is dangerous, epistemologically as well as ethically.

When such theorizing has waned (*kṣiṇe*), then there is cessation of grasping (*upādāna-nirodha*), which is freedom while living. The cessation of grasping eventually leads to the waning of rebirth (*janmanaḥ kṣayaḥ*).

5. *Karma-kleśa-kṣayān mokṣa karma-kleśā vikalpataḥ,*
te prapañcat prapañcas tu śūnyatāyāṃ nirudhyate.

On the waning of defilements of action, there is release. Defilements of action belong to one who discriminates, and these in turn result from obsession. Obsession, in its turn, ceases within the context of emptiness.

MKV(P) pp.349-350; *MKV(V)* p.149.

The fact that this statement of Nāgārjuna immediately follows his criticism of *theorizing* relating to "mine" and "I," that is, speculation relating to subject and object, becomes very valuable in determining the meaning of the term *vikalpa*, a term that has caused much confusion and misunderstanding.

Vikalpa can mean two different types of discrimination. One is the type of discrimination made at the phenomenal level. It is the discrimination referred to at XVIII.2, a discrimination that is empirically grounded, but which should be kept under control (*śama*). The second is the type of discrimination made at a metaphysical level. It is the discrimination referred to at XVIII.4, which has gone far beyond the empirical level and thus become theoretical or speculative.

For Nāgārjuna, the defilements of action follow from the latter, not from the former. It seems that this is the primary reason for his reference to and criticism of *vikalpa* at XVIII.5 rather than at XVIII.3.

Wrong actions (*mithyā-karmānta*), i.e., actions that are defiled, emanate from wrong beliefs (*mithyā-dṛṣṭi*), which are the results of wrong thoughts or discriminations (*mithyā-saṃkalpa, mithyā vikalpa*). Obsessions are the inevitable results of such wrong discriminations. When such obsessions are appeased, then a person does not get involved either in a notion of a permanent self or in a theory of complete annihilation. The realization that self-awareness is dependently arisen (III.7) is a realization that it is empty of a permanent substance (*svabhāva-śūnya*). This latter is the middle path that avoids eternalism and annihilationism.

6. *Ātmety api prajñapitam anātmety api deśitaṃ,*
buddhair nātmā na cānātmā kaścid ity api deśitaṃ.

The Buddha's have make known the conception of self and taught the doctrine of no-self. At the same time, they have not spoken of something as the self or as the non-self.

MKV(P) p.355; *MKV(V)* p.152.

If the distinctions made in XVIII.2 and 4 are not recognized, it is natural for the interpreters of Nāgārjuna to run into difficulties in explaining the contents of this verse. Here agin we have the use of the *iti*-formula, this time used with the terms *ātman* and *anātman*, as *ātma-iti* and *anātma-iti*. However, the difference between the Buddha's speculations and those of the metaphysicians in this regard is that the Buddha does not speculate on any entity (*kaścid*) as *ātman* or as *anātman*. In other words, he does not reify either *ātman* or *anātman*. Reifying *ātman* one ends up in eternalism; reifying *anātman* one is led to annihilationism. Without resorting to such reification, the Buddha has indicated the meaning of *ātman* (*ātmeti prajñapitaṃ*) and has spoken of the implications of *anātman* (*anātmeti deśitaṃ*). Both *ātman* and *anātman* are explained by the Buddha in terms of dependent arising (*pratītyasamutpāda*). This doctrine of dependent arising eliminates the need for postulating either permanence or annihilation.

As such, the distinction that Inada attempts to make between *prajñapitaṃ* as "provisionally employed" and *deśitaṃ* as "instructed" becomes untenable. If "provisional explanation" is to be achieved by the use of words, it could not be different from "instruction." Both need the use of language. Just as much as the Buddha could instruct on the "true idea of *anātman*," he could have instructed on the true idea of *ātman*, without falling into metaphysics in either case. If the use of the empirical terms can be utilized in one case, there is no reason to assume any difficulty in using them in the other. The problem then is not with regard to language as such, but only in regard to the way in which it is used.

7. *Nivṛttam abhidhātavyaṃ nivṛtte citta-gocare,*
anutpannāniruddhā hi nirvāṇam iva dharmatā.

When the sphere of though has ceased, that which is to be designated also has ceased. Like freedom, the nature of things is non-arisen and non-ceased.

MKV(P) p.364; *MKV(V)* p.154.

"Whereof thought has ceased, thereof speech also has come to cease."

Abhidhātavya means "that which is to be designated." It refers to the world of objects. It is the same as *abhidheya* which, if we follow Nāgārjuna's method of exposition, is mutually related to *abhidhāna,* "designation." Both *abhidheya* and *abhidhāna* would thus cease to be along with the cessation of the sphere of thought (*citta-gocara*).

"Whereof one cannot speak, thereof one must be silent."

It is possible for the interpreters of Nāgārjuna to assume that here is the identification of the "unspeakable" with "emptiness" (*śūnyatā*), generally referred to in negative terms as "non-arisen, non-ceased" (*anutpannāniruddha*), which is then identified with both "true nature" (*dharmatā*) and freedom (*nirvāṇa*). This is the easy route to the belief in the so-called "non-conceptual" (*nirvikalpa*) ultimate reality (*paramārtha, tattva*).

However, the first line of Nāgārjuna's statement should prevent anyone from reaching such a conclusion. Nowhere has Nāgārjuna asserted any form of knowledge that transcends the *six* senses. For him, what is perceivable is also conceivable. He may, reflecting upon the conceptualization of the metaphysicians, admit that what is *not* perceivable is also conceivable. Yet, it would be improper to assume that he will recognize the non-conceptual (*nir-vikalpa*) as being perceivable. Conceptualizing and conceiving are not two different activities. Hence his statement: "When the realm of thought has ceased, that which is to be designated also has ceased."

As pointed out in the introduction, a similar statement was made by the Buddha in relation to a *tathāgata* who has passed away, and the present context, in which the metaphysical notion of self (*ātman*) is discussed, is no more different from that in which the Buddha made that statement.

So far as Nāgārjuna's analysis is concerned, it has become clear that his negations pertained primarily to metaphysics, whether it be the notion of a permanent and eternal self (*ātman*) or a substance (*svabhāva*). Along with the negation of a permanent and eternal self, Nāgārjuna also rejected absolute "otherness" (*para-bhāva*). Existence and non-existence, in this metaphysical sense, were rejected by him. As pointed out in the analysis of the Dedicatory Verses, the "non-arising" (*anutpāda*) and "non-ceasing" (*anirodha*) were intended as criticisms of such metaphysics. If one recognizes a substance, Nāgārjuna would say it is non-ceasing; if one recognizes annihilation, Nāgārjuna would characterize is as non-arising. In other words, if absolute arising and absolute ceasing were to be accepted, these would negate empirical arising and ceasing which is the basis of "dependent arising" (*pratītyasamutpāda*). When both "the way of phenomena" (*dharmatā*) and freedom (*nirvāṇa*), which are explained in terms of "dependent arising" (*pratītyasamutpāda*), are referred to as "non-arisen and non-ceasing", it is more appropriate to assume that here they are to be distinguished from absolute arising and absolute ceasing. Arising and ceasing in an absolute sense represent inappropriate conceptualizations. Neither the nature of phenomena nor freedom should be the subject of such inappropriate conceptualizations.

8. *Sarvaṃ tathyaṃ na vā tathyaṃ tathyaṃ cātathyam eva ca,*
naivātathyaṃ naiva tathyam etad buddhānuśāsanaṃ.

Everything is such, not such, both such and not such, and neither such and not such: this is the Buddha's admonition.

MKV(P) p.369; *MKV(V)* p.157.

On the basis of this statement, Inada, following his predecessors in the interpretation of Nāgārjuna, reached the conclusion that "truth is non-relational, non-descriptive, non-differential. . . . it is thatness or thusness," (p.113). Referring specifically to XVIII.8, he says that here "Nāgārjuna introduces the famed Four-cornered Logic, . . . i.e., the possible conditions of is, is not, both is and is not, and neither is nor is not, in order to exhibit the fact that final truth transcends all these possibilities; it is *śūnyatā* per se" (ibid.)

So far, our analysis of Nāgārjuna's statements has failed to reveal any form of four-cornered logic that he used to *establish* an ultimate truth. Whenever he utilized it, he did so in order to reject metaphysical assumptions, rather than to establish something or some theory.

After stating the fact that metaphysical views, especially those relating to a *tathāgata* after death, take us beyond the sphere of thought (*citta-gocara*)(XVIII.7), Nāgārjuna is here expanding the discussion to include one of the most persistent problems of metaphysics, namely, "everything" (*sarvaṃ*). It is the problem that led the Sarvastivadins to uphold the view that "everything exists" (*sarvam asti*) in the form of substance (*svabhāva*). Nāgārjuna is simply allowing that metaphysical question to be settled by the use of the fourfold propositions that negate each other.

Indeed, this is not presented as the "teaching" or "message" (*śāsana*) of the Buddha, as Inada seems to understand. Quite on the contrary, it is an "admonition" or "advice" (*anuśāna*) in regard to the manner in which speculation about "everything" can be resolved, namely, by demonstrating the inevitable self-contradictions. In other words, he is stating that the question regarding "everything" cannot be settled by any form of discussion, a view clearly expressed by the Buddha in his famous "Discourse on Everything" (*Sabba-sutta*, see commentary on IX.3), which Nāgārjuna was probably conversant with.

9. *Apara-pratyayaṃ śāntaṃ prapañcair aprapañcitaṃ,*
nirvikalpam anānārtham etat tattvasya lakṣaṇaṃ.

Independently realized, peaceful, unobsessed by obsessions, without discriminations and a variety of meanings: such is the characteristic of truth.

MKV(P) p.372; *MKV(V(* p.158.

This is one of the most important statements of Nāgārjuna, quoted often by his classical as well as modern interpreters. The most recent translation and interpretation comes from Inada and, as such, it could be considered a digest of the existing views. Hence, it is appropriate to quote Inada's rendering of this verse in full. It reads as follows:

> Non-conditionally related to any entity, quiscent, non-conceptualized by conceptual play, non-discriminative and non-differentiated. These are the characteristics of reality (i.e., descriptive of one who has gained the Buddhist truth) (p.115).

The term *apara-pratyaya* is here taken to mean a special kind of relation that transcends any form of empirical conditionality. *Śānta* signifies "quiescence," a quiescence resulting from the avoidance of any conceptuality, probably the sort of peace and quiet experienced by one who has temporarily stopped the functioning of the six sense faculties by reaching the state of cessation (*nirodha-samāpatti,* or *saññā-vedayita-nirodha*). It is where the dichotomy of subject and object is completely dissolved (*nir-vikalpa*) and where the variegated experiences of the world, the variety of meanings or fruits (*nānārtha*), is eliminated. Truth, in such a context, cannot be very different from that of either the *Upaniṣads* or the Vedanta. It is the flushing out of all conceptual thinking (*citta-vṛtti-nirodha*), thereby transforming the empirical experience into one of absolute, ultimate truth or reality.

However, a glance at the "Discourse to Kātyāyana," the primary source for Nāgārjuna's formulation of the "middle way," will reveal the untenability of such an explanation.

Even though the verse seems to describe the characteristics of truth or reality (*tattvasya lakṣaṇam*), every preceding statement points to the *means* by which a conception of truth is arrived at. Hence, it is one of the most important statements on epistemology. The most salient features of this epistemolgoy are already clearly embodied in the Buddha's discourse to Kātyāyana, presented in the form of an answer to the question as to what "right view" (*sammā-diṭṭhi*) is. The contents of the verse can be analysed in the light of this discourse in the following manner.

The term *apara-pratyaya* does not refer to a truth that is non-conditionally related to any entity. Rather, it explains the manner in which knowledge (*ñāṇa*) is attained by one who has "right view" (*sammā-diṭṭhi*). After rejecting the metaphysical views pertaining to permanent existence (*atthitā*) as well as the belief in a permanent and substantial personal entity (*attā . . . me*), a belief that will require the *testimony* of some other person who claims to know the absolute beginning of things, the empiricist Buddha claimed that knowledge (of one who has right view) occurs without having to depend upon another person (*apara-paccayā ñāṇam evāssa ettha hoti*, *S* 2.17). It is knowledge for which one does not have to depend upon another, primarily because it pertains to arising and ceasing of empirical phenomena. It involves personal verification, a verification that can be accomplished by someone before one begins to formulate any right view.

Man's search for a permanent entity, while he is equipped with limited epistemological resources, leaves him with unresolved questions. He continues to doubt. He is constantly perplexed and troubled. Looking for permanence, he misses the empirically given. The search for the unseen "beauty queen" (*janapada-kalyānī*, *D* 1.193; *M* 2.40) makes him forget the immediatley relevant questions (*M* 2.40). As such, he has no peace of mind. However, if he were to direct his attention to what is immediately given, and understand the human predicament in its context without being inquisitive about metaphysical entities (***dukkham eva uppajjamānaṃ uppajjati dukkhaṃ nirujjhamānaṃ nirujjhatiti na kaṅkhati na vicikicchati, ibid.***), his mind would be peaceful (***śāntam***). The Buddha, in one of his very famous statements, insisted that when a reflecting person understands the arising and ceasing of phenomena, all his doubts disappear (*Ud* 1). Such peace of mind is achieved, not by ignoring what is relevant in the human context, but by ignoring the irrelevant and irresolvable metaphysical issues.

Such a state of peace (*śānti*) cannot be achieved so long as one is bound by one's prejudices (***upāyupādānābhinivesa-vinibandho, ibid.,***) This is the "obsession" (*prapañca*) that Nāgārjuna is referring to in the present context. The discourse to Kātyāyana has no reference to any conceptual proliferation.

How such obsessions have further strengthened and encouraged the search for ultimate truths, contributing to indiscriminate discriminations, such as those of existence and non-existence (***bhāva-abhāva***) or self-nature and other-nature (***svabhāva-parabhāva***), has already been explained by Nāgārjuna. These are the discriminations that are to be avoided in the search for truth. ***Nirvikalpa*** refers to the absence of such discriminations.

A pluralistic view of the world is not incompatible with dependent arising (***pratītyasamutpāda***). Pluralism in the context of dependent arising does not imply the existence of self-contradictory truths. It need not necessarily lead to a notion of an Absolute that transcends such self-contradictory truths. The criterion for deciding what is true in the context of dependent arising is consequence or fruit (***artha***). When the Buddha maintained that "truth is one; there is no second" (***ekaṃ hi saccaṃ na dutīyam atthi, Sn*** 884), he was certainly referring to this pragmatic criterion of truth based upon the notion of dependent arising, not an absolute truth that transcends all forms of duality and plurality. Nāgārjuna's characterization of truth as "not having a variety of meanings" (***anānārthaṃ***) reflects more the Buddha's own conception of truth.

To summarize, the conception of truth and the epistemological means on the basis of which it is formulated all point to the fact that the truth under consideration is the "dependently arisen" (*pratītyasamutpanna*). The principle of dependent arising (*pratītyasamutpāda*) is merely the expression of the manner in which "dependently arisen" phenomena are explained. They are two sides of the same coin.

Yet, as reiterated before, the greatest misunderstandings created by the metaphysicians were in regard to "dependently arisen phenomena" (*pratītyasamutpanna-dharma*). Therefore, after examining the epistemological means by which the conception of truth "as dependently arisen" is arrived at, Nāgārjuna, in the verse that follows immediately, takes up the metaphysical interpretations of the concept of dependence.

10. *Partītya yad yad bhavati na hi tāvat tad eva tat,*
na cānyad api tat tasmān nocchinnaṃ nāpi śāśataṃ.

Whatever that arises depending upon whatever, that is not identical nor different from it. Therefore, it is neither annihilated nor eternal.

MKV(P) p.375; *MKV(V)* p.150.

Whatever is arisen dependent upon (*pratītya*) another, that is, the dependently arisen (*pratītyasamutpanna*), is not appropriately explained in terms of identity or difference. As empahsized so often by Nāgārjuna, absolute identity involves permanence and absolute difference implies annihilation. Dependent arising is the middle way adopted by the Buddha in elucidating change and causation.

11. *Anekārtham anānārtham anucchedam aśāśvataṃ,*
etat tal lokanāthānāṃ buddhānāṃ śāsanāmṛtaṃ.

That is without a variety of meanings or one single meaning, it is not annihilation nor is it eternal. Such, it is reminisced, is the immortal message of the Buddhas, the patrons of the world.

MKV(P) p.377; *MKV(V)* p.160.

The metaphysics of identity or of difference, of one or of many, of permanence or of annihilation, may be proved or not proved. So far the evidence has not been found that would provide justification for any such notions. The only known evidence points to the fact that things are changing and are dependently arisen. Such change and dependent arising do not fall within the duality of one or many, of annihilation or permanence. Dependent arising is what has been known so far. Unless a radical change occurs in the constitution of things, this dependent arising will continue to be. Such is the immortal teaching of the Buddha.

This, again, is Nāgārjuna's reflection on the epistemology of dependent arising.

12. *Sambuddhānāmanutpāde śrāvakānāṃ punaḥ kṣaye,*
jñānaṃ prateyka-buddhānām asaṃsargāt pravartate.

When the fully enlightened ones do not appear; on the waning of disciples; the wisdom of the self-enlightened ones proceeds without association.

MKV(P) p.378; *MKV(V)* p.161.

The Buddha's teachings were perpetuated by a long line of disciples (*śrāvaka*). If that lineage were to be interrupted, still it is possible for his teachings to reappear. Nāgārjuna was probably aware of the metaphor of the "ancient city" (*nagara*) whose discovery is compared to the discovery of "dependent arising" by the historical Buddha himself (*S* 2.104-107; *Tsa* 12.5 [*Taisho* 2.80b]). Therefore, contradicting many a tradition that depended heavily on an unbroken continuity as the primary source of the knowledge of the Buddha's teaching, Nāgārjuna is here maintaining that such widsom (*jñāna*) can occur even without any contact or association (*asaṃsargāt*) through the self-enlightened ones (*pratyeka-buddha*).

CHAPTER NINETEEN
Examination of Time
(Kāla-parīkṣā)

1. *Pratyutpanno 'nāgataś ca yady atītam apekṣya hi,*
pratyutpanno 'nāgataṣ ca kāle 'tīte bhaviṣyati.

If the present and the future exist contingent upon the past, then the present and the future would be in the past time.

2. *Pratyutpanno 'nāgataś ca na stas tatra punar yadi,*
pratyutpanno 'nāgataś ca syātāṃ kathaṃ apekṣya taṃ.

Again, if the present and the future were not to exist therein [i.e., in the past], how could the present and the future be contingent upon that?

MKV(P) pp.382-383; *MKV(V)* p.163.

As mentioned at XVII.14, the conception of time was an important factor in the explanation of the fruits of action (***karma-phala***). All actions do not bear fruit immediately. Indeed, the problems were magnified by the Buddha's recognition of the possibility of the survival of the human personality through countless lives. The Abhidharma lists four categories of karma in terms of their fruitioning, all of which can be traced back to the discourses themselves. The four categories are as follows: (i) karma that fruitions immediately or in the present life (***diṭṭha-dhamma-vedanīya***); (ii) karma that fruitions in the next life (***upapajja-vedanīya***); (iii) karma that fruitions in some after life (***aparāpariya-vedanīya***); and (iv) karma that produces no fruitioning (***ahosi-kamma***)(*Vism* p.601). The use of the metaphor of "the imperishable promissory note" by Nāgārjuna was necessitated by the fact that some karmas produce consequences on a subsequent occasion.

Thus, the conception of time becomes invariably bound up with the notion of karma. As such, whatever metaphysical speculations that emerged with the doctrine of karma, such as those mentioned at XVII.7-10, also came to be associated with the conception of time. Analysing time as a separate entity, the metaphysicians assumed that if there were to be any mutual relationship between the present and the future on the one hand and the past on the other, then, since they are distinct entities, the present and the future will have to be inherent in the past. In other words, the past produces the present and future from within itself. This is the identity version of causation (*svatotpatti*). A further implication of this is that if one knows the past, one also knows with absolute certainty what the present and the future would be. These, indeed, represent some of the basic speculations of the Sarvāstivādins.

3. *Anapekṣya punaḥ siddhir nātītaṃ vidyate tayoḥ,*
pratyutpanno 'nagataś ca tasmāt kālo na vidyate.

Moreover, non-contingent upon the past, their [i.e. of the present and future] establishment is not evident. Therefore, neither a present nor a future time is evident.

MKV(P) p.383; *MKV(V)* p.163.

The present verse embodies Nāgārjuna's criticism of the notion of time referred to in XIX.1-2. Taken away from that context, this will appear to be a complete rejection of the very notion of time. However, Nāgārjuna's criticism pertains only to the contingence *(apekṣā)* understood in the light of a theory of inherence. On a previous occasion (X.8-12), Nagārjuna has convincingly demonstrated the difficulties involved in explaining contingence or relativity in the context of theories of identity (which is also implied in inherence) and difference.

Nāgārjuna's argument seems to read as follows:

1. *Major premiss:*
   The present and the future are not seen to be established non-contingent upon the past.
2. *Middle term.*
   Contingence of the present and the future on the past implies the substantial existence of the present and the future in the past, which is not evident.

3. *Conclusion:*
Therefore, the present and the future, as substantial entities, do not exist.

Ignoring the middle term, so clearly defined at XIX.1-2, Nāgārjuna's conclusion will appear to be an absolute rejection of time. It would then read as follows:

1. *First premiss:*
The present and the future are not contingent upon the past.
2. *Second premiss:*
The present and the future are not non-contingent upon the past.
3. *Minor premiss:*
The present and the future cannot be both contingent and non-contingent upon the past.
4. *Conclusion:*
The present and the future do not exist.

4. *Etenaivāvasiṣṭau dvau krameṇa parivartakau,*
uttamādhama-madhyādīn ekatvādīṃś ca lakṣayet.

Following the same method, the remaining two periods of [time] as well as related concepts such as the highest, the lowest and the middle, and also identity, etc. should be characterized.

MKV(P) p.384; *MKV(V)* p.164.

Nāgārjuna is insisting that the same argument be applied to the concept of the present in relation to the past and future, and to the future in relation to the past and present. In addition, he maintains that this analysis can be extended to similar concepts like the highest, the lowest, the middle, etc. In all these cases, the metaphysical issues emerge as a result of the *absolute distinctions* that are being made. Such absolute distinctions are being often made in logical analyses, and are not supported by empirical evidence. Time, *as experienced*, cannot be analysed into three water-tight compartments as past, present, and future. (See Introduction, for an explanation of the experienced time by a modern psychologist.)

5. *Nāstito gṛhyate kālaḥ sthitaḥ kālo na vidyate,*
yo gṛhyetāgṛhītaś ca kālaḥ prajñapyate katham.

A non-static time is not observed. A static time is not evident. Even if the unobserved time were to be observed, how can it be made known?

MKV(P) p.385; *MKV(V)* p.165.

A non-static time is a temporal flux. It is what the interpreters of the Abhidharma referred to as the "flowing present" (*santati paccuppanna, DhsA* 421), where the future continues to flow into the past through the present. Any attempt to grasp it would be futile, for by the time the attempt is made the present has disappeared into the past. In order to grasp it one has to stop the flow. Hence the metaphysicians recognized a static moment (*sthiti-kṣaṇa*). Nāgārjuna has already analysed the implications of such theories in Chapter VII. Thus, time understood in terms of distinct momentary entities could not account for experience. This metaphysical theory viewed the present as the momentary present (*khaṇa-paccuppanna*, loc.cit.). Even if the non-graspable time were to be grasped, Nāgārjuna's question is: "How can it be made known?" The empiricist is, therefore, left with a specious time (probably an *addhā-paccuppanna*). It is specious because, when any attempt is made to grasp it independent of temporal events, it vanishes like a mirage. It cannot be made known by any means. Absolute time makes no sense for Nāgārjuna.

6. *Bhāvaṃ pratītya kālaś cet kālo bhāvād ṛte kutaḥ,*
na ca kaścana bhāva 'sti kutaḥ kālo bhaviṣyati.

If it is assumed that time exists depending upon an existent, how can there be time without an existent? No existent whatsoever is found to exist. Where can time be?

MKV(P) p.387; *MKV(V)* pp.165-166.

An existent (*bhāva*), since it represents a metaphysical entity having its own nature (*svabhāva*), has already been rejected by Nāgārjuna. Time (*kāla*) denied by him is an absolute time. It is time that is real as momentary entities (*kṣaṇa*) or something that is fleeting (*santati*) on its own. In the present verse, Nāgārjuna is maintaining that two independent entities—an existent (*bhāva*) and time (*kāla*)—cannot be dependent upon one another. If they are dependent upon one another (*bhāvaṃ pratītya kālaś cet*), then there cannot be time independent of an existent. An existent as such is non-existent. Whence can there be time? This is a rejection not of temporal phenomena, but only of time *and* phenomena as well as their mutual dependence so long as they are perceived as independent entities.

CHAPTER TWENTY
Examination of Harmony
(Sāmagrī-parīkṣā)

1. *Hetoś ca pratyayānāṃ ca sāmagryā jāyate yadi,*
   phalam asti ca sāmagryāṃ sāmagryā jāyate katham.

If the effect were to arise from a harmony of cause and conditions, and if it were to exist in the harmony, how can it arise from the harmony?

2. *Hetoś ca pratyayānāṃ ca sāmagryā jāyate yadi,*
   phalaṃ nāsti ca sāmgryāṃ sāmagryā jāyate kathaṃ.

If the effect were to arise from a harmony of cause and conditions and if it were not to exist in the harmony, how can it arise from the harmony?

MKV(P) p.391; *MKV(V)* p.168.

The term used in the early discourses for "assemblage" is *saṅgati* (*M* 1.111-112). For example, the eye, the visible form, and visual consciousness are said to come together (*saṅgati*) in contact (*phassa*). Here, the eye, visible form, and visual consciousness are compatible factors, and not incompatible. However, as events came to be distinguished in the Abhidharma, the interpreters of the Abhidharma had to be concerned more with "harmony" (*sāmāgrī*) than with simple "assemblage" (*saṅgati*). The conception of "harmony" thus came to attract Nāgārjuna's attention, even though he will return to the notion of "assemblage" later on in this chapter.

Nāgārjuna's attempt at the beginning of this chapter is to examine the conception of harmony and to prevent any metaphysical interpretation of it. Metaphysical speculations were further advanced by the Sarvāstivāda distinction between cause (*hetu*) and condition (*pratyaya*). This latter distinction, supported by the Sarvāstivāda conception of self-nature (*svabhāva*), culminated in the idea of self-causation (*svata utpatti*).

For this reason, in the very first verse, Nāgārjuna takes up three ideas: (i) harmony, (ii) distinction between cause and conditions, and (iii) the arising of an effect *from* a harmony of cause and conditions. (Note Nāgārjuna's use of *hetu* in the singular and *pratyaya* in the plural.)

Nāgārjuna's criticism is mainly directed at the idea of self-causation. If the fruit arises *from* the harmony (*sāmagryā*, ablative case) of a cause and a set of conditions (*hetoḥ pratyayānāṃ ca*), then it is already existent in the harmony (*sāmagryāṃ*, locative case). How then can it arise *from* the harmony (*sāmagryā*)? The causal process presented in this manner implies the identity between "harmony of cause and conditions" and the fruit or effect that arises from it. The identity theory of causation was already criticized in Chapter I.

Similarly, as stated at XX.2, if the fruit or effect arising from such a harmony were not to be in the harmony, that is, if the effect is different from the harmony, it can never arise from that harmony. This is a criticism of the non-identity theory of causation discussed in Chapter I. These two verses, therefore, state the difficulties involved in accepting theories of identity and difference.

3. *Hetoś ca pratyayānāṃ ca sāmagryām asati cet phalaṃ,*
gṛhyeta nanu sāmagryāṃ sāmagryāṃ ca na gṛhyate.

If it is assumed that the effect exists in the harmony of cause and conditions, should it not be observed in the harmony? However, it is not observed in the harmony.

4. *Hetoś ca pratyayānāṃ ca sāmagryāṃ nāsti cet phalaṃ*
hetavaḥ pratyayāś ca syur ahetu-pratyayaiḥ samāḥ.

If the effect were not to exist in the harmony of cause and conditions, then the cause and conditions would be comparable to non-cause and non-conditions.

MKV(P) pp.392-393; *MKV(V)* p.169.

If the identity theory is valid, then the fruit could be observed (*gṛhyeta*) in the harmony itself, even before it is produced through such harmony. However, Nāgārjuna assumes that it is not observed or grasped in this manner. Once again this confirms our view that Nāgārjuna is not a mere dialectician, but an empiricist who appeals to experience, as he did at I.5.

If, on the contrary, the fruit is not found in the harmony, then the cause and the conditions would be rendered in-effective.

5. *Hetukaṃ phalasya dattvā yadi hetur nirudhyate,*
yad dattaṃ yan niruddhaṃ ca hetor ātma-dvayaṃ bhavet.

If the cause were to cease having passed on the causal status to the effect, then there would be two forms of the cause: the given and the ceased.

6. *hetuṃ phalasyādattvā ca yadi hetur nirudhyate,*
hetoḥ niruddhe jātaṃ tat phalam āhetukaṃ bhavet.

If the cause were to cease without passing on the causal status to the effect, then the effect that is born when the cause has ceased would be without a cause.

MKV(p) pp.394-395; *MKV(V)* p.170.

The metaphysicians recognized two types of causes—the concomitant (*sahabhū*) and the associated (*saṃprayuktaka*)—as being presently existing and producing the effect (*sahabhū-saṃprayuktaka-hetū vartamanau phalaṃ prayacchati, Akv* p.99). They are supposed to give rise to the effect at the same time (*samāna-kālaṃ . . . phaladāna,* ibid.) However, with the dominance of the linear view of causation as well as the theory of momentary destruction (*kṣaṇa-bhaṅga*) of phenomena, the question was raised as to how the cause in the present moment could give rise to the effect in the succeeding moment. The answer was that the effect comes to be without a pause or gap (*samanantara nirvarttanāt*). The effect is both given (*datta*), in the sense of being put forward (*prayacchati*) by the cause, and at the same time not given (*na punaḥ dattaṃ*, because it is not identical (*tad eva*) with the cause (ibid.).

These are some of the speculations referred to by Nāgārjuna. He insists that if a cause were to perform the dual task of providing causal efficacy and ceasing at the same time, then it should possess dual natures (*ātma-dvayaṃ*). If, on the contrary, it were to cease, without passing over the causal efficacy, then the effect would be without a cause. These indeed are the implications of the conclusions reached by the metaphysician that the effect is both given (*datta*) and not given (*na datta*), referred to in the *Abhidharmakośabhāṣya*.

7. *Phalaṃ sahaiva sāmagryā yadi prādurbhavet punaḥ,*
eka-kālau prasajyete janako yaś ca janyate.

If, again, the effect were to appear together with the harmony, then it would follow that the producer and the produce are contemporaneous.

8. *Pūrvam eva ca sāmagryāḥ phalaṃ prādurbhavet yadi,*
hetu-pratyay-nirmuktaṃ phalam āhetukaṃ bhavet.

If the effect were to appear even prior to the harmony, the effect, distinct from causes and conditions, would be without a cause.

MKV(P) pp.395-396; *MKV(V)* p.170.

Moving from the individual cause to the harmony of conditions (*sāmagrī*), Nāgārjuna raises similar questions. If the effect were to appear (*prādurbhavet*) along with the harmony of conditions, then the distinction between the producer and the produced would collapse. Similarly, if the effect were to precede the harmony, then causation would be rendered meaningless.

9. *Niruddhe cet phalaṃ hetau hetoḥ saṃkramaṇaṃ bhavet,*
purva-jātasya hetoś ca punar-janma prasajyate.

If it is assumed that when the cause has ceased to exist, the effect would

become the transformation of the cause, then it follows that there is a rebirth of a cuase that was already born.

MKV(P) p.396; *MKV(V)* p.171.

Among the variety of causes that were formulated to account for a continuous effect (*nisyanda-phala*) are complementary (*sabhāga*) and universal (*sarvatraga*) causes (*Akb* p.94). Explained in the light of the theory of moments, a universal cause would mean the continuous arising of the same cause in order to account for the continuous effect. The continuous effect (*niṣyanda-phala*) thus turns out to be a transformation (*saṃkramaṇa*) of the cause (*hetu*). Nāgārjuna refuses to recognize the rebirth of the *same* cause that has ceased.

10. *Janayet phalam utpannaṃ niruddho 'sthaṃgataḥ kathaṃ,*
tiṣṭhann api kathaṃ hetuḥ phalena janayed vṛtaḥ.

How can a cause that has ceased, has reached its end, give rise to an effect that is already arisen? How can a cause, even though enduring, produce an effect, when it is separated from the latter?

MKV(P) p.397; *MKV(V)* p.171.

Throughout the present analysis we have indicated that the philosophical method adopted in the Abhidharma did not create any metaphysical problems until the interpreters adopted a theory of moments that were followed by theories of identity and difference. The variety of causes (*hetu*) and conditions (*pratyaya*), even though not presented in such detail and in identical terminology in the discourses, is not incompatible with the teachings embodied therein. However, even a cursory glance at the manner in which the interpreters of the Abhidharma struggled with these different causes and conditions (see *ĀK* Chapter ii; *Akb* pp.38-110) is sufficient to indicate the magnitude of the problems they were faced with.

Nāgārjuna continues his analysis showing how a cause that has ceased (*niruddha*) or one that remains (*tiṣṭhan*), yet is distinct from the effect (*phalena vṛtaḥ*), could never give rise to an effect.

11. *Athāvṛtaḥ phalenāsau katamaj janayed phalaṃ,*
na hy adṛṣṭvā vā dṛṣṭvā vā hetur janayate phalaṃ.

What cause, even if it were not separated from the effect, will give rise to the effect? A cause does not produce an effect either imperceptibly or perceptibly.

MKV(P) pp.398-399; *MKV(V)* p.172.

When the analytical process was carried to its extreme, many events, which under normal contexts would not have been questioned, came to be doubted. For example, instead of a related event, analysis produced two: a relation and an event. When the normal empiricist criteria were adopted in the latter case, one was compelled to assume that the relation is not perceived in the same way as the event is perceived. The metaphysician was thus compelled to insist upon the substantial existence of the relation. "Birth is the arising of what is to be born and this does not take place without causes and conditions," so says the *Abhidharmakośa* (*janyasya janikā jātir na hetu-pratyayair vinā,* ii.49). The *bhāṣya* on this passage continues to argue about the nature of this "birth" (*jāti*), insisting that the genetive case (*ṣaṣṭhi*) (as in the statement, "arising *of* what is to be born") makes no sense if birth (*jāti*) is not perceived in the same way as "that which is to be born" (*janikā*) is perceptible. The Sautrantika Vasubandhu argues against this position saying that "numbers, limits, distinction, union, analysis, otherness, sameness" are recognized as reals (*sattva*) in the speculations of the heretics (*tīrthakāra*), and that these are needed only to establish the knowledge (*buddhi*) of the reality of "the one, the dual, the great, the individuated, the united, the separated, the other, the same, etc." To illustrate his point of view, he refers to the example of "the union of form" (*rūpasya saṃyoga*) and maintains that the genetive case indicates the own-nature (*svabhāva*) of "form." However, in his own Sautrantika view it is a mere designation (*prajñapti-mātram, Akb* p.79).

It is this controversy regarding the reality or unreality of numbers, conjunctions, disjunctions, etc. (a controversy that has continued to plague philosophers in the modern world) that Nāgārjuna is referring to in the present verse when he uses the terms *dṛṣṭvā* (seen) and *adṛṣṭvā* (unseen).

12. *Nātītasya hy atītena phalasya saha hetunā,*
nājātena na jātena saṃgatir jātu vidyate.

Indeed, the assemblage of a past effect with a past or a future or a present cause is not evident.

13. *Na jātasya hy ajātena phalasya saha hetunā,*
nātītena na jātena saṃgatir jātu vidyate.

Indeed, an assemblage of the present effect with a future or a past or a present cause is not evident.

14. *Nājātasya hi jātena phalasya saha hetunā,*
nājātena na naṣṭena saṃgatir jātu vidyate.

Indeed, as assemblage of the future effect with a present or a future or a past cause is not evident.

MKV(P) pp.400-401; *MKV(V)* pp.172-173.

After analysing the conception of "harmony" (*sāmagrī*), Nāgārjuna now returns to the earlier notion of "assemblage" (*saṃgati*)(see comments on XX.1). The notion of assemblage may not have caused philosophical problems for the early Buddhists who adopted an empiricist theory of change and causation. But, for Nāgārjuna, the conception of assemblage, like the notion of harmony, does not work, so long as it is associated with the metaphysical conception of time.

Vasubandhu, as a Sautrāntika, himself raises the more radical question as to how the mind (*manas*) that has already ceased can assemble with future and present concepts (*dharma*) and mental consciousness (*mano-vijñāna*) in order to produce contact (*Akb* p. 143, *manindriyasya punar niruddhasyānagatavartamānābhyāṃ dharma-manovijñānābhyāṃ kathaṃ saṃnipātaḥ*). He then refers to a variety of insights (*bhedaṃ gatā buddhayaḥ*) of different teachers, and the controversy appears to be too complicated. He dismisses them saying: "Enough of this argument" (*alaṃ prasaṅgena*). Nāgārjuna's reluctance to accept any one of these views is, therefore, the result of his realization that they are all metaphysical views not allowing for any definite answers or solutions.

15. *Asatyāṃ saṃgatau hetuḥ kathaṃ janayate phalaṃ,*
satyāṃ saṃgatau hetuḥ kathaṃ janayate phalaṃ.

When an assemblage does not exist, how can a cause produce an effect? When an assemblage exists, how can a cause produce an effect?

MKV(P) pp.401-402; *MKV(V)*p.173.

Here the cause (*hetu*) is defined in terms of assemblage (*saṃgati*) which is either existent (*sat*) or non-existent (*asat*). A cause defined in such a way turns out to be substantialist or non-substantialist. The former implies permanence and the latter, annihilation. Nāgārjuna rejects both.

16. *Hetuḥ phalena śūnyaś cet kathaṃ janayate phalaṃ,*
hetuḥ phalenāśūnyaś cet kathaṃ janayate phalaṃ.

If it is assumed that the cause is empty of an effect, how can it produce an effect? If it is assumed that the cause is not empty of an effect, how can it produce an effect?

MKV(P) p.402; *MKV(V)* p.173.

Turning around, Nāgārjuna now takes up the conception of the effect or fruit (*phala*). If the cause is empty (*śūnya*) of the effect, it can never produce an effect. Neither is it appropriate to assume that the effect is produced by the cause if it is already in the cause, hence not empty (*aśūnyaṃ*) of the effect.

17. *Phalaṃ notpatsyate 'śūnyam aśūnyaṃ na nirotsyate,*
aniruddham anutpannam aśūnyaṃ tad bhaviṣyati.

A non-empty effect will not arise; a non-empty effect will not cease. For, the non-ceased and non-arisen will also be the non-empty.

MKV(P) p.402; *MKV(V)* p.174.

This verse should clarify the meaning of the famous terms *aniruddhaṃ* ("non-ceased") and *anutpannaṃ* ("non-arisen") more than any other statement of

Nāgārjuna. Whatever phenomenon (*dharma*) is characterized by Nāgārjuna as "empty" (*śūnya*) is without self-nature. If something possesses a self-nature, then it is not empty (*aśūnya*). As such, it can neither cease nor arise (*anirodham anutpādam*). Thus, an effect or fruit that is not empty and therefore is possessed of self-nature will not arise (*notpatsyate*) nor cease (*na nirotsyate*).

18. *Katham utpatsyate śūnyaṃ katham śūnyaṃ nirotsyate,*
śūnyam apy aniruddhaṃ tad anutpannaṃ prasajyate.

How will the empty arise and how will the empty cease? If something is empty, it follows that it is non-ceased and non-arisen.

MKV(P) p.403; *MKV(V)* p.174.

Taken by itself, this verse can be used to justify the view that according to Nāgārjuna "emptiness" (*śūnyatā*) is the ultimate truth beyond all forms of description. Hence the negative description: "non-ceased" (*aniruddhaṃ*) and "non-arisen" (*anutpannaṃ*).

However, considered along with XX.17, which rejects the notion of identity presented by the Sarvāstivādins as self-nature (*svabhāva*), which according to Nāgārjuna is "non-empty" (*aśūnya*), what is referred to as "empty" (*śūnya*) in the present verse is more appropriately understood as a reference to the non-identity theory of the Sautrāntikas. It may be remembered that the first Buddhist school to deny the Sarvāstivāda theory of self-nature was the Sautrāntika school. How the Sautrāntika theory of "emptiness" or "absence of substance" (*niḥ-svabhāva*) and their theory of "momentary destruction" (*kṣaṇa-bhaṅga*) led to a denial of both arising and ceasing has already been pointed out (VII.17 ff.).

As such, the present statement of Nāgārjuna, following upon his refutation of identity, must involve a rejection of difference, the two extremes that he has persistently criticized. In other words, the Sarvāstivāda and Sautrāntika theories both render arising and ceasing meaningless.

19. *Hetoḥ phalasya caikatvaṃ na hi jatūpapadyate,*
hetoḥ phalasya cānyatvaṃ na hi jatūpapadyate,

The identity of cause and effect is indeed not appropriate. The difference between cause and effect is indeed not appropriate.

20. *Ekatve phala-hetvoḥ syād aikyaṃ janaka-janyayoḥ,*
pṛthaktve phala-hetvoḥ syāt tulyo hetur ahetunā.

If there were to be identity of cause and effect, then there would be oneness of producer and the produce. If there were to be difference between cause and effect, then the cause would be equal to a non-cause.

21. *Phalaṃ svabhāva-sadbhūtaṃ kiṃ hetur janayiṣyati,*
phalaṃ svabhāvāsadbhūtaṃ kiṃ hetur janayiṣyati.

How is it that a cause will produce an effect which comes to be on its own nature? How is it that a cause will produce an effect which does not come to be on its own nature?

MKV(P) pp.403-404; *MKV(V)* p.174.

The implications of the theories of identity and difference discussed at XX.17-18 are further elaborated in these three verse.

22. *Na cājanayamānasya hetutvam upapadyate,*
hetutvānupapattau ca phalaṃ kasya bhaviṣyati.

Moreover, the causal efficacy of something that is not producing is not appropriate. In the absence of causal efficacy, to what will the effect belong?

(*MKV(P)* p.405; *MKV(V)* p.175.

Identity and difference are thus shown to militate against not merely arising, but also causal or dependent arising. Causal efficacy (*hetutvaṃ*) is rendered meaningless if there were to be no production, that is, if the arising of an effect cannot be accounted for by a cause, which is the result of the Sarvāstivāda and Sautrāntika theories. If causal efficacy cannot be accounted for, how can one speak of an effect or fruit?

23. *Na ca pratyaya-hetūnām iyam ātmānam anātmanā,*
yā sāmagrī janayate sā kathaṃ janayet phalam.

Whatever harmony of causes and conditions there is, it is not produced by itself or by another. If so, how can it produce an effect?

MKV(P) p.406; *MKV(V)* p.175.

After producing an exhaustive analysis of the relationship between a cause (*hetu*) and fruit or effect (*phala*), Nāgārjuna returns to the question with which he began the chapter, the harmony of causes and conditions. Once again, refuting the identity and non-identity theories, he insists that whatever harmony there is, it is not produced by the causes and conditions either from within themselves (*ātmanā* = *svabhāvata*) or from outside (*anātmanā* = *parataḥ*). When harmony cannot be explained in any of *these two* ways, then it is not possible to assume that an effect can arise from a harmony so explained.

24. *Na sāmagrī-kṛtaṃ phalaṃ nāsāmagrī-kṛtaṃ phalaṃ,*
asti pratyaya-sāmagrī kuta eva phalaṃ vinā.

The effect is not made by the harmony, nor is it not made by a harmony. Where indeed can there be a harmony of conditions without an effect.

MKV(P) pp.406-407; *MKV(V)* p.176.

The effect is not produced by a harmony of causes and conditions explained in the above manner. Nor is it produced by a non-harmony. Nāgārjuna's final question is: Where can there be a harmony without a fruit or effect? This final conclusion need not be understood as a denial of fruit or effect. On the contrary, it can be the assertion of a pragmatist who insists that there cannot be a harmony of causes and conditions *without* a fruit or effect.

CHAPTER TWENTY ONE
Examination of Occurrence and Dissolution
(Saṃbhava-vibhava-parīkṣā)

1. *Vinā vā saha vā nāsti vibhavaḥ saṃbhavena vai,*
   vinā vā saha vā nāsti saṃbhavaḥ vibhavena vai.

Dissolution does not exist either without or with occurrence. Occurrence does not exist either without or with dissolution.

2. *Bhaviṣyati katham nāma vibhavaḥ saṃbhavaṃ vinā,*
   vinaiva janma maraṇaṃ vibhavo nodbhavaṃ vinā.

How can there be dissolution without occurrence, death without birth, dissolution without uprising?

MKV(P) pp.410-411; *MKV(V)* p.178.

The terms *saṃbhava* and *vibhava* need to be translated keeping in mind the purpose of this section. It is an attempt on the part of Nāgārjuna to explain the life-process (*saṃsāra*) or the human personality without resorting to a theory of self or soul (*ātman, pudgala*) considered to be eternal. As mentioned earlier, this whole section is devoted to the establishing of the idea of non-substantiality of the human person (*pudgala-nairātmya*). This has to be achieved not only by showing the untenability of the theory of permanence or eternalism, but also of a conception of annihilationism.

Thus, in this particular chapter *saṃbhava*, in the sense of occurrence, pertains to the "birth" (*janma*) of a human being conditioned by various factors, without any underlying permanent entity passing from one life to another. *Vibhava*, in the sense of dissolution, means "death" (*maraṇa*), and here there is no implication of complete annihilation. In the life-process, birth is thus not the absolute beginning, nor is death the absolute end.

The first two verses deny the occurrence of death without (*vinā*) birth or at the same time (*saha*). Just as much as death does not occur without birth, there is no up-rising (*udbhava*) without dissolution (*vibhava*). This is an empirical, rather than a logical, analysis of birth and death. A rationalist can argue that "all human beings are not mortal," for everyone who has been born has not died. Such a rational argument did not prevent the Buddha from accepting mortality as a fact of life. For him, the evidence lies in the fact that so far all human being who have died had been born. However, this does not lead the Buddha to assert the metaphysical view that death is inherent in birth.

3. *Saṃbhavenaiva vibhavaḥ kathaṃ saha bhaviṣyati,*
na janma-maraṇaṃ caivaṃ tulya-kālaṃ hi vidyate.

How can there be dissolution along with occurrence? Indeed, simultaneous birth and death are similarly not evident.

MKV(P) p.411; *MKV(V)* p.178.

This is an explicit rejection of the metaphysical view that death is inherent in birth. If the life-process (*saṃsāra*) were to be understood as a series of momentary existences (*saṃtāna, saṃtati*), as the Sautrāntikas believed, then the seeds of death should occur at the very moment of birth. This logical explanation was not acceptable to the empiricist Nāgārjuna.

4. *Bhaviṣyati kathaṃ nāma saṃbhavo vibhavaṃ vinā,*
anityatā hi bhāveṣu na kadācin na vidyate.

How can there be occurrence without dissolution, for the impermanence in existences is never not evident.

MKV(P) p.412; *MKV(V)* p.178.

Occurrence (*saṃbhava*), as an absolutely new beginning, is rejected here, when Nāgārjuna affirms that without dissolution occurrence does not take place.

Indeed, the discourse to Kātyāyana utilized the empirical argument that the belief in a permanent entity is abandoned when one perceives the cessation of the world (*loka-nirodhaṃ . . . yathābhūtaṃ sammappaññāya passato yā loke atthitā sā na hoti*). Nāgārjuna's argument here is not that "there is another realm or aspect of being which people have always overlooked. This is the realm or aspect of *bhāva*, [which] refers to the truly dynamic worldly existence" (as Inada seems to assume, see p. 125). Rather, it is a rejection of *bhāva*, primarily because impermanence (*anityatā*) is incompatible with *bhāva*, which implies permanence. In fact, Nāgārjuna was probably aware that the Buddha had always employed the term *bhava* to explain the process of "becoming," instead of the abstract term *bhāva*. Indeed *bhāva*, or its more restricted form *svabhāva*, is equivalent to *astitva* (*atthitā*) and more often Nāgārjuna understood the term in that sense.

5. *Saṃbhavo vibhavenaiva kathaṃ saba bhaviṣyati,*
na janma-maraṇaṃ caiva tulya-kālaṃ hi vidyate.

How can occurrence be evident along with dissolution? Indeed, simultaneous birth and death are similarly not evident.

MKV(P) p.414; *MKV(V)* p.179.

At XXI.3, Nāgārjuna questioned the feasibility of asserting that death occurs together with (*saha*) birth. In the present verse, he is questioning the validity of asserting the occurrence of birth together with (*saha*) death. In other words, he is questioning the feasibility of asserting an invariable connection between death and rebirth, an invariable connection that is never asserted by the Buddha. In fact, what the Buddha asserted was that a dying person, depending upon conditions, can be reborn. An invarible relationship between death and rebirth was admitted only by the substantialists.

6. *Sahānyonyena vā siddhir vinānyonyena vā yayoḥ,*
na vidyate tayoḥ siddhiḥ kathan nu khalu vidyate.

The occurrence of things, either together or separately, is not evident. If so, how can their establishment be evident?

MKV(P) p.415; *MKV(V)* p.180.

This conclusion of Nāgārjuna is related to his criticisms in the previous verses. He is simply questioning the metaphysical assertions relating to occurrence and dissolution, birth and death.

7. *Kṣayasya saṃbhavo nāsti nākṣayasyāsti saṃbhavaḥ,*
kṣayasya vibhavo nāsti vibhavo nākṣayasya ca.

Occurrence of that which is waning does not exist, nor is there occurrence of that which is not waning. Dissolution of that which is waning does not exist, nor is there dissolution of the not waning.

MKV(P) p.415; *MKV(V)* p.180.

The term *kṣaya* was used in the Buddhist texts in the context where waning or complete extinction is implied. Whereas the term *nirodha* could mean ceasing that could be followed by arising (*utpāda*) and, as such, they could be used as complementaries to explain change and impermanence as well as dependent arising, the term *kṣaya* had no such complementary term except its negation, *a-kṣaya*, which implies permanence. For this reason, Nāgārjuna was able to maintain that there is neither absolute cessation (*kṣaya*) nor permanence (*a-kṣaya*) of both occurrence (*saṃbhava*) and dissolution (*vibhava*).

8. *Saṃbhavo vibhavaś caiva vinā bhāvaṃ na vidyate,*
saṃbhavaṃ vibhavaṃ caiva vinā bhāvo na vidyate.

Without an existent, occurrence as well as dissolution are not evident. Without occurrence as well as dissolution, an existent is not evident.

9. *Saṃbhavo vibhavaś caiva na śūnyasyopapadyate,*
saṃbhavo vibhavaś caiva nāśūnyasopapadyate.

Either occurrence or dissolution of the empty is not appropriate. Either occurrence or dissolution of the non-empty is also not appropriate.

10. *Saṃbhavo vibhavaś caiva naika ity upapadyate,*
saṃbhavo vibhavaś caiva na nānety upapadyate.

It is not appropriate to assume that occurrence and dissolution are identical. It is not appropriate to assume that occurrence and dissolution are different.

MKV(P) pp.416-418; *MKV(V)* pp.180-181.

It is probably the use of the term *bhāva* at XXI.8 that led Inada to assume that it represents a unique realm of existence recognized by Nāgārjuna. However, if we are to keep in mind the two metaphysical schools—Sarvāstivāda and Sautrāntika—and their metaphysical doctrines of identity and difference, it is possible to interpret the statement in verse 8 as well as the two verses that follow as straightforward criticisms of these two schools.

For example, a Sautrāntika who denies a *bhāva* or *svabhāva* can maintain that occurrence and dissolution can take place without a permanent entity (*bhāva, svabhāva*). Occurrence and dissolution would then mean the absence of continuity. Nāgārjuna denies this.

On the contrary, a Sarvāstivādin can maintain that a *bhāva* or *svabhāva* can exist without occurrence and dissolution, and this would account for continuity but negate difference. This too is rejected by Nāgārjuna.

Similarly, occurrence and dissolution are incompatible with the "empty" (*śūnya*), as understood by a Sautrāntika, or the "non-empty" (*aśūnya*) as explained by the Sarvāstivādin (see XX.16-18).

Furthermore, occurrence and dissolution are neither identical (*naika*) nor different (*nānā*) in a metaphysical sense.

11. *Dṛśyate saṃbhavaś caiva vibhavaś caiva te bhavet,*
dṛśyate saṃbhavaś caiva mohād vibhava eva ca.

It may occur to you that both occurrence and dissolution are seen. However, both occurrence and dissolution are seen only through confusion.

MKV(P) p.419; *MKV(V)* p.181.

It would be a folly to assume that occurrence and dissolution are perceived (*dṛśyate*). Neither the Buddha nor Nāgārjuna would be willing to assert this. Occurrence and dissolution in themselves are not perceivable. They are seen only in relation to phenomena that occur and dissolve. The metaphysical issues that arose during Nāgārjuna's time as a result of the extremist analysis of phenomena into events and relations have already been referred to (see XX.11).

12. *Na bhāvāj jāyate bhāvo bhāvo 'bhāvān na jāyate,*
nābhāvāj jāyate 'bhāvo 'bhāvo bhāvān na jāyate.

An existent does not arise from an existent; neither does an existent arise from a non-existent. A non-existent does not arise from a non-existent; neither does a non-existent arise from an existent.

13. *Na svato jāyate bhāvaḥ parato naiva jāyate,*
na svataḥ parataś caiva jāyate jāyate kutaḥ.

An existent does not arise from itself, or from another or from both itself and another. Whence can it then arise?

MKV(P) pp.419–421; *MKV(V)* p.182.

Bhāva and *abhāva* referred to here may be compared with the *sat* and *asat* in the pre-Buddhist Indian philosophy. The unresolvable metaphysical questions that plagued Indian philosophy for centuries, questions such as "Did existence (*sat*) arise from non-existence (*asat*)?" or *vice versa*, have once again been introduced into Buddhist thought by the Sarvāstivādins and the Sautrāntikas. The identity and non-identity theories of causation, theories of self-causation and external causation, and many other metaphysical views that emerged in the Buddhist tradition are repeatedly mentioned and rejected by Nāgārjuna.

14. *Bhāvam abhyupapannasya śāśvatoccheda-darśanam,*
prasajyate sa bhāvo hi nitya 'nityo 'tha vā bhavet.

For him who is engrossed in existence, eternalism or annihilationism will necessarily follow, for he would assume that it is either permanent or impermanent.

MKV(P) p.421; *MKV(V)* pp.182–183.

Nāgārjuna is here presenting the inevitable conclusions that a person involved in speculations relating to *bhāva* will reach. If the *bhāva* is assumed to be permanent, he will end up with a notion of eternalism. If, on the contrary, the *bhāva* is looked upon as being impermanent, then he will assert annihilation.

It may be noted that the Sarvāstivādins who were involved in the notion of *bhāva*, came up with the belief in an eternal self-nature (*svabhāva*) or substance (*dravya*). The same involvement led them to assume the momentary destruction (*kṣaṇa-bhaṅga*) of impermanent qualities or characteristics of *bhāva*.

15. *Bhāvam abhyupapannasya naivocchedo na śāśvatam,*
udaya-vyaya-saṃtānaḥ phala-hetvor bhavaḥ sa hi.

[On the contrary,] for him who is engrossed in existence, there would be neither annihilationism nor eternalism, for, indeed, becoming is the series of uprising and ceasing of cause and effect.

16. *Udaya-vyaya-saṃtānaḥ phala-hetvor bhavaḥ sa cet,*
vyayasyāpunarutpatter hetucchedaḥ prasajyate.

If it is assumed that becoming is the series of uprising and ceasing of the cause and effect, then with the repeated non-arising of that which ceases, it will follow that there will be annihilation of the cause.

MKV(P) pp.422–423; *MKV(V)* p.183.

The Sautrāntika position was no more different. They assumed that *bhāva* is none other than *bhava*, the process of becoming represented by the series (*saṃtāna*) of arising and ceasing of effect and cause (*phala-hetvoḥ*) As such, they believed that their conception of existence does not come under either eternalism or annihilationism.

However, Nāgārjuna has a different perception. He assumes that if the process of becoming (*bhava*) is analysed into a series of arising and ceasing of effect and cause, as the Sautrāntikas did, one is compelled to recognize the non-rebirth (*a-punar-utpatti*) of that which has ceased, and there would be complete annihilation of the cause. This is similar to the argument used at XXI.7.

17. *Sadbhāvasya svabhāvena nāsadbhāvaś ca yujyate,*
nirvāṇa-kāle cocchedaḥ praśamād bhava-saṃtateḥ.

The non-existence of that which possesses existence in terms of self-nature is not appropriate. [On the contrary,] at the time of freedom, there will be annihilation as a result of the appeasement of the stream of becoming.

MKV(P) pp.423–424; *MKV(V)* pp.183–184.

Nāgārjuna's attention is now directed at the Sautrāntika view, for it is that which finally contributed to the "personalist theory" (*pudgala-vāda*) of the Vātsīputriyas. The Sautrāntika will dismiss the Sarvāstivāda view, insisting that there is no way in which *nirvāṇa* can be explained in terms of their notion of self-nature (*svabhāva*), especially because what is really existing (*sadbhāva*) on its own (*svabhāvena*) cannot become a non-existent (*asadbhāva*).

However, the Sautrantika will say that as a result of the appeasement of the series of becoming (*bhava-saṃtati*), there is annihilation at the time of *nirvāṇa*. Having stated this position, Nāgārjuna proceeds to analyse its implications.

18. *Carame na niruddhe ca prathamo yujyate bhavaḥ,*
carame nāniruddhe ca prathamo yujyate bhavaḥ.

It is not proper to assume that there is first becoming when the last has ceased. Nor is it proper to assume that there is first becoming when the last has not ceased.

MKV(P) p.425; *MKV(V)* p.184.

The Sautrāntika theory of a series of momentary existences is under investigation here. As mentioned before, the Sautrāntikas were often faced with the problem of explaining arising (*utpāda*). Thus, Nāgārjuna argues that the first (moment of) becoming (*prathamo bhavaḥ*) cannot occur when the last (*carama*) has ceased, for there will be nothing to give rise to the former. This is what was referred to as the cessation of the cause (*hetuccheda*) at XXI.16. The other alternative is to assume that the entity of the last moment has not ceased (*aniruddha*), and this, of course, makes it difficult for the first becoming to occur at all.

19. *Nirudhyamāne carame prathamo yadi jāyate,*
nirudhyamāna ekaḥ syāj jāyamāno 'paro bhavet.

If the first were to be born when the last is ceasing, then that which is ceasing would be one and that which is being born would be another.

MKV(P) p.426; *MKV(V)* 184.

Assume that the first becoming occurs at the time when the last is ceasing (*nirudhyamāna*). Nāgārjuna insists that, in that case, what is ceasing is one thing and what is arising is something completely different (*aparo*). Nāgārjuna is here referring to the implications of the theory of moments, namely, the recognition of absolute distinctions.

20. *Na cen nirudhyamānaś ca jāyamānaś ca yujyate,*
sārdhaṃ ca mriyate yeṣu teṣu skandheṣu jāyate.

If it is asserted that the ceasing is also the being born, this would not be proper. For, in that case, whatever that is born in relation to the aggregates, would also be dying at the same time.

MKV(P) p.426; *MKV(V)* p.185.

Further complications will arise if it is assumed that something that ceases is also arising. Nāgārjuna is not prepared to accept such an occurrence because this would mean the simultaneous death and birth of the aggregates. Therefore, an occurrence is not explained by a strictly momentary theory of existence advocated by the Sautrāntikas.

21. *Evaṃ triṣv api kāleṣu na yuktā bhava-saṃtatiḥ,*
triṣu kāleṣu yā nāsti sā kathaṃ bhava-saṃtatiḥ.

Thus, the stream of becoming is not proper in the context of the three periods of time. How can there be a stream of becoming that does not exist during the three periods of time?

MKV(P) p.427; *MKV(V)* p.185.

The conclusion is inevitable that the series of becoming (*bhava-saṃtati*) is not appropriately explained in terms of the three periods of time, a concept which, as shown in the previous chapter, is not empirically grounded.

CHAPTER TWENTY TWO
Examination of the *Tathāgata*
(Tathāgata-parīkṣā)

1. *Skandhā na nānyaḥ skandhebhyo nāsmin skandhā na teṣu saḥ,*
tathāgataḥ skandhavān na katamo 'tra tathāgataḥ.

The *tathāgata* is neither the aggregates nor different from them. The aggregates are not in him; nor is he in the aggregates. He is not possessed of the aggregates. In such a context, who is a *tathāgata*?

2. *Buddhaḥ skandhān upādāya yadi nāsti svabhāvataḥ,*
svabhāvataś ca yo nāsti kutaḥ sa parabhāvataḥ.

If a Buddha were to be dependent upon the aggregates, he does not exist in terms of self-nature. He who does not exist in terms of self-nature, how can he exist in terms of other nature?

MKV(P) pp.432–436; *MKV(V)* pp.187–189.

In addition to some of the terms used by the Buddha to refer to his own achievements, his disciples used a vast array of epithets in extolling his virtues. It is significant to note that none of these epithets caused so much misunderstanding as the one under discussion in the present chapter, namely, *tathāgata*. It seems that the very conception of *tathāgata* invited misunderstanding.

The term can be rendered into English as "thus-gone" (*tathā-gata*). The conception of one who has "thus-gone" immediately brings to mind the idea of an "agent" (see Chapter II). It was, therefore, inevitable that when questions relating to the "destiny" of the enlightened one were raised, they were always raised in relation to a *tathāgata*.

Nāgārjuna was aware that questions pertaining not only to the final destiny, but also to the nature of the living saint were raised during the Buddha's day. A discussion between Sāriputta and a monk named Yamaka, who had entertained the belief that a *tathāgata* is annihilated after death (*param maraṇā*) is reported in the *Saṃyutta-nikāya* (*S* 3.109-115; *Tsa* 5.2 [*Taishō* 2.30c-31c]). Reading the first part of this discussion, one gets the impression that Sāriputta was reluctant to identify the *tathāgata* with the five aggregates or to distinguish the *tathāgata* from the aggregates. On the basis of this, it is possible to come to the conclusions, that the *tathāgata* is linguistically transcendent.

However, if the discussion is followed to the very end, one can clearly see that such a conclusion is not warranted. For Sāriputta is not willing to admit a *tathāgata* in an absolute sense (*saccato thetato*), comparable to the metaphysical "self" (*ātman*) that was considered to be permanent and eternal. Indeed, toward the end of the discussion, Sāriputta moves from the conception of *tathāgata* to the notion of "self" (*atta*) and refuses to admit a self that is identical with or different from the aggregates.

Nāgārjuna, as if he had read this discourse, begins the present chapter in an identical way, first maintaining that the *tathāgata* is neither identical nor different from the aggregates, and then proceeding to question the existence or non-existence of the *tathāgata* after death. As in the *Saṃyutta* passage, Nāgārjuna immediately qualifies his reference to the living *tathāgata*, insisting that the *tathāgata* or the *buddha* under investigation is one possessed of self-nature (*svabhāva*) and hence similar to the notion of "self" (*atta*) rejected by Sariputta. Nāgārjuna thereupon uses his famous argument that if the *tathāgata* is not found in terms of self-nature, he cannot either be found in terms of other-nature (*para-bhāva*).

3. *Pratītya para-bhāvaṃ yaḥ so 'nātmety upapadyate,*
yaś cānātmā sa ca kathaṃ bhaviṣyati tathāgataḥ.

He who is dependent upon other nature would appropriately be without self. Yet, how can he who is without self be a *tathāgata*?

MKV(P) p.437; *MKV(V)* p.189.

If self-nature (*svabhāva*) were to be equivalent to self (*ātman*) as an entity in itself, then whatever is of "other-nature" (*para-bhāva*) will be "no-self" (*anātma*). "No-self" in this particular sense, which implies absolute difference, is not acceptable to Nāgārjuna, for it is a recognition of a difference between a *tathāgata* and the psychophysical personality.

4. *Yadi nāsti svabhāvaś ca para-bhāvaḥ kathaṃ bhavet,*
svabhāva-parabhāvābhyāṃ ṛte kaḥ sa tathāgataḥ.

If there exists no self-nature, how could there be other-nature? Without both self-nature and other-nature, who is this *tathāgata*?

MKV(P) p.437; *MKV(V)* p.190.

The idea that if there were to be no self-nature other-nature too would not be evident was already emphasized at I.3. A third metaphysical alternative that transcends both self-nature and other-nature is here denied.

5. *Skandhān yady anupādāya bhavet kaścit tathāgataḥ,*
sa idānīm upādadyād upādāya tato bhavet.

If there were to be a *tathāgata* because of non-grasping on to the aggregates, he should still depend upon them in the present. As such he will be dependent.

MKV(P) p.438; *MKV(V)* p.190.

In the early discourses, a person in bondage and therefore in a state of suffering (*dukkha*) is explained in terms of the five aggregates of grasping (*upādānakkhandha*). A person who is freed is said to be without grasping (*anupādāna*), but not without the aggregates. The gerund *upādāya* was used in the discourses to express two different meanings, namely, (i) "clinging to" (see *an-upādāya*, *Vin* 1.14; *A* 1.162; 4.290, etc.) and (ii) "depending upon" (*D* 1.205, *kālañ ca samayañ ca upādāya*). It was only in the former sense that a person was said to be freed from the aggregates, not in the latter sense. Yet, with the development of substantialism, that is, when a freed person came to be looked upon as being totally different from the one in bondage, each having his own nature (*svabhāva*)(see Chapter XXV), the freed one was perceived not only as one not grasping (*anupādāya*) on to the aggregates, but also as one who is independent of the aggregates. It is this substantialist interpretation that Nāgārjuna is criticizing when he points out that if a *tathāgata* were to exist without grasping on to the aggregates (*skandhān anupādāya*), he will still be dependent upon (*upādadyād*) them at the present time (*idānīṃ*), that is, as long as he is alive. Nāgārjuna was thus going back to the Buddha's own definition of a freed one.

6. *Skandhān cāpy anupādāya nāsti kaścit tathāgataḥ,*
yaś ca nāsty anupādāya sa upādāsyate katham.

There exists no *tathāgata* independent of the aggregates. How can he who does not exist dependently be grasped?

MKV(P) p.438; MKV(V) p.190.

Nāgārjuna seems to be using the passive very *upādāsyate* in an epistemological sense. In the previous verse, he maintained that a living *tathāgata* should be dependent upon the aggregates, even though he does not grasp on to them. Here Nāgārjuna is re-asserting the same position, when he says: "There exists no *tathāgata* who is independent of the aggregates." The reason for this is that such an independent *tathāgata*, being a metaphysical entity like the *ātman*, cannot be grasped or known.

7. *Na bhavaty anupādattam upādānaṃ ca kiṃcana,*
na cāsti nirupādānaḥ kathaṃcana tathāgataḥ.

There is no sphere of non-grasping, nor is there something as grasping. Neither is there someone who is without grasping. How can there be a *tathāgata*?

MKV(P) p.439; MKV(P) p.190.

The metaphysical speculations regarding identity and difference (*svabhāva, parabhāva*) leave the dependent or the grasped (*upādatta*), dependence or grasping (*upādāna*) as well as the one who is free or independent (*nirupādānaḥ*), without any basis. How can there be a *tathāgata*? The fact that it is only an explanation in terms of identity and difference that is rejected here is clearly indicated in the verse that follows.

8. *Tattvānyatvena yo nāsti mṛgyamāṇaś ca pañcadhā,*
upādānena sa katham prajñapyate tathāgataḥ.

He who, sought for in the fivefold manner, does not exist in the form of a different identity, how can that *tathāgata* be made known through grasping?

MKV(P) p.439' *MKV(V)* p.190.

The substantialiast explanation of a *tathāgata* would imply that he has completely transformed himself into a different entity, that is, a *tathāgata* having his own-nature (*svabhāva*) with no relationship to the person in bondage. However, examining the fivefold aggregates, no such entity can be discovered. Such a *tathāgata* cannot be explained in terms of dependence (*upādānena*).

Thus, the conception of dependence (*upādāna*) is incompatible with both identity and difference. What is denied here is neither dependence nor a *tathāgata*, but merely the metaphysical approaches to both dependence and *tathāgata*.

Instead of translating *tattva* and *anyatva* and as identity and difference, we have rendered the phrase as "different idenity" since it occurs in the singular.

9. *Yad apīdam updānaṃ tat svabhāvān na vidyate,*
svabhāvataś ca yan nāsti kutas tat parabhāvataḥ.

This grasping is not found in terms of self-nature. How can that which does not exist in terms of self-nature come to be in terms of other-nature.?

MKV(P) pp.439-440; *MKV(V)* p.191.

Just as much as a *tathāgata* cannot be explained satisfactorily by relying upon a theory of identity (*svabhāva*) or difference (*parabhāva*), even so grasping itself (*upādāna*) cannot be found in terms of self-nature or other nature. In other words, it would not be appropriate to explain grasping as an inevitable act or tendency in human beings.

10. *Evaṃ śūnyam upādānam upādātā ca sarvaśaḥ,*
prajñapyate ca śūnyena katham śūnyas tathāgataḥ.

Thus, grasping and grasper are empty in every way. How can an empty *tathāgata* be made known by something that is empty?

MKV(P) pp.440-441; *MKV(V)* p.191.

Thus, grasping as well as the one who grasps are empty in every possible way. They are devoid of any substance.

For the substantialist, the *tathāgata* as well as the aggregates have substance or own-nature, even though they are different from one another. The substantialist can explain the *tathāgata*, whose self-nature (*svabhāva*) is freedom, contrasting him with the one who is in bondage as a result of his being a "grasper" (*upadātṛ*) and whose nature is distinct (*para*) from that of the *tathāgata*. However, with Nāgārjuna's denial of self-nature, that sharp dichotomy also is dissolved. Hence Nāgārjuna's insistence that an empty *tathāgata* cannot be made known in relation to an equally empty "grasper" (*upādātṛ*) or "grasping" (*upādāna*) referred to in the previous verse.

11. *Śūnyam iti na vaktavyam aśūnyam iti vā bhavet,*
ubhayaṃ nobhayaṃ ceti prajñapty arthaṃ tu kathyate.

"Empty," "non-empty," "both" or "neither"—these should not be declared. It is expressed only for the purpose of communication.

MKV(P) p.444; *MKV(V)* pp.192-193.

Note again the use of the *iti*-formula. Nāgārjuna is rejecting any *theorizing* regarding either the "empty" or the "non-empty" or both or neither. Neither the empty nor the non-empty should be reified. These terms are used only for the sake of communicating or expressing an experience which, being dependent (*pratītyasamutpanna*), has no static self-nature (*svabhāva*), and as such cannot be demarcated and reified. The subtle difference between ***vaktavya*** ("should be declared") and ***kathyate*** ("is spoken of, is expressed") should not go unnoticed. For Nāgārjuna, declaration and expression are two different activities, the former calling for unquestioned acceptance, a sort of categorical imperative, the latter leaving room for modification depending upon the context.

This statement of Nāgārjuna is better understood in the light of the analysis of concepts provided by a modern philosopher like William James who recognizes a pragmatic view of language and truth, in contrast to substantialist philosophers like Plato for whom "concepts" are the incorruptible reals.

12. *Śāśvatāśāśvatādy atra kutaḥ śānte catuṣṭayaṃ,*
antānantādi cāpy atra kutaḥ śānte catuṣṭayaṃ.

How can the tetralemma of eternal, non-eternal, etc., be in the peaceful?
How can the tetralemma of finite, infinite, etc., be in the peaceful?

MKV(P) p.446; *MKV(V)* p.194.

Śānta is an appeased one. It is the *tathāgata* who has appeased the dispositions, obsessions as well as the object (see comments on V.8). For him, the fourfold metaphysical alternatives either regarding the duration of phenomena such as eternality (*śāśvata*) and non-eternality (*aśāśvata*) or regarding the extent of phenomena such as the finite (*anta*) and the infinite (*ananta*) do not exist. He has stopped brooding over the past and running after the future.

13. *Yena grāho gṛhītas tu ghano 'stīti tathāgataḥ,*
nāstīti sa vikalpayan nirvṛtasyāpi kalpayet.

Discriminating on the basis of grasping or the grasped, and firmly in-

sisting that a *tathāgata* "exists" or "does not exist," a person would think similarly even of one who has ceased.

MKV(P) p.447; *MKV(V)* p.194.

The Buddha's reasons for the rejection of the notion of *tathāgata* in the *Saṃyutta* passage referred to above (see comments on XXII.1-2) are clearly emphasized by Nāgārjuna. The Buddha rejected a *tathāgata* because his existence was asserted in a real and absolute sense (*saccato thetato*). When Nāgārjuna speaks of a dogmatic grasping (*grāha*) on to something as the real or substantial (*ghana*) existence or non-existence (*astīti . . . nāstīti*) of the *tathāgata*, he was expressing the sentiments similar to those of the Buddha. Furthermore, arguing in a similar way as the Buddha did, Nāgārjuna maintains that the same sort of substantialist speculations lead to the views regarding the existence and non-existence of the *tathāgata* even after his death.

Here there is no denial of a *tathāgata*, but only of a substantial entity. The verse that follows is unequivocal in this regard.

14. *Svabhāvataś ca śūnye 'smiṃś cintā naivopapadyate,*
paraṃ nirodhād bhavati buddho na bhavatīti vā.

When he is empty in terms of self-nature, the thought that the Buddha exists or does not exist after death is not appropriate.

MKV(P) p.447; *MKV(V)* p.194.

Here the term *asmin*, in the locative absolute construction (*asmin svabhāvataś ca śūnye*), refers to the *tathāgata*. If the *tathāgata* who is alive is empty of self-nature, then it is not appropriate to assume that he exists or does not exist after death. It is only the substantialist thinking (*cintā*) that leads to the metaphysical questions which were left undeclared (*avyākṛta*) by the Buddha.

15. *Prapañcayanti ye buddhaṃ prapañcātītam avyayam,*
te prapañcahatāḥ sarve na paśyanti tathāgatam.

Those who generate obsessions with great regard to the Buddha who has gone beyond obsessions and is constant, all of them, impaired by obsessions, do not perceive the *tathāgata*.

MKV(P) p.448; *MKV(V)* p.195.

Here we radically differ from the prevailing explanations that *prapañca* means thought distinct from reality (see Inada, p. 135). Having rejected the more widespread view that Buddhism recognizes an "unspeakable" (*avācya*) and "indefinable" (*anirvacanīya*) truth or reality (*tattva*), which leads to the above interpretation of *prapañca*, we have rendered the term as "obsession."

The Buddha remains aloof from obsessions (*prapañcātītam*). As such, he is not understood or grasped by those who are obsessed. A person who is obsessed with the idea of identity will understand the Buddha in a way different from one who is obsessed with the idea of difference. One will say that he "exists" (*asti*) and the other will insist that he "does not exist" (*nāsti*).

The Buddha who has overcome such "obsessions" is "not so variable" (*avyayaṃ*). His perceptions are not variable in the same way as those of the unenlightened ones who are dominated by obsessions. Nāgārjuna could not have been unaware of the definition of the Buddha as "one who has become stable and steady" (*ṭhitaṃ ānejjappattaṃ*, *A* 3.377; *ṭhitaṃ cittaṃ*, *S* 5.74). The term *avyaya* in the present context expresses the same idea of stability and steadfastness achieved by a Buddha. This is not to assume his permanent existence.

16. *Tathāgato yat svabhāvas tat svabhāvam idaṃ jagat,*
tathāgato niḥsvabhāvo niḥsvabhāvam idaṃ jagat.

Whatever is the self-nature of the *tathāgata*, that is also the self-nature of the universe. The *tathāgata* is devoid of self-nature. This universe is also devoid of self-nature.

MKV(P) pp.448-449; *MKV(V)* p.195.

The first statement of Nāgārjuna may be taken to mean that there *is* a self-nature of the *tathāgata* which is identical with that of the universe. This would be justification for the belief in a permanent entity which is identical with the reality of the universe, comparable to the *ātman* and *brahman* of the Hindu tradition. However, Nāgārjuna immediately sounds the warning that there is not such self-nature either in the *tathāgata* or in the universe. This would mean that non-substantiality (*nairātmya*) applies not only to the individual (*pudgala* = *tathāgata*) but also to all phenomena (*dharma* = *jagat*).

CHAPTER TWENTY THREE
Examination of Perversions
(Viparyāsa-parīkṣā)

1. *Saṃkalpa-prabhavo rāgo dveṣo mohaś ca kathyate,*
śubhāśubha-viparyāsān saṃbhavanti pratītya hi.

Lust, hatred, and confusion are said have thought as their source. Perversions regarding the pleasant and the unpleasant arise depending upon these.

MKV(P) p.451; *MKV(V)* p.197.

Following upon a discussion of the *tathāgata* in relation to the world, a discussion that avoided absolute identity and absolute difference, Nāgārjuna takes up the question regarding perversions (*viparyāsa*) which makes a difference between a person in bondage and one who is freed.

The four perversions are discussed by the Buddha at *Aṅguttara* 2.52. They pertain to perceptions (*saññā*), thoughts (*citta*), and views (*diṭṭhi*). Perversion (*vipallāsa*) of perception or thought or view occurs with the identification of

i. the impermanent with the permanent (*anicce niccan ti*),
ii. the not unsatisfactory with the unsatisfactory (*adukkhe dukkhan ti*),
iii. the non-substantial with the substantial (*anattani attā ti*), and
iv. the unpleasant with the pleasant (*aśubhe śubhan ti*).

It is important to note that perversion ii is based upon perversion i, and perversion iv is based upon perversion iii. While perversions ii and iv relate to subjective attitudes, perversions i and iii are cognitive in nature.

The recognition of subjective perversions (i.e. ii and iv) does not mean that those experiences relating to which perversions arise do not exist. Indeed, experiences of the pleasant (*śubha* = *manāpa*) and unpleasant (*aśubha* =

amanāpa) sensations occur even in the enlightened ones (*Itivuttaka* 38). Perversion is the wrong identification of these experiences. However, the same cannot be said of the cognitive perversions, for the Buddha would be reluctant to assume that there is an experience corresponding to something that is either permanent or substantial.

For Nāgārjuna, perversions ii and iv are not due to purely intellectual or cognitive incapacity on the part of the individual. They are due more to the subjective elements dominating thoughts such as lust and hatred, which arise along with thoughts (*saṃkalpa-prabhavo*), even though these latter are not part of the world of experience. This explanation of Nāgārjuna is based upon a passage in the *Saṃyutta* wherein the Buddha identifies desire (*kāma*) with thoughts of lust (*saṃkappa-rāga*) without confusing it with whatever is beautiful (*citrāni*) in the world (see *S* 2.22; *Tsa* 48.20 [*Taishō* 2.345b]).

As such, it is not surprizing to see Nāgārjuna beginning his analysis with the last of the perversions, namely, the identification of the pleasant with the unpleasant (*aśubhe śubhan ti*), a subjective perversion that is based upon the cognitive confusion (i.e., *anattani attā ti*). Nāgārjuna was probably interested in beginning his analysis with the subjective perversion because the metaphysicians, who carried the analytical process beyond its limit, had difficulty in accounting for the emergence of sensations such as the pleasant and the unpleasant.

2. *Subhāśubha-viparyāsān saṃbhavanti pratītya ye,*
te svabhāvān na vidyante tasmāt kleśa na tattvataḥ.

Whatever perversions of the pleasant and the unpleasant that occur dependently are not evident in terms of self-nature. Therefore, the defilements are not in themselves.

MKV(P) p.453; *MKV(V)* p.197.

The perversions of the pleasant and the unpleasant are dependently arisen. As mentioned before, they are the products of lust and hatred; they arise within the individual. For this reason, they are not found in themselves (*na svabhāvataḥ*). Whatever defilments (*kleśa*) occur as a result of such perversions cannot be part of the experienced world. Rather they related to the way in which the world is perceived by the individual. It is only in this sense that they are looked upon as being unreal (*na tattvataḥ*).

3. *Ātmano 'stitva-nāstitve na kathamic ca sidhyataḥ,*
tam vināstitva-nāstitve kleśānāṃ sidhyataḥ katham.

The existence or the non-existence of the self is not established in any way. Without that, how can the existence or the non-existence of defilements be established?

MKV(P) p.453; *MKV(V)* p.198.

The perversion regarding what is pleasant and unpleasant has been traced back to the perversion where the non-substantial (*anātman*) is identified with the substantial (*ātman*). The substantial and the non-substantial, in the eyes of the metaphysician, pertain to existence (*astitva*) and non-existence (*nāstitva*) respectively (see V.8; XV.7, 11). The discourse to Kātyayana rejects both these views as being metaphysical.

Nāgārjuna is here insisting that neither the existence nor the non-existence of a metaphysical self can be proved. If there were to be no such self, then the defilements associated with such a self also cannot exist. In the absence of a substantial self, if only the defilements were to exist, then they should have self-existence, which was an idea denied at XXIII.2. Thus, neither the substantial existence of a self nor the substantial existence of defilments can be established.

4. *Kasyacidd hi bhavantīme kleśāḥ sa ca na sidhyati,*
kaścid āho vinā kiṃcit santi kleśā na kasyacit.

These defilements, indeed, belong to someone. Yet, such a person is not established. In other words, in the absence of anyone, these defilments seem to exist without belonging to anyone.

MKV(P) p.453; *MKV(V)* p.198.

Not only are the defilments not established as substantial elements, they cannot be proved to exist even as attributes. If defilements are considered as belonging to someone (*kaścid*) who is substantially existing, the absence of such a substantial entity would mean the absence of defilements as attributes.

5. *Svakāya-dṛṣṭivat kleśāḥ kliṣṭe santi na pañcadhā,*
svakāya-dṛṣṭivat kliṣṭaṃ kleśeṣv api na pañcadhā.

The defilments are like the view of one's own personality. Within the defiled, they are not found in the fivefold way. The defiled is like the view of one's own personality, for even within the defilements it is not found in the fivefold way.

MKV(P) p.454; *MKV(V)* p.198.

This is a further criticism of the substantialist notions of "defilements" (*kleśa*) as well as of the "defiled" (*kliṣṭa*). Such substantialist perspectives are comparable to the views regarding an "embodied person" (*svakāya-dṛṣṭi*), who is not obtainable when that personality is analysed into the five aggregates.

6. *Svabhāvato na vidyante śubhāśubha-viparyayāḥ,*
pratītya katamān kleśāḥ śubhāśubha-viparyayān.

The perversions regarding the pleasant and the unpleasant are not evident from the standpoint of self-nature. Depending upon which perversions of the pleasant and the unpleasant are these defilements?

MKV(P) p.455; *MKV(V)* p.199.

Just as much as both the defilements (*kleśa*) and the defiled (*kliṣṭa*) are not evident in substantial form, so are the perversions that give rise to defilements. They too are not found in any substantial way. The question then is: What is the nature of the perverson relating to the pleasant and the unpleasant depending upon which defilements are said to arise?

Here there is no denial of perversions nor the defilements. What has been questioned is only the *way* in which these are conceptualized.

7. *Rūpa-śabda-rasa-sparśā gandhā dharmāś ca ṣaḍvidhaṃ,*
vastu rāgasya dveṣasya mohasya ca vikalpyate.

Material form, sound, taste, touch, smell and concepts—these are discriminated as the sixfold foundations of lust, hatred, and confusion.

MKV(P) p.456; *MKV(V)* p.199.

Analysing lust, hatred, and confusion in terms of the four perversions, it may be maintained that lust and hatred are subjective attitudes, while confusion refers to the cognitive aspect of understanding (see comments on XXIII.1), even though the cognitive and attitudinal aspects are dependent upon one another. The present statement of Nāgārjuna implies the dependence of the attitudinal as well as the cognitive aspects of experience upon the sixfold objects of sense experience.

8. ***Rūpa-śabda-rasa-sparśā gandhā dharmāś ca kevalāḥ,***
gandharvanagarākārā marīci-svapna-saṃnibhāḥ.

Material form, sound, taste, touch smell as well as concepts—all these are comparable to the city of the *gandharvas* and resemble mirages and dreams.

MKV(P) p.457; *MKV(V)* pp.199-200.

The similes of the "dream" (*svapna*) and the "city of the *gandharvas*" (*gandharva-nagara*) have already been employed, along with "illusion" (*māyā*), to refute the substantialist explanation of the dispositionally conditioned phenomena (*samskṛta*)(see VII.34). The six objects of experience referred to at XXIII.7 are indeed dispositionally conditioned. They are not objects that are found in themselves (*svabhāvataḥ*). Nor are they absolutely non-existent.

9. ***Aśubhaṃ vā śubhaṃ vāpi kutas teṣu bhaviṣyati,***
māyā-puruṣa-kalpeṣu pratibimba-sameṣu ca.

How can the pleasant and the unpleasant come to be in people who are fabrications of illusion or who are comparable to mirror images?

MKV(P) p.458; *MKV(V)* p.200.

What Nāgārjuna has been criticizing so far is a substantialist theory of the pleasant and the unpleasant (*svabhāvato . . . śubhāśubhaviparyayān* XXIII.6). His argument in the present verse is directed against the belief that such substantial experiences can occur in thoughts of human beings who are themselves ***non-substantial***, and who are comparable to mirror images or reflections (see commentary on XVII.31-32).

10. *Anapekṣya śubhaṃ nāsti aśubhaṃ prajñapayemahi,*
yat pratītya śubhaṃ tasmāc chubhaṃ naivopapadyate.

We make known that the unpleasant does not exist without being contingent upon the pleasant, and that the pleasant, in its turn, is dependent upon that [i.e. the unpleasant]. Therefore, the pleasant [in itself] is not appropriate.

11. *Anapekṣyāśubhaṃ nāsti śubhaṃ prajñapayemahi,*
yat pratītyāśubhaṃ tasmād aśubhaṃ naiva vidyate.

We make known that the pleasant does not exist without being contingent upon the unpleasant, and that the unpleasant, in its turn, is dependent upon that [i.e., the pleasant]. Therefore, the unpleasant [in itself] is not evident.

MKV(P) pp.458-459; *MKV(V)* p.200.

This is a clear refutation of the substantialist views of both the pleasant and the unpleasant. Nāgārjuna insists that they are dependent upon one another. They are not independent experiences where one is replaced by another, as in the case of the theory of "attainment" (*prāpti*) and "non-attainment" (*aprāpti*)(see comments on XVI.10, XXIV.32).

12. *Avidyamāne ca śubhe kuto rāgo bhaviṣyati,*
aśubhe avidyamāne ca kuto dveṣo bhaviṣyati.

When the pleasant is not evident, whence can there be lust? When the unpleasant is not evident, whence can there be hatred?

MKV(P) p.459; *MKV(V)* p.201.

In addition to being mutually dependent, the pleasant and the unpleasant provide a foundation for the subjective tendencies such as lust and hatred. Thus, lust would be non-existent if the pleasant were not evident. Similarly, hatred would be non-existent, if the unpleasant were not evident. This, indeed, is the conclusion of the *Saṃyutta* passage referred to at XXIII.1. In that context, the Buddha was not denying the pleasant and the unpleasant experiences in the world. He was simply insisting that when such experiences occur a wise man restraints his yearning (*chanda*) for it.

13. *Anitye nityam ity evaṃ yadi grāho viparyayaḥ,*
nānityaṃ vidyate śūnye kuto grāho viparyayaḥ.

If there were to be grasping on to the view, "What is impermanent is permanent," then there is perversion. The impermanent is not evident in the context of the empty. How can there be grasping or perversion?

MKV(P) p.460; *MKV(V)* p.201.

So far Nāgārjuna has endeavored to show that the perversion regarding the pleasant and the unpleasant is the result of a cognitive confusion which led to the belief in a substance or self (*ātman*). With the present statement, Nāgārjuna begins to analyse the conception of impermanence (*anitya*) in order to explain the *tathāgata's* cognitive understanding of the world of experience. This understanding enables the *tathāgata* to eliminate the perversion relating to happiness and suffering.

Here, the perversion pertains to grasping of the impermanent as the permanent. If so, the perspective in which the *tathāgata* looks at the world should be one of impermanence. Unfortunately, the notion of impermanence that dominated the Buddhist tradition during Nāgārjuna's day was more a metaphysical one (see commentaries on Chapter VII) than an empirical one. For the metaphysician, the absence of permanence implied the reality of the momentary. Nāgārjuna rightly believes that as much as grasping after permanence is a perversion, so is grasping after the reality of the momentary (= *kṣaṇika*). The denial of permanence does not commit oneself to the other extreme of momentary destruction (*kṣaṇa-bhaṅa*). Emptiness (*śūnyatā*) does not imply any such momentariness.

14. *Anitye nityam ity evaṃ yadi grāho viparyayaḥ,*
anityam ity api grāhaḥ śūnye kiṃ na viparyayaḥ.

If grasping on to the view, "What is impermanent is permanent," is perversion, how is it that even the grasping after the view, "What is empty is impermanent," does not constitute a perversion?

MKV(P) p.462; *MKV(V)* p.202.

It is possible for someone to raise the question as to whether grasping after the empty would itself be a perversion, just as much as grasping after the permanent or the impermanent would constitute perversions. Nāgārjuna is here raising this question and then proceeds to answer it in the following verse.

15. *Yena gṛhṇāti yo grāho grahītā yac ca gṛhyate,*
upaśāntani sarvāṇi tasmād grāho na vidydate.

That through which there is grasping, whatever grasping there is, the

grasper as well as that which is grasped—all these are appeased. Therefore, no grasping is evident.

MKV(P) p.465; *MKV(V)* p.203.

The middle path enunciated in the discourse to Kātyāyana avoided the two extremes relating to philosophical understanding and explanation. This was achieved through the appeasement of dispositions and the elimination of grasping. Because of non-grasping, all the metaphysical questions relating to the faculties (*yena gṛhṇāti*), the process of understanding (*grāha*), the person involved in such understanding (*grahītā*) as well as the object of understanding (*yac ca gṛhyate*), come to be appeased. The appeased one (*śanta*) does not continue to raise questions or doubts beyond a *certain limit*, not because he knows everything nor because he does not care to know, but because he is aware of the conflicts generated by any pursuit of knowledge that goes beyond experience.

The fact that grasping for emptiness can constitute a sort of perversion (*śūnyatā dṛṣṭi*) has already been explained by Nāgārjuna (XIII.8). This does not mean that the very conception of emptiness is invalidated in the same way as the concepts of permanence and momentariness would be invalidated. The reason for this is that the notions of permanence and substance as well as of momentariness are not empirically grounded compared with dependent arising, non-substantiality, or emptiness. Both the Buddha and Nāgārjuna would categorize the former under wrong thoughts (*mithyā saṃkalpa*), while they would consider the latter as right or appropriate thoughts (*samyak saṃkalpa, kalpanā yātra yojyate*, XVII.13). The verse that follows should be understood in such a context. This indeed is the final conclusion of Nāgārjuna in the *Kārikā* (see XXVII.30).

16. *Avidyamāne grāhe ca mithyā vā samyag eva vā,*
bhaved viparyayaḥ kasya bhavet kasyāviparyayaḥ.

When grasping, wrongly or rightly, is not evident, for whom would there be perversion and for whom would there be non-perversion?

MKV(P) p.466; *MKV(V)* p.204.

With grasping gone, whether it be for the right thing or the wrong thing, the enlightened one does not involved himself in any substantialist thinking relating to perversion or non-perversion. This is the state of the saint who has attained freedom from grasping (*anupādāya vimukti*).

17. *Na cāpi viparītasya saṃbhavanti viparyayāḥ,*
na cāpy aviparītasya saṃbhavanti viparyayāḥ.

Perversions do not occur to one who is already subjected to perversion. Perversions do not occur to one who has not been subjected to perversions.

18. *Na viparyasyamānasya saṃbhavanti viparyayāḥ,*
vimṛśasva svayaṃ kasya saṃbhavanti viparyayāḥ.

Perversions do not occur to one who is being subjected to perversions. Reflect on your own! To whom will the perversions occur?

MKV(P) p.467; *MKV(V)* p.204.

Upon reaching such a level of moral and intellectual development (as referred to in the previous verse), one does not get involved in metaphysical speculations such as whether perversions arise in one who is already afflicted by perversions, or not afflicted, or is being afflicated. The speculation that is avoided pertains not only to the past and the future but also the present. As such he avoids the metaphysics discussed in Chapter II. When perversions themselves are not perceived as being substantial, how can one consider a perverse person as a substantial entity.

19. *Anutpannā kathaṃ nāma bhaviṣyanti viparyayāḥ,*
viparyayeṣv ajātesu viparyaya-gataḥ kutaḥ.

How could there be non-arisen perversions? When perversions are not

born, whence can there be a person who is subjected to perversions?

MKV(P) pp.467-468; *MKV(V)* p.205.

Picking up the argument from the previous verse, Nāgārjuna is here specifically rejecting the substantialist notions of perversions as well as persons who are perverse. If perversions are substantial or having self-nature (*svabhāva*), they cannot be considered as arisen (*utpanna*). When they are non-arisen or unborn (*ajāta*), there cannot be a person in whom these would arise, for they cannot serve as attributes.

20. *Na svato jāyate bhāvaḥ parato naiva jāyate,*
na svataḥ parataś ceti viparyaya-gataḥ kutaḥ.

An existent does not arise from itself, nor does it arise from another, nor both itself and other. If so, whence can there be a person who is subject to perversions?

MKVP) p.468; *MKV(V)* p.205.

This verse, which is not available in Kumārajīva's translation, represents aņ application of the analysis of substantial existence (*bhāva*) in Chapter I to the problems of a substantial person or entity. It is almost identical with XXI.13.

21. *Ātmā ca śuci nityaṃ ca sukhaṃ ca yadi vidyate,*
ātmā ca śuci nityaṃ ca sukhaṃ ca na viparyayaḥ.

If either the self, the pleasant, the permanent, or the happy is evident, then neither the self, the pleasant, the permanent, nor the happy constitutes a perversion.

MKV(P) p.468; *MKV(V)* p.205.

Nāgārjuna began his examination of perversions (*viparyāsa*) utilizing the same terms used by the Buddha at *A* 2.52. In the present verse, he adopts a slightly different terminology in referring to the perversions. Instead of *śubha* and *aśubha*, he uses the pair of terms *śuci* and *aśuci*, and instead of *adukkha* he has *sukha*. This latter terminology was indeed utilized by the interpreters of Abhidharma when discussing the perversions (see *Akb* p.286). As such, it is a clear indication that Nāgārjuna was conversant withg the early discourses as much as he was familiar with the Abhidharma commentarial literature.

Nāgārjuna's argument in the present verse could lead to misunderstanding unless it is seen in the context of his previous statements about the perversions, expecially at XXIII.20. If the self, the pleasant, the permanent, and the happy are evident *as self-existent entities*, then, indeed, they do not constitute perversions. Unfortunately, Inada's translation does not seem to bring out this strong sense of "exist" that Nāgārjuna is implying here.

22. *Nātmā ca śuci nityaṃ ca sukhaṃ ca yadi vidyate,*
anātmā 'śucy anityaṃ ca naiva duḥkhaṃ ca vidyate.

If neither the self, the pleasant, the permanent, nor the happy is not evident, then neither the non-self, the unpleasant, the impermanent, nor the suffering would also be evident.

MKV(P) p.469; *MKV(V)* p.205.

Having rejected the substantial existence of the four perversions, Nāgārjuna is here emphasizing their relativity. However, relativity in this context need not be understood as applying in an identical way to all the four perversions. As pointed out earlier (see comments on XXIII.1), the four perversions deal with two different categories, the cognitive and the attitudinal. The fact that *anātman* and *anitya* are conceptually related to *ātman* and *nitya* does not mean that the latter are cognitively based. They are relative only at the conceptual level. On the contrary, *śuci* and *aśuci* as well as *sukha* and *duḥkha* are part of experience, even though there could be confusion regarding their identification.

23. *Evaṃ nirudhyate 'vidyā viparyaya-nirodhanāt,*
avidyāyāṃ niruddhāyāṃ saṃskārādyāṃ nirudhyate.

Thus, with the cessation of perversions, ignorance ceases. When ignorance has ceased, the dispositions, etc. come to cease.

MKV(P) p.469; *MKV(V)* p.206.

The distinction between the two kinds of perversions mentioned earlier (XXIII.1,22) seems to be justified by the present statement. When the perversions cease, the immediate result would be the cessation of ignorance (*avidyā*). This would pertain to the more cognitive perversions (i and iii). The cessation of ignorance would also mean the cessation of the perversions relating to dispositions, that is, perversions ii and iv.

24. *Yadi bhūtāḥ svabhāvena kleśāḥ kecidd hi kasyacit,*
kathaṃ nāma prahīyeran kaḥ svabhāvaṃ prahāsyati.

If, indeed, certain defilements of someone have come to be on the basis of self-nature, how could they be relinquished? Who ever could relinquish self-nature?

25. *Yady abhūtāḥ svabhāvena kleśāḥ kecidd hi kasyacit,*
kathaṃ nāma prahīyeran ko 'sadbhāvaṃ prahāsyati.

If, indeed, certain defilements of someone have not come to be on the basis of self-nature, how could they be relinquished? Who ever could relinquish non-existence?

MKV(P) p.471; *MKV(V)* pp.206-207.

Nāgārjuna's conclusion in this chapter is that the defilements (*kleśa*), which are the results of the perversions discussed above, cannot be eliminated, and, therefore, there could be no *tathāgata*, if these defilements are looked upon as being either substantial, i.e., something that has come to be (*bhūta*) having self-nature (*svabhāva*) or non-substantial, i.e., something that has not come to be (*abhūta*) because of its having no real nature (*asadbhāva*). In either case, there can be no abandoning of defilements and hence the achievement of the state of *tathāgata*.

CHAPTER TWENTY FOUR
Examination of the Noble Truths
(Ārya-satya-parīkṣā)

1. *Yadi śūnyam idaṃ sarvam udayo nāsti na vyayaḥ,*
caturṇām ārya-satyānām abhāvas te prasajyate.

If all this is empty, then there exists no uprising and ceasing. These imply the non-existence of the four noble truths.

MKV(P) p.475; *MKV(V)* p.209.

Nāgārjuna's discussion of the four truths was an inevitable consequence of his analysis of perversions (Chapter XXIII) which, in its turn, was occasioned by a need to explain the perspective of a *tathāgata* (Chapter XXII). The four truths refer to the problem of suffering, the subject matter of two of the perversions, namely, mistaking the unpleasant for the pleasant (*aśubhe śubhan ti*) and non-suffering for the suffering (*aduḥkhe duḥkhan ti*).

Verses 1-6 in the present chapter pose one major problem faced by the Buddhist (or even by the non-Buddhist) in explaining suffering (*duḥkha*) and, therefore, the four noble truths, when placed in the context of "emptiness" (*śūnyatā*). The important questions are: Who are these Buddhists (or non-Buddhists)? Why are they faced with such a problem? The answers to these questions are found in the *Abhidharmakośa-bhāṣya* of Vasubandhu.

Vasubandhu refers to a theory proposed by *some*: "There indeed is no feeling of happiness" (*nāsty eva sukhā vedanā*) and "Everything is suffering or unsatisfactory" (*duḥkhaiva tu sarvaṃ*)(*Akb* p.330). There is very little doubt that this interpretation of the Buddha's teaching emerged with and was continued until modern times by thinkers and scholars belonging to the Brahmanical tradition. By ignoring a simple yet extremely important pronoun (namely, *idaṃ*, "this"), the Brahmanical interpreters transformed the Buddha's teaching from an empirical to an absolutistic system. Thus, the Buddha's statement: *sarvam idaṃ duḥkhaṃ* ("all this is suffering") turns out to be an unqualified universal statement: *sarvaṃ duḥkhaṃ* ("everything is suffering"). Similarly, a specific statement such as *sunyam idaṃ sarvaṃ* ("all this is empty") turns out to be another absolutistic one, *sunyaṃ sarvaṃ* ("everything is empty," a problematic not noticed by Inada, p. 144).

Threatened by such a problematic situation, the Buddhist metaphysicians were driven to the extreme position of asserting absolute forms of happiness, when they insisted: "Happy feelings do indeed exist in terms of unique character" (*asty eva svalakṣaṇataḥ sukhā vedanā, Akb* p.331). Yet, realizing that the Buddha did not present the world as a "bed of roses," they were compelled to admit that there are come experiences that are inherently unsatisfactory (*svabhāvenaiva duḥkhā*, ibid., p.329).

Thus, not realizing that this was all due to a Brahmanical misreading of the Buddha's discourses and assuming that there is a genuine problem, the Buddhist metaphysicians came to admit both suffering or unsatisfactoriness (*duḥkha*) and happiness (*sukha*) as substantially existing. Instead of correcting the Brahmanical misreading, they struggled for an explanation:

> When [the Buddha] declared: 'One should perceive happy feelings as suffering,' [i.e., the perception of one who has eliminated the perversions,] both [happiness and suffering] are available therein. Happiness is inherently so, because there is pleasantness. However, eventually there is suffering, because of its changing and impermanent nature. When that [feeling] is perceived as happiness, it contributes to enlightenment, through its enjoyment. When it is perceived as suffering, it leads to release, by being non-attached to it. (*Akb* p.331, *Yad uktaṃ "sukhā vedanā duḥkhe ti draṣṭavye" ti ubhayaṃ tasyām asti. Sukhatvaṃ ca svabhāvato manāpatvāt, duḥkaṃ ca paryāyato vipariṇāmānitya-dharmatvāt. Sā tu sukhato dṛśyamānā buddhāya kalpate, tad āsvādanāt, duḥkhato dṛśyamānā mokṣāya kalpate, tad vairāgyād iti.*)

The substance-terminology in the above passage should make it clear as to which Buddhist school was presenting this explanation. There seems to be no question that it was authored by the Sarvāstivādins. Thus, it was their desire to uphold the conception of substance that made them uncomfortable with the notion of "the empty" (*śūnya*). The substantialists were prepared to wrestle with the conceptions of substance and causation and, as shown earlier, they produced substantialist theories of causation. However, they could not do the same with the conception of "the empty" (*śūnya*), even though "emptiness" itself may be amenable to such substantialist interpretations (see XXIV.14).

It is in order to highlight this problem that Nāgārjuna begins the chapter with a reference to "the empty" (*śūnya*, as in *yadi śūnyam idaṃ sarvaṃ*) rather than to the abstract conception of "emptiness" (*śūnyatā*). In Nāgārjuna's mind, to preserve the non-substantialist and non-absolutistic standpoint of the Buddha, what needs to be restored is "the empty" rather than "emptiness," because the latter is dependent upon the former, whereas any emphasis on the latter could wipe out the former, as it happened in the case of the absolutists and the substantialists. In presenting the metaphysicians dilemma in this manner, Nāgārjuna was more concerned with the mistake of his Buddhist counterparts than with the misreadings of the Buddhist texts by the Brahamincal thinkers. For this reason, he makes no reference to such misreadings as "*sarvaṃ śunyaṃ.*"

2. *Parijñā ca prahāṇṃ ca bhāvanā sākṣikarma ca,*
caturṇām ārya-satyānām abhāvān nopapadyate.

In the absence of the four noble truths, understanding, relinquishing, cultivation, and realization will not be appropriate.

MKV(P) p.477; *MKV(V)* p.210.

Understanding (*parijñā*) pertains to the first of the four noble truths, namely, that suffering exists. Relinquishing (*prahāṇa*) refers to the second, namely, the cause of suffering, which is explained as craving (*tṛṣṇā*). Realization (*sākṣikarma*) applies to the third, namely, the state of freedom from suffering, which is nirvana. Cultivation or practice (*bhāvanā*) involves the fourth, namely, the path leading to the cessation of suffering.

3. *Tad abhāvān na vidyante catvāry ārya-phalāni ca,*
phalābhāve phalasthā no na santi pratipannakāḥ.

In the absense of this [fourfold activity], the four noble fruits would not be evident. In the absence of the fruits, neither those who have attained the fruits nor those who have reached the way [to such attainment] exist.

MKV(P) p.477; *MKV(V)* p.210.

The non-absolutistic standpoint of early Buddhism is clearly embodied in the doctrine of the four fruits (*ārya-phala*). Even though freedom without grasping (*anupādā vimukti*) is sometimes referred to as the one goal (*ekāyana*), yet a deliberate attempt to assert degrees of attainments where some are considered to be inferior to others is conspicuously absent. Like the relay of chariots (*rathavinīta*), one segment of the path is as important as the other, "dispassion" (*vairāgya*) being one dominant attitude permeating all segments. This has an important bearing on the conception of truth to be discussed soon.

4. *Saṃgho nāsti na cet santi te 'ṣṭau puruṣa-pudgalāḥ,*
abhavāc cārya-satyānāṃ saddharmo 'pi na vidyate.

If the eight types of individuals do not exist, there will be no congregation. From the non-existence of the noble truths, the true doctrine would also not be evident.

MKV(P) p.478; *MKV(V)* p.210.

Inada was probably assuming that *cet* refers to thought (*citta*) when he translated part of the first line as "the eight aspirations of men do not exist," whereas it could be more appropriately read as a conditional particle.

The association of the true doctrine (*sad-dharma*) with the four noble truths (*ārya-satya*) to a point where the absence of the latter implies the non-existence of the former should naturally raise questions regarding the more popular assignment of doctrines to the various schools where the four noble truths are assigned to the so-called Hinayana with the superior Mahāyāna having something more to offer. Such an assignment becomes really questionable when a great Mahāyāna thinker like Nāgārjuna himself admits of such a correlation (XXIV.30).

This equation is also significant for another very important reason. *Dharma*, as "teaching" also means a "statement" of doctrine. Some modern linguistic philosophers would prefer to use the term "truth" primarily in referring to statements rather than to facts. *Sad-dharma*, identified with truth, seems to accommodate such a perspective.

5. *Dharme cāsati saṃghe ca kathaṃ buddho bhaviṣyati,*
evaṃ trīṇy api ratnāni bruvāṇaḥ pratibādhase.

6. *śūnyatāṃ phala-sadbhāvam adharmaṃ dharmam eva ca,*
sarva-saṃvyavahārāṃś ca laukikān pratibādhase.

When the doctrine and the congregation are non-existent, how can there be an enlightened one? Speaking in this manner about emptiness, you contradict the three jewels, as well as the reality of the fruits, both good and bad, and all such worldly conventions.

MKV(P) pp.478-489; *MKV(V)* 210-213.

At this point the metaphysician brings up the notion of "emptiness" (*śūnyatā*). For him, emptiness is a problem, not because of any other reason, but because it implies "the empty" (*śūnya*), and this latter leaves no room for substantial existence (*sad-bhāva*) of the fruits (*artha*) of both good and bad as well as all the worldly conventions.

Inada's translation of *dharma* and *adharma* as proper and improper acts is a corrective to his earlier rendering of these two terms as factor and non-factor at VIII.5. However, his translation of *saṃvyavahāra* as something additional to *dharma* and *adharma* can be questioned in the light of the use of *vyavahāra* at XVII.24, where a similar, but not idential, set of categories (*puṇya-pāpa*, "merit and demerit") is referred to as *vyavahāra*. Indeed, this particular use of the term *vyavahāra* (= *saṃvṛti*) will throw much light on an understanding of the distinction between the two truths discussed at XXIV.8.

7. *Atra brūmaḥ śūnyatāyāṃ na tvaṃ vetsi prayojanaṃ,*
śūnyatāṃ śūnyatārthaṃ ca tata evaṃ vihanyase.

We say that you do not comprehend the purpose of emptiness. As such, you are tormented by emptiness and the meaning of emptiness.

MKV(P) p.490; *MKV(V)* p.213.

Looking at the nature of the objections raised by the Buddhist metaphysicians against the notion of "emptiness," Nāgārjuna is insisting that they do not understand "the purpose of emptiness," (*śūnyatāyāṃ prayojanaṃ*). Does this mean that "emptiness" has a functional or pragmatic value, rather than being an absolute concept? Does it need to be substantiated by "the empty," rather than merely substantiating "the empty." Which is more important, "the empty" or "emptiness," or are they of equal importance? If "the empty" is considered to be important, "emptiness" would be a mere idea with no grounding in experience. If the "emptiness" is looked upon as being important, the empty would turn out to be a fabrication. If both are considered to be equally important, there could be circularity in reasoning based upon them. However, if the empty is considered to be the basis of experience, and emptiness is derived from that experience, this latter could be provisional and remain to be corrected in terms of future experience. In such a case, the circularity involved in arguing about them could be easily eliminated. In the next three verses, Nāgārjuna proceeds to provide very specific answers to most of these questions.

8. *Dve satye samupāśritya buddhānāṃ dharma deśanā,*
loka-saṃvṛti-satyaṃ ca satyaṃ ca paramārthataḥ.

The teaching of the doctrine by the Buddhas is based upon two truths: truth relating to worldly convention and truth in terms of ultimate fruit.

MKV(P) p.492; *MKV(V)* 1p.214.

This has turned out to be one of two most discussed verses in Nāgārjuna's *Kārikā*. Modern disquisitions on the conception of two truths could perhaps fill several substantial volumes. Instead of plodding over trodden ground, the present discussion will be confined to a comparison of the conception of two truths in early Buddhism and the metaphysical version presented by the interpreters of the Abhidharma, with a view to clarifying Nāgārjuna's position. Nāgārjuna's version will be examined in the light of the problems posed at the beginning of the present chapter, as well as his reference to worldly conventions in the previous chapters.

In the *Sutta-nipāta,* the Buddha condemned any attempt to uphold a view (*diṭṭhi*) as the ultimate (*paramaṃ*)(*Sn* 796ff.). Refusing to recognize any knowledge of "things as they really are," and making a more sober claim to knowledge of "things as they have come to be" (*yathābhūta*), the Buddha was reluctant to accept any notion of *paramattha* as "ultimate reality." Instead, he claimed to know "the dependently arisen" (*paṭiccasamuppanna*) and, on that basis, formulated the conception of "dependent arising" (*paṭiccasamuppāda*). In such a context, it was more meaningful for him to speak of *attha* (Sk. *artha*) and *paramattha* (Sk. *paramārtha*) in the sense of fruit, consequence, or result (= *phala*, as in *sāmañña-phala*, "the fruit of recluseship"). Thus, a good action is one that is fruitful (*attha-saṃhita*) and a bad, unfruitful (*an-attha-saṃhita*).

The Buddha also recognized that views about good and bad, purity and impurity, are in most cases relative conventions (*Sn* 878-894). According to the same text, good (*kusala*) and bad (*akusala*) are conventions that vary depending upon contexts (*sammutiyo puthujjā*, *Sn* 897). These are the ways of the world (*loka*), often characterized as *sammuti, vohāra* (*D* 3.232) or *paññatti* (*S* 4.39-40). However, there is no indication that, since these are relative conventions, the Buddha advocated the transcendence of both good and bad.

Having defined the good as the fruitful, the Buddha characterized the ultimate good as the ultimately fruitful. The term *paramattha* was thus used to refer to the "ultimate fruit" rather than "ultimate reality." *Sammuti* and *paramattha* are therefore not two contrasting truths. The former is a mixed bag, while the latter represents the ultimate ideal. As a result of attaining *nibbāna*, which is the complete eradication of lust (*rāga*), hatred (*dosa*), and confusion (*moha*), the Buddha found himself enjoying an ultimate fruit, without hurting himself or others (*na attantapo na parantapo, D* 3.232). *Paramattha* thus becomes the moral ideal as reflected in the Buddha's own attainment of freedom and happiness.

The theory of dependent arising (*praṭiccasamuppāda*) explaining the phenomena that are dependently arisen (*paṭiccasamuppanna*) thus accommodates the four truths as well as the two truths. All truths being pragmatic, there is here no place for an "absolute or ultimate reality." The Buddha's epistemological standpoint does not allow for such speculations.

This, however, was not the case with the metaphysicians. It is significant to note that when the Buddhist metaphysicians were faced with the problem of reconciling the four truths with their conception of substance (*svabhāva*), they were compelled to fall back on the conception of two truths (*Akb* p.33). However, their interpretation of the two truths is totally different from the Buddha's and, in fact, seems to be contrary to it. Here again, Vasubandhu is our source.

As a Sautrāntika metaphysician, Vasubandhu refers to the two truths (*satya*) and surreptitiously moves on to a discussion of existents (*sat*): *saṃvṛti-sat* and *paramārtha-sat* (*Akb* p.334). He then provides two examples to illustrate the nature of *saṃvṛti-sat*. The first is a 'pot' (*ghaṭa*). There cannot be knowledge of a pot when it is broken into pieces. The second is water (*ambu*). Water is not known independent of the knowledge of "form" (*rūpa*). Contrasted with these two is knowledge of the *paramārtha-sat*. 'Material form' (*rūpa*) is an example of such existence. In this case, when an object is broken down into its ultimately irreducible elements, namely, atoms (*paramāṇu*), there is knowledge of the "unique nature" (*svabhāva* = *svalakṣaṇa*?) of such atoms. For the metaphysician, that unique nature, whether it is called *svabhāva* or *svalakṣaṇa*, has always remained an epistemological enigma.

This interpretation of the two truths is totally absent either in the early discourses or in the canonical Abhidharma. In the so-called Theravada tradition, it appears for the first time in the non-canonical texts (*Miln* 160), contributing, as it did in the case of the Sarvāstivāda and Sautrāntika schools, to insoluble problems such as the duality of mind and matter. Vasubandhu's statement of the two truths—*saṃvṛti* and *paramārtha*—in the above context, where he was recording the interpretation of the Sautrāntika view, remains in sharp contrast to the spirit of the Buddha's teaching on "non-substantialism." This should certainly provide an interesting background to the analysis of Nāgārjuna's own version of the two truths.

9. *Ye 'nayor na vijānanti vibhāgaṃ satyayadvayoḥ,*
te tattvaṃ na vijānanti gambhiraṃ buddha-śāsane.

Those who do not understand the distinction between these two truths do not understand the profound truth embodied in the Buddha's message.

MKV(P) p.494; *MKV(V)* p.215.

Nāgārjuna is, of course, criticizing his opponents for not understanding the Buddha's message. If so, Nāgārjuna's own explanation of these two truths should not come anywhere close to the one discussed by Vasubandhu, according to which the *saṃvṛti* represents a mere designation, not an ultimate reality or *paramārtha*. It is an ontological speculation which is not supported by the Buddha's own conception of dependent arising.

10. *Vyavahāram anāśritya paramārtho na deśyate,*
paramārtham anāgamya nirvāṇaṃ nādhigamyate.

Without relying upon convention, the ultimate fruit is not taught. Without understanding the ultimate fruit, freedom is not attained.

MKV(P) p.494; *MKV(V)* p.216.

Unless one is committed to upholding a theory of linguistic or conceptual transcendence of ultimate truth or reality, there seems to be no reason to restrict the use of the terms *saṃvṛti, vyavahāra,* or *prajñapti* to refer primarily to linguistic convention. These terms could and did stand for any kind of convention, whether it be linguistic, social, political, moral, or religious. As mentioned earlier (see comments on XXIV.8), all such conventions are pragmatic and contextual. As such, truth relating to them would also be pragmatic and contextual.

The fact that in the two previous instances when Nāgārjuna used the term *vyavahāra* (XVII.24; XXIV.6), he used it in the context of a discussion of morality, is of utmost significance. It is in this same context that the Buddha used the term *vohāra* (*D* 3.232 *anariya-vohara = musāvāda,* etc., and *ariya-vohara = musāvādā veramaṇī,* etc.) as well as the term *sammuti* (= *saṃvṛti, Sn* 897, 911). These, therefore, are the moral conventions of the world (*loka, laukika,* see XXIV.6) that are pragmatic, yet contextual. However, an ideal moral truth cannot be strictly confined to a particular context. It needs to be more universal and comprehensive. This, indeed, was the Kantian problem. If Nāgārjuna was following the Buddha's solution to this problem (see comments on XXIV.7), he could not have ignored the pragmatic component in the universal moral principle formulated by the Buddha. A moral law that is incapable of accommodating any exceptions can be utterly useless and even harmful. As William James once remarked, "There is always a *pinch* between the ideal and the actual which can only be got through by leaving part of the ideal behind" ("Moral Philosophies and Moral Philosophers," in *Essays in Pragmatism*, ed. Albury Castell, New York: Hafner, 1948, p. 78). This is because the ideal is an abstraction out of the concrete and, therefore, needs to be modified in the light of new concrete situations.

Nāgārjuna's statement "Without relying upon the conventional, the ultimate fruit is not expressed" (*vyavahāram anāśritya paramārtho na deśyate*), explains only a one-way relation, not a one-one relationship. He is *not* saying: "Without relying upon the ultimate fruit, the conventional is not expressed." Thus, he was rejecting a deontological moral principle that provides an absolute source of all moral ideas with no concessions made for individual or concrete situations.

The second line emphasizes the need to have some understanding of that moral principle before one could think of attaining freedom (*nirvāṇa*). However, it is possible to argue that this moral principle issued out of the Buddha's attainment of nirvana, and that without attaining nirvana one will not be in a position to understand what that principle means. Neither the Buddha nor Nāgārjuna would advocate such a position. If one were to first attain freedom and then look for a moral principle to account for it, one could sometimes end up in wayward fancies, utopias, and hallucinations. For this reason, an understanding of *saṃvṛti* ("worldly fruit, *laukika artha*) and, depending upon that, gaining some knowledge of *paramārtha* ("ultimate fruit," *lokuttara artha*) could serve as a guide for the attainment of freedom (*nirvāṇa*). In the *Therīgatha* we come across an instance where a disciple claimed that he perceived the faultless *dhamma* (*addasaṃ virajaṃ dhammaṃ*) and the path to freedom, while she was still leading a household life (*agārasmiṃ vasantī 'haṃ*). Subsequently, she left the household life and attained freedom from all defilements (*Thig* 97 ff.). It is true that the Buddha attained enlightenment and freedom by sheer accident. This is why he was reluctant to recognize any teacher (see *M* 1.171). Yet, before preaching about it to to the world, he spent much time reflecting upon it, as a scientist continues to verify a discovery he has made before making it public. Nāgārjuna probably assumed that people could have the benefit of the Buddha's experience and not waste time experimenting with practices that the Buddha himself found to be fruitless (*an-artha*).

11. *Vināśayati durdṛṣṭā śūnyatā mandamedhasam,*
sarpo yathā durgṛhīto vidyā vā duṣprasādhitā.

A wrongly perceived emptiness ruins a person of meager intelligence. It is like a snake that is wrongly grasped or knowledge that is wrongly cultivated.

MKV(P) p.495; *MKV(V)* p.216.

Having explained the two truths, and establishing an important relationship between the conventional and the ideal, the particular and the universal, Nāgārjuna returns to the conception of "emptiness" (*śūnyatā*) that gave rise to the metaphysicians' problems. The abstract conception of emptiness (*śūnyatā*, representing an abstract noun), derived from the experience of "the empty" (*śūnya*), could be as destructive and fatal as a wrongly grasped snake. How the emphasis on the ideal and the universal to the utter neglect of the particular or the situational has wrought havoc can be known through a careful and unbiased study of human history.

12. *Ataś ca pratyudāvṛttaṃ cittaṃ deśayituṃ muneḥ,*
dharmaṃ matvāsya dharmasya mandair duravagāhatāṃ.

Thus, the Sage's (the Buddha's) thought recoiled from teaching the doctrine having reflected upon the difficulty of understanding the doctrine by people of meager intelligence.

MKV(P) p.498; *MKV(V)* p.217.

This is a reference to the incident related in the "Discourse on the Noble Quest" (*Ariyapariyesana-sutta, M* 1.167-168) where the Buddha explains the nature of his enlightenment as well as the events immediately preceding and succeeding his attainment of enlightenment. Nāgārjuna could not have been unaware of the nature of the Buddha's enlightenment as described in this discourse and also the reasons for the Buddha's reluctance to preach the doctrine. The Buddha's statement reads thus:

> It occurred to me monks: "This *dhamma* won by me is deep, difficult to see, difficult to understand, tranquil, excellent, beyond *a priori* reasoning, subtle, intelligible to the learned. But these human beings are delighting in obsessions (*ālaya*), delighted by obsessions, rejoicing in obsessions. So that for the human beings who are rejoicing in obsessions, delighted by obsessions and rejoicing in obsessions, this were a matter difficult to see, that is to say, dependent arising. This too were a matter difficult to see, that is to say, the appeasement of all dispositions, the renunciation of all attachment, the waning of craving, the absence of lust, cessation, freedom. But if I were to teach the *dhamma* and others were not to understand me, that would be a weariness to me, that would be a vexation to me.' (*M* 1.167)

This passage should dispel any doubts regarding the nature of the Buddha's reasons for his initial reluctance to preach. It was not because of any intellectual incapacity on the part of the human beings, but mostly because of the emotional difficulties they would have in breaking away from the accepted theories in which they have found safety and comfort, a sort of 'mooring' (*ālaya*), especially in accepting a less absolutistic and fundamentally non-substantialist (*anatta*) philosophy and a way of life. As indicated above, the phrase used by the Buddha to refer to the attitude of the human beings is *ālaya-ratā* ("delighting in *ālaya*," where *ālaya* is derived from *ā* + √*li* implying some sort of mooring or obsession). *Ālaya* represents an obsession for not only the pleasures of sense, but also ideas, dogmas, theories, etc.

13. *Śūnyatāyām adhilayaṃ yaṃ punaḥ kurute bhavān,*
doṣa-prasaṅgo nāsmākaṃ sa śūnye nopapadyate.

Furthermore, if you were generate any obsession with regard to emptiness, the accompanying error is not ours. That [obsession] is not appropriate in the context of the empty.

MKV(P) p.499; *MKV(V)* p.217.

Adhilaya has been rendered as "repeatedly refuted" (Inada, p.147). However, the term is more closely related to *ālaya* (see commentary on XXIV.12) utilized by the Buddha to refer to emotional attachment or obsession for views. Nāgārjuna seems to be saying that the metaphysicians are generally fascinated by clear-cut and well-formed theories, abstract concepts, which they revere as divine, while the concrete percepts are looked upon as belonging to the brute (see William James, *Some Problems of Philosophy,* p.34). This paves the way for an extremely important statement by Nāgārjuna regarding *śūnyatā* and *śūnya.*

14. *Sarvaṃ ca yujyate tasya śūnyatā yasya yujyate,*
sarvaṃ na yujyate tasya śūnyaṃ yasya na yujyate.

Everything is pertinent for whom emptiness is proper. Everything is not pertinent for whom the empty is not proper.

MKV(P) p.500; *MKV(V)* p.218.

This terse statement of Nāgārjuna, representing an extremely valuable assessment of the two concepts of "emptiness" (*śūnyatā*) and "the empty" (*śūnyaṃ*), can be comprehended only in the background of his previous statement (XXIV.13). It is a criticism of the absolutistic and substantialist enterprise wherein abstract concepts like "emptiness" receive a divine status thereby becoming compatible with anything and everything in human experience, like the Platonic "forms", whereas any emphasis on the concrete leaves everything hanging in the air. Plato's "forms", Spinoza's "substance", Vedānta "Brahman" and Lao-tzu's "Tao" – all these are fascinating abstract concepts that fit in with everything. Even if one does not have to move on to the other extreme, as did Hume with his "impressions", and the Sautrantikas with their "atoms" (*paramāṇu*), any recognition given to the concrete, to plurality, to the flux tends to disrupt the sense of security one enjoys in a world of abstractions. The Sarvāstivādins raised objections against "the empty" (*śūnya*)(XXIV.1-6) not because there is an actual conflict between the notion of "the empty" and the theory of four truths, but because the conception of "the empty" conflicted with their notion of substance (*svabhāva*) which they were holding on to with great enthusiasm. The fault, as Nāgārjuna points out in the following verse, is theirs.

15. *Sa tvaṃ doṣān ātmanīyān asmāsu paripātayan,*
aśvam evābhirūḍhaḥ sann aśam evāsi vismṛtaḥ.

You, attributing your own errors to us, are like one who has mounted his horse and confused about it.

MKV(P) p.502; *MKV(V)* p.218.

As mentioned previously (see comments on XXIV.14), the problem faced by the Buddhist metaphysicians was in regard to reconciling "the empty" (*śūnya*) with the four noble truths. This was because they were explaining the four truths in relation to the notion of substance (*svabhāva*) and the notion of substance clearly conflicted with the concept of "the empty." If Nāgārjuna had merely relied upon the abstract concept of "emptiness" (*śūnyatā*), ignoring "the empty" (*śūnya*), the Buddhist metaphysicians would not have run into difficulties, for "emptiness," being the abstract concept could easily be reconciled with the notion of substance. As such, the problem was created by the metaphysicians when they emphasized the non-empirical "substance" to the neglect of the empirical phenomena, as is clearly evident from Nāgārjuna's statement that follows. Nāgārjuna was, therefore, reminding them that they were riding their own horse without realizing it.

16. *Svabhāvād yadi bhāvānāṃ sad-bhāvam anupaśyasi,*
ahetu-pratyayān bhāvāṃs tvam evaṃ sati paśyasi.

If you perceive the existence of the existents in terms of self-nature, then you will also perceive these existents as non-causal conditions.

MKV(P) p.502; *MKV(V)* p.219.

For Nāgārjuna, any existent is a causally conditioned existent. Such an existent is clearly imcompatible with a self-nature or substance, the latter being permanent and eternal by definition. This would mean that Nāgārjuna's conception of "emptiness" (*śūnyatā*) does not partake of any such characteristics. Even though "emptiness" and "self-nature" are both abstractions from concrete experiences, Nāgārjuna would continue to maintain the primacy of such concrete experiences, which are "the empty," and insist that "emptiness" is *dependent upon* "the empty," while the metaphysicians would consider self-nature to be *independent*, thereby divorcing it from the concrete.

17. *Kāryaṃ ca kāraṇaṃ caiva kartāraṃ karaṇaṃ kriyāṃ,*
utpādaṃ ca nirodhaṃ ca phalaṃ ca pratibādhase.

You will also contradict [the notions of] effect, cause, agent, performance of action, activity, arising, ceasing, as well as fruit.

MKV(P) p.503; *MKV(V)* p.219.

How the recognition of self-nature (*svabhāva*) contradicts all forms of empirical knowledge, knowledge recognized by the Buddha relating to dependent arising, moral behavior (*karma*), and responsibility (*karma-phala*), has already been explained in detail in the numerous chapters that precede. Here Nāgārjuna is simply summarizing all his conclusions.

18. *Yaḥ pratītyasamutpādaḥ śūnyatāṃ tāṃ pracakṣmahe,*
sā prajñaptir upādāya pratipat saiva madhyamā.

We state that whatever is dependent arising, that is emptiness. That is dependent upon convention. That itself is the middle path.

MKV(P) p.503; *MKV(V)* p.219.

There seems to be no other statement of Nāgārjuna more controversial than this one. An entire school of Chinese Buddhism emerged as a result of the interpretation (or misinterpretation) of this verse, [see Hajime Nakamura, "The Middle Way and the Emptiness View," *Journal of Buddhist Philosophy*, ed. Richard S. Y. Chi, (Indiana University, Bloomington, Indiana,) 1 (1984):81-111].

In the first line, Nāgārjuna is presenting an equation: Dependent arising (*pratītyasamutpāda*) is "emptiness" (*śūnyatā*). Inada's rendering of this line is an improvement on Nakamura's, since the latter assumes that here there is a reference to the events (op. cit., p.81), rather than the principle in terms of which the events are explained. As emphasized earlier, "dependent arising" and "emptiness" are abstract concepts derived from concrete empirical events, "the dependently arisen" (*pratītyasamutpanna*) and "the empty" (*śūnya*) respectively. Unless this relationship between the abstract and the concrete is clearly observed, the interpretation of the second line of the verse will remain for ever obscure, as seems to have happened since Nāgārjuna composed this treatise.

The second line refers to the middle path (*madhyamā pratipat*). The question is: In what way can dependent arising and emptiness, which are synonymous, represent a middle path? The answer to this question is in the statement, *sa prajñaptir upādāya.*

If this phrase were to be translated as, "It is a provisional name" (Inada, p.148) or as "That is a temporary designation" (Nakamura, p.81), which are standard translations offered by most scholars, then in the explanation of dependent arising and emptiness one will be committed either to an extreme form of nominalism or a similiarly extremist absolutism. In such a case, dependent arising or emptiness would either be a mere description with *no* basis in cognitive experience or it would be an experience that is ineffable. The former alternative would conflict with everything Nāgārjuna was trying to establish, namely, the reality of arising and ceasing, of human behavior, etc. (XXIV16-17). The latter alternative would render any philosophical enterprise meaningless and would undermine Nāgārjuna's assertion at XXIV.10.

Taking *saṃvṛti, vyavahāra,* and *prajñapti* as synonyms, as was intended by the Buddha himself (*D* 3.202), and considering the contexts in which Nāgārjuna was using the terms *saṃvṛti* and *vyavahāra* (XVII.24; XVIV.6,8)—namely, in relation to discussions of worldly conventions, the most important among them being good and bad, *dharma/adharma* (and this sense is captured by Inada's own translation of *saṃvṛti* and *vyavahāra*, see p. 146)—it would be more appropriate to characterize both "dependent arising" and "emptiness" as being the ***universal*** truths rather than ***absolute*** truths. This would mean that both *saṃvṛti* (and, therefore, *vyavahāra* and *prajñapti*) and *paramārtha* are "thought constructions" founded on experience. As such, they are not absolutely real or absolutely unreal. This, then, would be the middle position (*madhyamā pratipat*). This middle path could be adopted in understanding all forms of experience, whether they be linguistic, social, political, moral, or religious. While all conventions, whether they be situational (*saṃvṛti*) or ideal (*paramārtha*), are explained in terms of dependent arising, the conception of "the empty" (*śūnya*) eliminates the absolutistic sting at the level of the situational, and "emptiness" does so at the level of the universal. (See comments on XXIV.19 that follows.)

19. *Apratītya-samutpanno dharmaḥ kaścin na vidyate,*
yasmāt tasmād aśūnyo hi dharmaḥ kaścin na vidyate.

A thing that is not dependently arisen is not evident. For that reason, a thing that is non-empty is indeed not evident.

MKV(P) p.505; *MKV(V)* p.220.

After clarifying the nature of the universal conventions, Nāgārjuna returns to the situational, for it was this latter that caused problems for the metaphysicians. The metaphysicians realized that "the dependently arisen" (*pratītyasamutpanna*), so long as it is considered to be "the empty" (*śūnya*), conflicted with their notion of substance (*svabhāva*). Therefore, they were looking for "the dependently arisen" that is not empty of substance.

However, for Nāgārjuna, substance (*svabhāva*) is not dependently arisen (XV.2). A thing that is not dependently arisen is not evident. Therefore, a substance is also not evident. A substance being non-empty, the absence of a substance would mean the absence of the non-empty (*a-śūnya*).

This is a clear and unequivocal denial of substance (*svabhāva*), of the non-empty (*a-śūnya*) and of the in-dependent (*a-pratītyasamutpanna*), and the assertion of the non-substantial (*niḥ-svabhāva*), the empty (*śūnya*) and the dependently arisen (*pratītysamutpanna*). In the hope of being an *absolute non-absolutist,* if someone were to propose that both alternatives—*svabhāva* and *niḥsvabhāva, aśunya* and *śūnya, apratītyasamutpanna* and *pratītyasamutpanna*—are true (or false), the empiricist Nāgārjuna, following the Buddha (*Sn*

884) would insist that only one of these alternatives is true (*ekaṃ hi saccaṃ*), and not the second (*na dutiyaṃ*). This means that neither the Buddha nor Nāgārjuna could be characterized as absolutists.

However, if the two alternatives were to be two metaphysical alternatives, then both the Buddha and Nāgārjuna would be compelled to negate them. Taken out of context, *svabhāva* and *niḥsvabhāva* could appear as metaphysical alternatives. So could *aśūnya* and *śūnya*. Yet, *apratītyasamutpanna* and *pratītyasamutpanna*, as understood by the Buddha and Nāgārjuna, could not be easily converted to metaphysical alternatives. The reason for this is that the term *pratītyasamutpanna*, being a past participle, does not refer strictly to any *one* temporal experience, whether it belongs to the past, present or future, nor does it transcend temporality altogether. While it has a present connotation, it is not divorced from the past. It is, therefore, a term most appropriately used to describe the events perceived by the Buddha through his "knowledge of things as they have come to be" (*yathābhūta-ñāṇa*). It refers to the events experienced in the so-called "specious present" (see comments on XIX.4).

It is this empiricist *prajñapti* that serves as a corrective to any proposal which would turn either *pratītyasamutpāda* or *śūnyatā* into an absolute truth, ineffable and a-temporal. It is, indeed, the philosophical middle path referred to at XXIV.18 and the Buddha's discourse to Kātyāyana.

20, *Yady aśūnyam idaṃ sarvam udayo nāsti na vyayaḥ,*
caturṇām āryasatyānām abhāvas te prasajyate.

If all this is non-empty, there exists no uprising and ceasing. These imply the non-existence of the four noble truths.

MKV(P) pp.505-506; *MKV(V)* p.220.

By rescuing the philosophical middle path from any absolutistic or substantialist interpretation, Nāgārjuna has set the foundation for the explanation of the Buddha's doctrine of the four noble truths. The facts of arising and ceasing are central to the four noble truths. If there ever has been a permanent entity, an entity that is not empty of a substance, then dependence as well as the four noble truths would have been falsified. No such entity *has been* discovered so far. Hence the four truths have remained valid.

21. *Apratītya-samutpannaṃ kuto duḥkhaṃ bhaviṣyati,*
anityam uktaṃ duḥkhaṃ hi tat svābhāvye na vidyate.

How can there be suffering that is not dependently arisen? Suffering has, indeed, been described as impermanent. As such, it is not evident in terms of self-nature.

MKV(P) p.506; *MKV(V)* p.220.

Nāgārjuna is here returning to the interpretation of suffering by the substantialist metaphysicans (see comments on XXIV.1), who held that suffering exists in terms of self-nature. He is reminding the metaphysicians that the Buddha's conception of suffering is founded not only on the idea of dependent arising but also the notion of impermanence. In fact, the perversion regarding the notion of impermanence is also the cause of the perversion regarding the conception of suffering (see comments on XXIII.1).

22. *Svabhāvato vidyamānaṃ kiṃ punaḥ samudeṣyate,*
tasmāt samudayo nāsti śūnyatāṃ pratibādhataḥ.

How can that which is evident in terms of self-nature rise again? Therefore, for one who contradicts emptiness, there exists no [conception of] arising.

MKV(P) p.506; *MKV(V)* p.221.

Throughout the treatise, Nāgārjuna was refusing to recognize that the conception of self-nature or substance leaves any room for the recognition of arising and ceasing. This was contrary to the attempt on the part of the metaphysicians. Nāgārjuna is here insisting that the conception of arising (*samudaya*) makes no sense at all when applied to self-nature.

Self-nature is not something that comes and goes. It is not an occurrence. It is there for ever. As such, it contradicts the theory of emptiness which is intended to explain the occurrence of events. Emptiness, as mentioned earlier (XXIV.18), is synonymous with "dependent arising."

23. *Na nirodhaḥ svabhāvena sato duḥkhasya vidyate,*
svabhāvaparyavasthānān nirodhaṃ pratibadhāse.

The cessation of suffering that exists in terms of self-nature is not evident. You contradict cessation by adhering to a notion of self-nature.

MKV(P) p.507; *MKV(V)* p. 221.

Just as the notion of self-nature contradicts the idea of arising, it also renders the conception of cessation meaningless. Note the emphasis on the present participle, *santa* (left untranslated by Inada, p. 149), used in relation to *duḥkha*, implying "suffering that exists" in terms of self-nature. The notion of existence defined in this manner has already been criticized by Nāgārjuna (I.6). In effect Nāgārjuna is saying that the notion of existence (*sat*) may be compatible with the conception of self-nature, but it is not appropriate in the context of "that which has come to be" (*bhūta*).

24. *Svābhāvye sati mārgasya bhāvanā nopapadyate,*
athāsau bhāvyate mārgaḥ svābhāvyaṃ te na vidyate.

When self-nature exists, the cultivation of the path is not appropriate. And if the path were to be cultivated, then no self-nature associated with it [i.e., the path] would be evident.

MKV(P) p.507; *MKV(V)* p.221.

The principle of self-nature (*svābhāvya*, note the use of the abstract noun instead of *svabhāva*) explains the way in which self-nature functions. Thus, if somethings are assumed to have self-nature, what is assumed is that things happen on their own (*svo bhāvo*) without the support of anything else. In this sense, they are independent. If the path (*mārga*) leading to the cessation of suffering (*duḥkha*) were to be explained in terms of self-nature, it means that the way will work out on its own, without any effort on the part of one who is expected to cultivate it. If one is expected to cultivate the path, it means that one has to make an effort. It does not happen automatically.

25. *Yadā duḥkaṃ samudayo nirodhaś ca na vidyate,*
mārgo duḥkha-nirodhatvāt katamaḥ prāpayiṣyati.

When suffering as well as its arising and ceasing are not evident, through the cessation of suffering where will the path lead to?

MKV(P) p.508; *MKV(V)* p.221.

Insisting upon the recognition of self-nature, the metaphysicians were compelled to deny the fact of suffering as well as its arising and ceasing. It would, therefore, be meaningless to speak of a path leading to the cessation of suffering. Substantialist speculation leaves only two alternatives: either there is cessation of suffering or there is no cessation of suffering. If the fact is that there is cessation of suffering (*duḥkha-nirodhatva*), there is no room for a path. It happens in any case. If the fact is that there is no cessation of suffering, then it is meaningless to think of a path. Fatalism being the consequence of both standpoints, the notion of a path leading to any goal is rendered utterly meaningless.

26. *Svabhāvenāparijñānaṃ yadi tasya punaḥ kathaṃ,*
parijñānaṃ nanu kila svabhāvaḥ samavasthitaḥ.

If non-understanding is due to self-nature, how can one come to possess understanding subsequently. Is it not the case that self-nature is fixed?

MKV(P) p.508; *MKV(V)* p.222.

Inada's rendering of *nanu kila svabhāvaḥ samavasthitaḥ* as "self-nature, indeed, never remains fixed," seems to be based upon a misunderstanding of the import of the particle *nanu* which simply means: "is it not the case that," rather than a simple negation. If self-nature is something that "never remains fixed," what we are presented here is the so-called Spinozan solution to the problem of substance. Nāgārjuna was not willing to accept such an interpretation of self-nature, for if self-nature were understood as changing, the whole purpose of formulating the notion of self-nature by the substantialists would be defeated. Therefore, he was simply asking the question: "Is it not the case that self-nature is fixed?" He is, in fact, insisting that if it is not fixed, it is not a self-nature. A change of substance was, in the eyes of Nāgārjuna, a self-contradiction.

Hence he argues: If there is any inability to understand suffering because such inability is inherent, is through self-nature, then there can never be its understanding. Something that is inherently unknowable can never be subsequently known. This is the most telling criticism of self-nature (*svabhāva*) as it is employed in the explanation of the path to freedom (*nirvāṇa*).

27. *Prahāṇa-sākṣātkaraṇe bhāvanā caivam eva te,*
parijñāvan na yujyante catvāry api phalāni ca.

As in the case of understanding, this [i.e., the explanation in terms of self-nature] is not proper in relation to the activities of relinquishing, realizing as well as cultivating. And so would the four fruits be [improper].

MKV(P) p.509; *MKV(V)* p.222

An understanding (*parijñā*) of the nature of suffering (*duḥkha*) is a necessary prerequisite for its relinquishing, the realization of freedom, and the cultivation of the path leading to freedom. In the previous verse, Nāgārjuna explained how a belief in self-nature would create difficulties in explaining understanding (*parijñā*) or its absence (*aparijñā*).

The same difficulties are associated with the explanation of the relinquishing (*prahāṇa*) of suffering, the realization (*sākṣātkaraṇa*) of freedom and the cultivation (*bhāvanā*) of the path. To highlight these difficulties, Nāgārjuna concentrates on the fruits or consequences (*phala*).

28. *Svabhāvenādhigataṃ yat phalaṃ tat punaḥ katham,*
śakyaṃ samadhigantuṃ syāt svabhāvaṃ parigṛhṇataḥ.

How could it be possible for a person, who upholds a theory of self-

nature, to realize a fruit that has already been realized through self-nature?

MKV(P) p.510; *MKV(V)* p.222.

A person believing in self-nature also admits that a fruit is obtained by that means. If a fruit has not been achieved through self-nature it can never be achieved in any other way. It is an either/or situation. Accept it as occurring on its own or it will never occur. This is a substantialist view of freedom (*nirvaṇa*, which will be taken up for detailed treatment by Nāgārjuna later on). This, indeed, is a fatalistic or a deterministic explanation of causality. Either the effect exists in the cause or it does not (see discussion of *artha* [= *phala*] at I.6).

29. *Phalābhāve phalasthā no na santi pratipannakāḥ,*
saṃgho nāsti na cet santi te 'ṣṭau puruṣa-pudgalāḥ.

In the absence of the fruits, there are neither those who have attained the fruits nor those who have reached the way [to such attainment]. If the eight types of individuals do not exists, there will be no congregation.

30. *Abhāvāc cārya-satyānāṃ saddharmo 'pi na vidyate,*
dharme cāsati saṃghe ca kathaṃ buddho bhaviṣyati.

From the non-existence of the noble truths, the true doctrine would also not be evident. In the absence of the doctrine and the congregation, how can there be an enlightened one?

MKV(P) p.510; *MKV(V)* p.222.

Having shown that the explanation of the attainment of the fruits (*phala*) of life is rendered impossible or meaningless by the adherence to the notion of self-nature, Nāgārjuna turns the table on the metaphysicians, showing them how the denial of emptiness (*śūnyatā*), rather than its assertion, leads to a denial of all that they were trying to explain.

31. *Apratītyāpi bodhiṃ ca tava buddhaḥ prasajyate,*
apratītyāpi buddhaṃ ca tava bodhiḥ prasajyate.

Your [conception of the] enlightened one implies an independent enlightenment. Also, your [conception of] enlightenment implies an independent enlightened one.

MKV(P) p.510; *MKV(V)* p.223.

Explained in terms of self-nature, the enlightened one would be so irrespective of conditions (*apratyaya*). Similarly, enlightenment would be achieved irrespective of whether it is a person who makes an effort or not. This substantialist explanation of enlightenment and the enlightened one, in terms that are strictly naturalistic or deterministic, would render the activities of the one seeking enlightenment and freedom utterly meaningless.

32. *Yaś cābuddaḥ svabhāvena sa bodhāya ghaṭann api,*
na bodhisattva-caryāyāṃ bodhiṃ te 'dhigamiṣyati.

Whosoever is by self-nature unenlightened, even though he were to contend with enlightenment, would not attain enlightenment through a career off a *bodhisattva*.

MKV(P) p.511; *MKV(V)* p.223.

This is the one and only time Nāgārjuna, the so-called patron of Mahāyāna, refers to the way (*caryā*) of a *bodhisattva*. Yet, the kind of criticism he is presenting here offers no consolation to those who accept certain doctrines of popular Mahāyāna. Any substantialist theory, according to Nāgārjuna's view, militates against the career of a *bodhisattva*.

To uphold the view that a person is by nature unenlightened is tantamount to saying that he can never attain the fruit of enlightenment and freedom by exerting himself. Similarly, to assert the view that a person is by nature enlightened, is a potential *buddha*, or possesses a *bodhi-citta*, makes the attainment of enlightenment meaningless (XXIV.28) or impossible.

This, indeed, is reminiscient of the long drawn controversy between the Sarvāstivādins and the Sautrāntikas regarding the nature as well as the functioning of good (*kusala* = *dharma*) or bad (*akusala* = *adharma*) thoughts (*citta*). The metaphysical problems generated by an extremist analysis in relation to phenomena in general have been explained in Chapters I and II. The selfsame metaphysical problems appeared in the explanation of moral phenomena. The Sarvāstivāda-Sautrantika controversy relating to the "seeds that are of good nature" (*kusala-dharma-bīja*) reflects their involvement in such metaphysical issues.

The atomistic (and, therefore, non-empirical) analysis of thought (*citta*) led the metaphysicians to assume a sharp distinction not only between good thoughts (*kusala-citta*) and bad thoughts (*akusala-citta*), but also between individual moments of thought in each series, whether they be of good thoughts or bad thoughts. As such, several questions came to be raised: How does one good thought moment give rise to another similar thought moment? How can two different thought moments, one which is good and the other which is bad, co-exist in one moment, especially when they are distinct as light and darkness (*āloka-tamas*, see *Adv* p.170)? If they cannot co-exist, how can a bad thought moment give rise to or be followed by a good thought? While the Sarvāstivādins utilized the conceptions of *prāpti* and *aprāpti* to explain the manner of their occurrence, the Sautrāntikas employed the notion of seed (*bīja*) to elucidate these problems.

The substantialist Sarvāstivādins, who adhered to a notion of self-nature (*svabhāva*) were compelled to maintain that each variety of thought has its own-nature. Yet, when they were called upon to explain the occurrence or non-occurrence of good or bad thoughts in an individual person's stream of thought (*saṃtāna*), they assumed that the non-attainment (*aprāpti*) of one kind of thought could make room for the attainment (*prāpti*) of another kind. The Sautrantikas, rejecting the notion of self-nature, emphasized the idea of potentiality (*śakti*) existing in the form of seed (*bīja*). Thus, when a good thought moment occurs, the bad thought moment can remain latent without manifesting itself. Thus, we are left with two potentialities, one manifesting itself when the other is not. The terms *śakti, bīja,* and *vāsanā* were all employed to refer to such potentiality.

A distinction came to be admitted not only between good (*kusala*) and bad (*akusala*), but also among the good seeds themselves. Thus, there are defiled good seeds (*sāśrava-kusala-bīja*) and non-defiled good seeds (*anāśrave-kusala-bīja*), the former accounting for worldly goodness and the latter leading to freedom (*nirvāṇa*). These seeds were considered to be extremely subtle (*susūkṣma*) and remain uncorrupted or undestroyed (*na samudghāta*). They were compared to gold (*kañcana*). A popular statement runs thus:

I perceive his extremely subtle seed of release like a seam of gold concealed in a cleft of elemental rocks. (*Mokṣa-bījam ahaṃ hy asya susūkṣmam upalakṣaye, dhātu-pāṣāṇa-vivare nilīam iva kañcanam*, *Sakv* p. 644, see also Jaini, *Adv* Introduction, p.116.)

Even though this substantialist view is attributed to the Buddha himself (see Jaini, loc cit.) on the basis of the Buddha's statement regarding the "luminous thought" (*pabhassaraṃ cittaṃ*), we have already provided evidence to the contrary (see Introduction), where thought is compared with "gold-ore" (*jāta-rūpa*) rather than with gold (*suvaṇṇa*). As such, neither the theory of the "seeds of release" (*moksa-bija*) nor of the "originally pure mind" (*prakṛti-prabhāsvara-citta*), which is a predecessor, the Mahāyāna notion of a *bodhi-citta*, can be reconciled with the Buddha's conception of non-substantiality (*anatta*) or Nāgārjuna's view of "emptiness (*śūnyatā*). The present statement of Nāgārjuna is a clear rejection of the substantialist standpoint of the later interpreters, which represents a recurrent desire to go back to a *primordial source*.

33. *Na ca dharmam adharmaṃ vā kaścij jātu kariṣyati,*
kim aśūnyasya kartavyaṃ svabhāvaḥ kriyate na hi.

No one will, indeed, do good or bad. What could the non-empty do? For, self-nature does not perform.

MKV(P) p.511; *MKV(V)* p.223.

Inada, once again, renders the terms *dharma* and *adharma* as factors and non-factors of experience, thereby reading more ontology than axiology into the statement of Nāgārjuna. A substantialist interpretation of good and bad allows no room for their cultivation or performance. If someone is good in terms of self-nature, he does not have to perform the good; it is simply there. Similarly with bad. Self-nature (*svabhāva*) implies absolute existence (*sad-bhāva*), not occurrence (*sambhava*, XXIV.22).

34. *Vinā dharmam adharmaṃ ca phalaṃ hi tava vidyate,*
dharmādharma-nimittaṃ ca phalaṃ tava na vidyate.

As for you, the fruit would be evident even without good or bad. This means that for you a fruit occasioned by good and bad would not be evident.

MKV(P) p.512; *MKV(V)* p.223.

The consequence of upholding a notion of self-nature in moral philosophy are explicated here. If good and bad were to be explained in terms of self-nature or substance, then there would be goodness and badness "in themselves." These would always be existent. A fruit, if it were to arise at all, from a good action will always be good and, as such, there would be identity of cause and effect (see Chapter I). If a good action were to lead to a bad consequence, it would not matter at all, as it is assumed to be the case with, for example, "good-will." This notion of intrinsic good or bad would render the concept of a cause (*nimitta*) almost meaningless.

35. *Dharmādharma-nimittaṃ vā yadi te vidyate phalaṃ,*
dharmādharma-samutpannam aśūnyaṃ te kathaṃ phalaṃ.

If, on the contrary, a fruit occasioned by good or bad is evident to you, how can you maintain the fruit that has arisen from good or bad to be [at the sametime] non-empty?

MKV(P) p.512; *MKV(V)* p.223.

Thus, Nāgārjuna insists that moral discourse and a substantialist world-view are incompatible. If something is good by nature, good in terms of self-nature, good in itself, then it must be *always* good. It cannot be otherwise. Such an absolutistic theory will fail to accommodate some individual or particular situations that are in conflict with the theory, but which would certainly be valid in certain contexts. This was a serious defect in the absolutistic theory, as explained by Nāgārjuna in the following verse.

36. *Sarva-saṃvyavahārāṃś ca laukikān pratibādhase,*
yat pratītyasamutpāda-śūnyatāṃ pratibādhase.

You will contradict all the worldly conventions when you contradict the emptiness associated with dependent arising.

MKV(P) p.513; *MKV(V)* p.224.

This, once again, highlights the significant relationship between worldly conventions, that are situational or contextual and the principle of dependent arising which, as explained earlier, is a universal. The only way the universal can accommodate the situational is when the universal is not looked upon as corresponding to an "ultimate reality." The substantialists who assumed that there is an ultimate reality, therefore, were faced with all the insoluable metaphysics. Thus the actual function of emptiness is the elimination of this substantialist sting (see comments on XXIV.18).

37. *Na kartavyaṃ bhavet kiṃcit anārabdhā bhavet kriyā,*
kārakaḥ syād akurvāṇaḥ śūnyatāṃ pratibādhataḥ.

For one who contradicts emptiness there would be nothing that ought to be done; activity would be uninitiated and an agent would be non-acting.

MKV(P) p.513; *MKV(V)* p.224.

The unfortunate consequences of upholding a substantialist theory and denying emptiness are listed here. Interestingly, all of them pertain to human behavior and moral responsibility. This says much about the concerns of Nāgārjuna, who by popular acclaim is more a logician primarily concerned with language and truth and therefore with ultimate reality, rather than a moral philosopher interested in axiology and, for that reason, emphasizing the conception of "ultimate fruit." He is supposed to have scorned any speculation about human behavior (***karma***), what human behavior ought to be (***kartavya***), and who a responsibile human agent (***kurvāṇa***) is.

In brief, a substantialist view leads to a denial of the human element functional in this world, an element that is generally described as "disposition" (***saṃskāra***). Not only does it negate the world conditioned by human dispositions (i.e., the ***saṃskṛta***), it also denies any activity and creativity in the natural world (see XXIV.38 that follows).

38. *Ajātam aniruddhaṃ ca kūṭasthaṃ ca bhaviṣyati,*
vicitrābhir avasthābhiḥ svabhāve rahitaṃ jagat.

In a substantialist view, the universe will be unborn, non-ceased, remaining immutable and devoid of variegated states.

MKV(P) p.513; *MKV(V)* p.224.

The assumption of a substance (*svabhāva*) would deprive the natural world, the world of dependent arising, of all the variety (*vicitra*) and freshness and leave it sterile and unproductive. This, indeed, is the Buddha's criticism of eternalism (*sassata-diṭṭhi*) when he maintained that according to this view the self and the world are sterile, immovable, and remaining stable like a pillar," (*D* 1.14; *S* 3.202, 211, etc., *yathā sassato attā ca loko ca vañjho kūṭaṭṭho esikaṭṭhāyiṭṭhito*).

39. *Asamprāptasya ca prāptir duḥkha-paryanta-karma ca,*
sarva-kleśa-prahāṇaṃ ca yady aśūnyaṃ na vidyate.

If the non-empty [is evident], then reaching up to what has not been reached, the act of terminating suffering as well as the relinquishing of all defilements would not be evident.

MKV(P) p.515; *MKV(V)* p.225.

The substantialist view would not only negate the world determined by human dispositions (*saṃskṛta*) and the natural world of dependent arising (*pratītysamutpanna*), but also the ideal world, the world of freedom. Nirvana would remain inexplicable in the context of a substantialist world-view. This is the subject matter of the next chapter. Before proceeding to explain freedom, Nāgārjuna has a quotation from the Buddha (XXIV.40).

40. *Yaḥ pratītyasamutpādaṃ paśyatīdaṃ sa paśyati,*
duḥkhaṃ samudayaṃ caiva nirodhaṃ mārgam eva ca.

Whoever perceives dependent arising also perceives suffering, its arising, its ceasing and the path [leading to its ceasing].

MKV(P) p.515; *MKV(V)* p.225.

The Buddha maintained that he who perceives dependent arising perceives the *dhamma* (*M* 1.190-191; *Chung* 7.2 [*Taishō* 1.467a). Perceiving dependent arising is not merely perceiving "things as they have come to be" (*yathābhūta*), but also seeing how a human being placed in such a context of dependent arising experiences suffering (*duḥkha*); what causes such suffering; what kind of freedom can be attained and what the path is that leads to the attainment of freedom and emancipation. Dependent arising and the four noble truths are, therefore, the foundations on which the whole edifice called Buddhism is built. Any school of Buddhism that refuses to recognize the centrality of these doctrines would loose its claim to be a legitimate part of that tradition. These constitute the truths that Nāgārjuna was attempting to explicate in the present chapter.

CHAPTER TWENTY FIVE
Examination of Freedom
(Nirvāṇa-parīkṣā)

1. *Yadi śūnyam idaṃ sarvam udayo nāsti na vyayaḥ,*
prahāṇād vā nirodhād vā kasya nirvāṇam iṣyate.

If all this is empty, there exists neither arising nor ceasing. [As such,] through the relinquishing and ceasing of what does one expect freedom?

MKV(P) p.519; *MKV(V)* p.227.

Even though some of the problems relating to freedom (*nirvāṇa*) have already been discussed in the context of a *tathāgata* (Chapter XXII) and the four noble truths (Chapter XXIV), Nāgārjuna singles out this topic for further analysis, especially in view of certain grave misconceptions that emerged as a result of a substantialist world-view. Without making any attempt to determine what these metaphysical views were, many a scholar has plunged himself into assertions about Nāgārjuna's conception of freedom and produced views that are no less metaphysical than those rejected by Nāgārjuna.

The present verse explains the difficulties the metaphysicians, who accepted substantial phenomena, experienced when they attempted to elucidate freedom. While the previous chapter dealt with the problems the substantialists faced when they accepted a notion of self-nature and tried to account for the four noble truths, especially the empirical fact of suffering (*duḥkha*), the present context Nāgārjuna is primarily concerned with the question of freedom from suffering. The substantialist dilemma here would be: How can freedom (*nirvāṇa*) be explained, if the conception of emptiness is utilized not only to explain the empirical fact of suffering but also to elucidate *nirvāṇa*) which, even though described as the cessation of suffering (*duḥkha-nirodha*), was also the ultimate or absolute reality.

After denying any substance (*svabhāva*) in the conventional or the contextual (*vyavahāra*), if Nāgārjuna had *not* proceeded to extend that denial to the ideal (*paramārtha*), the substantialist could have remained silent. However, when Nāgārjuna universalized "the empty" (*śūnya*) by saying "all this is empty" (*sar-*

vam idaṃ śūnyaṃ)—and that included the substantialists' conception of "ultimate reality" (*paramārtha*) understood in various ways, either as "atomic reality" (*paramāṇu*) or the "seed of release" (*mokṣa-bīja*) or the "originally pure thought" (*prakṛti-prabhāsvara-citta*)(see XXIV.32)—he was threatening the very foundation of substantialist metaphysics. In the next twenty-three verses, Nāgārjuna proceeds to demolish that foundation.

2. *Yady aśūnyam idaṃ sarvam udayo nāsti na vyayaḥ,*
prahāṇād vā nirodhād vā kasya nirvāṇam iṣyate.

If all this is non-empty, there exists neither arising nor ceasing, [As such,] through relinquishing and ceasing of what does one expect freedom?

MKV(P) p.521; *MKV(V)* p.227.

As in the previous chapter, it is because of his preference for an empirical explanation of things in terms of arising and ceasing (*udaya-vyaya*) that Nāgārjuna is not willing to accept a metaphysical substance. Hence his argument that relinquishing (*prahāṇa*) and ceasing (*nirodha*) are meaningless in the context of the "non-empty" (*aśūnya*). Thus, for Nāgārjuna, the non-empirical view is the one expressed in the form, "All this is non-empty (*sarvam idam aśūnyaṃ*), rather than the view presented as "All this is empty" (*sarvam idaṃ śūnyaṃ*). If, on the contrary, the substantialists were to accept the empirical phenomena to be empty, but not *nirvāṇa,* still Nāgārjuna could ask the question: If *nirvāṇa* is a permanent and eternal substance, why talk of arising and ceasing, relinquishing and abandoning, for suffering (*duḥkha*) or defilements (*kleśa*) that need to be relinquished actually do not affect the originally pure existence?

For Nāgārjuna and the Buddha, neither the empirical events nor the ultimate fruit were substantial. Neither *saṃsāra* nor *nirvāṇa* were absolute in any sense. As such, what Nāgārjuna is presenting is not different from the empirical view of bondage and freedom explained in the Buddha's discourse to Kātyāyana.

3. *Aprahīṇam asamprāptam anucchinnam aśāśvataṃ,*
aniruddham anutpannam etan nirvāṇam ucyate.

Unrelinquished, not reached, unannihilated, non-eternal, non-ceased and non-arisen—this is called freedom.

MKV(P) p.521; *MKV(V)* p.228.

Having rejected a permanent and eternal substance which, as explained earlier (XXIV.38), "is unborn, unceased, remaining immovable and devoid of variegated situations," if Nāgārjuna were to explain freedom in almost idential terms, his philosophy would not be any different from those of his substantialist opponents. Furthermore, it is the substantialists themselves who considered freedom (*nirvāṇa*) as well as the non-defiled good seeds (*anāśrava-kusala-bīja*) or the seeds of release (*mokṣa-bīja*) to be subtle (*susūkṣma*) and uncorrupted or undestroyed (*na samudghāta*)(see XXIV.32). This leaves the interpreter of the present verse with only one escape-route, namely, to consider the six negations presented here to be simple negations of metaphysical existence (*sat*) or its associate, non-existence (*asat*).

How relinquishing (*prahāṇa*) becomes problematic if one were to accept a self-nature (*svabhāva*) has been explained at XXIV.27. The substantialists, as mentioned in the discussion of XXIV.32, were left with two distinct self-natures: the good (*kusala*) and the bad (*akusala*). Their problem was how any one of them, being permanent and eternal, could be relinquished.

If it is assumed that the "seed of release" (*mokṣa-bīja*) is subtle and incorruptible and produces freedom (*nirvāṇa*) as the "ultimate fruit" (*parama artha* or *phala*), Nāgārjuna's refutation of it is clearly stated at XXIV.28. He explained how the reaching (*saṃprāpti* = *samadhigamana*) of a fruit (*phala*) is made impossible by the recognition of a permanent and incorruptible self-nature. Thus, when freedom (*nirvāṇa*) is explained as reqlinquishing (*prahāṇa*) and reaching (*saṃprāpti*), these should not be understood in a substantialist way. *If they were so understood,* the only way to explain the empirical conception of freedom is by *negating* them. Thus, in freedom there is "no thing" (*na kaścit*)(XXV.24)—a thing understood as being substantial or having self-nature—that is either relinquished (*prahīṇa*) or reached (*saṃprāpta*).

The other four negations were discussed in relation to the Dedicatory Verses (as part of the eight negations). There too, it was pointed out that the eight negations were intended to eliminate the metaphysical notions of existence (*astitva*) and non-existence (*nāstitva*). The same could be said of the two couplets in the present verse: *anucchinnaṃ/aśāśvataṃ* and *aniruddhaṃ/anutpannaṃ*.

Thus, the sixfold activity—relinquishing, reaching, interruption, remaining constant, ceasing and arising—*as explained by the metaphysicians* need to be negated before an empiricist theory could emerge. Such metaphysical explanations can easily be abandoned if their foundations, namely, the metaphysical concepts of substantial existence (*sat* or *astitva*, *bhāva* or *svabhāva*) and nihilistic non-existence (*asat* or *nāstitva*, *abhāva* or *parabhāva*), were to be given up. This, indeed, is the task that Nāgārjuna sets up for himself in the following verses.

4. *Bhāvas tāvan na nirvāṇaṃ jarā-maraṇa-lakṣaṇam,*
prasajetāsti bhāvo hi na jarā-maraṇaṃ vinā.

Freedom, as a matter of fact, is not existence, for if it were, it would follow that it has the characteristics of decay and death. Indeed, there is no existence without decay and death.

MKV(P) p.524; *MKV(V)* p.229.

Inada takes *bhāva* in the present context as the nature of ordinary existence. Instead, the term is better explained as a reference to metaphysical existence (*astitva*), as has been the case with Nāgārjuna (see especially, XXI.15-16; also XXV.10). The metaphysicians who admitted *bhāva* or *svabhāva* as eternal and permanent entities never attempted an empirical justification of these entities. They seem to have assumed that these are known through "ominscience" (*sarvajñatva*). Nāgārjuna, realizing the Buddha's attitude toward such knowledge-claims (see discussion of *Sabba-sutta* at IX.3) and, therefore, making no reference to such knowledge at all in the present text, simply noted the implications of this metaphysical speculation and insisted that such existence (*bhāva*, *svabhāva*) is invariably associated with characteristics (*lakṣaṇa*), like decay and death (*jarā-maraṇa*). Thus, freedom will not include freedom from decay and death and this would contradict the Buddha's claim that he is freed from the recurrent cycle of births and deaths. On the contrary, if the metaphysicians insisted that there is no invariable connection between existence (*bhāva*) and characteristics (*lakṣaṇa*), then they could claim that after *parinirvāṇa* a freed person can retain the eternal existence and drop the characteristics. Nāgārjuna was quite certain that this is an extension of the metaphysical position and is in conflict with the non-substantialist teachings of the Buddha (see XXV.17).

5. *Bhāvaś ca yadi nirvāṇaṃ nirvāṇaṃ saṃskṛtaṃ bhavet,*
nāsaṃskṛto hi vidyate bhāvaḥ kvacana kaścana.

Moreover, if freedom were to be existence, then freedom would be conditioned. Yet, an existence that is unconditioned is not evident anywhere.

MKV(P) p.526; *MKV(v)* p.230.

In rendering the terms *saṃskṛta* and *asaṃskṛta* as "conditioned" and the "unconditioned" respectively, we have, in the present context, tried to retain the interpretation of the metaphysicians, for it is this particular interpretation that is being questioned by Nāgārjuna. Undoubtedly, it is the Sarvāstivāda theory which equated *saṃskṛta* and *pratītyasamutpanna* that Nāgārjuna has in mind (see comments on VII.1). The implication of this equation is that "the unconditioned" (*asaṃskṛta*) is also the "independent" or "uncaused" (*apratītyasamutpanna*), an implication not acceptable to both Nāgārjuna and the Buddha.

In fact, XXV.4-6 highlight the sharp distinction the metaphysicians assumed between freedom and bondage (see Chapter XVI, Examination of Bondage and Release). It is this sharp distinction, which is the foundation of the substantialist explanation of freedom and bondage, that is being analysed by Nāgārjuna. Unless this metaphysical explanation is kept in view, speculatoins about Nāgārjuna's own conception of freedom can turn out to be as weird as those of the metaphysicians.

6. *Bhāvaś ca yadi nirvāṇam anupādāya tat kathaṃ,*
nirvāṇaṃ nānupādāya kaścid bhāvo hi vidyate.

Furthermore, if freedom were to be existence, how can that freedom be independent, for an independent existence is certainly not evident?

MKV(P) p.526; MKV(V) p.230.

Here again we have a metaphysical interpretation of *upādāya* (see IV.1-2) where existence (*bhāva*), as the permanent and the eternal, becomes not only the "unconditioned" (XXV.5), but also the absolutely "independent" (*anupādāya*)(see also XXII.5). Nāgārjuna is not prepared to equate freedom with such non-empirical existence.

7. *Yadi bhāvo na nirvāṇam abhāvaḥ kiṃ bhaviṣyati,*
nirvāṇaṃ yatra bhāvo na nābhāvas tatra vidyate.

If freedom is not existence, will freedom be non-existence? Wherein there is no existence, therein non-existence is not evident.

MKV(P) p.527; *MKV(V)* p.230.

The metaphysical notions of existence and non-existence expressed in such terms as *astitva* and *nāstitva* are here referred to as *bhāva* and *abhāva*. They bring back the problems of identity and differences (see I.3). Nāgārjuna's argument, as at I.3, is that these two are relative concepts.

8. *Yady abhāvaś ca nirvāṇam anupādāya tat katham,*
nirvāṇaṃ na hy abhāvo 'sti yo 'nupādāya vidyate.

If freedom is non-existence, how can freedom be independent? For there exists no non-existence which evidently is independent.

MKV(P) p.527; *MKV(V)* p.231.

If there were to be no permanent existence, there could be no permanent non-existence. If there were to be no absolute existence, there could be no nihilistic non-existence. Just as much as freedom is not absolute existence, it is also not nihilistic non-existence. Nāgārjuna's attempt in the present chapter is directly aimed at getting rid of such a metaphysical explanation of freedom. The Buddhists, throughout history, were prone to make such distinctions, sometimes ignoring the empirical middle position advocated by the Buddha. This is what Nāgārjuna intends to explain in the next verse.

9. *Ya ājavaṃ-javī-bhāva upādāya pratītya vā,*
so 'pratītyānupādāya nirvāṇam upadiṣyate.

Whatever is of the nature of coming and going that occurs contingently or dependently. Freedom is, therefore, indicated as being non-contingent and independent.

MKV(P) p.529; *MKV(V)* p.231.

Even though the Buddha empahsized the avoidance of metaphysical extremes, there was indeed a tendency to distinguish ***saṃsāra*** and ***nirvāṇa***. The cycle of births and deaths, "comings and goings" (***ājavaṃ-javiṃ***), was looked upon as having its own nature (***bhāva***) which is dependence. This is contrasted with the nature (***bhāva***) of freedom which is independent. The intrusion of the substantialist notions in the form of ***saṃvṛti*** (convention) and ***paramārtha*** ("ultimate reality") into the Buddhist doctrine during the scholastic period has already been referred to (see comments on XXIV.8). Even though most Buddhist thinkers were able to avoid such ontological speculations in explaining the nature of the world and freedom, the Buddhist metaphysicians had difficulty in avoiding such a dichotomy. Therefore, in the next verse, Nāgārjuna proceeds to remind the Buddhists of the Buddha's teaching on becoming and other-becoming (***bhava-vibhava***).

10. *Parhāṇaṃ cābravīc chastā bhavasya vibhavasya ca,*
tasmān na bhāvo nābhāvo nirvāṇaṃ iti yujyate.

The teacher has spoken of relinquishing both becoming and other-becoming. Therefore, it is proper to assume that freedom is neither existence nor non-existence.

MKV(V) p.530; *MKV(V)* p.232.

In addition to the two concepts of ***saṃbhava*** and ***vibhava***, discussed previously (Chapter XXI), Nāgārjuna introduces another pair: ***bhava*** and ***vibhava***. It is significant to note that when Nāgārjuna rejected ***astitva*** and ***nāstitva*** he was quoting the Buddha (XV.7). He does the same when he refers to ***bhava*** and ***vibhava*** (XXV.10). Yet, when he rejects ***bhāva*** and ***abhāva***, two concepts that do not appear in the early discourses, except as suffixes, Nāgārjuna merely indicates that the Buddha realized their implications (*bhāvābhāva-vibhāvinā*, XV.7) and does not present it as a statement of the Buddha. This supports our previous contention that *bhāva* and *abhāva* represent an attempt to reintroduce *astitva* and *nāstitva* into philosophical discussions by the Brahmanical and Buddhist metaphysicians.

One significant difference between the concepts of *bhāva* and *abhāva* (*astitva* and *nāstitva*), on the one hand, and *bhava* and *vibhava*, on the other, is that the former are metaphysical assumptions and the latter describe empirical events. As such, the reasons for their rejection would be different. *Bhāva* and *abhāva* are rejected because they are metaphysical and, as such, unverifiable in terms of the epistemological standpoint adopted by the Buddha. On the contrary, *bhava* and *vibhava* are experienced processes of life, namely, becoming and other-becoming, and the reason for their being rejected is that they lead to suffering (*duḥkha*). *Bhava* is the process of becoming conditioned by dispositions. Hence the Buddha spoke of "craving for becoming" (*bhava-taṇhā*), a constant thirsting to become this or that. *Vibhava* could mean either "becoming something different" or annihilation of this process of becoming (namely, suicide). This was also referred to as a form of craving (*vibhava-taṇhā*). However, the process of becoming and becoming otherwise could be explained in terms of metaphysical and, therefore, wrong beliefs (*mithyā-dṛṣṭi*) in absolute existence (*bhāva*) and nihilistic non-existence (*abhāva*), respectively, instead of dependent arising (*pratītyasamutpāda*). Neither of the metaphysical explanations, according to the Buddha, could serve as the basis for freedom.

11. *Bhaved abhāvo bhāvaś ca nirvāṇaṃ ubhayaṃ yadi,*
bhaved abhāvo bhāvaś ca mokṣas tac ca na yujyate.

If freedom were to be both existence and non-existence, then release would also be both existence and non-existence. This too is not proper.

MKV(P) p.531; *MKV(V)* p.232.

It is possible for someone to assume that "freedom" represents a special kind of existence which combines both existence and non-existence. If it is understood as some mysterious existence beyond existence and non-existence, Nāgārjuna reminds his opponents that it is no more than simple "release" (*mokṣa*), and this latter need not be described as both existence and non-existence. Release is no more than the release from suffering and there is nothing transcendental about it.

12. *Bhaved abhāvo bhāvaś ca nirvāṇam ubhayaṃ yadi,*
nānupādāya nirvāṇam upādāyobhayaṃ hi tat.

If freedom were to be both existence and non-existence, freedom could not be independent, for existence and non-existence are, indeed, dependent upon one another.

MKV(P) p.531; *MKV(V)* p.232.

As pointed out earlier, the substantialist definition of freedom implied independence, rather than non-grasping or non-clinging (see comments on XXII.5). Thus, if the metaphysicians were to define freedom as both existence and non-existence, it could not be independent as they expect it to be. This is because existence and non-existence are dependent.

13. *Bhaved abhāvo bhāvaś ca nirvāṇam ubhyaṃ kathaṃ,*
asaṃskṛtaṃ ca nirvāṇaṃ bhāvābhāvau ca saṃskṛtau.

How could freedom be both existence and non-existence, for freedom is unconditioned while existence and non-existence are conditioned?

MKV(P) p.531; *MKV(V)* p.233.

As in the previous verse, here too Nāgārjuna is taking the definition proffered by the opponent and criticizing his conception of freedom. This is similar to the argument adduced by Nāgārjuna at XXV.6, except that in the present case Nāgārjuna is insisting that if something is both existence and non-existence, it could not appropriately be called an "unconditioned." The "unconditioned," by the metaphysician's definition, is the "independent" (*apratītyasamutpanna*), and an element with two entities as parts of it will always be conditioned by those two parts.

14. *Bhaved abhāvo bhāvaś ca nirvāṇam ubhayaṃ kathaṃ,*
na tayor ekatrāstitvam āloka-tamasor yathā.

How could freedom be both existence and non-existence, for their simultaneious existence in one place is not possible, as in the case of light and darkness?

MKV(P) p.532; *MKV(V)* p.233.

This brings out another aspect of the metaphysicians' conception of freedom, namely, the monistic implication. *Nirvāṇa,* looked upon as the "ultimate reality" (*paramārtha*), could not accommodate variety and multiplicity. For them, it is the one ultimate truth, everything else being provisional. However, Nāgārjuna is insisting that they could not maintain that *nirvāṇa* is both existence and non-existence.

15. *Naivābhāvo naiva bhāvo nirvāṇam iti yā 'ñjanā,*
abhāve caiva bhāve ca sā siddhe sati sidhyati.

The proposition that freedom is neither existence nor non-existence could be established if and when both existence and non-existence are established.

MKV(P) p.532; *MKV(V)* 233.

Añjanā from (√*anj*, "to annoint") can mean a symbol. Here Nāgārjuna is not speaking of logical proof to decide the validity of a symbolism, or a proposition. Rather, he is interested in the empirical justification. Thus, unless both existence and non-existence, as explained by the metaphysician, can be shown to have empirical validity, their negations too would mean nothing.

16. *Naivābhāvo naiva bhāvo nirvāṇaṃ yadi vidyate,*
naivābhāvo naiva bhāvo iti kena tad ajyate.

If freedom as neither existence nor non-existence is evident, by means of what is it made known as neither existence nor non-existence?

MKV(P) p.533; *MKV(V)* p.233.

This seems to be a rather devastating criticism of the more popular view that freedom cannot be expressed either as existence or as non-existence. That is, it is linguistically transcendent or is ineffable. If the statement, "Freedom is neither existence nor non-existence," is intended to express the ineffability of *nirvāṇa*, Nāgārjuna is questioning the meaningfulness of that very statement. This means that absolute negation is as metaphysical as absolute assertion, "absolute nothingness" is as meaningless as "absolute thingness," and these are the absolutes that are expressed by terms like *bhāva* and *abhāva*.

17. *Paraṃ nirodhād bhagavān bhavatīty eva nohyate,*
na bhavati ubhayaṃ ceti nobhayaṃ ceti nohyate.

It is not assumed that the Blessed One exists after death. Neither is it assumed that he does not exist, or both, or neither.

18. *Tṣṭhamāno 'pi bhagavān bhavatīty eva nohyate,*
na bhavaty ubhayaṃ ceti nobhayaṃ ceti nohyate.

It is not assumed that even a living Blessed One exists. Neither is it assumed that he does not exist, or both or neither.

MKV(P) p.534; *MKV(V)* p.234.

These, indeed, are the metaphysical assertions made regarding the *tathāgata* (XXII) which both Nāgārjuna and the Buddha rejected. The foundations of these metaphysical views were the theories of identity and difference. This very important problem is next taken up for examination by Nāgārjuna.

19. *Na saṃsārasya nirvāṇāt kiṃcid asti viśeṣaṇam,*
na nirvāṇasya saṃsārāt kiṃcid asti viśeṣaṇam.

The life-process has no thing that distinguishes it from freedom. Freedom has no thing that distinguishes it from the life-process.

MKV(P) p.535; *MKV(V)* p.234.

This statement of Nāgārjuna has contributed to a major and wide-spread assertion regarding the uniqueness of Mahāyāna philosophy, namely, the ultimate identity of *saṃsāra* and *nirvāṇa*. This assertion may appear to be correct, if we are to ignore all that has been said by Nāgārjuna regarding the metaphysical doctrines of identity (*ekatva*) and difference (*nānatva*), especially in the chapters dealing with the *tathāgata* (XXII) and the four truths (XXIV).

Those who upheld the view that this statement is an assertion of the identity of *saṃsāra* and *nirvāṇa* do not seem to have paused for one moment to reflect on the question regarding the nature of the identity they were implying; nor have they attempted to place that conception of identity (if there is one) in the historical context.

The fact that there was a great urge on the part of the Buddhists, especially after the Buddha's death, to raise him to the level of a supreme being, having no real connections with the ordinary human world, can easily be seen from the more popular Mahāyāna texts like the *Lalitavistara* and the *Saddharmapuṇḍarīka* as well as the Theravada treatises like the *Jātaka-nidāna-kathā*. Through that popular perspective, substantialist views regarding the nature of the Buddha began to emerge among philosophers. These philosophical views were prominent with the early metaphysicians like the Sarvāstivādins and the Sautrāntikas.

Nirvāṇa, understood as the "ultimate reality" (*paramārtha*), came to be distinguished from *saṃsāra*, the unreal, the convention, the impermanent. The Buddha's own view that *nirvāṇā* is the "ultimate fruit" (*paramattha*), a culmination of the fruit (*attha*) of everyday life, the highest moral perfection involving the eschewing of all immoral conduct (*sabba-pāpassa akaraṇaṃ*) and the *promotion* of good (*kusalassa upasampadā*), was gradually being forgotten. *Dharma* was gradually being distinguished from the *dharma* in the *dharma-adharma* context. The inappropriate equation of the *puṇya-pāpa* distinction with the *dharma-adharma* distinction (see comments on XVII.24) led to the belief in a *Dharma* that transcends the *dharma-adharma* distinction.

However, this was not Nāgārjuna's understanding. *Vyavahāra*, the contextual or the conventional, is not provisional in a cheap pragmatic sense and, therefore, unreal. It is the concrete without which the ideal (*paramārtha*) makes no sense at all (XXIV.10). It is the absolute distinction between *vyavahāra* and *paramārtha* that is denied in the present verse.

The fact that the Buddhist metaphysicians were involved in long-drawn philosophical disputes with the Brahmanical schools of thought and, therefore, the possibility of mutual influences should not be discounted. For example, the Sautrāntika philosophical standpoint resembles in many ways the standpoint of the Vaiśeṣikas. This latter philosophy is founded on the basic methodology of making "distinctions" (*viśeṣaṇa*). Nāgārjuna's present statement can be properly evaluated in the background of such a methodology.

Indeed, the most significant part of the statement is: *na kiṃcit asti viśeṣaṇam*, i.e., "there is no thing that can be taken as a distinction," or "there is no distinct thing." (see XXV.20 and 24). The reference to some metaphysical entity as "some thing" (*kiṃcit*) is a popular feature in the early discourses as well as in the *Prajñāpāramitā-sūtras*.

20. *Nirvaṇasya ca yā koṭiḥ koṭiḥ saṃsaraṇasya ca,*
na tayor antaraṃ kiṃcit susūkṣmam api vidyate.

Whatever is the extremity of freedom and the extremity of the life-process, between them not even a subtle something is evident.

MKV(P) p.535; MKV(V) p.235.

Having rejected a sharp dichotomy between *saṃsāra* and *nirvāṇa*, Nāgārjuna is not willing to let the metaphysician discover something extremely subtle (*kiṃcit susūkṣmam*), comparable to the extremely subtle and incorruptible seed of release (*mokṣa-bīja*)(see comments on XXIV.32), between *saṃsāra* and *nirvāṇa*. The identity theories of both Sarvāstivāda and Sāṅkhya school posited such subtle entities to explain continuity. Nāgārjuna's present statement should be understood in the background of the ideas expressed by these schools.

Therefore, the translation of the first line as "The limits of *nirvāṇa are* the limits of *saṃsāra*" (Inada, p.158), is not very appropriate. Furthermore, the first line does not make a complete sentence. The emphasis in the complete sentence is on the phrase *kiṃcit susīkṣmaṃ* (see XXV.19), which is Nāgārjuna's major concern here.

21. *Paraṃ nirodhād antādyāḥ śāśvatādyāś ca dṛṣṭayāḥ,*
nirvāṇam aparāntaṃ ca pūrvāntaṃ ca samāśritāḥ.

Metaphysical views relating to the finite, etc., to the eternal, etc., after death are associated with [the problems of] freedom as well as the posterior and prior extremities.

MKV(P) p.536; *MKV(V)* p.235.

Herein, reference is made to eight of the ten "undeclared" (*avyākṛta*) issues. Nāgārjuna perceives them to be associated with the question of freedom, a freedom looked at from two of the major concerns of the human beings, namely, the first beginning and the ultimate end, the first cause and the final cause. Human concerns like "Where did I come from?" or "Where would I go after this?" (as will be exlained in the final Chapter on "Examination of Views") have influenced human thinking and often led to metaphysical views about freedom and bondage.

22. *Śūnyeṣu sarva-dharmeṣu kim anantaṃ kim antavat,*
kim anantam antavac ca nānantaṃ nānantavac ca kiṃ.

23. *Kiṃ tad eva kim anyat kiṃ śāśvataṃ kim aśāśvataṃ,*
aśāśvataṃ śāśvataṃ ca kiṃ vā nobhayam apy ataḥ.

When all things are empty, why [speculate on] the finite, the infinite, both the finite and the infinite and neither finite nor the infinite? Why [speculate on] the identical, the different, the eternal, the non-eternal, both or neither?

MKV(P) p.537; *MKV(V)* p.235.

Empiricist Nāgārjuna's final final question, after presenting such a detailed analysis of all the metaphysical views to which he has devoted twenty-five chapters, is "Why raise all these metaphysical issues, when all experienced things are empty?" (*śūnyeṣu sarva-dharmeṣu kiṃ* . . .). As reiterated before in the commentary, he is speaking about things that are empty (*śūnya*), which are the empirically given and which are seen to be dependently arisen (*pratītyasamutpanna*). He is not emphasizing the abstract concept, "emptiness" (*śūnyatā*).

24. *Sarvopalambhopaśamaḥ prapañcopaśamaḥ śivaḥ,*
na kvacit kasyacit kaścid dharmo buddhena deśitaḥ.

The Buddha did not teach the appeasement of all objects, the appeasement of obsession, and the auspicious as some thing to some one at some place.

MKV(P) p.538; *MKV(V)* p.236.

Inada has broken up the above into two distinct statements and thereby lost its significance. The first line contains qualifications of ***dharma*** occurring in the second. Nāgārjuna's emphasis is on the phrase: ***kaścit dharmaḥ***, as it was in the case of the two important statements made previously in the present chapter (XXV.19-20). When the Buddha spoke of freedom (***nirvāṇa***), which he qualified as the appeasement of all objects (***upalambha*** = ***ālambana*** = ***drāṣṭavya***, cf. ***draṣṭavyopaśama*** at V.8) or the appeasement of obsessions (***prapañcopaśama***) or auspicious (***śiva***, see Dedicatory Verses), he was not referring to them as "some thing," that is, some entity having a specific distinction (***viśeṣaṇa***) or subtlety (***susūkṣmatva***). He was not speaking of freedom in the way the substantialist conceived of it.

All these twenty-five chapters are, therefore, negative in character and tone. They were devoted to a refutation of the two metaphysical but related views of existence and non-existence (***astitva-nāstitva***). Having cleared up the dust that had gathered around all the doctrines preached by the Buddha, Nāgārjuna is now ready to go on to the positive description of bondage and freedom as enunciated by the Buddha in the discourse to Kātyāyana. Nāgārjuna's treatment of the metaphysical issues that emerged in relation to all these doctrines—doctrines pertaining to causation, change, the human personality, survival, karma, moral responsibility, and freedom—is so exhaustive and complete that he can proceed to explain the Buddha's conception of bondage and freedom without any fear of ***any*** one raising ***any*** question. For he has already answered them all. Herein lies the greatness of Nāgārjuna as a philosopher.

CHAPTER TWENTY SIX
Examination of the Twelve Causal Factors
(Dvādasāṅga-parīkṣā)

1. *Punarbhavāya saṃskārān avidyā-nivṛtas tridhā,*
abhisaṃskurute yāṃs tair gatiṃ gacchati karmabhiḥ.

A person enveloped by ignorance forms such dispositions in the threefold ways leading to re-becoming, and through such actions he moves on to his destiny.

MKV(P) p.542; *MKV(V)* p.238.

This chapter is of little significance to most Nāgārjunian scholars. Inada argues:

> With the discussion of *Nirvāṇa* in the last chapter the treatment from the standpoint of the Mahayana had basically come to a close. In this chapter and the final one to follow, Nāgārjuna goes into the analysis of the Hīnayānistic doctrines. . . . The discussion is Hīnayānistic and it reveals that the source of trouble lies in ignorance which in turn initiates all kinds of mental conformations *(saṃskāra)* (*Nāgārjuna*, p.160).

While disagreeing totally with this interpretation, I propose to show that this chapter represents the most positive explanation by Nāgārjuna of the Buddha's teachings on bondage and freedom as enunciated in the vast collection of discourses, with the discourse to Kātyāyana as the pivotal text. Indeed, without the positive teachings presented here coming after the negative analysis in the last twenty-five chapters, it is rather difficult to see how Nāgārjuna could claim to be restating the Buddha-word, as he openly expressed it in several places earlier (see XV.6; XVII.6, 8, 11; XXIV.8-9). It is indeed surprising to see how most interpreters of Nāgārjuna are looking for positive statements of the doctrine primarily through negations (XXV.3 and Dedicatory Verses), while ignoring all the positive statements of Nāgārjuna.

XXVI.1 is a further explanation of the Buddha's statement: "Depending upon ignorance are dispositions" (*avijjāpaccayā saṅkhārā*). Its elaboration is also the Buddha's and is presented in the *Kukkuravatika-sutta* (M 1.390).

2. *Vijñānaṃ saṃnivisate saṃskārapratyayaṃ gatau,*
saṃniviṣṭe 'tha vijñāne nāmarūpaṃ niṣicyate.

Consciousness, with disposition as its condition, enters [the new] life. When consciousness has entered, the psychophysical personality is infused.

MKV(P) p.543; *MKV(V)* p.238.

This represents the explanation of the relationships described in the statement, "Depending upon dispositions is consciousness" (*saṅkhārapaccayā viññāṇaṃ*) and "Depending upon consciousness is the psychophysical personality" (*viññāṇapaccayā nāmarūpaṃ*). The explication of the first of these is found at *S* 3.87 (*Tsa* 2.14 [*Taishō* 2.11c]) where it is said: "Disposition is so called because it processes . . . consciousness that has already been dispositionally conditioned, into its present state." The dispositions are thus responsible for providing an individuality to consciousness, and it is this individuated consciousness that comes to be established in a psychophysical personality. This latter event is explained at *D* 2.63 (*Chang* 10.2 [*Taishō* 1.61b]), where it is stated that the psychophysical personality formed in the mother's womb will not grow into maturity (*na vuddhiṃ viruḷhiṃ āpajjati*) if consciousness were not to enter it and get established therein. In fact, the Chinese translation of Kumārajīva refers to such attainment of maturity of the psychophysical personality.

Those who are unwilling to attribute a doctrine of survival to Nāgārjuna may interpret the relation between consciousness and the psychophysical personality as no more than the explanation of the act of being conscious during ordinary day to day experiences. If so, it would have been possible for Nāgārjuna to say so at this point. Instead, he prefers to speak of a life (*gati*), generally understood as a future life or destiny, and proceeds to explain the process of perception only after outlining the emergence of the six sensory faculties associated with the psychophysical personality.

3. *Niṣikte nāmarūpe tu ṣaḍāyatana-sambhavaḥ,*
ṣaḍāyatanam āgamya saṃsparśaḥ saṃpravartate.

When the psychophysical personality has been infused, the occurrence of the six spheres (of sense) takes place. Depending upon the six spheres proceeds contact.

MKV(P) p.552-553; *MKV(V)* p.242.

The Buddha's statement, "Depending upon the psychophysical personality are the six spheres of sense" (*nāmarūpapaccayā saḷāyatanam*), explains an important pre-requisite for the emergence of human knowledge. If the psychophysical personality is not properly formed or if the sensory faculties were to be defective, the sensory spheres such as material form, sound, smell, taste, touch, and concepts would not provide a foundation for contact. Thus, the visual organ, which is part of the psychophysical personality should be unimpeded (*aparibhinna*) and should function properly. The external object should come into focus (*bahirā ca rūpā āpatham āgacchati*) and attention (*samannāhāra*), which is a function of consciousness, should be available (*M* 1.190; *Chung* 7.2 [*Taishō* 1.467a]). Then only there will emerge consciousness which is a necessary condition for contact. This idea is then elaborated by Nāgārjuna in the next verse.

4. *Cakṣuḥ pratītya rūpaṃ ca samanvāhāram eva ca,*
nāmarūpaṃ pratītyaivaṃ vijñānaṃ saṃpravartate.

5. *Saṃipātas trayāṇāṃ yo rūpa-vijñāna-cakṣuṣām,*
sparśaḥ saḥ tasmāt sparśac ca vedanā saṃpravartate.

Thus, depending upon the eye and material form, and attention too, and depending upon the psychophysical personality proceeds consciousness. Whatever is the harmonious concurrence of the three factors: material form, consciousness, and eye, is contact. Feeling proceeds from such contact.

MKV(P) p.553-554; *MKV(V)* p.242.

The twelvefold formula presents feeling as being conditioned by contact (*phassapaccayā vedanā*). However, Nāgārjuna feels the need to explain what contact is all about. He, therefore, inserts the explanation of contact provided by the Buddha in the *Madhupiṇḍka-sutta* (*M* 1.111-112; *Chung* 28.3 [*Taishō* 1.604b]). Contact is the harmonious concurrence (*saṅgati*) of three factors: material form, (visual) consciousness, and eye. It is this harmonious concurrence that provides a foundation for feeling (*vedanā*).

6. *Vedanāpratyayā tṛṣṇā vedanārthaṃ hi tṛṣyate,*
   tṛṣyamāna upādānam upādatte caturvidhaṃ.

Conditioned by feeling is craving. Indeed, craving is feeling-directed. The one who craves, grasps on to the fourfold spheres of grasping.

MKV(P) p.554-555; *MKV(V)*p.243.

Here Nāgārjuna has an interesting explanation of craving (*tṛṣṇā*) when he says: *vedanārthaṃ hi tṛṣyate*, i.e, "it is for feeling that one craves." It is a reference to the pleasant feelings (*śubha, manāpa,* or *sukha*). The fourfold spheres of grasping are: grasping for desires (*kāma*), for views (*diṭṭhi*), for rules and rights (*sīlabbata*), and for theories of self (*attavāda*)(*M* 1.51).

7. *Upādāne sati bhava upādātuḥ pravartate,*
   syādd hi yady anupādāno mucyeta na bhaved bhavaḥ.

When grasping exists, becoming on the part of the grasper proceeds. If he were to be a non-grasper, he would be released, and there would be no further becoming.

MKV(P) p.556; *MKV(V)* p.243.

It is interesting to note that at this point in the explanation of the twelvefold formula Nāgārjuna speaks of freedom or release (*mokṣa*). It is a point at which the process of bondage can be interrupted. Nāgārjuna is problably emphasizing this because he witnessed how his fellow Buddhists, in spite of their enormous intellectual capacities, constantly adhered to metaphysical views and were caught in "Brahma's Net" (*brahma-jāla*). Some of these intellectual giants, who were able to write commentary after commentary, even though they had abandoned household lives were enamored with their views and involved in ceaseless diatribes. Realizing the emphasis placed by the Buddha upon "non-grasping" (*anupādāna*), Nāgārjuna interrupts his exposition of the process of bondage to explain freedom.

8. *Pañca skandhāḥ sa ca bhavaḥ bhavāj jātiḥ pravartate,*
jarā-maraṇa-duḥkhādi sokāḥ saparidevanāḥ.

9. *Daurmanasyam upāyāsā jāter etat pravartate,*
kevalasyaivam etasya duḥkha-skandhasya saṃbhavaḥ.

The five aggregates constitute this becoming. From becoming proceeds birth. Suffering relating to decay and death, etc., grief, lamentation, dejection, and dispair—all these proceed from birth. Such is the occurrence of this entire mass of suffering.

MKV(P) p.556-557; *MKV(V)* p.243-244.

The elimination of craving for becoming (*bhava-taṇhā*), as mentioned earlier (see XXV.10), was encouraged by the Buddha. The reason for this is not merely because craving causes suffering in this life, but also because it could lead to birth in another life (*jati*), which would also involve the repetition of all the unfortunate experiences of the present life. The phrase *duḥkha-skandha* is used in the sense of heap or mass of suffering rather than "suffering attached to the *skandhas*," (Inada, p.162).

10. *Saṃsāra-mūlān saṃskārān avidvān saṃskaroty ataḥ,*
avidvān kārakaḥ tasmān na vidvāṃs tattva-darśanāt.

Thus, the ignorant forms dispositions that constitute the source of the

life process. Therefore, it is the ignorant who is the agent, not the wise one, because of his [the latter's] perception of truth.

MKV(P) p.558; MKV(V) p.244.

The enlightened one who had attained the appeasement of dispositions (*saṃskāropaśama*) does not contribute to the perpetuation of the life-process (*saṃsāra*). Hence, he is not an agent (*kārakaḥ*) responsible for such perpetuation. This seems to indicate Nāgārjuna's awareness of the Buddha's famous statement that upon attaining enlightenment he perceived the builder of the house (*gaha-kāraka, Dh* 154).

Reading too much metaphysics into the phrase *tattva-darśana* can destroy all that Nāgārjuna attempted to do in the preceding twenty-five chapters. Instead of explaining it as "the perception of an absolute reality," it could be more appropriately understood as the perception of the empirical truth that "all this is empty" (*sarvam idaṃ śūnyaṃ*) of a substance (*svabhāvataḥ*).

11. *Avidyāyāṃ niruddhāyāṃ saṃskārāṇām asaṃbhavaḥ,*
avidyāya nirodhas tu jñānenasyaiva bhāvanāt.

When ignorance has ceased, there is no occurrence of dispositions. However, the cessation of that ignorance takes place as a result of the practice of that [non-occurrence of dispositions] through widsom.

MKV(P) pp.558-559; *MKV(P)* p.244.

The mutual relationship between cessation of ignorance and the non-arising of dispositions is emphasized by Nāgārjuna, keeping in mind the distinction between the appeasement of dispositions (*saṃskāropaśama*) in the present life and their waning (*saṃskāra-kṣaya*) at the time of death, thereby not providing another opportunity for rebirth.

12. *Tasya tasya nirodhena tat tan nābhipravartate,*
duḥkha-skandhaḥ kevalo 'yam evaṃ samyag nirudhyate.

With the cessation of these, these othere factors [of the twelvefold formula] would not proceed. In this way, this entire mass of suffering ceases completely.

MKV(P) p.559; *MKV(V)* p.244.

The emphasis is probably on the cessation of ignorance and the non-arising of dispositions. These two factors are taken to predominate the entire life-process. The attainment of enlightenment and the appeasement of dispositions through non-grasping (***anupādāna***) account for "freedom with substrate" (***saupādiśeṣa-nirvāṇa***), while the elimination of dispositions provides for non-re-becoming (***a-punar-bhava***)(cf. XXVI.1) and the waning of birth (***jāti-kṣaya***), which is freedom "without substrate" (***nirupādiśeṣa-nirvāṇa***).

CHAPTER TWENTY SEVEN
Examination of Views
(Dṛṣṭi-parīkṣā)

1. *Dṛṣṭayo 'bhūvaṃ nābhūvaṃ kiṃ nv atīte 'dhvanīti ca,*
yās tāḥ śāśvatalokādyāḥ pūrvāntaṃ samupāśritāḥ.

Whatever views asserting an eternal world, etc. based upon [the perception]: "Did I exist or not exist in the past?" are associated with the prior end [of existence].

MKV(P) p.571; *MKV(V)* p.249.

The first line of the verse has been reconstructed by Poussin on the basis of the Tibetan translation.

In the *Pārileyyaka-sutta* (*S* 3.94-99; *Tsa* 2.25 [*Taishō* 2.13c-14a]), the Buddha maintained that views such as "The self and the world are eternal" (*sassato attā ca loko ca*) are metaphysical because they are dispositional answers (*saṅkhāro so*) to querries about the past such as: "Did I exist in the past or not?" As such, they are not based *entirely* upon empirical facts. Indeed, they are attempts to go back to the prior end of existence (*pubbanta*). While the Buddha recognized them as futile attempts, mostly because of the limitations of human knowledge and understanding (see Chapter XI), he was not unwilling to accept whatever evidence available through veridical memories (*sadi, pubbenivāsānussati*). On the basis of such evidence, he characterized the past existences as impermanent (*anicca*), dispositionally determined (*saṅkhata*), and dependently arisen (*paṭiccasamuppanna*), and not as permanent (*nicca*), immutable (*dhuva*), and eternal (*sassata*).

Nāgārjuna's explanation of the metaphysical views of eternalism (*śāśvata*), etc. is, therefore, a vivid representation of the Buddha's attitude regarding such views.

2. *Dṛṣṭayo na bhaviṣyāmi kim anyo 'nāgate 'dhvani,*
bhaviṣyāmīti cāntādyā aparāntaṃ samupāśritāḥ.

Whatever views asserting the finite, etc. based upon [the perception]: "Would I not exist in the future or would I become someone else?" are associated with the posterior end [of existence].

MKV(P) p.573; *MKV(V)* p.249.

The assumptions that the self and the world are finite or infinite are similarly based upon one's dispositions (*saṅkhara*). Those who are enamored with life as it is would insist upon the world being infinite. Those who are averse to life would advocate finiteness, insisting that there will be no way in which life could continue. This is tantamount to annihilation (*uccheda-diṭṭhi*, *S* 3.99; *Tsa* 2.25 [*Taishō* 2.14b]).

3. *Abhūm atītam adhvānam ity api etan nopapadyate,*
yo hi janmasu pūrveṣu sa eva na bhavaty ayaṃ.

The view that I existed in the past is not appropriate, for whosoever was in the previous birth, he, indeed, is not identical with his person.

MKV(P) p.573; *MKV(V)* p.250.

This statement may appear, at first sight, to mean a denial of rebirth or survival; that is, it would be inappropriate to say: "I existed in the past." However, if one is careful in observing the emphasis in the second line, namely, *sa eva* ("he himself"), it will become apparent that what is denied is not any relationship between two lives, but the *identity* of the two persons in different existences. Therefore, the statement, "I existed in the past," becomes metaphysical only if an absolute identity is posited, which indeed was the proclivity of the metaphysician.

4. *Sa evātmeti tu bhaved upādānaṃ viśiṣyate,*
upādāna-vinirmukta ātmā te katamaḥ punaḥ.

If it were to occur [to someone]: "He, indeed, is the self," then grasping is identified. Separated from grasping, what constitute your self?

MKV(P) pp.574-575; *MKV(V)* p.250.

The Buddha explained self-consciousness expressed in such statements as "I am . . . " (*asmīti*) as dependent upon (*upādāya*) the five aggregates. It is like seeing one's own reflection on a clean mirror or a pan of clear water. In this case, one cannot perceive one's reflection unless there is a personality that is reflected, and these constitute the five aggregates (*S* 3.105). However, converting this self-consciousness to a *cogito*, a "self" that is permanent and eternal, is also the work of *upādāna*, meaning "grasping or clinging." It is sometimes described as thirsting or craving (*taṇhā*) and this could be for becoming (*bhava*) or other-becoming (*vibhava*)(*S* 3.26; *Tsa* 3.23 [Taisho 2.19a].

Thus, neither self-consciousness nor a "self" would be found independently (*upādāna-vinirmukta*). However, the attainment of freedom, described as *anupādā vimukti*, does not imply the negation of self-consciousness, but only of the "thirsting for becoming," (*bhava-taṇhā*), which otherwise could lead to the belief in a permanent and eternal self that is independent of the aggregates, and idea already rejected by Nāgārjuna in Chapter XXV.

5. *Upādāna-vinirmukto nāsty ātmeti kṛte sati,*
syād upādānam evātmā nāsti cātmeti vaḥ punaḥ.

When it is assumed that there is no self separated from grasping, grasping itself would be the self. Yet, this is tantamount to saying that there is no self.

MKV(P) p.575; *MKV(V)* p.251.

The assertion that there is no self apart from grasping (*upādāna-vinirmukta*) provides the identity theorists with the opportunity of identifying the self with grasping. Thus, when the Buddha, having denied a self, maintained that consciousness (*viññaṇa*) provides a link between two lives (*D* 3.105; *Chang* 12.2

[*Taishō* 1.767a]), one of his disciplies, Sāti, immediately assumed that "this consciousness itself transmigrates, and not another" (*idam eva viññāṇaṃ sandhāvati saṃsarati anaññaṃ, M* 1.256; *Chung* 54.2 [*Taishō* 1.767a]), thereby attributing an identity theory to the Buddha. The Buddha's immediate response was to deny such identity by asserting that consciousness is dependently arisen (*paṭiccasamuppanna*). Then the Buddha proceeded to show how consciousness, when explained in terms of causal dependence, leads to a denial of such identity. This, indeed, is what Nāgārjuna endeavors to do in the present context.

6. *Na copādānam evātmā vyeti tat samudeti ca,*
   katham hi nāmopādānam upādātā bhaviṣyati.

Grasping is not identical with the self, for that [i.e., grasping] ceases and arises. Furthermore, how can grasping be the grasper?

MKV(P) p.576; *MKV(V)* p.251.

As was done by the Buddha, (see comments above XXVII.5), Nāgārjuna is rejecting the notion of self (*ātman*) on two grounds. First, it is assumed to be permanent and eternal, whereas grasping that is identified with the self is subject to arising and ceasing. Secondly, the self is also assumed to be the agent behind all human action and, therefore, of grasping. If so, how can it be both action and agent at the same time?

7. *Anyaḥ punar upādānād ātmā naivopapadyate,*
   gṛhyeta hy anupādāno yady anyo na ca gṛhyate.

Furthermore, a self that is different from grasping is not appropriate. A person who is without grasping can be observed. However, if he were to be different [from grasping], he could not be observed.

MKV(P) p.577; *MKV(V)* p.251.

For the Buddha as well as for Nāgārjuna, the denial of a substantial entity is based upon empirical evidence, namely, the perception of an individuality consisting of the five aggregates. The five aggregates do not appear individually as insulated discrete elements. They appear as a lump (*puñja*) which retains its individuality (based upon dispositions) and continuity (founded upon consciousness). In such a context he is called a person (*hoti satto ti sammuti*, *S* 1.135; *Tsa* 45.5 [*Taishō* 2.327a]). In the context of a society, he becomes a social being with relationships to others (as son, father, or daughter, mother, etc.) In the context of moral behavior, he becomes good or bad (see the explanation of empirical self by William James, *The Principles of Psychology*, vol.1,291-293). However, if the self were to be considered different from the perceived individuality, it would turn out to be a rather mysterious entity and hence unknowable through the available means of knowledge.

Candrakīrti, who prefers a transcendentalist interpretation of Nāgārjuna, gives a negative explanation of what is very clearly a positive statement of Nāgārjuna.

8. *Evaṃ nānya upādānān na copādānam eva saḥ*
ātmā nāsty anupādānaḥ nāpi nāsty eṣa niścayaḥ.

Thus, he is neither different from grasping nor identical with it. A self does not exist. Yet, it is not the case that a person who does not grasp does not exist. This much is certain.

MKV(P) pp.577-578; *MKV(V)* p.252.

Candrakīrti, who favored a transcendentalist interpretation of Nāgārjuna, makes this a negative statement. The positive reading given above is justified on two grounds. First, in the previous instances, Nāgārjuna was clearly asserting an empirically known (= *gṛhyeta*) *anupādānaḥ* (that is, a person freed from grasping), while at the same time rejecting an *ātman* different from both grasping and non-grasping. Secondly, the positive reading is clearly justified by Kumārajīva's Chinese rendering of this verse.

As such, what Nāgārjuna is denying is both identity (*upādānam eva saḥ*) and difference (*anya upādānaṃ*). A rejection of metaphysical identity and difference does not necessarily mean that Nāgārjuna was abandoning an empirical personality. For Nāgārjuna, language need not be necessarily metaphysical in character.

9. *Nābhūm atītam adhvānam ity etan nopapadyate,*
yo hi janmasu pūrveṣu tato 'nyo na bhavaty ayaṃ.

The statement, "I did not exist in the past," is not appropriate, for this person is not different from whosoever existed in the previous lives.

MKV(P) p.578; *MKV(V)*p.252.

This, then is a clear denial of absolute difference. Just as much as the statement, "I existed in the past," is not appropriate so long as it is interpreted to mean absolute identity, even so the statement, "I did not exist in the past," is not appropriate as long as it is taken to mean absolute difference.

10. *Yadi hy ayaṃ bhaved anyaḥ pratyākhyāyāpi taṃ bhavet,*
tathaiva ca sa saṃtiṣṭhet tatra jāyeta vāmṛtaḥ.

If this person were to be different [from that person in the previous existence], then he would come to be even forsaking that person. In that case he would remain the same and, in such a context, an immortal would emerge.

MKV(P) p.579; *MKV(V)* p.252.

Absolute difference implies absolute identity. Nāgārjuna has already shown that "other-nature" (*para-bhāva*) means the self-nature (*svabhāva*) of another (XV.3, *svabhāvaḥ parabhāvasya parabhāvo hi kathyate*). Absolute identity as well as absolute difference, this involves complete independence, and as such it would constitute immortality. Nothing is to be *achieved*. Kumārajīva renders the phrase *tatra jāyeta vāmṛtaḥ* as "The *ātman* will be self-caused."

11. *Ucchedaḥ karmaṇāṃ nāśas tathā 'nyena kṛta-karmaṇāṃ,*
anyena paribhogaḥ syād evam ādi prasajyate.

[If that were the case,] there would be annihilation and destruction of ac-

tions. This implies that the fruit of action performed by one will be experienced by another.

MKV(P) p.580; *MKV(V)* p.253.

The verse has been reconstructed by Poussin on the basis of the Tibetan translation.

How a metaphysical conception of difference would lead not only to a denial of survival but also a repudiation of moral responsibility has been already discussed by Nāgārjuna (Chapter XII). There it was shown that he depended upon a discourse of the Buddha to explain this problem. The present is simply a restatement of that argument.

12. *Nāpy abhūtvā samudbhūto doṣo hy atra prasajyate,*
kṛtako vā bhaved ātmā saṃbhūto vāpy ahetukaḥ.

Yet, in that context, the error of assuming an emergent without prior existence does not follow. Either the self would be caused or, if it has occurred, it would be without a cause.

MKV(P) p.580; *MKV(V)* p.253.

The concept of self (*ātman*) was posited in order to account for the continuity in the human personality which could also explain moral responsibility. However, the denial of an eternal self led to the opposite view that there is no continuity, but annihilation (*uccheda*). The denial of an eternal self and the consequent assertion of annihilation do not imply (*na prasajyate*) the further metaphysical view that something that did not exist before comes to be (*abhūtvā sambhoti*), which came to be interpreted as the *abhutvā bhāva utpāda* in the Sautrantika school (see Kalupahana, *Causality*, p.p.152-254). In other words, there is no implication here that existence is completely independent, without any prior connections. As such, if there were to be any self (*ātman*), it would be "made" (*kṛtaka*, see *kāraka* at XXVI.10). If it is not, and if it were assumed to arise, the self would be causeless.

13. *Evaṃ dṛṣṭir atīte yā nābhūm aham abhūm aham,*
ubhayaṃ nobhayaṃ ceti naiṣā samupapadyate.

Thus, whatever view there is such as, "I existed in the past; I did not exist; both or neither," is not really appropriate.

MKV(P) p.581; *MKV(V)* p.253.

The views (*dṛṣṭi*) referred to here are the metaphysical views relating to identity. difference, both or neither. It should be noted that the reasons for rejecting these views are empirical. Empiricism, in the Buddha as well as in Nāgārjuna, allows for the recognition of continuity without having to posit absolute identity or absolute difference.

14. *Adhvany anāgate kiṃ nu bhaviṣyāmīti darśanam,*
na bhaviṣyāmi cety etad atītenadhvanā samaḥ.

A view such as "Will I exist in the future?" or "Will I not exist in the future?" is comparable to those associated with the past.

MKV(P) p.582; *MKV(V)* p.254.

Here again, the views that are inappropriate are those involving identity and difference, not any explanation of what the future *could be* based upon one's experience of the process of dependent arising.

15. *Sa devaḥ sa manuṣyaś ced evaṃ bhavati śāśvatam,*
anutpannaś ca devaḥ syāj jāyate na hi śāśvatam.

If it is thought that a human is the same as a divine being, then there would be the eternal. If the divine being were to be non-arisen, then he would not be born and that would constitute the eternal.

16. *Devād anyo manuṣyaś ced aśāśvatam ato bhavet,*
devād anyo manuṣyaś ced saṃtatir nopapadyate.

If it is thought that a human is the same as a divine being, then there would be the non-eternal. If it is thought that a human is different from a divine being, then continuity is not appropriate.

MKV(P) p.583; *MKV(V)* p.254.

In addition to the attainment of the ultimate goal of life (*paramārtha*) which is freedom (*nirvāṇa*), the Buddha allowed for the possibility of a human being reaching up to the status of a deity or a divine being (*deva*), assumed to be one who is materially as well as morally superior to ordinary human beings, yet not coming anywhere close to the ultimate goal (see *S* 1.228; *Tsa* 40.1 [*Taishō* 2.290b]). However, the Buddha refused to recognize these divine beings as eternal and permanent entities (*D* 1.20, see *Chang* 14.1 (*Taishō* 1.90b-c]).

The recognition of the above possibility could prompt the substantialists to discover "some-thing" (*kiṃcit*) in the human being that is identical with the divine. Nāgārjuna is here rejecting any such identity, as well as any alternate theory that could make divinity uncaused.

Furthermore, the emphasis on absolute difference would not only lead to the belief in non-eternality (*aśāśvata*), which would imply a denial of continuity in or the process of becoming (*saṃtati*), the latter being distinguished from the metaphysical process referred to earlier (see XVII.7-10).

17. *Divyo yady ekadeśaḥ syād ekadeśaś ca mānuṣaḥ,*
aśāśvataṃ śāśvataṃ ca bhavet tac ca na yujyate.

If a part were to be divine and the other part to be human, then there would be both the eternal and the non-eternal, and this too would not be proper.

MKV(P) p.584; *MKV(V)* p.255.

The combination of two metaphysical views does not provide for a non-metaphysical one. The Buddha's rejection of such views is clearly stated in the *Brahmajāla-suttanta* (*D* 1.21). Nāgārjuna is simply reiterating that position here.

18. *Aśāśvataṃ śāśvataṃ ca prasiddham ubhayaṃ yadi,*
siddhe na śāśvataṃ kāmaṃ naivāśāśvatam ity api.

Supposing both the eternal and the non-eternal are established, then it is not possible to either assert the eternal or the non-eternal.

MKV(P) p.585; *MKV(V)* p.255.

Nāgārjuna is here refusing to accept a conclusion which is only a part of a conjunctive proposition.

19. *Kutaścid āgataḥ kaścit kiṃcid gacchet punaḥ kvacit,*
yadi tasmād anādis tu saṃsāraḥ syān na cāsti saḥ.

If anyone has come from somewhere and again were to go somewhere, then the life-process would be beginningless. Such a situation does not exist.

MKV(P) p.585; *MKV(V)* p.255.

The metaphysics rejected in Chapter II is referred to in the first line. The second line emphasizes the ideas expressed in Chapter XI.

20. *Nāsti cec chāśvataḥ kaścit ko bhaviṣyaty aśāśvataḥ,*
śāśvato 'śāśvataś cāpi dvābhyām ābhyāṃ tiraskṛtaḥ.

If it is thought that there is nothing eternal, what is it that will be non-eternal, both eternal and non-eternal, and also what is separated from these two?

MKV(P) p.586; *MKV(V)* p.256.

Here again, we have Nāgārjuna's analysis of "something" (*kaścit*), an entity that he was determined to get rid of on previous occasions (XXV.19,20,24). The theories of identity, difference, both or neither, are associated with such metaphysical entities. Hence Nāgārjuna's refusal to accept such theorizing.

21. *Antavān yadi lokaḥ syāt paralokaṃ kathaṃ bhavet,*
athāpy anantavāṃl lokaḥ paralokaḥ kathaṃ bhavet.

If the world were to have a limit, how could there be another world? Furthermore, if the world were to have no limit, how could there be another world?

MKV(P) p.587; *MKV(V)* p.256.

Having discussed the metaphysical views relating to duration, i.e., eternality, etc., of the world and the self, Nāgārjuna moves on to a discussion of the theories relating to the extent of the world.

The rejection of the metaphysical notions of the finite and the infinite are based upon a recognition of the possibility of a future world (*para-loka*). According to Nāgārjuna's analysis, a finite (*anta*) implies absence of continuity (*uccheda*), and as such militates against any conception of a future world explained in terms of dependent arising (*pratītyasamutpāda*). The infinite (*ananta*) implies permanence or eternality (*śāśvata*) and, as such, it would be meaningless to speak of a future world as an "other world" (*para-loka*), for it would be identical with the previous world.

22. *Skandhānām eṣa saṃtāno yasmād dīpārciṣām iva,*
pravartate tasmān nāntānantavattvaṃ ca yujyate.

As this series of aggregates proceeds along like a flame of a lamp, [speculation about] its finitude or its infinitude is not proper.

MKV(P) p.587; *MKV(V)* p.256.

The simile of the lamp (*padīpa*) was popular among the Buddha and his disciples, especially in their explanation of freedom (*nibbāna*). As the flame of a lamp is extinguished, because of the absence of the conditions necessary for its continuous burning, so is a person's mind freed when the fuel that feeds its continuous burning with anxiety is exhausted. Explaining this process in terms of dependence, it would be most inappropriate to speak of its finitude or infinitude, independent of any conditions that are involved in its continuity or lack of continuity. This is a clear indication that an absolutistic conception is incompatible with an explanation based upon conditionality.

23. *Pūrve yadi ca bhajyerann utpadyeran na cāpy amī,*
skandhāḥ skandhān pratītyemān atha loko 'ntavān bhavet.

If the prior aggregates were to be destroyed and these aggregates were also not to arise depending upon these other [aggregates], then the world would be finite.

24. *Purve yadi na bhajyerann utpadyeran na cāpy amī,*
skandhāḥ skandhān pratītyemān loko 'nanto bhaved atha.

If the prior aggregates were not to be destroyed and these aggregates were also not to arise depending upon these other [aggregates], then the world would be infinite.

MKV(P) p.588; *MKV(V)* p.256.

The above is a criticism of an explanation of the continuity in the aggregates which does not take into consideration their causal dependence. If the aggregates were looked upon as things that appear and disappear with no causal relations, then only can one speak of a finite world. In other words, the conception of a finite world involves one of the extreme views discussed earlier, namely, annihilation (*uccheda*).

The non-arising of the aggregates dependent upon other aggregates would then imply permanence, and this is what is involved when one speaks of an infinite world.

25. *Antavān ekadeśaś ced ekadeśas tv anantavān,*
syād antavān anantaś ca lokas tac ca na yujyate.

If the world were to be partly finite and also partly infinite, it would be both finite and infinite, and this too is also not proper.

MKV(P) p.589; *MKV(V)* p.256.

The rejection of both the finite and the infinite, the eternal as well as the non-eternal, as constituting the reality, was prompted by the Buddha's refusal to recognize two different levels of reality: a changing and finite world contrasted with an eternal and infinite ultimate reality or an Absolute. As such, neither in the Buddha's philosophy, nor in Nāgārjuna's thinking is there any room for an Absolute of any sort.

26. *Kathaṃ tāvad upādātur ekadeśo vinaṅkṣyate,*
na naṅkṣyate caikadeśaḥ evaṃ caitan na yujyate.

How can it be possible that one part of a grasper is destroyed and the other part is not destroyed. This too is not proper.

27. *Upādānaikadeśaś ca kathaṃ nāma vinaṅkṣyate,*
na naṅkṣyate caikadeśo naitad apy upapadyate.

How can it be possible that one part of grasping is destroyed and another part is not destroyed. This too is not appropriate.

MKV(P) pp.589-590; *MKV(V)* p.257.

Nāgārjuna leaves no room for the recognition of an eternal and absolute entity either in the person grasping (*upādātṛ*) or in grasping (*upādāna*).

28. *Antavac cāpy anantaṃ ca prasiddham ubhayaṃ yadi,*
siddhe naivāntavat kāmaṃ naivānantavad ity api.

Supposing both the finite and the infinite are established, then it is not possible to assert either the finite or the infinite.

MKV(P) p.590; *MKV(V) p.257.*

This rejection of the finite and the infinite is comparable to the rejection of the eternal and the non-eternal (XXVII.18).

29. *Athavā sarva-bhāvānāṃ śūnyatvāc chāśvatādayaḥ,*
kva kasya katamaḥ kasmāt sambhaviṣyanti dṛṣṭayaḥ.

Thus, because of the emptiness of all existents, where, to whom, which and for what reason views such as the eternal could ever occur?

MKV(P) p.591; *MKV(V)* p.258.

The recognition of dependently arisen phenomena (*pratītyasamutpanna dharma*) means the acceptance of the non-substantiality or emptiness of all these things. If things are non-substantial, how can there be views about the eternal and the non-eternal, the finite and the infinite? The answer to this question has been provided by the Buddha and clearly restated by Nāgārjuna. It is the result of an urge on the part of human beings to find absolute answers to questions such as "Where did I come from?" or "Where do I go from here?" These questions would be raised and attempts to answer them be made so long as human beings are propelled by a "craving for becoming" (*bhava-tṛṣṇā*) or "craving for other-becoming" (*vibhava-tṛṣṇā*). This was the riddle of human existence faced by the Buddha. Understanding that riddle of existence, the Buddha attained freedom (*nirvāṇa*) by spewing out craving (*tṛṣṇā*) and abandoning any grasping (*upādāna*).

30. *Sarva-dṛṣṭi-prahāṇāya yaḥ saddharmam adeśayat,*
anukampam upādāya taṃ namasyāmi gautamaṃ.

I reverently bow to Gautama who, out of compassion, has taught the true doctrine in order to relinquish all views.

MKV(P) p.592; *MKV(V)* p.258.

This final statement of Nāgārjuna referring to the Buddha's preaching of the doctrine (*sad-dharma*) is to be contrasted with his statement at the end of the chapter on freedom (*nirvāṇa*)(XXV.24), where he says that the Buddha did not "preach anything as . . ." (*na . . . kaścid dharmo buddhena deśitaḥ*), and should open the eyes of those who stick to a completely negative interpretation of Nāgārjuna. Nāgārjuna's remarks clearly show that he was aware that the Buddha did not speak "metaphysically" but only "empirically."

INDEX TO THE *KĀRIKĀ*

NOMINAL FORMS

VERBAL FORMS

GENERAL INDEX